PUBLICATIONS

OF

THE AMERICAN FOLKLORE SOCIETY

BIBLIOGRAPHICAL AND SPECIAL SERIES

GENERAL EDITOR, TRISTRAM P. COFFIN

VOLUME I

REVISED

1964

NATIVE AMERICAN BALLADRY

Native American Balladry

A DESCRIPTIVE STUDY AND A BIBLIOGRAPHICAL SYLLABUS

by

G. MALCOLM LAWS, JR.

REVISED EDITION

PHILADELPHIA

THE AMERICAN FOLKLORE SOCIETY

1964

International Standard Book Number 0–292–73500–6

Library of Congress Catalog Card Number 64–17007

Copyright © 1964 by G. Malcolm Laws, Jr.

Printed in the United States of America

Revised edition, 1964

Second printing, 1975

Published for the American Folklore Society by the
University of Texas Press, Austin and London

For MacEdward Leach
whose friendship and enthusiasm
have been a continuing source
of pleasure and inspiration.

Contents

Preface To The Revised Edition

Since the first edition of this work was published in 1950, a number of major folksong collections have appeared and some important work on native balladry has been done. The present edition gives me the opportunity to bring *Native American Balladry* up to date and to increase its usefulness as a work of reference.

The content of Chapters I-VIII remains substantially the same, although I have made various additions, corrections, and revisions and have incorporated the results of recent study in many of the generalizing statements. Chapter IX, which appears in this work for the first time, was originally an article in the *Journal of American Folklore*.

I have completely revised the reference material of Appendix I (Ballads Current in Oral Tradition) with three main purposes in mind. First, I have greatly increased the number of references to specific texts in the older collections. Second, I have added references to texts in the various collections of the last dozen years, including such major contributions as Volume II (*Folk Ballads*) of the *Frank C. Brown Collection of North Carolina Folklore*, Helen Creighton's *Traditional Songs from Nova Scotia* and *Maritime Folk Songs*, Volumes III and IV of Vance Randolph's *Ozark Folksongs*, William Doerflinger's *Shantymen and Shanty-boys*, William Owens's *Texas Folk Songs*, Olive Wooley Burt's *American Murder Ballads*, Alton Morris's *Folksongs of Florida*, and Lester Hubbard's *Ballads and Songs from Utah*. Third, I have added substantially from these and other sources to the list of ballads current in oral tradition.

Most of the additions to Appendix I result from the appearance in new collections of pieces not previously reported or not established, according to my criteria, as clearly traditional. These include a number of ballads which appeared in the first edition in Appendix II (Ballads of Doubtful Currency in Tradition). Also added are several pieces previously omitted through oversight or because I was uncertain about their native origin. The only major change in policy involves ballads collected in Canada. In the first edition I excluded Canadian ballads if they had not been reported from singing in the United States. This now seems less logical to me than including all the Canadian material as a part of substantially the same ballad tradition. Appendix I now contains exactly sixty-nine new ballads. (In the table of contents for each type, a double line separates the ballads of the first edition from those just added). About seventy ballads have also been added to Appendix II. Most of these are either from the older Canadian collections or from the works cited above. Their traditional status does not seem firmly enough established to warrant their inclusion with the titles in Appendix I.

I should like to express once more my continuing appreciation of the work of ballad collectors and scholars and to acknowledge my indebtedness to them. And I wish particularly to thank Dr. Kenneth Goldstein and Professors MacEdward Leach, Tristram P. Coffin, and D. K. Wilgus for advice, encouragement, and material assistance.

Philadelphia
October, 1963

Preface to the First Edition

Thanks to the tireless work of regional collectors of folksong during the past few decades, American literature has been enriched by the printed texts of hundreds of songs previously preserved in the memories of folk singers. As the quantity of this material has grown, so has the need for classifying and studying it on a nationwide basis. I have undertaken a part of this task by attempting to winnow out the traditional American ballads from the great body of native and imported folksong. The large number of ballads thus garnered as well as the wide distribution of many of them offers convincing evidence that the United States has a vigorous tradition of balladry based on native themes.

In describing and analyzing the ballads of America and in discussing their origin, I have frequently felt the need of more information than was available. Despite the noble efforts of a handful of scholars, ballad study has not kept pace with ballad collection. Further research will undoubtedly produce solutions to some of the mysteries surrounding a study of this kind. But if one may judge from the study of balladry in other lands, many of the puzzles must remain unsolved.

In order to supplement the information in the text and to increase the usefulness of this book as a reference work, I have made the appendices as complete as possible. The bibliographies and summaries provided under each ballad title should be found helpful both in themselves and as a starting point for further research. Each ballad has been provided with an identifying number in an effort to overcome the present confusion of ambiguous titles. The system of numbering is flexible enough to allow for the inclusion of additional ballads, since the collectors' work is far from finished. Field workers are constantly making and reporting new discoveries, either of unrecorded ballads or of additional versions of pieces already in print. Much more intensive collecting must be done, especially in regions hitherto neglected, before the number of American ballads can be stated with any certainty.

It is my pleasant duty to express here my deep appreciation for the generous assistance I have received since I began this study. First of all, my thanks go to my colleagues and teachers at the University of Pennsylvania. Professors Matthew W. Black, E. Sculley Bradley, and Harold S. Stine kindly read the manuscript and made helpful observations and suggestions. To Professor MacEdward Leach, Secretary-Treasurer of the American Folklore Society, under whose guidance this study was produced,

I owe a special debt of gratitude for his unfailing good-nature, constant encouragement, and valuable advice. Professor Wayland D. Hand of the University of California, Editor of the *Journal of American Folklore,* proofread the manuscript and offered a number of useful references. Professor Samuel P. Bayard of Pennsylvania State College, an associate editor of the *Journal,* after a close and critical reading of the manuscript, submitted detailed notes and comments based on his many years of ballad study. These officers of the American Folklore Society graciously recommended the publication of my book in the present series. They are not responsible, of course, for any errors which may have crept into it or for the opinions which I have expressed.

It would be difficult to overestimate my obligation to all those collectors and scholars whose anthologies and studies have laid the groundwork for this book. Without their labors the study could not have been undertaken. I am also grateful to all those who have so generously supplied me with information. Without exception my queries have received courteous and helpful response. Permission to reprint various ballads has been graciously granted and is specifically acknowledged in the appropriate sections of the text.

My thanks go finally to my sister, Elizabeth Laws, for her many weeks of assistance in typing the manuscript.

Philadelphia
March, 1950

Chapter I

A Definition of Native American Balladry

Before entering into a discussion of native American balladry, it is necessary to define the term "popular ballad" with some precision. We are not, of course, dealing with an isolated phenomenon but rather with a kind of verse which for centuries has been popular in various languages among the peoples of Europe. American balladry is closely connected with the balladry of the British Isles, which itself is related to that of the Continent. A broad definition of the popular ballad must ignore the barriers of language and include great variations in form, spirit, subject matter, and literary quality.

Having surveyed the entire field of European balladry, Professor William J. Entwistle came to the conclusion that a ballad was "any short traditional narrative poem sung, with or without accompaniment or dance, in assemblies of the people."[1] As an accurate general statement, this definition is entirely adequate. Without elucidation, however, it does not reveal a great deal about the nature of ballads. Professor Gordon H. Gerould uses a similar but much compressed definition when he says, "the ballad is a folk-song that tells a story."[2] Many years before, Professor Kittredge had summed up the matter in much the same way when he wrote the oft-quoted sentence, "A ballad is a song that tells a story, or—to take the other point of view— a story told in song."[3] These definitions and many more like them identify the ballad as a type of narrative song. From this starting point scholars expand and make more specific their definitions in an attempt to distinguish balladry from other types of literature, oral and written.

Continuing his definition, Professor Kittredge goes on to say that a ballad "more formally . . . may be defined as a short narrative poem adapted for singing, simple in plot and metrical structure, divided into stanzas, and characterized by complete impersonality so far as the author or singer is concerned." This more descriptive definition cannot be accepted without reservation. Entwistle says that "three out of four principal types of European ballad are not stanzaic at all,"[4] and it is easy to show that

[1] *European Balladry*, pp. 16-17.
[2] *The Ballad of Tradition*, p. 3.
[3] Sargent and Kittredge, *English and Scottish Popular Ballads* (one volume edition), p x.
[4] *Op. cit.*, p. 16.

1

even in the English traditional balladry with which Kittredge was concerned "complete impersonality" is not an invariable rule.

Professor Gerould sums up his analysis of the ballad type in the following illuminating paragraph:

> We may, then, safely amplify our original definition by adding to it the statement that in at least three respects all European ballads are alike, and that by virtue of these common qualities we recognize them to be ballads. We may say that a compressed and centralized episode is the ordinary narrative unit, that dramatic presentation of action is the ordinary narrative method, and that impersonality of approach to the theme is the ordinary narrative attitude. A ballad is a folk-song that tells a story with stress on the crucial situation, tells it by letting the action unfold itself in event and speech, and tells it objectively with little comment or intrusion of personal bias."[5]

It will be observed that this definition admirably summarizes several ballad characteristics without insisting too strongly upon any one of them.

The scholars I have quoted have presumably derived their definitions from ballad collections already made. They have not been faced with our problem, which is to distill the American ballads from a vast body of native and imported folksong and popular song. What we need is a working definition which will serve to distinguish the popular ballad from a large number of related verse forms. From the definitions given above and from an analysis of many of the pieces in the Child collection and elsewhere, I have worked out a broad definition which will serve to identify the ballad and to distinguish it from other forms. This definition is by no means radical, but it opens the way for the inclusion of many pieces not admitted by Child. *A ballad is a narrative folksong which dramatizes a memorable event.* Everyone agrees that a ballad must tell a story. Calling it a folksong indicates the importance not only of singing but of oral transmission, with its attendant phenomenon of variation. The dramatic element is so constant and so important that its inclusion in the definition seems advisable, even though an occasional ballad may be weak in this respect. By a memorable event is meant one which is sufficiently gripping or entertaining to be repeatedly narrated in song. A single event is indicated, because, as Professor Gerould has said, a ballad usually concentrates on only one episode or occurrence. Impersonality, the third quality which Professor Gerould felt was important enough to be included, I have not mentioned for reasons which I hope to make clear.

Because this study deals only with ballads in English—though not with English ballads—it seems natural to turn for further enlightenment about the nature of balladry to the great compilation of Professor Francis James Child, *The English and Scottish Popular Ballads.* The 305 narrative songs

---
[5] *Op. cit.,* pp. 10-11.

included in his work have been generally accepted under the term "Child ballads" as the virtually complete body of English traditional balladry. That subservience to the Child canon has resulted in some unjustifiable conclusions about balladry I shall attempt to point out later. For the moment, however, the Child collection will serve to illustrate certain features which the best of the British ballads have in common. Needless to say, any general statement will have its exceptions. The analysis which follows is intended only as the broadest kind of survey of the ballad type.

That these ballads belong to the folk would be apparent, if for no other reason, because of the large number of varying texts recovered from tradition. Words, phrases, or entire stanzas are altered or relocated or disappear. New stanzas sometimes replace them and are themselves subjected to changes. The effect of such changes is debatable. Many ballads obviously degenerate, but others seem to improve with age. At any rate, generations of folk singers have impressed upon the ballads an atmosphere very different from that of professional poetry. The niceties of rhyme, meter, and even of syntax are often ignored. The diction becomes simple; there is no obvious striving for effect, no dwelling upon words for their own sake. The result is verse of highly uneven quality but usually of great sincerity. Fine poetry is present, not necessarily by accident, in many of these ballads, but the ballads themselves are rarely fine poems. They lack the polished perfection and the unity of form and style which a trained poet can impart to a poem of his own creation. This is not to say that ballad style is purely a matter of chance. Even ballads known to have been composed centuries apart may seem to have been cast from the same mold, for the conservative folk cherish the narrative techniques, the stock situations, the very phraseology which tradition has sanctioned. Thus conventionality takes the place of originality and serves as a distinguishing feature of popular balladry.

Although ballads vary greatly in length and stanzaic form, typical pieces contain from one to three dozen quatrains, roughly alternating iambic tetrameter and iambic trimeter, and rhyming a b c b. Their lyricism is far from constant, but most of them can be sung effectively to relatively simple tunes.

Dialogue is generously employed throughout the ballads, and some ballad stories are told entirely in this form. This large amount of dialogue, which is a feature of dramatic rather than expository narrative, tends to exclude all but indirect descriptive details. The stories are told directly, almost hurriedly, without waste of words. The narrator remains in the background and does not reflect upon the action. His attitude toward the story may be inferred, but it is not usually stated as part of the narrative.

Perhaps the most striking characteristic of these ballads is the large amount of action which they compress into a small space. Murder, battle, and suicide are common, as are other forms of violence. Thought flames into deed, and death strikes suddenly, almost without warning. Love, with its attendant complications is a favorite theme, as is treachery. Both result in those conflicts which are the mainspring of vigorous action. Humor appears, too, usually of the broad type familiar in the fabliau, which depends upon deeds rather than words. Ghosts walk in the ballads and magic transformations occur. Ships are sunk, houses are burned, men and women are pierced through with swords and pen knives. But cruel and bloody as many of the ballads are, the narrator retains his composure and air of detachment as he swiftly finishes his story. When the event has been narrated the ballad ends, and the listener may draw from it what implications he will.

That these austere and anonymous verse narratives have emotional impact has been recognized for centuries. Because of their dignity and power, they strike chords of response within even the sophisticated listener. Admittedly they are simple in diction and in style, but the adjectives "crude" and "artless" should not be applied to them. Professor Gerould sums up the matter nicely when he writes: "Ballads are very far from being primitive poetry, indeed; they are rather the flower of an art formalized and developed among people whose training has been oral instead of visual."[6]

That Professor Child's collection contains the finest of British traditional ballads no one denies, but in it he neither defined the ballad nor fully explained his method of deciding what to include. It is becoming increasingly apparent that subjective considerations must have influenced his inclusion of some pieces and his rejection of others.[7]

Professor Entwistle points out that had Child's criteria been different he might have included some of the wares of the 16th century ballad-mongers whose broadsides were popular in England.[8] And Gerould writes: "No one, it seems to me, ought to dispute, even though he holds very firmly to the tradition of Child, the acceptance as ballads of a great many songs that are not to be found in our monumental collection."[9] The editors of a recent American folksong collection have this to say:

> Unfortunately for methods of exact classification, the line which Child endeavored, following Jamieson,[10] to drawn between "popular" ballads and "vulgar" ballads turns out to be a very artificial one. It is becoming more and more clear that many so-called vulgar ballads have as much

---

[6] *Ibid.*, p .12.

[7] For an illuminating analysis of the pieces finally included in and excluded from Child's definitive edition, see Thelma G. James, "The English and Scottish Popular Ballads of Francis J. Child", *JAF* 46 (1933), 51-66. Miss James concludes that "a 'Child ballad' means little more than one collected and approved by Professor Child" (p. 59).

[8] *Op. cit.*, p. 228.

[9] *Op. cit.*, p. 32

[10] Robert Jamieson was, of course, but one of many earlier editors whose collections Child studied and used.

right to rank as "popular", in every sense in which Child understood the word, as any in his corpus. . . .[11]

It is vital for the purposes of this study to realize that British balladry does not begin and end with *The English and Scottish Popular Ballads.*

Preserved in oral tradition here and in the British Isles are many English, Scottish, and Irish folksongs which might have been included in Child's collection had they been less obviously journalistic. Although we do not know Child's standards of acceptability, we may judge from his work that among the prime considerations were a measure of antiquity, traditional ballad style, as he conceived it, and evidence that a piece had existed as traditional song or was in some way connected with folk tradition. Most of the ballads which Child did not include had wide distribution as broadsides, that is single sheets containing one or more songs and sold very cheaply. In general those which are of concern to us have appeared from the eighteenth century on and hence are much later than the ballads of Child. It is likely that folk singers originally learned them from the printed sheets. (Sometimes a familiar tune was indicated to which the broadside ballad should be sung.) But the fact remains that very few people who sing those ballads have ever seen them in print. They have been handed down traditionally along with the Child ballads and have been subjected, though for a shorter time, to the vicissitudes of oral transmission.

To be sure, these later pieces as a rule are inferior to the best of the Child ballads. Frequently they are insipid or sentimental, and many of them do not have that objectivity which contributes to the excellence of the older balladry. The first person becomes more and more intrusive, and the narrator pauses more frequently to reveal his own attitudes. Because the later balladry has become increasingly subjective I have excluded impersonality from the definition given earlier. In my opinion, a narrative folk-song which dramatizes a memorable event does not cease to be a ballad merely because the narrator comments on the action or tells his own story.

Furthermore, we cannot refuse to call the later pieces popular ballads merely because of their inferior quality. To quote Professor Gerould again, "The excellence of a ballad according to literary standards . . . or its total lack of such excellence, has nothing directly to do with its status as a ballad."[12]

When first composed and printed, a broadside ballad has, of course, no standing as folksong. It becomes a popular ballad only after it has passed into tradition and become a part of folk literature. It may well be that Professor Child omitted many of the later pieces not because of their broadside origin but because he could not be certain that they had become

[11] Flanders, Ballard, Brown, and Barry, *The New Green Mountain Songster*, p. 69.
[12] *Op. cit.*, p. 31.

established folksongs. Had he been able to benefit by the work of twentieth century collectors here and abroad, Child would have seen clearly the continuing vitality of folk balladry and might have altered his somewhat antiquarian attitude toward the form. I do not mean to imply that Professor Child ignored all the products of the ballad press. Many of his oldest texts are printed from broadsides,[13] but he usually indicates that such ballads had found their way into print from tradition, instead of starting their lives as broadsides. Occasionally, however, he does imply that a printed text represents the original form of a ballad.[14]

Since the traditional ballad may be printed in broadside form and the broadside ballad may become traditional, it is rather misleading to make the term "broadside" synonymous with inferior, implying that it means a composition of little worth. Actually there is no clear dividing line between the two forms. The great majority of broadside ballads have not remained in the memory of the folk, but those which have are certainly entitled to consideration along with the best of the popular ballads.

Partly as a result of having to some degree freed English balladry from the limits imposed by Child's collection, we are faced with a new and hardly less important problem, that of distinguishing between ballad and song. Kittredge, Cecil Sharp, and other scholars emphasize the impersonality of the ballads and contrast them with highly subjective songs of some narrative content. For example, Professor Kittredge says of the ballad, "Unlike other songs, it does not purport to give utterance to the feelings or the mood of the singer". In a footnote to this statement he remarks, "This distinguishes the ballad, strictly so called, from the purely lyrical poem. Such a song as 'Waly, waly, gin love be bony' is, then, not a ballad, though it tells a story".[15] This song expresses the desolation of a girl whose lover has left her. The first and last stanzas will give some idea of its spirit:

> O Waly, Waly, up the bank!
> And Waly, Waly, down the brae!
> And Waly, Waly yon burn-side,
> Where I and my love wont to gae!
>
> Oh, oh, if my young babe were born,
> And set upon the nurse's knee,
> And I my sell were dead and gane
> For a maid again I'll never be.[16]

She remembers the happiness of their life together, and she keeps repeating half unbelievingly the statement that her lover has grown cold to her. Certainly the piece is charged with emotion, but to say that it is not a

---

[13] See nos. 199, 211, 243, 272, 273, etc.

[14] See for example "Bonny Lizie Baillie" (no. 227), "The Crafty Farmer" (no. 283), and "The Sweet Trinity" (no. 286).

[15] *Loc. cit.*

[16] *English and Scottish Popular Ballads* (one volume edition), p. 667.

ballad because of the emotion it expresses would seem to place too much emphasis on the necessity for impersonality in balladry. As has been said, subjectivity in balladry is not uncommon outside Child's collection.

A much more useful and dependable means of distinguishing between ballad and song is to consider the strength and organization of the narrative elements. Kittredge has said that "Waly, waly" tells a story. Let us compare it with the opening and closing stanzas of "Barbara Allen":

> It was in and about the Martinmas time,
> When the green leaves were a falling,
> That Sir John Graeme, in the West Country,
> Fell in love with Barbara Allen.

> "O mother, mother, make my bed!
> O make it soft and narrow!
> Since my love died for me today
> I'll die for him tomorrow!"[17]

The action of this ballad is carried on during a considerable time interval from the moment of first love, through the misunderstanding, Sir John's sickness and death, and Barbara's final statement. In short, the ballad action is dramatized from beginning to end. In "Waly, waly", on the other hand, the narrative and dramatic elements are weak. We know almost as much about the girl's love affair from the song, but we know it largely by inference. It is reflected upon in the manner of soliloquy rather than dramatized. The story is not so much told as implied or suggested. Thus, setting aside the matter of subjectivity, we may say that in contrast to songs, ballads dramatize their central events. Moreover, the primary purpose of the ballad is to tell a story, while that of the song is to express a state of mind. It should be added that in many narrative folksongs ballad-like and song-like qualities are so evenly distributed that classification becomes arbitrary rather than logical. In such cases one can hardly do more than make a decision and hope that it will find acceptance.

So much space has been devoted to the problem of definition because it has been largely ignored by editors of folksong collections in this country. Most editors present a wide variety of native and imported ballads and songs without attempting to separate and classify them, except that they give the Child ballads first. Cox's *Folk-Songs of the South* may be called typical of the carefully edited scholarly compilations. It contains 185 folksongs of various types consecutively numbered and without division, the first 33 and the last of which are Child ballads. Some editors distinguish half-heartedly between native and imported pieces without separating ballads and songs. Others print extinct ballads beside those in oral tradition, or make classifications on the basis of subject matter alone. Many editors use the words "ballad" and "song" loosely and even interchangeably. And so

[17] *Ibid.*, p. 180.

many interpretations have been placed upon the word "folksong" that one frequently comes upon pieces which, so far as can be demonstrated, have never existed in oral tradition.

Where attempts have been made to set boundaries, the results have sometimes been misleading. Thus Cecil Sharp, after admitting that the line between ballad and song is hard to draw, says that a ballad is a romantic and impersonal narrative, while a song is emotional "and is usually the record of a personal experience—very frequently of an amatory nature".[18] The result of working with such an unsatisfactory definition is that Sharp's large printed collection contains not a single native American folksong which he calls a ballad.

In defining the popular ballad and in distinguishing between ballad and song I have attempted to bring some order out of confusion. Definitions based on the Child ballads alone do not take into account more recent developments in balladry. They largely ignore the often subjective products of the broadside ballad press which have passed into tradition, and the ballads composed under the influence of such models. Defining a ballad merely as a narrative folksong which dramatizes a memorable event frees it from the necessity of impersonality and admits a wider variety of material than Child included. Of course, all definitions can be objected to for one reason or another. Professor Gerould, for example, prints "The Old Chisholm Trail" among his "Specimen Ballads of American Origin",[19] while I prefer to consider the piece a song. Yet his definition of a ballad is more explicit than mine. At the same time, I have probably included in this study several pieces which he and others would not wish to call ballads. The most useful of definitions can only point the way in doubtful cases. Occasionally subjective considerations must rule.

The problem of definition should not be set aside without some observations on the different meanings of the word "folksong". In its loosest sense it may refer to almost any verse collected from the people either in manuscript form or from singing. Fortunately most scholars employ the word more precisely, but still with varying connotations. The distinction between the narrative ballad and the lyrical folksong (or simply song) has already been discussed. When used in its broader sense, folksong designates a branch of folklore of which balladry is a part. Since folklore is always understood as traditional material, folksong must then be the possession of those in whose minds such material is stored. Some scholars would stop at this point and say that any songs traditionally sung by the folk are folksongs. It is more usual, however, to eliminate the songs which also circulate widely in print and to consider as folksong those pieces which are dependent for their continuing existence upon oral transmission. But even this limitation

---

[18] *English Folk Songs from the Southern Appalachians*, Vol. I, pp. xxviii-xxix.
[19] *The Ballad of Tradition*, p. 284.

may not be sufficient.. It sometimes happens that various songs which are preserved only in tradition retain an obviously literary style which is alien to that of the folk. It seems wisest to attempt to reserve the designation folksong for those pieces which exhibit that forthright and unaffected style which is characteristic of unsophisticated people. From the standpoint of definition, it makes little difference whether this style was originally present in the composition or has come about as the result of folk variation. Thus the word "folksong" and hence the word "ballad", as used in this study, will usually connote a traditional piece bearing some evidence of folk style.

There are three great bodies of traditional balladry in America, the Child ballads, the broadside ballads imported from the British Isles, and the native American ballads. These types intermingle and are known and sung by the same people. Many of the same influences have been brought to bear upon them. In addition to these types, dozens of imported and native narrative songs which cannot quite be called ballads are traditional in this country. It is the purpose of this study to separate the native American ballads from all the other songs and to consider them as a group with certain convenient divisions.

This study is largely confined to ballads which have originated in the United States and the Maritime Provinces of Canada. Ballads imported from the British Isles are not considered unless they have been sufficiently reworked in this country to acquire separate identity as American pieces. Minor variations, such as the localization of place names, which do not significantly alter the content of a piece, cannot be said to affect its origin, and consequently the large group of only slightly Americanized British ballads is not considered.

Having defined ballads as narrative folksongs, I am confining this study to ballads actually recovered from tradition and then printed by collectors. Hundreds of broadside ballads written in America have become extinct, either because they were not of enduring interest to ballad singers or because they were "simply and literally unsingable."[20] It would be misleading to resurrect them and consider them along with those which are currently traditional. Since most American ballads are less than a century old, it has often been difficult to decide what constitutes a traditional ballad. A ballad printed by only one collector may be known to no one but the singer. On the other hand, it may be widely known within a small area or among singers overlooked by collectors. Some of the conclusions reached in this study may have to be revised as ballad collecting continues. Native ballads have received far less attention than imported ones, particularly the Child ballads. Large areas of the country have been either ignored or only sketchily investigated, if we may judge by the collections which have been published.

---

[20] For the latter observation I am indebted to Professor Samuel P. Bayard.

Even the fine regional collections have often drawn their material from only three or four counties of a state. Then, too, many private collections remain unedited in manuscript form throughout the country and consequently are unavailable for study. I have decided to discuss only those ballads which have been collected from singers since about 1920. Native ballads collected earlier and not printed since will be listed in Appendix II to await further searching. Among them are a few ballads printed only from old manuscripts, and some others which collectors have printed since 1920 but without clear evidence of their having been sung. A substantial group in Appendix II consists of ballads sung for collectors in recent years which are not clearly traditional. (Such pieces, for example, may have been learned directly from print, from phonograph records or from their authors). I have further decided to exclude ballads known to have been composed within the last thirty years in the belief that it is too soon to call any of them traditional.

In addition to the ballads, collectors have recovered many narrative songs which are now traditional in America but which are not treated here because they are different in form and spirit from popular ballads. Many of them are sentimental or comic stage or parlor songs of the nineteenth century. Some are designed to frighten drunkards into sobriety. Still others are melodramatic and artificial tales of death and desertion. A representative list of these songs is given in Appendix III, along with my reasons for excluding them from the ranks of balladry.

Having thus limited the field, we find remaining some 250 native American ballads. Almost all of them fit the definition previously given and are in the writer's opinion properly designated popular ballads. The list in Appendix I upon which this study is based is offered somewhat apologetically. Undoubtedly as other collections are published it will have to be further expanded. Each ballad scholar will have his own perfectly legitimate ideas concerning what should be included. Complete agreement is hardly to be hoped for, particularly since some of the folksongs listed in the appendices were shifted from one category to another before a final decision was made. It is also possible that further research will show that some of the ballads here listed as native are actually importations. Since ballads of much the same type have been produced by English-speaking people on both sides of the Atlantic, clues which help reveal the national origin of a piece are often lacking. Of course, the British origin of many ballads recovered from American tradition can be clearly demonstrated. Not infrequently, however, one can only assume that a piece is imported. Thus, though ballad movement westward across the Atlantic has been the rule, an occasional piece may have travelled in the opposite direction and added to the confusion. Appendix IV gives a selection of ballads which, though they do not appear in Child's collection, are probably or certainly of British origin.[21]

---

[21] Such ballads are treated in detail in my *American Balladry from British Broadsides.*

Chapter II

American Ballad Types

Some editors of American folksong anthologies print all the pieces they have collected without attempting to classify them further than to place together compositions of similar origin or subject matter. The collections of Cox,[1] Eddy,[2] Henry,[3] and Brewster[4] number their ballads and songs consecutively, leaving the student free to derive his own classifications from them. In his preface, Professor Belden explains the arrangement of his material but then adds, "The categories are by no means mutually exclusive, and are therefore not divided in the text."[5] Cecil Sharp's collection is divided broadly, and from our point of view unsatisfactorily, into "Ballads" and "Songs".[6] Lomax[7] and Sandburg[8] use their own subjective and colorful designations. Each editor faces the problem of classification anew, and either devises his own list of headings or presents his findings without reference to type.

All collectors must be aware of the need for uniformity even when they realize the difficulty of achieving it. As Professor Belden puts it, "Scientific classification of folksong is, so far as I know, a desideratum not yet attained."[9]

The problem of classifying native American ballads is, of course, less complex than that faced by editors of miscellaneous collections of American folksongs. But the problem does exist, and the necessity for classification is much greater in a study of this kind than in an anthology. In deciding upon the nine classes of ballads listed in Appendix I, I have made free use of designations which have already appeared as titles or chapter headings in published collections, tailoring them to fit the material at hand. Native ballads will be treated in this and later chapters under the following headings: War Ballads, Ballads of Cowboys and Pioneers, Ballads of Lumberjacks, Ballads of Sailors and the Sea, Ballads about Criminals and Outlaws, Murder Ballads, Ballads of Tragedies and Disasters, Ballads of the Negro, and Ballads on Various Topics. It will be seen that this list emphasizes

---

[1] J. H. Cox, *Folk-Songs of the South.*
[2] M. O. Eddy, *Ballads and Songs from Ohio.*
[3] M. E. Henry, *Folk-Songs from the Southern Highlands.*
[4] P. G. Brewster, *Ballads and Songs of Indiana.*
[5] H. M. Belden, *Ballads and Songs Collected by the Missouri Folk-Lore Society*, p. xii.
[6] *English Folk Songs from the Southern Appalachians.*
[7] J. A. and A. Lomax, *American Ballads and Songs.*
[8] Carl Sandburg, *The American Songbag.*
[9] *Loc. cit.*

occupations and events rather than theme, form, style, place of origin, or any other criterion upon which classifications may be based. Admitting that the types have been arbitrarily chosen, I offer them without apology in the belief that they will be useful in various ways in making clear some of the directions which native balladry has taken. It will perhaps seem odd that all native balladry can be gathered together under so few headings without making the list of miscellaneous ballads unwieldy, but, as will be shown later, most of the types contain a wide variety of material.

Examination of the ballads will show that a great many of them could have been placed in several of the categories here given. "Frankie and Albert," for instance, which I list among the Negro ballads, would also qualify as a ballad of tragedy, a murder ballad, or a ballad about a criminal. As a matter of fact, so many ballads could be classified as tragic that I have tried to find more specific categories whenever possible. Among the Ballads of Outlaws and Criminals are included those in which the emphasis is upon the lawbreaker. "Charles Guiteau," for example, is concerned mainly with the assassin's career and with the fate he is about to meet. When the emphasis is with the victim, as in "Mary Phagan," or when it is about equally divided, the designation Murder Ballad is used.

These divisions are based mainly upon subject matter; they are made without reference to the circulation of the ballads. It is not unusual for collectors to find lumberjacks who sing ballads of the sea, for example, because lumbering and sailing, on fresh or salt water, often attracted the same men and because both types of balladry originated largely in the north. White singers and Negroes have repertories which overlap, and most ballads about criminals are sung by law-abiding citizens. To place a ballad in a class is merely to indicate in a general way its relation to other ballads of its kind. The reason for considering Negro ballads as a unit are given in Chapter VII. It would be foolish, of course, to establish boundaries between ballads and then restrict discussion to fit these artificial limits. Consequently I shall cross freely from one main group to another in discussing the ballads and shall create further informal categories and sub-types as they seem necessary.[10]

---

[10] Some misunderstanding regarding the purposes of this system of classification seems to have arisen. (See D. K. Wilgus, "Ballad Classification," *Western Folklore* 5 (1955), 95-100). Each ballad is listed under a particular heading and given a number so that it may be readily identified and distinguished from similar pieces. Other arrangements will be found more suitable for other purposes. Designating a ballad "C 19" does not mean that it should always be studied as a lumberjack ballad or that "C 18" and "C 20" should be regarded as most nearly like it. Nor should the reader be too disturbed to find that "G 1" and "G 31" are widely separated (since the latter has been added in this edition), though both are about railroad accidents. Both may be located fairly easily under "Ballads of Tragedies and Disasters." While it may be theoretically desirable to have a logical system of classification of all Anglo-American ballads, I have seen no indication that such a system can be devised.

Those who are accustomed to the archaic style and the medieval atmos-phere of some of the best known Child ballads may have some difficulty in adjusting themselves to the realistic immediacy of native American ballads. The British ballads frequently imply more than they state; they have some of the suggestive qualities of real poetry. American ballads leave relatively little to the imagination. They are explicit and detailed, often tiresomely so. Their subject matter, too, is markedly different from that of most of the British ballads. The knights and ladies, the gold and silver, the magic transformations, and the evil stepmothers of Child balladry have no place in the native balladry of America. Even love, the most popular of all narrative and dramatic topics, is rarely treated by the American ballad maker. Crafty plottings, deep seated jealousies, seductions, disguises, strife within families, duels to the death—such topics are almost unheard of in our balladry. We hear, instead, of the difficulties and perils of various occupations, of sordid crimes committed by insignificant people, of fires and mine blasts and rail-road wrecks, of struggles against the frontier, of death by snake-bite or freezing, of trips on clipper ships and lake schooners, of death in dozens of different forms. The analyses which follow are designed primarily to indicate broadly the subject matter dealt with in various ballads within each main group and various sub-groups. Readers who find certain titles ambiguous or unfamiliar are referred to Appendix I, which contains a description of every ballad treated in this study.[11]

WAR BALLADS

With the possible exception of "Springfield Mountain," "Brave Wolfe" is apparently the only native ballad to have survived in tradition from Colonial times. This laudatory account of the general's gallant death at the Battle of Quebec is in 18th century broadside style. It is clearly not of folk origin, but the folk accepted and cherished it. The fact that it was frequently reprinted in songsters is an indication of its popularity in the nineteenth century. The Revolution has left us only three ballads. (The allegorical piece "Revolutionary Tea" is presumably of later origin). "Paul Jones's Victory" and "Paul Jones, the Privateer", both written in the fluent manner of the professional, are patriotic accounts of the American hero's prowess on the high seas. "Major André's Capture", which must originally have been an awkwardly written broadside, is a sympathetic account of the young British spy's capture and execution. It is perhaps significant that these four eighteenth century ballads are concerned primarily with men whose heroism in times of great danger is recorded and admired in the ballads. One ballad, "Bold Dighton," remains precariously in tradition from

---

[11] It should be remembered that discussion is limited to ballads still current in oral tradition.

the Napoleonic Wars, and four more come down to us from the War of 1812. "Brave General Brock" records a military victory from the Canadian point of view. In "The *Constitution* and the *Guerrière*" honors are about equally divided between the American master, Captain Hull, and his famous frigate which was victorious over the British ship. This is a rollicking and cleverly rhymed broadside which has barely survived. One of the most unusual of American ballads is "James Bird." After a long and tender account of Bird's parting from his family and friends to join Perry in the Battle of Lake Erie, the ballad glowingly praises his valor in the battle and then regretfully reports his desertion from his ship and his eventual execution. No attempt is made to excuse the hero, but the balladist's sympathy for him never wavers. This intensely human account of a dramatic turn of events has remained deservedly popular. In "The Battle of New Orleans" the successes of General Andrew Jackson's forces are celebrated. "The Hunters of Kentucky" deals with the same battle but is of post-war composition.

Two ballads remain to remind us of the Indian Wars. "The Texas Rangers" describes the battle through the eyes of a young volunteer who lives through it, and watches sadly as many of his fellow Rangers are struck down by Indian arrows. As Professor Belden points out the version given in Sharp transfers the scene to the Civil War.[12] The Indians become Yankees, and the narrator grieves for the Texas boys who lie dead at Manassas. It is probable that "The Dying Ranger" was another product of the Indian fights, though it, too, has Civil War versions. Here a wounded ranger or soldier speaks sadly of home before he dies with his comrades around him. The man who speaks sentimentally and at some length before death is a familiar figure in both native and foreign balladry; several ballads of the Civil War are of this type, and other pieces might have been included if they had contained more narrative action.[13] "The Drummer Boy of Shiloh", "A Soldier from Missouri", and "The Battle of Mill Springs" are alike in that each gives a detailed report of a young soldier's dying speech, without saying much about the battle in which he has been wounded. Pieces of this sort, when they are clearly traditional, cannot be dismissed on the grounds of sentimentality alone. In a war in which thousands of boys in their teens died, there must have been far too many such heartrending scenes. Some variety is added in "The Last Fierce Charge" by having two soldiers give their last instructions to each other before riding to death in battle. Five of the Civil War ballads contain broad descriptions of various battles, usually from a partisan point of view. In "The Battle of Shiloh Hill," however, we are given a general account of the horrors of the conflict and are not told on which side the narrator fought. Interestingly enough, "The Battle of Elkhorn Tavern," a long and detailed account containing satiric thrusts at the enemy,

---

[12] Belden, p. 336.
[13] See the ballad-like piece "Brother Green", for example. (Appendix III).

exists with appropriate alterations in both a Northern and a Southern form. "The Battle of Shiloh" and "The Battle of Bull Run" both celebrate the glory of Southern arms and belittle the Northern forces, and in "The Sweet Sunny South" the Southerner looks forward to the day when his land will be free of the hated invaders. The two sea-ballads which remain in tradition from the war are "The *Cumberland's* Crew" and "The *Cumberland,*" which describe the heroic but disastrous battle of the Northern frigate and the ironclad *Merrimac.* Reminiscent of and hardly inferior to "The Star-Spangled Banner," which may in part have inspired it, "The *Cumberland's* Crew" is a rousingly patriotic piece in broadside style. In the little-known ballad called "The Rebel's Escape," a Southern soldier flees from a Northern prison and is aided by his family to return to friendly territory.

When we realize that hundreds, perhaps thousands of ballads must have been composed between, let us say, 1750 and 1865, it comes as a shock to find so few remaining in tradition. A good many songs of the Civil War are still sung, but only a handful of ballads. Earlier wars have left us very little, and the dozens of important national and political events which occurred between the beginning of the Revolution and the Civil War have left us no traditional ballads at all. Many historical ballads still exist in collections of old American broadsides,[14] and there is some evidence to support the logical assumption that a large number of them were temporarily popular. But they seem to have passed completely out of the folk memory. One explanation is that most ballad singers are unconcerned with events of purely historical importance. Their interests lie in the fate of human beings, whose experiences they can understand and share. Whatever additional causes may be offered to explain the failure of historical ballads to survive, the fact remains that, at least so far as recent collections show, most of these pieces are totally extinct.

The survival of only about a dozen real ballads of the Civil War supports the theory that singers tend to forget ballads which no longer have much meaning for them. The war, needless to say, is preserved in the folk memory, especially in the South as an event of tremendous importance. But now that all who fought in it are dead, descriptions of engagements have little more than antiquarian interest. It will be seen that in half these ballads interest is centered on a young man who is dying; the war is merely the stage upon which the smaller and more meaningful event is taking place. This type of ballad has a much better chance of survival than the type which emphasizes the event rather than the individual.[15]

---

[14] For example, Neeser's specialized collection, *American Naval Songs and Ballads,* contains 85 naval pieces of various kinds on the War of 1812 alone, most of them anonymous broadside ballads.

[15] No real ballads from World War I seem to have survived in tradition. The war was fought far from home in an era of declining ballad composition; such ballads as were composed would probably have found little favor among folk singers in the United States.

Ballads of Cowboys and Pioneers

Despite the fact that some of them are based on older models or contain borrowed material, the ballads of the cowboys and pioneers display an independence of spirit which sets them apart from other types of American balladry. The inhabitants of the old West were independent people; they had renounced the settled life of long established communities, and had gone to vast, largely unexplored regions where life was frequently dangerous and always difficult. The West offered freedom, but it gave in exchange hardship and often death. Yet living close to nature appealed to many men and a few women. Perhaps these people, having made a choice, were unwilling to turn back. More probably, they were of that rugged breed which is exhilarated by pioneer life, which preserves its sense of humor in the face of difficulties, and which finds its reward in overcoming obstacles, and living free of the obligations which bind those in civilized regions. Yet not all of them achieve complete freedom, for frequently they express the empty longing of the homeless and the exiled.

Death, the favorite subject of all balladry, occurs time and again in the ballads of the West. Like the soldiers we have mentioned, the cowboys die far from their families and homes, thinking and speaking of the life they once knew. Loneliness vies with independence as a predominant theme in Western balladry. In "The Cowboy's Lament" the young man who has been shot surveys his wasted life and grieves both for himself and for his distant family. We never learn the cause of death in "The Dying Cowboy", but we can sympathize with the boy's request to be taken home for burial. Although both these ballads are reworkings of older material, Western treatment has given them dignity and poignancy. Somehow we have more sympathy for the cowboys than for either of their ballad ancestors, the young rake of the English ballad "The Unfortunate Lad" and the man who pleads sentimentally and at great length not to be buried "in the deep, deep sea." In "Little Joe the Wrangler", "When the Work's All Done This Fall", and "Utah Carroll", death comes suddenly to the cowboys during their efforts to halt stampedes. Bill Vanero is fatally wounded by Indian arrows, and A Fair Lady of the Plains meets the same fate while helping her husband herd cattle. Despite the prevalence of homicide in the West, only one ballad about murder has survived in tradition, and in that the crime was committed elsewhere. The conscience-stricken young man in "The Wandering Cowboy" has gone West to escape punishment for killing a rival in love. It is true that the dishonest boss in "The Buffalo Skinners" meets death at the hands of his men, but the killing is mentioned only incidentally and cannot be called the subject of the ballad.

Pioneer hardships are still remembered in a few ballads. "Sweet Betsy from Pike" is a satiric and jovial account of a migration from Missouri,

which is included among the ballads somewhat hesitantly because its narrative element is so diffuse. Still, it seems to belong with other ballads of the
chronicle type in which the subject is an extended adventure rather than a
sharply defined incident. "The Buffalo Skinners", which is closely related to
the lumberjack ballad "Canaday-I-O", is of similar construction, though the
parts of the latter ballad are more firmly held together. This ballad is a
serious and bitter account of the buffalo hunters' dangerous and unpleasant
life. In "The Trail to Mexico" interest is about evenly divided between the
cowboy's work and his lack of success in love. After a rambling beginning,
the old Mormon ballad "The Sioux Indians" settles down in the conventional
manner to recount a battle between emigrants and Indians, and "The
Mountain Meadows Massacre" records the gruesome and needless killing of
another group of emigrants.

The line between ballad and non-ballad must be drawn somewhere if the
definition of the type is to have any meaning. I have decided to exclude
"The Old Chisholm Trail" and others of its kind, because they are not
consecutively developed narratives. Lumbermen, cowboys, sailors, and others
have produced many traditional songs about their work. These have a certain
narrative framework, and usually string together a long series of typical but
unrelated incidents. They have no clear beginning or ending, and they
could not be said to recount a single event. The Lomaxes have printed
110 stanzas of "The Old Chisholm Trail" in *Cowboy Songs* and *American
Ballads and Songs* and say that hundreds of stanzas are unprintable.[16] This
song, like "Mademoiselle from Armentières", is a catch-all piece of great
popularity. There seems no need to call it a ballad. Many other occupational
songs describe typical working days or hardships. But the true ballad
concentrates on a particular dramatic occurrence instead of merely setting
forth a general state of affairs.

People whose lives are full of difficulties are likely to have a well-
developed sense of humor which occasionally spills over from folksong and
folk tale in folk ballad. We have already spoken about "Sweet Betsy from
Pike." "Joe Bowers", the amusing story of a pioneer whose girl had married
their home-town butcher instead of waiting for him, has been accepted by
the folk, though it sounds like a professional creation. Two drunken cowboys
defeat the devil, who has come to take them away, in "Tying a Knot in the
Devil's Tail."[17] In "Zebra Dun" a practical joke misfires when the "tenderfoot" demonstrates his ability to ride an outlaw horse, and in "Strawberry
Roan" the overconfident broncho rider comes to grief. But humor is relatively
rare in cowboy balladry, as it is in American folk balladry generally.

Except for "Joe Bowers", "The Cowboy's Lament" and "The Dying

---

[16] Lomax, *American Ballads*, p. 376.
[17] Compare "The Farmer's Curst Wife," Child no. 278.

Cowboy", which all can understand and appreciate, the texts of the cowboy and pioneer ballads have not usually commended themselves to ballad singing Americans in other regions. Artistically, they have relatively little to recommend them, and their specialized nature has probably kept them from being widely popular. But they are full of vigor and drama, and they reflect an era which is rapidly fading into history.

BALLADS OF LUMBERJACKS

The lumbering industry of the Northern woods attracted great numbers of footloose and rugged men just as did the Western plains. Like the cowboys, the lumberjacks, or shanty-boys, as they were more frequently called, lived away from society and had to depend on their own resourcefulness for entertainment. Because many of them were Irish or of Irish extraction,[18] they turned naturally to the singing of old songs and inevitably to the creation of new ones. As might be expected, their ballads deal mainly with the dramatic events of their own dangerous occupation, particularly with the constant battle against the forces of nature. One might suppose that falling trees and branches would be the great hazard of lumbering, but I have found only one traditional ballad on that subject. In "Harry Dunn" a youth is crushed to death by a hanging limb while working in the Michigan woods. Death by drowning was apparently much more common, to judge from the ballads, in eleven of which lumbermen meet that fate. The most widely known of these, "The Jam on Gerry's Rock", reports the death of Young Monroe, who is tossed into the swirling chaos of a breaking log jam. The heroes of several other ballads die under almost identical circumstances.[19] Rocks, logs, and rushing water must have given a man little chance to emerge alive. One misstep might be fatal to a lumberman working on the fast Northern rivers. In the semi-satirical ballad "The Shanty-boy on the Big Eau Claire", we are told simply that the youth "fell off a rapids piece on the falls at Mosinee." The shanty-boys for whom the ballad was written would understand. The danger did not end with a successful river trip, for the large mechanical saws of the mills could mangle a man in a few seconds. The ballad of "Harry Bale" describes such an accident. Even if he escaped accidents, the lumberjack had other hardships to contend with. "Canaday-I-O" and the "Three MacFarlands" describe winters of intense cold and back-breaking work in the snowy woods. That the work had its lighter side, too, can be learned from a ballad like "The Little Brown Bulls" in which the lighter team of oxen wins a log-snaking contest. Then there was always the night in town to look forward to; that would be exhilarating if not restful. One account of such a night is given in "The Green Mountain Boys".

---

[18] See Rickaby, *Ballads and Songs of the Shanty-boy*, p. xxv.
[19] See ballads C 3-C 10 in Appendix I.

The shanty-boy might sing of a faithless girl, as in "Jack Haggerty", or laugh about another lumberman's mishap, as in "Joe Thomas." Despite the dangers and difficulties of their job, the men would return to the woods year after year because lumbering was in their blood. They have greatly enriched our folksong with a series of well-made ballads which are superior in lyricism and emotional impact to all others produced in America except those of the Negro.

BALLADS OF SAILORS AND THE SEA

Some lyricism but less substance is to be found, too, in the ballads of American sailors. Their chanteys, and those of the British—the two can hardly be separated[20]—are fine things of their kind—but the narrative element in most chanteys is so weak that they cannot be called ballads. Among the true ballads which have come down to us are a few accounts of successful trips on the ocean or on the Great Lakes. In "Red Iron Ore", "The *Bigler's* Crew", "The *Dom Pedro*", "The *Dreadnaught*," and "The Schooner *Fred Dunbar*" a ship begins its voyage, now and then passes a familiar landmark, makes a stop or two, and eventually arrives at its destination. The crew looks forward to getting ashore. The stories, such as they are, are told in a lively and vigorous manner, and the stanzas are interspersed with ringing refrains. Though they are full of the spirit of fresh winds and open water, these chronicles, like those of the cowboy, the pioneer, and the shanty-boy, lack the drama to be found in ballads which are built upon a single striking incident or event. "The *Persian's* Crew," "Fifteen Ships on Georges' Banks," and "The Death of Herbert Rice" have greater power to move the hearer because of their elegaic tone and their emphasis upon the men who have met their deaths. "The Loss of the *Albion*," a rare old sea ballad, is weak poetically but strong in its sympathy for the passengers and crewmen who died when their ship was split upon the rocky Irish coast. Late nineteenth century disasters are recounted in the Lake Michigan ballad "The Beaver Island Boys" and in "The Wreck of the *Huron*," which tells of the loss of a Navy ship. The sinking of the *Titanic* is also recorded in this group. But "The Flemings of Torbay" alters the gloomy pattern by joyfully recounting the rescue of two young Maritime fishermen.

The sea has also contributed a few pieces which because of their subject matter stand pretty much alone. "Bound Down to Newfoundland" tells of a voyage under a captain ill with smallpox. "Charles Augustus Anderson" is a tale of murder and mutiny. And "The Ghostly Crew" is a reminder that belief in revenants is still current among some seafaring men. "Dixie Brown" follows part of the career of a lonely sailor who fares badly both ashore and

---

[20] See Colcord, *Songs of American Sailormen*, p. 31.

at sea. Of greater merit is "Bold Manan the Pirate", a semi-humorous account of the depradations and eventual downfall of a villainous sea-rover. Among the oldest and most interesting of native ballads is "The Bold Northwestern Man," a piece dating from 1791, when the crew of the *Lady Washington* successfully repulsed the attack of a band of Indians with whom they were trading. The event took place in the northern waters of the west coast, but the ballad is remembered in Maine and New Brunswick. Many other stirring events must once have been remembered in song, and yet most of the old ballads seem to have gone the way of the ships which inspired them.

Ballads About Criminals and Outlaws

For hundreds of years the outlaw has been a familiar figure of British balladry. There are more ballads about Robin Hood than about any other character of English history or legend. Johnny Armstrong and other Scots were celebrated in later balladry, and ballads about Sam Hall and Dick Turpin are still sung in America. Whatever may be the cause of this interest in the outlaw, the fact remains that he is still popular in folk tradition.[21] Frequently he is admired for his prowess, but, if not, he is at least found sufficiently colorful to sing about. Occasionally he reaches the status of a folk hero.

Such a man was Jesse James, about whom two ballads are still popular. Both of them—here designated "Jesse James I" and "Jesse James II"—are stories of the treacherous shooting of the outlaw by Robert Ford, a member of his own gang. The sympathies of the narrators are clearly with the victim. Other bandits of the reckless post-Civil War period have been sufficiently notorious to have ballads composed about them. Charles Quantrell, the leader of a guerilla band was one of these, but unfortunately the ballad which celebrates one of his exploits has come down to us only in fragmentary form.[22] Cole Younger, who was one of Quantrell's men, as well as a confrere of the James boys, has been more fortunate. An inartistic but graphic ballad recounting some of his felonies has been reported from several Western states. "Sam Bass", the rambling life-story of another Western robber, has been even more popular. It, too, is hardly more than doggerel. The South has produced its share of badmen, among whom Sidney Allen, Wild Bill Jones, and Kenny Wagner are the subjects of folk ballads. These men are all murderers, but the ballads about them emphasize their bravado, and pass rather lightly over the killings. The central incident of the New England ballad "Wilkes Lovell," the recapture of two prisoners after a jail break,

---

[21] This fact is commented upon in Flanders-Barry, *The New Green Mountain Songster*, p. 215.

[22] See Appendix II.

is set forth in some detail, but we are not told why the men were imprisoned in the first place.

"Wilkes Lovell" ends with a warning against criminal activities. Like so many other British and American ballads, it has been composed on the "crime does not pay" theme. Time and again condemned criminals, usually murderers, have, according to folk tradition, composed ballads about their downfall as a warning to all who might be tempted to stray from the straight and narrow path. Most of these ballads must have been written by experienced creators of broadsides to capitalize on sensational events of the moment.[23] A few of them, however, may actually have been composed by prisoners awaiting execution.[24] Probably the best known ballad of the confessional or "good-night" type is "Charles Guiteau," the story of the decline and fall of a man whose life might have been happy had he not chosen the road of crime. Several ballads containing the same details, but different names, are known, and it seems certain that Charles Guiteau was not the first murderer to tell his story in this form. Another ballad of the same general content is "Ewing Brooks", the more detailed story of an escaped murderer who is finally apprehended and sentenced. Not infrequently ballads of this kind base their appeals for pity upon the unhappy state of the culprit's family. Thus in "Gambling on the Sabbath Day" the condemned murderer berates himself and speaks sadly to the tearful members of his family who have come to say farewell. In the jailhouse ballad "Twenty-One Years", the lonely and apparently guiltless young man bemoans his fate and soliloquizes about his fickle girl and the dishonest judge who sentenced him. The central character of "Young Companions" not only admits that he has murdered a young woman, but speaks at length about breaking his mother's heart and living a sinful life. He seems to feel that execution is about what he deserves. Of course a ballad composer or singer feels obligated in cases of this kind to emphasize the unpleasant fate of those who disregard the law.

The ballads of border warfare which form such a colorful part of the Child collection have been replaced in this country by a few ballads about mountain feuds. Jean Thomas prints several of these in *Ballad Makin' in the Mountains of Kentucky*,[25] but because her book is largely undocumented, it is difficult to say whether or not they should be called traditional. "The J. B. Marcum Song" and "The Rowan County Crew" are known to be authentic accounts of old feuds, composed in a somewhat plodding style. Feuds involved so many plots and counter plots that it was difficult to

---

[23] At least, this was the practice in England. Sir Henry Mayhew refers to a London ballad singer who composed Newgate ballads and who was paid a shilling for "a copy of verses written by the wretched culprit the night previous to his execution". Quoted from *London Labour and the London Poor*, by W. Henderson, *Victorian Street Ballads*, p. 11.

[24] See for example "Ellen Smith", "The Vance Song", and "Frankie Silvers".

[25] Pp. 11-24.

compress the story of even one killing into a smooth ballad; this was particularly true if the ballad-maker wanted to remain neutral and still to give all the pertinent facts. Considering its specialized nature, "The Rowan County Crew" has had surprisingly wide oral circulation in the South and Middle West. In general, though, it may be said that feud ballads are mainly of local interest.

MURDER BALLADS

That murder is a subject of wide interest needs no demonstration. Those who feel that ballads are unusually morbid or gruesome may compare them not only with the stories that make the headlines but with many of the classics of written literature from pre-Christian times to the present. Since most ballads owe their very existence to sensational events, it is inevitable that murder should have a prominent place in balladry. There is no need to assume that the balladist is bloodthirsty or that he delights in murder. Even the supposedly impersonal Child ballads reveal their sympathy for the victims of crime. Because American balladry as a whole is more personal and subjective, native balladists usually feel free to condemn the murderer and grieve for his victim.

"The Jealous Lover", which we shall claim as a native product until some one offers indisputable proof that it is not, is one of the most popular ballads in this country. Its basic situation, that of the girl lured from her home and brutally disposed of by her lover or fiancé, is echoed in quite a few American texts. The Jealous Lover stabs the girl. In several American ballads including "Poor Omie" and "On the Banks of the Ohio" the lover takes the girl to a lake or river and drowns her despite her pleas.[26] These murders are usually unmotivated in the ballads, apparently because of tabus against the mention of pregnancy or illegitimacy. This is in sharp contrast to Child balladry, which is usually frank and explicit where sex is concerned. In "Murdered by a Brother" a man punishes his dishonored sister and her lover by drowning them both. A new horror is added in "Pearl Bryan I": the girl's head is never found. In "Henry Green" and "McAfee's Confession" murder by poisoning takes place after marriage. McAfee is attracted to another woman, but no motivation is provided for Henry Green.

In one of these ballads the sympathy is clearly on the side of the murderer. The composer of "Fuller and Warren" apparently felt that Fuller was driven to murder his rival because of that man's treachery and the fickleness of the girl they both loved. And in "Ellen Smith" the lover who has been arrested for the murder of his sweetheart mixes moving statements about his love for the girl with vigorous protestations of his innocence.

The wide currency of ballads of this type is not difficult to understand.

---

[26] See also "Grace Brown and Chester Gillette" and "Lula Viers".

They do not require the specialized knowledge of the occupational ballads. They can be appreciated by people of all kinds in all regions because they are based on elemental human passions and situations. They are truly tragic, and they excite both the interest and the pity of those who hear them.

Murder ballads which tell stories of sheer brutality have less currency probably because the murderers seem inhuman and the events basically incomprehensible to the average person. In "Poor Goins", "John Funston", and "The Peddler and His Wife" innocent people are wantonly killed and robbed. Ballads under the title "The Ashland Tragedy" describe the murder of two girls and a boy by thugs who had invaded their house, and the pieces entitled "Meeks Family Murder" describe the slaughter of an entire family. Little Josie in "Suncook Town Tragedy" is attacked from ambush and done away with. The somewhat similar story of Mary Phagan, who was attacked and killed in the pencil factory where she worked, is achieving some circulation, apparently because the ballad builds up sympathy for the girl before briefly describing the crime. Almost as a rule, American murder ballads avoid sordid details and concentrate on the tragic aspects of the crimes they report.

BALLADS OF TRAGEDIES AND DISASTERS

This group is somewhat miscellaneous, for it consists of all those tragic ballads which could not be included under earlier headings. Ballads of two more occupations, mining and railroading, are considered here, along with those of several major disasters, and a few individual tragedies.

Mining has long been one of the most hazardous peacetime occupations in which large numbers of men engage. Mine cave-ins, fires, and explosions kill dozens, sometimes hundreds, of men at once and leave whole villages in mourning. Naturally ballads are written about these events and are printed at the time to underline the horrors of such disasters and the bravery of the men involved in them. But the ballads rarely pass into general circulation, nor do they become popular, even among the miners themselves. Considering the large amount of song material which George Korson collected from hard- and soft-coal miners, he found relatively few ballads which were still sung. Perhaps the magnitude of these disasters prevents a singer from vicariously sharing the experience recorded. Or to take another view, the miners may find no particular pleasure in singing about tragedies like those which they themselves may have to face. At any rate, only one mine disaster, that which occurred at Avondale, Pennsylvania, in 1869, seems to have made much impression on the folk memory. One ballad on the subject, "The Avondale Disaster I", has been recovered from as far away as Nova Scotia and another, "The Avondale Disaster II", from Michigan. The two ballads are similar. They describe the unexpected fire which traps the men below ground, the anguish of their families, the futile and heroic attempts to save them, and finally the recovery of more than one hundred bodies. Disasters of similar magnitude are recounted in "The Cross Mountain Explosion" and "The Miners' Fate". "Charley Hill's Old Slope", reports the death of nine men in an elevator accident, and "The Dying Mine Brakeman", describes the death of a young man in a train accident below the surface. A very different sort of tragedy is recorded in "The Driver Boy." In this a young mule driver from the mines dies of pneumonia after having been cruelly beaten by his drunken father. That the miner was frequently cheerful and even gay is shown in his songs, but his ballads are as cheerless as the mines which produced them.

It seems strange that railroading, which is such a familiar and fascinating occupation to most Americans, has produced only three ballads which are widely sung. In all three, "Casey Jones", "The Wreck of Old 97" and "The Wreck on the C & O" the engineer dies largely as a result of trying to make up time in a fast train. The ballads give detailed accounts of these trips and comment favorably upon the skill and courage of the men at the throttle. All are looked upon as heroes, though their trips end in disaster. It is worth pointing out that the ballad with a single victim or hero has a much better chance of popularity than one in which many are killed. Mass tragedies can be looked upon with some detachment, but the death of an individual whose character has been delineated is far more moving and meaningful.

The weakness of the usual ballad-maker's attempt to encompass a great disaster within a few stanzas is illustrated by "The Milwaukee Fire" and "The Burning of the Granite Mill." Neither of these ballads has achieved much popularity, probably because the scene shifts constantly and little but the horror and confusion of the event is transferred to the ballad. Much the same may be said of "The Miramichi Fire" and "The Brooklyn Theatre Fire." The victims never achieve any stature as individuals.

The popularity of ballads about personal tragedies has already been commented upon in earlier sections of this chapter. A few more of these should be mentioned. Two of the oldest and most generally distributed native ballads have as their subject sudden and unexpected death. "Springfield Mountain" tells of a young farmer who is bitten by a rattlesnake while mowing his father's field. Unfortunately this ballad became a ludicrous stage song, and is better known in that form than as a serious piece. "Young Charlotte", the story of a girl frozen to death while driving to a ball with her fiancé, though more than a century old, has been preserved almost intact by several generations of singers. The work of a professional writer, it is more smoothly constructed than most native products. But in situation and general treatment it is of the folk, and it has been accepted and treasured by them. In "Stratton Mountain Tragedy", another ballad by the author of

"Young Charlotte", a young mother freezes to death in a blizzard but is able to protect her baby from the cold. Suicide as a result of unrequited love occurs in "Willie Down By the Pond", a ballad made the more tragic because the girl actually loved Willie when she teasingly refused his hand. In a complementary ballad, "The Silver Dagger", a young girl stabs herself when parental objections prevent her marrying the man she loves. Finally may be mentioned the relatively recent ballad "Floyd Collins", which describes the death of a young man trapped in a cave.

BALLADS ON VARIOUS TOPICS

Most of the pieces in this last group may be roughly divided into four sub-classes: sports ballads, ballads about wanderers, religious ballads, and ballads about love and women. Since most sports events are of only temporary interest, it is not surprising to find only a handful of such pieces in tradition. Three ballads about prize fights, "Morrissey and the Russian Sailor," "Morrissey and the Black," and "Heenan and Sayers" are all more than a century old, have been found but rarely by collectors, and may soon become extinct. The same may be said for the slightly more recent ballad "Ten Broeck and Mollie," which celebrates a Kentucky horse race. Several fragments have recently appeared, but the most coherent texts are those of a professional writer and a professional singer.

Among the wanderers we find the Arkansas Traveller, a character with a sense of humor, who satirizes life in a backwoods town. Then there is the Gambling Man, who may originally have been English, but who is now convincingly Americanized. He is a carefree wanderer, in contrast to the men depicted in "The Dying Hobo" and "Ten Thousand Miles from Home," which hint at the loneliness and hopelessness of the hobo's life.

Although Dr. George Pullen Jackson published several large collections of religious folk songs,[27] these volumes contain very few pieces that can be called ballads. "The Little Family", "Death Is a Melancholy Call", and "Wicked Polly" are, in my opinion, the only religious pieces which fulfill the requirements of the type. All of them have also been published in general collections of folksong. "The Little Family" retells in touchingly simple ballad verse the story of the raising of Lazarus. The other two pieces are "funeral ballads", that is, religious songs which are sung mainly at funerals in the South. Both describe the demise of young people who, according to their elders, have lived sinfully and as a result deserve the fate which is theirs.

Native balladry has dealt only infrequently with the subject of love. Since it is hardly conceivable that American composers have had little interest in the subject, we must look elsewhere for an explanation. Many imported love ballads are popular in this country. In "Barbara Allen" and various

---

[27] See the Bibliography.

other Child ballads built on love, as well as in a large body of British broadsides, the subject has been pretty thoroughly treated. Many of these imported ballads are excellent things of their kind, and it is easy to imagine the American balladists' deciding that it was futile to try to compete against them.

Although we are including it in this group, we cannot even say that "The Little Mohea" is definitely a native product. The Indian maid lives apparently on some tropical isle and might more properly if less poetically be called a South Sea Islander. Similar British broadsides are known, but none exactly like the ballad so popular in America. A ballad of much the same content, in which the stranger half falls in love with a Creole girl, is known as "The Lake of Ponchartrain." Barry suggests that this may be an imitation of "The Little Mohea."[28] Earl C. Beck has found and printed two more ballads of this type in both of which the girl is obviously an American Indian. It is possible that both "The Chippewa Girl" and "On the Banks of the Pamanaw" will eventually be traced to Britain, but until they are, we shall claim them, along with the others of like kind, as native products. Another Indian ballad, "The White Captive," is a romantic, not to say melodramatic, account of a young Indian chief's rescue of a white girl from torture. Although the ballad did not originate among the folk, they have disseminated it widely.

Ballads presumably of variety stage origin but distantly related to the *fabliaux* of British broadside balladry are "The Old Maid and the Burglar," "The Warranty Deed," "Courting the Widow's Daughter," and "The Girl That Wore a Waterfall." In the first two, men are shocked to discover that women who seem physically sound are actually wearers of wigs, false teeth, and glass eyes. In the third, a young man faces the wrath of a lonely and unattractive widow, and in the fourth, an appealing and apparently unattached girl has her victim beaten and robbed by her husband. In somewhat more serious vein are "The Lonesome Scenes of Winter" and "The Young Man Who Wouldn't Hoe Corn." In the former, a young man changes his mind about marriage and refuses the girl who has previously refused him. In the latter, the girl decides against marrying a man who is too lazy to look after his crops.

It will be seen from this chapter that although native American ballads deal with situations of many different kinds and treat various phases of life, their subject matter is fairly simple and obvious. Native ballads deal in the main either with death, the most spectacular and final of tragedies, or with the hardships and vicissitudes of life. Occasionally the ballad-maker finds a fresh subject or a new approach, but usually he confines himself to the type of material which his predecessors have handled successfully.[29]

---

[28] Flanders-Barry, *The New Green Mountain Songster*, p. 148.
[29] Ballads of the Negro are separately discussed in Chapter VII.

Chapter III

American Ballads as Dramatic Narratives

It may as well be admitted at the start of this discussion that, taken as a whole, native American balladry is inferior to the British balladry published by Child. This belief is so generally held that it will probably not be disputed. In fact, if we may judge largely by negative evidence, folklorists in general have considered American balladry beneath criticism. The amount of material collected increases enormously year by year, and new anthologies are constantly being published. Editors trace origins and refer in detail to the location of variant versions. But the ballad scholars usually stop there. Perhaps they feel that readers can draw their own judgments from the folksongs presented. Whatever their reasons may be, the fact remains that they have paid little attention to the techniques of the ballad makers. It is a welcome relief to come upon collections like *Minstrelsy of Maine*[1] and *The New Green Mountain Songster*,[2] which include snatches of pungent criticism with the illuminating historical accounts accompanying the ballad texts. Far too many anthologies have the take-it-or-leave-it atmosphere of a museum.[3]

Professor Gerould writes as follows of American ballads and ballad-makers:

> Let us grant at once that ballads of American origin have not gone very far in structure and texture towards the form of the European traditional ballad. Most of them betray the hands of their makers, who were either journalistic scribblers, hacks in the employ of broadside and songbook publishers or theatrical managers, or else country folk in whom the impulse to compose lingered though the art of composition had perished.[4]

This is sound, if somewhat severe, criticism. Significantly enough, much the same might be said of those ballads which were being produced abroad. The makers of ballads, like other authors, are conditioned by the age in which they live. As might be expected, American balladry, for the most part, is similar to that which appeared in the British Isles during the same period. Thus in style and in substance it is more closely related to the products of the ballad press than to the older and finer traditional balladry of Child. Striking contemporary events such as crimes of violence, stirring

---

[1] Edited by Eckstorm and Smyth.
[2] Edited by Flanders, Ballard, Brown, and Barry.
[3] Editors of Negro folksongs have also found their material worthy of comment, but most of their criticism has been casual and highly subjective.
[4] *The Ballad of Tradition*, p. 262.

adventures, and disasters were grist for the ballad-maker's mill on both sides of the Atlantic, and not a few American ballads have their counterparts abroad.[5]

Far from being a new development in America, the plebian ballad was well established in England long before Shakespeare was born and continued to flourish for more than two centuries thereafter. Many stall ballads were still being produced in the nineteenth century, but the type had passed its prime and was showing signs of decline. Thus when American balladry reached its zenith after the Civil War, the British street ballad had fallen upon evil days and was losing its former vigor as a form of printed literature. Under such circumstances it is little wonder that many native ballads have slight literary value. Because the British street ballad antedates the ballad of America, it may be said that the native author is ultimately indebted to England and Ireland for most of his stanzaic forms and for his narrative method. It is not necessary to assume, however, that he slavishly imitated the foreign broadside ballads which had traveled to America. Once he had become familiar with the type, he was free to handle his material as he saw fit. The purpose of this chapter is not to underline the inferiority of the native ballads, but in the space available to investigate the way in which the author tells his story and to see what results he achieves.

The late British broadsides should not alone be given credit for inspiring the American composer. The extraordinarily popular Child ballads could hardly have failed to influence him. Even if he was unable to reproduce their style, the native balladist may well have found in them some of the drama and the dignity which were often lacking in the broadsides. Nor should it be forgotten that American balladry mirrored the vigorous and varied life of the nation which produced it. In the last analysis, the native balladist was inspired by events which had real significance for him. Such evidence as can be gathered indicates that he was not usually a professional composer satisfying the demands of a hungry press. He was, on the contrary, one who composed for the entertainment of his fellows and who spoke with sincerity of the life he knew.

The balladry under discussion here has had sufficient appeal to work its way into the fabric of American life. It has not been looked upon lightly by singers and their audiences. Although we might wish it to be of higher literary quality, we must accept it for what it is, the native

---

[5] The following pieces in Henderson's *Victorian Street Ballads* are not unlike certain native American products: "The Albion Mills on Fire", "Execution of Alice Holt", "The Last Moments of A. Dalmas", "Shocking Rape and Murder of Two Lovers", and "Fearful Colliery Explosion". Other examples of late British broadsides may be found in Ashton's *Modern Street Ballads* and, printed mainly from tradition, in O'Lochlainn's *Irish Street Ballads*. In these collections and others the word "ballad" indicates merely a product of the ballad press. Thus many street ballads are topical songs which make no attempt at narration.

traditional balladry of the United States and British Canada. It will be enlightening from time to time to contrast our ballads with the best known traditional ballads in English, those in the Child collection. From the standpoint of literary excellence, such comparisons are patently unfair. Dozens of the Child ballads have been distilled through hundreds of years of tradition, while our native balladry never came to full maturity. At the same time, the method of contrast is too useful to be discarded, for it emphasizes those qualities of American balladry which are most pronounced.

The conviction that various narrative folksongs in the first person may properly be called ballads has been expressed in Chapter I. American balladry would suffer a great loss if we made exclusions on the basis of subjectivity alone. Such ballads as "The Sioux Indians", "The Texas Rangers", and "McAfee's Confession" would have to be discarded. Each of the ballads named is made, if anything, more vivid by the use of the first person. They exist primarily for the dramatic stories they tell. If, incidentally, the feelings of the narrator are revealed, that seems a poor reason for denying them admission to the ballad class. As a matter of fact, American singers display a fondness for the personal approach; many of our ballads recount the experiences of the narrator. In at least one case this tendency was carried too far. Rickaby reports that he heard a version of "The *Persian's* Crew" which the singer began as if he had been aboard the ship, apparently forgetting that all the crew were to die before the end of the ballad.[6] This illustrates the principal disadvantage of the first-person ballad. Most ballad stories end in the death of the main character. In a first-person ballad, death may be fearfully anticipated, but it cannot be dramatized, and thus such ballads are not neatly rounded off. The first-person plural is not unusual in chronicles of adventure; it may be found, for instance, in "The *Dreadnaught*" and "The Buffalo Skinners." In neither ballad does it interfere with a direct narrative approach.

The most objectionable feature of the subjective ballad is its tendency toward drawing a moral from stories of crime or tragedy. Even ballads about accidental death are not free from moralistic endings. Such endings may indicate attempts to mollify those who consider ballads worldly and sinful songs. Sensational stories with an avowedly moral purpose have long been popular, and street ballads of this type have been circulated in England for centuries. The Child ballads, by contrast, are conspicuously free from this convention. If any moralizing is to be done, the singer or his audience may do it. Of course the American ballad maker may be quite sincere in drawing a moral from his sad story. He may feel that good will result from giving his ballad an obvious purpose. The old Kentucky minstrel, Jilson Setters (James W. Day) had ethical as well as monetary reasons for composing

---

[6] *Ballads and Songs of the Shanty-boy*, p. 225.

ballads. He once spoke as follows to Jean Thomas:

> Try as a body will to pint out the wickedness of the world, meanness
> goes on. . . . They tell me a young fellow by the name of Bernard Friley
> was stobbed and clubbed plum to death. I've made up a warnin' piece
> about it. Though I don't know as it will do any good.[7]

Not a few native ballads may be called "warnin' pieces." The most obvious
examples are the funeral ballads "Wicked Polly" and "Death Is a Melancholy
Call." The last stanza of the former makes the following admonition:

> Oh. sinners, take this warning far, (i.e. "fair")
> And for your dying bed prepare;
> Remember well your dying day,
> And seek salvation while you may.[8]

The tragic story of Harry Dunn ends with this bit of advice to prospective
lumbermen:

> Don't leave your aged parents but stay home while you can;
> And when you go out to have a time, stay away from the
>   woods of Michigan.[9]

The action-filled ballad "The Wreck of Old 97" ends, in some versions, as
follows:

> Come, all you young ladies, and take warning;
> Take warning from this time.
> Never speak rash words to your sweetheart—
> He may go and never return.[10]

Cambiaire suggests that this moral is a later addition.[11] In any case, it is
rather inappropriate; no indication is given in the ballad that harsh words
were spoken to anyone. The author of "Young Charlotte" had the good
sense to let his tale end on a dramatic note, and, though the folk have added
several stanzas, most singers do the same. But at some time during its
wanderings Miss Pound's version acquired this distressing ending:

> Young ladies, think of this fair girl
> And always dress aright,
> And never venture thinly clad
> On such a wintry night.[12]

One more example of the American weakness for moralizing will suffice. In
one of Brewster's versions of "Pearl Bryan", the narrator becomes quite
violent about the perfidy of men:

---

[7] *Ballad Makin'*, p. 135. Mrs. Thomas prints Setters' ten-stanza ballad, "The Death of
Bernard Friley", on pp. 135-136.
[8] Eddy, *Ballads and Songs from Ohio*, p. 306.
[9] Gardner and Chickering, *Ballads and Songs*, p. 283.
[10] R. W. Gordon, *Adventure*, Jan. 30, 1924, p. 191.
[11] *East Tennessee and Western Virginia Mountain Ballads*, p. 97.
[12] *American Ballads and Songs*, p. 107.

Young ladies, now take warning; young men are so unjust
It may be your best lover, but you know not whom to trust.
Pearl died away from home and friends, out on that lonely
    spot;
Take heed! take heed! believe me, girls; don't let this
    be your lot![13]

It is unfortunate that advice-giving in ballads is inconsistent with artistry. The ballad-makers should realize that tragic stories can be made to carry their own implications, as the Child ballads do. But apparently such skillful construction is usually beyond their powers. Even if they resist the temptation to point a moral, the folk may take the matter into their own hands and supply one. These endings are by no means general in American balladry, but they occur frequently enough to merit discussion.

As has been shown in the preceding chapter, sensational material is the stock in trade of the American ballad-maker. Most native ballads tell tales of crime or tragedy which usually ends in death. Although its subject matter could easily be presented in a shocking manner, native balladry is surprisingly restrained. For example, sex, which is an important theme in the two main streams of British balladry, rarely finds its way into American folksong. Physical love is dealt with constantly and frankly in the older balladry, but is almost completely absent from the balladry of America. It is true that few American ballads tell love stories, but the explanation goes deeper than that. American balladry had its greatest development in the Victorian era, when even in the hinterland of America, female virtue and modesty were held in high esteem. The American ballad heroine, even when she is about to be murdered, is ladylike in word and deed. The tabu against sex leads the ballad-maker into certain difficulties when he attempts to recount an event in which sex played a vital part. The weak motivation in many murder ballads can be explained in this way. The man becomes a scheming villain who, for no apparent reason but innate fiendishness kills the woman who loves and trusts him.[14] The British traditional ballads take these and other sordid subjects in their stride. People who enjoyed witnessing executions were made of stern stuff; they wanted and got balladry that did not mince words.

American audiences preferred watered-down sensationalism. Killing is taken as a matter of course in many British ballads;[15] in America murder has been treated as the shocking deed that it is. Bloody details are avoided or are passed over quickly both in murder ballads and in other ballads of

---

[13] *Ballads and Songs of Indiana*, p. 286.
[14] See "The Jealous Lover", "Pearl Bryan", and other murder ballads in Appendix I.
[15] Most of the bluntness has been expurgated from British balladry in this country, though some gruesome details remain. In "The Brown Girl" ("Lord Thomas and Fair Annet"), Lord Thomas still cuts off the girl's head and throws or kicks it against the wall. See Randolph, *Ozark Folksongs*, vol. 2, p. 95.

tragedy. This is understandable in pieces sung by family groups, but it applies equally to the ballads created for male audiences. Death in these ballads, too, is treated tenderly, even reverently. We are not told that the Dying Cowboy is bleeding or in pain, or that the Dying Mine Brakeman has been mangled in the accident. After all, the folk set their own standards of taste and decide what shall survive; it is easy for them to censor a line or to omit an entire piece from their repertories. Eckstorm and Smyth have shown, for example, that in older versions of "The Jam on Gerry's Rock", only Monroe's head is found, while later versions do not mention decapitation.[16] Most singers probably found the tragedy keen enough without this extra horror. No doubt both composers and singers had their part in giving American balladry its high moral tone. In general, the folk neither condone vice nor discuss it in detail. Unlike British balladry, which exhibits the mores of many centuries, American balladry, having been compressed into relatively few decades, is consistent in its disapproval of deviations from the strict moral standards which are accepted if not always practiced by the people among whom it flourishes.

Because of their objective style the Child ballads may seem unsympathetic or cold blooded in their handling of tragedy. Actually, of course, they seethe with feeling, but they mask emotions under an exterior of reserve. The same cannot be said of most American ballads. Their subjective style leaves the way open for frequent emotional comments on the action. Sympathy for the victims of crime or disaster is expressed rather than implied. While kindness of heart and sympathy for the unfortunate are praiseworthy in themselves, they lead almost inevitably to sentimentality, another characteristic of the age of Victoria. American balladry is undeniably sentimental. But with a few exceptions the sentimentality is not of that objectionable kind once so beloved of female, and sometimes of male, poets and novelists. That is to say American balladry does not invent essentially false situations in order to weep over them.[17] Its sentimentality lies partly in a lack of selectivity in bestowing sympathy. A character in a desperate situation is wept over even if he is responsible for the condition in which he finds himself. The confessional ballads are the worst offenders in this respect. In these, the condemned criminal describes his crimes at some length and then becomes tearful because he is about to pay for them. Ballad sentimentality thrives, too, on stories of untimely death. Here the mistake, if I may so speak of it, comes not from the choice of subject matter, but from the attenuation of the death scene far beyond artistic limits. "Young Charlotte" is a notable exception. The girl speaks four memorable words and is silent.

---

[16] *Minstrelsy of Maine*, p. 188.

[17] While this statement holds true for the ballads under discussion, it should be explained that some narrative songs have been excluded from consideration because they combine a literary or pseudo-literary style with extreme sentimentality. See Appendix III.

But dying soldiers, cowboys, and others speak on, stanza after stanza, until one becomes more interested in the length of the monologue than in the tragedy being enacted. The event being recounted, however, is realistic enough; one encounters no difficulty in believing that these people are dying under the circumstances described. For this reason the sentimentality of the ballad is much easier to endure than is that in which both subject matter and treatment are unconvincing.

Suspense is not a conspicuous feature of native ballad construction. Those who are used to the delayed climax of Child ballads like "Lord Randall" and "Edward" may be disappointed to find that American ballads often use the journalistic method of telling a story. That is, they reveal what has happened in the first stanza and then recount the story in detail. To use Jilson Setters' work as an example once more, his ballad "The Murder of Pearl Bryan" begins as follows:

> A horrible crime was committed
> Soon was brought to light;
> For parents to look on their headless girl,
> What a sad and terrible sight.
> The girl who was beheaded,
> Pearl Bryan was her name.
> It was done by dental students
> A studying for fame.[18]

This résumé is more complete and less artistic than most. It may be defended in that it immediately excites one's interest to read or listen further. But the same can be said of the British ballads which save their dramatic revelations and end powerfully. Many of the first stanzas given in Appendix I illustrate this method of beginning a ballad. In some of them the device is used with enough restraint so that the drama of the tale is not seriously interfered with. In others it may be called a fault in story construction.[19]

Most American ballads, however, tell their stories in the usual narrative way, setting the scene, recounting preliminary events, and then treating in detail the central event and the climax. The not infrequent moralizing ending has already been discussed. Other journalistic devices than the one mentioned are found constantly in native ballads. One is reminded of that doggerel quatrain in which Kipling offers sound advice for reporters:

> I keep six honest serving men
> (They taught me all I knew);
> Their names are What and Why and When
> And How and Where and Who.[20]

It has been said that American balladry is sometimes weak in explaining

---

[18] *Ballad Makin'*, pp. 131-133.

[19] The journalistic beginning may be found, among others, in "The Brookfield Murder", "The Burning of the Granite Mill", "The Cross Mountain Explosion", "Floyd Collins", "Henry Green", and "The Wreck of Old 97".

[20] "The Elephant's Child", stanza 1.

the "why", the motivation of a story. It is usually strong, however, in reporting the details of time and place, and in explaining to whom and under what circumstances events happened.[21] This desire to be specific, to get as many facts into a ballad as possible, is responsible for much of the heavy-handed and awkward construction one encounters. Perhaps the American ballad-maker's regard for truth is stronger than his artistic sense; at any rate, he uses most of the material at hand, without considering its dramatic or poetic qualities or its appropriateness. "Jesse James II", for instance, begins with comments about the bandit's notoriety, and then plunges into an account of a bank robbery which Jesse staged. Not until the fifth stanza does the author get around to beginning the story of Jesse's death, which is the real subject of the ballad. This example is rather extreme. Usually the extraneous material is less prominent. Sometimes it consists only of an occasional stanza or phrase that one might wish revised or omitted entirely. Clumsy constructions, faulty diction, and other signs of poetic weakness, however, are typical of our balladry.[22]

It is patently unfair, of course, to apply the standards of true poetry to pieces which were composed hurriedly by untrained and often unlettered authors. In a sense these folk artists had deadlines to meet; those ballads which are based on fact had to be composed while their events were still fresh in the public mind. The ballad-makers usually had only hazy ideas about rhyme and meter, and none at all about the manipulation of intricate stanzaic forms. Technical weakness is so widespread in native balladry that it becomes almost a test of genuineness. One may be reasonably sure that any native ballad which shows evidence of real poetic skill either originated outside the folk or was modeled upon some ballad or poem of outside origin. After all, we should expect this to be true. Very little of real merit in literature is produced by accident. There is no good reason to expect miracles in folk balladry. The balladist may express himself sincerely, forcefully, touchingly, and, on the whole, effectively. But original poetic excellence is beyond his knowledge or ability.[23]

Almost any past era assumes color and romance for those who look back upon it from the prosaic present. The older Child ballads have long been thought of as epitomizing the romantic spirit of medieval Britain. American

---

[21] These details are of obvious value in connecting ballads with the events which inspired them. See Chapter V.

[22] For awkwardness in handling details, see the opening stanzas of "Ewing Brooks" and "The Brookfield Murder" in Appendix I. For wordiness, see the first stanza of "The Battle of Shiloh Hill". Of course, alterations always occur in folk transmission. One should be cautious about assigning either praise or blame to ballad authors unless original texts are available.

[23] Some native ballads which show poetic skill have never been traced to origins outside the folk (e.g. "The Jealous Lover" and "Lost Jimmie Whalen"), but this fact does not nullify the argument stated above. Further research may uncover sources now unknown; if a few ballads remain as exceptions to the rule, so much the better.

ballads, by contrast, seem compounded of ordinary events not unlike those which greet us daily in the newspapers. Actually, some of the romance of English balladry is contributed by the reader or listener. Already a similar phenomenon is beginning to take place in the ballads of America. Ballad collectors keep reminding us that the old West has disappeared, that machinery has replaced the shanty-man's axe, that sailing ships and old salts are relics of the past—in short, that many of the conditions and occupations which produced balladry have passed from the American scene. The folksongs of the nineteenth century are acquiring, for the people who collect and study them, an antique flavor and a charm which verge on the romantic.

There are, however, essential differences between traditional British and American balladry which not even time can overcome. American ballads are democratic. They fail to recognize class distinctions, and hence they largely ignore the theme of social conflict. Because they show no interest in people of wealth or position, they will never acquire the romantic flavor possessed by stories of royalty and nobility. Pageantry and the supernatural, two important ingredients of romance, have almost no place in our balladry.[24] Even love, the most universal of romantic themes, has been almost completely ignored by the native balladist. On the other hand, physical labor, which is rarely mentioned in the traditional balladry of the British Isles is responsible for many of the best known American ballads. Americans have long had a realistic attitude toward life which is inevitably mirrored in their folksong. If we analyze the truly romantic British ballads, we find that much of their action is basically quixotic and unreal. The characters are frequently finding themselves in tragic situations which people of ordinary sense could have avoided. The American tragic ballad, by contrast, has a certain blunt honesty about it which increases its impact and makes it entirely believable. It sounds factual rather than fictional because it deals in a straightforward manner with realistic subject matter.

Because American ballads follow a variety of patterns in form and style, it may be misleading to call any particular ballad typical. The two examples which follow, however, have no qualities which differentiate them sharply from other native products. I present these full versions, as they were recorded by collectors from singing, to give a general idea of the way native subject matter is handled.

ON SPRINGFIELD MOUNTAIN

On Springfield mountain there did dwell
A handsome youth, was known full well,
Lieutenant Merrill's only son,
A likely youth, near twenty-one.

---

[24] The only native ballads which deal with the supernatural are "Lost Jimmie Whalen" a piece decidedly Celtic in form and spirit, "The Ghostly Crew," another story about revenants, and "Tying a Knot in the Devil's Tail."

On Friday morning he did go
Down to the meadows for to mow.
He mowed, he mowed all around the field
With a poisonous serpent at his heel.

When he received his deathly wound
He laid his scythe down on the ground.
For to return was his intent,
Calling aloud, long as he went.

His calls were heard both far and near
But no friends to him did appear.
They thought he did some workman call
Alas, poor man, alone did fall.

Day being past, night coming on,
The father went to seek his son,
And there he found his only son
Cold as a stone, dead on the ground.

He took him up and he carried him home
And on the way did lament and mourn
Saying, "I heard but did not come,
And now I'm left alone to mourn."

In the month of August, the twenty-first.
When this sad accident was done.
May this a warning be to all,
To be prepared when God shall call.[25]

This may be the oldest of native ballads now current to have originated with the folk. The event it describes occurred in Massachusetts in 1761, and the ballad was presumably written at that time.[26]

Sympathy for the victim and later for his father is apparent throughout the ballad. With characteristic restraint, the ballad omits any account of the victim's agony. Although the youth is described only in a word or two and the father not at all, we can visualize both clearly enough to be moved by the tragedy. The author plunges directly into his story and almost immediately reaches the dramatic climax, which, however, is sufficiently extended to include the father's discovery of his son's body. Thus the ballad is built upon the detailed narration of a single event. Logically it should end with stanza six, but the author could not resist the temptation to add a moral. The final stanza weakens the structure of the narrative without adding significant infor-

---

[25] Printed in Flanders and Brown, *Vermont Folk-Songs and Ballads*, pp. 15-16, with music and the following headnote: "Recorded by Mr. Brown in Townshend, Vermont, from the singing of Mr. Josiah S. Kennison. Mr. Kennison's version of this truly New England folk-song differs from almost all others in that it is entirely serious, and without a trace of the caricature and clownishness that usually characterize this piece." This ballad is reprinted with the kind permission of Professor Arthur W. Peach, General Editor of the Green Mountain Series.

[26] See, however, the articles referred to under this title in Appendix I.

mation. The rather awkward and repetitious quality of the phraseology may be attributed both to the author and to generations of singers. Despite its deficiencies in grammar and vocabulary, and its lack of polish, the ballad is sincere and effective. Most of the faults which are so apparent here would disappear in singing. But even the coldness of the printed page cannot completely destroy its appeal.

"The Texas Rangers" is a mid-nineteenth century ballad still well established in tradition. The version given below is of average length and substance.

COME, ALL YE ROVING RANGERS[27]

Come, all ye roving rangers
Whoever you may be,
And listen to the troubles
That's happened unto me.

My name 'tis nothing extra,
But it I will not tell;
I am a roving ranger
And I'm sure I wish you well.

It was at the age of sixteen
I joined a jolly band;
We marched from San Antonio
Unto the Rio Grande.

Our captain he informed us,
Perhaps he thought it right,
Before we reached the station,
"Boys, we will have to fight."

I saw the black smoke rising,
I saw it bathe the sky;
The very first thought struck me,
"Now is my time to die."

I saw the Indians coming,
I heard them give a yell,
I saw their glittering glances,
And the arrows 'round me fell.

But full nine hours we fought them
Before the strife was o'er;
The like of dead and wounded
I never saw before.

Six of the noblest rangers
That ever saw the west,
We buried by these comrades,
There ever for to rest.

[27] Eddy, pp. 291-293, with music and this reference: "From Galen W. Summer, Canton, Ohio." Reprinted by permission.

I thought of my old mother
In tears to me did say,
"To you they are all strangers,
With me you'd better stay."

I thought she was old and childish,
And this she did not know;
My mind was bent on roving,
And I was bound to go.

Perhaps you have a mother,
Likewise a sister, too,
Perhaps you have a sweetheart
To weep and mourn for you.

If this be your condition,
Although you love to roam,
I advise you by experience,
You had better stay at home.

One trouble with ballads in the first person is that they are often seriously lacking in unity. This is not so bad as some, but the last four stanzas could certainly have been condensed, and might even have been omitted entirely.[28] Actually, stanzas three to eight contain all that is essential of the ballad. If we consider these alone, we find a fast-moving story told with vigor, one which contains half a dozen vivid phrases. No one would call its author a real poet, and yet the ballad has some of the suggestive power of poetry. From the outline sketched, one can visualize many details of the fierce battle. This piece illustrates fairly well the quality of the American popular ballad.

As practically every student of the subject has pointed out, ballads were designed for singing. Criticism based on theories of verse alone are decidedly unfair. To hear American ballads sung is to get an entirely new slant on them. The awkwardness disappears or is greatly smoothed over, and lines which seem merely trite in print acquire meaning and beauty. Sometimes, in fact, one finds it hard to believe that he is encountering the same ballad. This is perhaps most strikingly true of the Negro ballads, but the white ballads, too, should be heard if one is to understand the hold they have on the folk. American balladry is admittedly naïve. It has very little cleverness and no depth. Its primary purpose is to tell an interesting story in a dramatic way. Often showing serious deficiencies in vocabulary and syntax, it nevertheless has the virtues of clear expression and direct narrative style. Sincere and serious to the point of gloom, it rarely confuses right and wrong, and never is uncharitable toward the unfortunate. Joining as it does innate refinement and dignity with a strongly democratic spirit, native balladry has made no inconsiderable contribution to the oral literature of America.

---

[28] Hudson's version in *Folksongs of Mississippi*, pp. 227-228, contains the equivalent of four more stanzas; these give further information about the narrator, but no more about the battle.

Chapter IV

The Origin and Distribution of American Ballads

1.

An analysis of the place of origin of native American ballads, when that can be determined, shows that the South leads all other parts of the country, followed in order by the North, the Middle West, and the Far West. Considering the matter from the standpoint of wide distribution, the predominant position of the South becomes even more striking. Many of the Northern ballads have been confined to the region which produced them or have become almost extinct. Southern balladry, on the other hand, has flourished and has travelled more widely. With some notable exceptions, Northern ballads may be reported by only two or three collectors, while Southern pieces are found by many, often in places far distant from their point of origin.

Several explanations may be offered for these phenomena. In the first place, the heavily populated rural South of the late nineteenth and early twentieth centuries contained the largest number of unsophisticated communities in which ballad composers could find appreciative general audiences. Since few highly specialized occupations were widely practiced there, the ballads treated of outlawry, murder, tragedy, and other topics of wide appeal. Such pieces could travel easily to the Midwest and Far West as the population expanded and dispersed.

The population of the Northern United States was more concentrated in and near large cities where other forms of entertainment replaced folksinging. Furthermore, the sailors, lumbermen, and fishermen of New England, the Great Lakes region, and the Maritimes, while great singers and composers of ballads, created songs dealing with their own dramatic occupations which were of less general appeal than those of the South. Where these occupations have declined in importance, their balladry had tended to die away. Also, the more stable Northern population has kept Northern balladry geographically confined.

Although it is often relatively easy to determine, in a general way, the region to which a ballad belongs, such information is not likely to be of great help in solving the vexing problem of its origin. Many American ballads have been subjected to searching and sometimes disheartening investigations in

39

an attempt to trace them to their sources. Before attempting many general statements it may be well to consider some ballads about which the facts of authorship are known.

At present the authorship of about seventeen percent of the ballads in tradition can be stated with some confidence. More doubtfully or vaguely ascribed ballads add another eight per cent. Thus three-quarters of all the ballads are of unknown authorship.[1] Considering the relatively short history of most native ballads, it is rather surprising to find how few of them can be traced to specific authors. Investigators have found that statements made by singers are frequently so unreliable and misleading that further searching has almost always been necessary before a conclusion could be reached. Even at that, scholars have on occasion revised their original opinions about authorship. We cannot, of course, assert with confidence that first-person ballads of the confessional type were actually written by the convicts themselves. The first person is an old conventional device to add the appearance of veracity to the ballad story.[2] Ballads of which many variants are known are even harder to trace to a definite source. The tendency to localize place names in such ballads only adds to the confusion. Other difficulties will be cited as this discussion proceeds; for the moment let us examine a few claims of authorship.

Professor Rickaby had the rare good fortune to meet the author of two of the more popular lumberjack ballads. He discusses at some length the life and work of Mr. W. N. ("Billy") Allen, a roving woodsman who wrote "On the Banks of the Little Eau Pleine" and "The Shanty-Boy on the Big Eau Claire."[3] Mr. Allen's method, apparently, was to combine his own considerable powers of invention with the free use of imported material to produce ballads which are in Professor Rickaby's phrase "a peculiar composite of humor and pathos."[4] He would then sing his compositions to familiar tunes in the lumber camps where he worked. From the texts which Mr. Allen supplied, and from his conversations about his "poems" with Professor Rickaby, it is entirely clear that he actually wrote the ballads. On occasion Mr. Allen found himself in the curious position of hearing other lumberjacks given credit for the composition of his own ballads. The author "considered the joke a good one," says Professor Rickaby, "but kept it to himself, mainly

---

[1] Satisfactory ascriptions of authorship have been made for the following forty-three ballads: A 5, 15, 21, 25; B 5, 6, 9, 14, 18; C 2, 9, 11, 17, 25, 27; D 14, 16, 27; E 7, 8, 20, 23, 24; F 17, 18, 25, 31, 32, 33; G 9, 11, 12, 18, 22, 26, 27, 29, 30, 31; H 2, 15, 17, and 21. The following pieces are among those with vaguer or more doubtful ascriptions: B 2, 3, 4, 15, 27; C 7, 12, 13, 15; D 4, 17, 22, 23; E. 13; F 16, 27, 29, 35; G 2, 32; and I 6.

[2] See footnote 23, Chapter II.

[3] Rickaby, *Ballads and Songs of the Shanty-Boy*, pp. xxix-xxxvii and notes, pp. 196-198, 205-206.

[4] *Ibid.*, p. 197.

because he would not have been believed, I imagine."[5] This is a good example of the way in which confusion about origins can arise within a short time after composition. Scientific accuracy is hardly to be expected, either in the transmission of ballads or in the presentation of supplementary information about them. In cases of this sort, the singer may firmly believe he is telling the truth about authorship. But even if he does not, he is at least trying to entertain his fellows and perhaps bolster his own ego a bit. A singer who says he received a ballad from the lips of its author and then describes him may be merely trying to impress his listeners or command their attention. Ones does not have to go to a lumber camp to find similar examples of innocent fabrication.

Since Billy Allen is a good example of the composer-singer, let us turn for variety to a ballad written by someone outside "the folk." "James Bird" was written by Charles Miner and published in his newspaper *The Gleaner* at Wilkes-Barre, Pennsylvania in 1814.[6] Although based on events which now seem to most of us far in the past, it is still current and even popular among the folk. Professor Rickaby's comment on this ballad is worth quoting:

> Mr. Miner was a Congressman, an editor, a man of affairs, of good education and possessing considerable literary sense—all of which qualities would normally be set down as inimical to any feeling for popular balladry. Yet in "James Bird" he composed a ballad which clung in the hearts of the American folk for nearly a century; a ballad which, in my experience at least, varies less in its countless folk-versions than any other popular song. No detail in it has seemed superfluous, no stanza unnecessary, no sentiment false to the emotional realities of the thousands who heard, learned, sung, and believed it.[7]

But Charles Miner was not the only educated American to produce a successful ballad. Thanks to the tireless researches of Phillips Barry, we now know that "Young Charlotte" was written by Seba Smith (1792-1868) a New England literary man who was best known for his *Jack Downing Letters*. Professor Belden calls it "perhaps the most widely known and best loved of native American folksongs."[8] "Young Charlotte", too, has been accepted and remembered by the folk without essential change. Despite its somewhat literary flavor, it was almost completely congenial to their tastes. The ballad is based upon an event which took place in 1840. A young woman was frozen to death while riding to a ball with her escort. Smith dramatized the newspaper account which he had read, adding many effective details, and created one of the finest ballads produced in this country. As Belden points out,

---

[5] Ibid., p. xxx.
[6] Tolman and Eddy, "Traditional Texts and Tunes", *JAF* 35 (1922), 380.
[7] Rickaby, p. xxxv. This ballad is far from extinct. The Library of Congress collection, for example, contains recordings made between 1937 and 1939 by singers in New Jersey, Ohio, Michigan, and California.
[8] Belden, *Ballads and Songs*, p. 308.

"Young Charlotte" is "traditionally known in Georgia and Mississippi, where sleighs, let alone freezing to death on a sleigh-ride, must be unknown."[9]

N. Howard Thorp, a former cow-hand, included some of his verse in a small anthology called *Songs of the Cowboys*. Among them was "Little Joe the Wrangler", a ballad which has passed into oral tradition on a limited scale. The piece has enough pathos and local color to make it appeal to folk singers. Its versification is above average for a folk ballad, and its story is of a type popular among the cowboys. Although the author uses the first person plural, he gives no indication that his ballad is based on fact.

"The Dying Mine Brakeman", which is sung by miners in Virginia and West Virginia, was written as the result of a tragedy witnessed by its author. Having recorded the ballad from four singers, within three months, George Korson was naturally anxious to discover who had composed it. His fifth singer, Orville J. Jenks, gave him the answer. Korson reports the incident as follows:

> After Jenks sang I put the inevitable question to him:
> "Who made this ballad?"
> "I did," he replied casually, almost apologetically.[10]

Mr. Jenks told the collector that when he was working in a West Virginia mine one day in 1915, he saw a brakeman fatally injured in the wreck of a mine train. Part of Mr. Jenks' statement to Dr. Korson is germane to our purpose:

> . . . The idea for the ballad came to me as I was lifting the boy's body from the bloody mess. All the words did not come at once, but after mulling the idea over in my mind for a week, the ballad was finally finished and I wrote it down on paper. Then I suited a tune to it.[11]

Since both Thorp and Jenks wrote about accidents of a sort likely to happen to men engaged in their occupations, it is not surprising that cowboys and miners understood and appreciated their efforts. Orville Jenks was not the only author from whom Dr. Korson obtained the original version of a ballad which had become popular. John A. Murphy, a Pennsylvania miner, wrote that he had composed "The Driver Boy" in 1900 after having witnessed a beating similar to the one described in the ballad.

> "Some weeks after," wrote Murphy, the boy, who was a mule driver in the mines, caught a most severe cold, pneumonia set in and he died. My thoughts drifted back to the night of the beating and being of a poetical turn of mind, it gave me an inspiration to put my little talent to use . . . [12]

---

[9] *Loc. cit.*

[10] Korson, *Coal Dust on the Fiddle*, p .246.

[11] *Ibid.*, pp. 120-121. Mr. Jenks is the author of several other pieces printed by Dr. Korson.

[12] Korson, *Minstrels of the Mine Patch*, p. 106. Another example of Mr. Murphy's talent is a ballad called "The Twin-Shaft Disaster" (pp. 199-201). I have not found it elsewhere, and Dr. Korson does not indicate that it became traditional.

Although the last three ballads we have mentioned are inferior to "Young Charlotte" and "James Bird", just as the older pieces in turn cannot be compared with great poetry, it is a constant source of surprise to find how capably executed such pieces are. Sentimental, or occasionally awkward they may be, but they are also moving and effective. Their authors had the ability to see drama in life and to record it tellingly.

It should be pointed out that the authors we have discussed did not casually compose successful ballads without any previous practice in verse. Educated or not they were, to re-use Mr. Murphy's phrase, "of a poetical turn of mind." Their ballads were not produced by accident, but were the result of a feeling for verse combined with an urge to create. Not all of them were of the folk, but even those who were not supplied a need of the folk for ballads that could be sung and enjoyed. It would be unwise to draw final conclusions from these scattered examples, but we might at least suggest that a considerable portion of American balladry has been produced by part-time song-makers who had talent for telling a story in ballad form. Of course, almost anyone can sit down and dash off a ballad on some local event. Nearly every regional collection contains a few pieces which seem to have been created in this way.[13] If they have enough intrinsic interest to hide their structural weaknesses, such ballads may occasionally become popular. These few relatively good ballads which can be traced to specific authors seem, however, to have come mainly from people who were, if only in a small way, conscious artists.

I shall speak briefly of another folk composer whose history is of interest. Professor Cox gathered information about "The Vance Song" from three reliable sources and printed it as a headnote to his versions of the ballad. From these we learn that the ballad was composed, shortly before his execution for murder, by a Baptist preacher named Abner Vance. About 125 years ago, Vance shot a man who had seduced his daughter and refused to marry her. After an unfair trial, he was sentenced to be hanged.[14] The ballad, written while the minister was in prison, is about what one would expect it to be under the circumstances. In it the author combines wistful longing for the country scenes he must leave, condemnation of his enemies, and a sad farewell to his family, in which he expresses the hope of meeting them "on fair Canaan's shore." Somewhat incoherent in spots, the ballad, nevertheless, is a human document of considerable impact. It contains echoes of hymns and pastoral poetry which, while in strange surroundings, are not entirely inappropriate. If the stories of its origin can be believed, this is a good example of a single ballad forced, as it were, from the lips of a man whose talents presumably lay in other directions.

The problem of native ballad origins is by no means solved because a few

---

[13] Most of these pieces are outside the province of this study because they have not passed into oral tradition.

[14] See Cox, *op. cit.*, p. 207.

authors have been identified. A great deal of research by ballad enthusiasts was necessary to gather the small amount of information now available, to say nothing of the time spent on investigations which have proved fruitless. For every ballad of known authorship there are three others which remain anonymous. But if it is too late to identify the authors of most American ballads, we can at least theorize about them, and perhaps show why they have never emerged from obscurity. We are able to do this because collectors and scholars have been indefatigible in their search for material which would throw light on this problem.

How do ballads pass into folk tradition? The most obvious answer is that usually they are first sung locally when the events they recount are still fresh in the minds of the folk. Once they have become lodged in the folk memory, they will be passed along to singers of new regions and new generations. In general, however, the longer a ballad has been in circulation, the more difficult it is to obtain accurate and consistent information about it. The best course is to study ballads of recent origin and draw analogies from them. Jean Thomas's *Ballad Makin' in the Mountains of Kentucky* is the only long study yet published which gives much insight into the creation and circulation of new native balladry.[15] It is valuable because it describes the way of life of ballad singers and colorfully reproduces their manner of speech. Even more important than its contribution to one's understanding of the people is the information it provides about the origin of individual ballads.

Apparently the most prolific ballad maker of Mrs. Thomas's acquaintance was Jilson Setters (James W. Day),[16] who was blind until late in life, and who, in her words, "composed and 'suited to tune' more than fifty ballads, some of which critics declare, will live as classics."[17] The composer of "The Rowan County Crew" (E 20), although unable to read or write, would get the details of a story, construct a ballad, and then play and sing it on court days at Morehead, Kentucky. On at least one occasion he attended a hanging well supplied with printed ballads of his own composition. The young man to be executed had been convicted of murdering his wife while she was nursing their baby. Mrs. Thomas quotes Jilson as saying, many years later:

> "I had my pockets plum full of my song-ballet that I had made up
> about Bush and that a printer had run off for me on a little hand press
> at the county seat. I sold every one I had.

---

[15] Most of Mrs. Thomas's ballads have been excluded from Appendix I because I have been unable to find evidence that they are traditional. Unfortunately, *Ballad Makin'* is almost completely without documentation.

[16] "James W. Day, a blind street singer, is built into the romantic figure of Jilson Setters, the mountain minstrel. The J. W. Day of Morehead who composed 'The Rowan County Troubles' is more important than 'The Singin' Fiddler of Lost Hope Hollow'" (D. K. Wilgus, *Anglo-American Ballad Scholarship Since 1898*, p. 205).

[17] *Ballad Makin'*, p. x. Setters' ballad about Pearl Bryan may be heard on L. C. Record 1017 Al.

"The day of the hangin' men and boys hovered around me like bees to buy the ballet of Simpson Bush. You see," Jilson ever made certain his motive should not be misunderstood, "me a-bein' blind I had to earn a livin' for my family, and bein' as God gifted me with makin' song-ballets I follered that. Though I don't fancy such horrible tales, it seems like most folk do. . . ." [18]

Unfortunately I have no evidence to show that the ballad of Simpson Bush ever became traditional. But Setters' statement is of great interest and importance for many reasons. For one thing it shows that a new ballad could easily be sold. By having his composition ready on the day of the hanging, Jilson was sure of a good demand for it. The statement shows, too, the journalistic rapidity with which the ballad maker could operate. We may assume, furthermore, that, under the circumstances, a composer would be careful not to deviate from the facts as he had learned them. Too many people would be quick to point out errors in his story. Of course, since the ballad was composed before the hanging, that important event could not be described in it. On the other hand, if he had waited until after the execution, he would have lost his chance for a quick and almost effortless sale. Several other native ballads report that a criminal has been sentenced to death, but fail to describe the execution. One's credulity is not strained by imagining that they were produced and distributed under similar conditions.

Mrs. Thomas's findings offer concrete evidence to show that new ballads, at least in her state, are frequently first circulated in print. This helps to account for the striking similarity among various versions of certain ballads collected later from widely scattered regions. Certain students of folksong have spoken of ballad sheets of this kind as if they were a familiar commodity, but they almost never reprint a ballad from one of these sheets. The rural printed ballad that scholars talk about so glibly has almost become a part of folklore itself. A few references will illustrate what I mean. Vance Randolph, who has spent years combing the mountains for ballads, writes as follows:

> I have heard some mention of ballads printed hand-bill fashion, brought into the Ozarks in the early days: Belden (*Ballads and Songs*, 1940, p. xi) says that "single sheet ballads are not by any means out of circulation yet" in Missouri, but I have found very few of these. The ballets which I have seen are usually written in ink on yellow foolscap paper . . . [19]

I cannot tell from his remarks whether Mr. Randolph has unearthed any printed ballads at all. Turning to Belden, I find that he supports his statement by referring to a printing of "The Little Rosewood Casket" containing a

---

[18] *Ballad Makin'*, pp. 129-130. It should, perhaps, be pointed out that Jilson's ballads usually have a high moral and even religious tone.

[19] *Ozark Folksongs*, Vol. I, pp. 33-34. Randolph explains (p. 33) that "ballet" means a written copy of a song.

copyright notice and to another of "The Dying Girl", by Rev. J. H. Lewis, which is priced at five cents. The first piece is not, strictly speaking, a folk ballad; the second which was obtained from a Negro washerwoman is an undocumented narrative which might have originated almost anywhere. There is no good reason to consider this sheet an "original" printing.

Professor N. I. White speaks of . . . "the printed songs of those half folk composers, the 'ballet' writers, who", he says, "come into printing offices with doggerel verses pencilled on ruled tablet paper and, . . . order printed broadsides, which are sung and sold wherever there is a gathering of Negroes."[20] John and Allan Lomax have this to say on the subject:

> During the World War and for a generation before it, the business of "ballit" or broadside selling among Negroes had its heyday. Wandering singers, many of them itinerant ministers, made a good thing of hawking, for a price that ranged from a nickel to twenty-five cents, copies of the songs they sang, printed on one side of sheets of vari-colored paper.[21]

As far as I know the White anthology does not include any songs from print; the Lomaxes' book is limited to songs actually sung by Lead Belly. Most "ballets" are, perhaps literally, gone with the wind. That they once existed would be obvious from the foregoing quotations, even if some of them had not found their way into the hands of collectors. Of course nothing is more ephemeral than a single sheet of printed matter. If these "ballets" had been printed in large quantities—and there is little reason to believe that they were—it would still be astonishing for many of them to be found by collectors years later. One can only assume that most of them have been irretrievably lost. If by some miracle all these printed slips could be made available to students, much light would be shed on the problems of ballad origins.[22] As it is, we can only assume that many native ballads were first circulated in this form. How these originals may have differed from the versions now extant we have no way of determining with precision.

So far we have discussed three ways in which a ballad first circulates. It might be published by its author in a magazine or newspaper; it might be sung by its composer but not printed; it might be printed and distributed locally by its composer or by wandering minstrels. Then, too, a few native ballads still current in tradition got their start as broadsides published in the eighteenth and early nineteenth centuries by ballad printers in Eastern cities. Most American ballads seem to have been originally distributed by one of these methods. The ballads first distributed on phonograph records will be discussed later.

---

[20] *American Negro Folk-Songs*, p. 186.

[21] *Negro Folk-Songs as Sung by Lead Belly*, p. 181.

[22] Single-sheet ballads, however, are not necessarily originals. It would be dangerous to draw conclusions from undated broadsides without supplementary evidence of their origin.

After a ballad had become popular it was likely to find its way back into print. Many old broadsides were reprinted in nineteenth century songsters,[23] and later folk ballads were issued by city printers in broadside form.[24] A significant number of ballad texts have been transmitted in still another way. Carrying on an old tradition, many Americans, during the last century, copied into manuscript books the ballads and songs which they treasured. Many of these are traditional texts obviously taken down from singing or recitation. Aside from their value to the collectors and students of folksong, these manuscripts must have played an important part in preserving good texts by assisting the flagging memories of folk singers.[25]

Nothing has been said about possible communal origin of native ballads.[26] Could some American ballads have been composed by groups of people improvising stanzas on topics of common knowledge? Perhaps they could; some songs may have been created in this way by the folk. But until someone offers definite proof that certain native ballads were communally created, it will be assumed that all our ballads were originally the work of individual authors. There is no sound evidence to show that any American folksong of white origin which can properly be called a ballad was communally composed.[27] Most American ballads are anonymous, but there is no necessary connection between anonymity and group creation. Anonymity is almost inevitable in balladry. The ability of the folk to alter ballads significantly is beyond question. But this seems to be a gradual process, quite different from original composition. Supported as it is by the incontestible abilities of some people in rapid and clever improvisation, the communal theory of balladry has understandable appeal. But its weakness lies in its being merely a theory; it has the fact of individual composition to contend with.[28]

2.

Approximately forty-five per cent of some 250 native American ballads can be precisely dated, usually by the events which they recount. Of these only half a dozen remain in tradition, somewhat precariously, from the

---

[23] See for example Mackenzie, *Ballads and Sea Songs from Nova Scotia*, pp. 198, 205 for bibliographies of "Brave Wolfe" and "Paul Jones" ("Paul Jones's Victory").

[24] Finger, *Frontier Ballads*, p. 57, reproduces the broadside of "Jessie (sic) James" published by H. J. Wehman of New York, who offered a "catalogue of over 3000 popular English and German songs."

[25] One of these manuscript books is reproduced by Ruth Ann Musick under the title "The Old Album of William A. Larkin", *JAF* 60 (1947), 201-251.

[26] The communal theory of ballad origin is effectively summarized by Kittredge in his one volume edition of Child's *English and Scottish Popular Ballads*, pp. xviii-xxii.

[27] Now and again a student of the ballad will make an unsubstantiated claim for communal composition. See "The Battle of New Orleans" in Appendix I.

[28] This matter is discussed further near the end of Chapter VII.

eighteenth century, while the first two quarters of the nineteenth century have contributed about a dozen ballads each. Twenty-seven ballads of known date have survived from the third quarter of the last century and thirty-two from the final quarter. Since only sixteen ballads of the twentieth century (through 1930) have been definitely dated, it will be seen that the late nineteenth century has left us more pieces of certain date than all the other periods of our history combined.

Many other ballads can be roughly dated by their style and subject matter or by the statements of contributors. Of these only a few seem to be of earlier date than the mid-nineteenth century, while more than sixty can with some confidence be attributed to the period between 1850 and 1900. The twentieth century may be credited with about twenty-five of the undated pieces.

If the figures given above are combined, it will be seen that about half the ballads traditionally sung were produced in the last half of the nineteenth century, while the period before 1850 and the twentieth century have contributed approximately one-eighth and one-sixth of the total number. Remaining are some forty-five ballads of doubtful age, or slightly less than one-fifth the number extant in tradition. Even if students determine the date of some of these, the proportions attributed to each period will probably not be seriously affected.

Although detailed conclusions from these statistics would be unwise, a few generalizations may safely be made. To a rather large extent, American ballads have been based on events of interest at the time of their composition. As the decades pass, many of these cease to have meaning for folksingers and consequently drop out of tradition. The scantiness of native balladry more than a century old may be partly explained in this way. It is probable, too, that British balladry inhibited in large measure the early production of native pieces. Gradually, as the nation grew, there arose groups of people who needed a new body of folksong to meet the altered conditions of their lives. The Civil War, the increase in lumbering operations, the growth of the West, these and other developments made the latter half of the nineteenth century the time for American folksong to become firmly established and to flourish. Later, as the frontiers disappeared and the country settled down to life in an age of science and steel, much of the impulse toward folksong was lost and ballad production naturally declined. Many of our oldest ballads must be irretrievably lost, but fortunately for ballad study, collectors were extremely busy between 1915 and 1935. As a result, they were able to record from the lips of middle-aged and elderly people many ballads which were composed in the best days of American folksong and which otherwise might never have been preserved.

3.

Most American ballads arose too late to be distributed widely over this country by the migrations of the people. Some of the older pieces, it is true, benefited by these migrations and became established in folk tradition over wide areas. But even for these, conditions were not completely favorable, because they were first known in only one region in the East or South, while British ballads, having arrived with the early settlers, were known in many.[29] Later balladry had the fact of a relatively settled population to contend with. Yet, although the great migrations were over, native restlessness, the requirements of various occupations, and other motives kept considerable numbers of people on the move. Some of these people knew ballads and could be counted upon to take them wherever they went. The small proportion of wandering singers among them must have played an especially significant part in the distribution of new balladry; unfortunately we have no way of estimating their contribution. Thus it was that under relatively favorable circumstances a native ballad might gradually find its way to many parts of the country and become firmly established in national as well as in local tradition. On the other hand, a ballad composed on some event of local interest might never achieve popularity outside the region which produced it. And for every ballad which has been preserved in tradition, several others of similar kind must have been completely forgotten.[30]

The parts played by the phonograph and, more recently, by radio and television in the distribution of American ballads is far from clear. Certainly their influence on balladry must be considered. Commercial recordings of folk-songs have had huge sales. It is reported, for example that the Victor Talking Machine Company issued five million records of "The Wreck of Old 97."[31] "Casey Jones", "Frankie and Albert" in its modernized "Frankie and Johnny" form, "The Cowboy's Lament", and numerous other ballads have long been successfully distributed by the record companies. Charles Seeger presents the following astonishing statement concerning the number of folksong recordings made in this country:

> Amateur and trained folklorists reached rather gradually the fairly considerable tempo of collection of the last decade. But the phonograph companies had been doing a tremendous business even in the 1920's. Estimates of the quantity run from twenty to thirty thousand titles. The number of original masters must have been many times as great. How many of these pressings and masters now are or may ever be available for study—that is to say, in a state of preservation as in an archive—it

---

[29] The dominant position of British balladry is discussed in Chapter VIII.

[30] It seems probable that many ballads were lost because no one supplied them with tunes, or because they were found practically unsingable.

[31] Freeman H. Hubbard, *Railroad Avenue*, p. 260.

is impossible to say. No survey seems ever to have been made. Company files are often inaccessible, incomplete or nonexistent.[32]

Probably only a small percentage of these were native American ballads. Mr. Seeger goes on to say that "the limited duration of the ten-inch disc at 78 r.p.m. has in many cases required undesirable cutting of stanzas. . . . "[33] This is putting it mildly. Some record versions have been so drastically cut that only the introduction and conclusion of the ballad stories remain. In such fragmentary versions the narrative often loses its point and becomes almost meaningless. This restriction, of course, does not apply to the long-playing records which have helped revitalize the phonograph industry in the fifties and sixties. Here the problem is not the length of the text but its authenticity. While many excellent traditional texts are available on records, particularly those issued by the Library of Congress and by several commercial firms, more and more ballad texts of doubtful provenience are being foisted upon the public. Many of these are heavily edited versions of traditional pieces which commercial purveyors of folksong have found successful with undiscriminating audiences.

It seems that almost anyone with a reasonably pleasing voice and a miscellaneous repertory can make a good living or even become rich by catering to the present demand for what are loosely known as folksongs in the coffee houses, on college campuses, and in nightclubs. Such singers and others with better credentials have flooded the market with ballad and folksong recordings ranging from the most blatantly artificial to the genuinely traditional. Since demand begets supply, more and more ballads never before available outside the printed collections or archives are suddenly appearing for all to buy and learn. It is too early to see what results such recordings will have on future collections, but it may become increasingly difficult to recognize genuine traditional patterns of transmission and diffusion.

The regional collections contain a number of ballad texts which seem to have been learned directly or indirectly from phonograph recordings. In a few cases this indebtedness is made clear by the editors,[34] but in most it must be deduced from internal and external evidence. Professor D. K. Wilgus has shown, for example, that one-third (59) of the ballads listed in Appendix I of the first edition of this work were available on no fewer than 578

---

[32] *JAF* 61 (1948), p. 215 (from a review of commercial record albums).

[33] *Ibid.*, p. 216.

[34] Morris, *Folksongs of Florida*, p. 93: " 'John Hardie.' Recorded from the singing of Mrs. Jenks Hart, Newberry, who learned the song from a phonograph record several years previously." *Colorado Folksong Bulletin* 2 (1963), 2: "Mr. Ellis K. Skinner . . . learned most of his songs 1) from radio broadcasts over station WSM in Nashville, Tennessee, and KIDW (the first station in Lamer, Colorado), 2) from a column called 'Fiddlin' Joe's Song Corral,' published in Street & Smith's *Wild West Weekly*, and 3) by exchanging songs with other singers in the rural community of Walsh, which is near Lamer."

different hillbilly phonograph records, most of them made during the twen-
ties.[35] Thus for those who learned their songs relatively late, the influence
of this medium of distribution must have been considerable.

But the regional collections of the last thirty-five years have consisted
largely of texts learned long before the phonograph influence existed, and
the anthologies are remarkably free of ballads obtained from sources which
the folklorist would consider questionable.

A distinction should be made between ballads taken from tradition and
sung, sometimes considerably altered, on commercial phonograph records
and those pieces which were originally composed for the record industry
with its special demands and limitations in mind. Ballads of the latter type
have passed into tradition fairly frequently and represent an increasing
percentage of the pieces of relatively recent origin. Obviously in these cases
the phonograph text would not be a distortion of the original but the original
itself. For example, I have from Professor Wilgus the following account by
the composer of "Floyd Collins":

> In April, 1925, Mr. P. C. Brockman, a dealer and 'scout' for Okeh
> records, . . . while seated on the piazza of a Florida hotel first conceived
> the idea of the song of the tragedy in Sand Cave. He immediately wired
> me, 'Get song on Floyd Collins in Sand Cave.' Immediately upon receiv-
> ing the wire I went to the piano and in three hours the song was com-
> pleted and on its way to Florida. Mrs. Irene Spain, my eldest step-
> daughter, who assisted me in making the song, began the musical
> arrangement at once, and in less than forty-eight hours the song was
> on its way to Washington for copyright.

The composer was paid twenty-five dollars for the song and another twenty-
five dollars for the recording he later made of it. This is a significant example
of a twentieth century author making a ballad to order for the phonograph
trade. The composer was the Reverend Andrew ("Blind Andy") Jenkins, of
Atlanta, Georgia, newsboy, preacher, folksinger, and ballad maker, who is
also, according to Dr. Wilgus, the author of "Kenny Wagner," "Kenny
Wagner's Surrender," "Frank Dupree," "Lee Bible," "Edward Hickman,"
and "Marian Parker III". All the pieces listed are based upon sensational
events from various parts of the country. All were widely distributed on
phonograph records, and all found their way into tradition.

The influence of nineteenth century broadside and songster texts on the
distribution of the older American ballads has not been studied in detail, but
it is not negligible.[36] Ballads printed on single sheets were sold in enormous

---

[35] "Recorded Hillbilly Analogues of Laws' Native American Ballads," a paper read at
the Madison, Wisconsin, meeting of the American Folklore Society in September, 1957.
Dr. Wilgus lists the following native ballads on records: A8, 17; B1-7, 9-11, 13-15, 17;
C1; E1-5, 7, 8, 10, 11, 13-19; F1, 2, 4-6, 11, 14, 20; G1-3, 11, 17, 19, 22, 23; H1-4, 8, 9,
13; I1, 2, and 4.
[36] For a further discussion of this matter, see "Printed Texts and Ballad Survival," in
my *American Balladry from British Broadsides*, pp. 58-62.

quantities throughout the century, and all kinds of songbooks, including those containing ballads now traditional, were extremely popular. The first major catalogue of American song sheets and broadside ballads[37] includes such pieces as "Joe Bowers," "The Blue-Tailed Fly," "The *Cumberland's* Crew," "The Fellow That Looks Like Me," "The Hunters of Kentucky," and "The Banks of Brandywine," along with dozens of verse narratives no longer sung. And this catalogue is limited to the present holdings of one library for the period 1850-1870. *The Forget Me Not Songster*, which was first published about 1840 and continued to be reprinted in great quantities for many years, contains "Bold Dighton," "Brave Wolfe," "James Bird," "The Loss of the *Albion*," and "Paul Jones's Victory". That such printed texts were influential in spreading balladry seems obvious. At the same time, their impact on the twentieth century collections is rarely direct. Most collected texts of the pieces listed show those marked variations which are the best evidence of independent traditional life.

In general, however, American ballads have been distributed by individual singers performing non-professionally before small audiences in homogeneous communities and within families in the form of private singing. Ballads pass in the latter way from one generation to another without being diffused through the community. What we may call vertical transmission as opposed to the horizontal transmission of the public performer helps explain why so many ballads must be patiently searched for before finally being discovered by ballad collectors. Although non-commercial ballad singing is a long way from dying out, it has lost much of its prominence as a form of traditional entertainment among the folk, and the few remaining singers are not always easy to find.

Information about the geographical distribution of each traditional ballad is presented in Appendix I, but it may be well here to analyze and supplement some of this data. For purposes of illustration, one or two pieces from each of our nine main types have been chosen. The possible influence of commercial media is here disregarded.

Versions of "The Texas Rangers," in which the enemies are variously described as Indians, Rebels, and Yankees, have been reported from almost every state in the South and Middle West. The piece is sung also in Utah, Pennsylvania, and New England, and has even reached Nova Scotia.[38] More than two dozen texts are available for study—a fairly large number for a native ballad. As has been said, "James Bird" is still sung traditionally in more than one region. I have found it printed in this century from New York, Pennsylvania, West Virginia, Kentucky, North Carolina, Ohio, Missouri,

---

[37] Edwin Wolf, 2nd, *American Song Sheets, Slip Ballads, and Poetical Broadsides, 1850-1870: a Catalogue of the Collection of the Library Company of Philadelphia*, Phila., 1963.

[38] Flanders-Barry, *The New Green Mountain Songster*, p. 228.

Wisconsin, Nebraska, and Utah.[39] Knowing that this ballad was first published in Pennsylvania makes its present distribution interesting to trace.
"The Dying Cowboy" flourishes all over the South and has been reported
from many places in the Midwest and West. The fact that so many cowboys
came originally from the South may help explain its popularity in that
region. More than twenty printed versions are available, including that in
Lomax's *Cowboy Songs* which is said to be "amalgamated from thirty-six
separate sources."[40] Its companion piece, "The Cowboy's Lament," has general distribution throughout the United States. More than thirty versions
appear in scholarly collections.

That fine ballad of the shanty-boy, "The Jam on Gerry's Rock" has been
reported principally from the northern lumbering states, as well as from
West Virginia, North Carolina, Florida, Newfoundland, Nova Scotia, Ontario,
and even Aberdeenshire, Scotland.[41] More than thirty versions have been
printed. By way of contrast the Great Lakes ballad "Red Iron Ore" might
be mentioned. Apparently only one version of this has been printed, that of
M. C. Dean of Minnesota, which Rickaby and Sandburg reprint.[42] Those
familiar with the ballad will understand its limited appeal. "Sidney Alllen"
presumably originated at Hillsville, Virginia, in 1912. All the versions reported are so nearly identical that a printed original must be behind them.
The best text comes from Virginia by way of Michigan. Others have been
reported from Virginia via Rhode Island,[43] from Tennessee, Virginia, Kentucky, Alabama, Mississippi, and Nevada. The piece has been printed seven
times. Another outlaw ballad, "Sam Bass", has been printed about a dozen
times, usually from Missouri and Texas, but also from Arkansas, Colorado,
and Utah.[44]

To continue this illustration of distribution, we may take the murder
ballads "Henry Green" and "Mary Phagan". The former originated in New
York State. It has been printed from New York, Vermont, Michigan,
Missouri, and Arkansas, and has been collected also from Maine, New Hampshire, New Jersey, Virginia and Florida. The movement of this ballad in
various directions from its point of origin presents a typical pattern of
transmission. The ballad of Mary Phagan, based on her murder in Georgia
in 1913, has been printed about fifteen times, from Georgia, Alabama, Kentucky, Alabama via Illinois, North Carolina, Florida, Virginia via Michigan,[45] Ohio, Tennessee and Utah. Here the transmission is mainly northern

---

[39] See also footnote 6 above.
[40] P. 48.
[41] Flanders-Barry, *op. cit.*, p. 45.
[42] Three other singers, from Michigan and Ohio, have contributed versions to the Library
of Congress collection.
[43] Obtained by Horace P. Beck.
[44] The Library of Congress has a recording from Kentucky.
[45] Gardner and Chickering's *Ballads and Songs of Southern Michigan* is enriched by a
number of ballad texts from Virginia.

and westward. "The Burning of the Granite Mill", one of the least artistic of American ballads, must have originated in Massachusetts, where the event occurred. It has been printed only three times, from Vermont, Nova Scotia, and Maine. The much wider distribution of another tragic ballad, "Young Charlotte", has been outlined earlier in this chapter. Especially well known in the northern states, it has been reported from every major section of the country. About forty full texts have been printed.

"Frankie and Albert" seems as popular among white singers as among Negroes. More than three dozen good texts, most of them varying widely from one another, may be found in print. Although reported mainly from the South, the ballad appears to be known in all parts of the country. According to Lomax, Dr. R. W. Gordon collected three hundred variants of it.[46] "The Coon Can Game" evidently has much less appeal, even among the Negroes who created it, having been printed only eight times, from South Carolina, Kentucky, Texas, and Montana, with a composite text from Arkansas and California. The two dozen texts of "The Little Mohea" have come from all sections of the country, with concentration in the South. As a final example of distribution we find "The Arkansas Traveler" printed more than two dozen times. Most of the versions are from the South and Midwest.

The foregoing analysis was based on about five per cent of the traditional native ballads. Although it contains a higher than average representation of ballads which are truly popular, it gives a general indication of the way ballads spread from their region or place of origin. As would be expected, gradual oral transmission among neighboring states seems to be the rule. As collecting continues, more detailed analyses will become possible. Undoubtedly many pieces are much more widely diffused than this study indicates.

---

[46] *American Ballads and Songs*, p. 103.

Chapter V

The American Ballad as a Record of Fact

For hundreds of years the British broadside ballad served as a special kind of news sheet. Hastily composed and carelessly printed, it was distributed largely among people of little education, who desired sensational stories simply and dramatically told. With its woodcut illustration and its superficial reporting, the street ballad may be compared to the present-day tabloid newspaper. The ballad was not seeking after truth in any philosophical sense. It dealt usually with factual material, but since its primary purpose was to entertain, and since its verse form was somewhat confining, its author felt under no obligation to present a complete and unbiased report. At times, perhaps, the ballad maker wrote with tongue in cheek disbelieving various statements in the very story he was telling, but feeling that it was remarkable enough to pass along. Journalists who produced anonymous ballads for the gullible had no reputations for veracity to uphold; thus we find dozens of old ballads which tell stories, parts of which are so fantastic that no one of judgment from Elizabethan times on could possibly have credited them.[1] Apparently these were enjoyed by the public and accepted at face value. Although often partisan in their approach, many other broadsides and a large number of the Child ballads seem to be honest attempts to present factual information dramatically.[2] Such ballad stories when compared with historical accounts of the events they describe exhibit a striking fidelity to fact. To confuse the matter further, a third class of broadside ballads exists. This consists of obviously or apparently fictitious stories designed purely to be enjoyed but not to be believed.[3] Time and oral transmission, however, play strange tricks, and eventually it becomes difficult if not impossible to distinguish between fact and fiction in many ballads not based on well-known historical events.

Native American balladry, which is the product of a more enlightened age than the older English balladry, contains few fantastic or supernatural elements. No particular effort is required to believe the central events. But since it is known that a few ballads have no basis in fact, it is dangerous to jump to conclusions about them. Each ballad presents investigators with a

---

[1] See for example *The Shirburn Ballads*, edited by Andrew Clark, nos. X, XVI, XXXIII, and XXXVIII.
[2] See Child nos. 167-208 and *The Shirburn Ballads*, nos. LX, LXII, LXVII and LXXIX.
[3] See *The Shirburn Ballads*, nos. I, XV, XXXVII, and XLIX.

separate problem to be worked with and perhaps solved. The recent development of American balladry has been extremely helpful in this regard. Students have frequently been able to trace ballad stories if not to their authors at least to newspaper accounts or court records. As a working rule, the investigator assumes that the American ballad is based on fact. In most cases this assumption has proved correct; documentary evidence which corroborates information given in one ballad or another is constantly being discovered. American balladry in general is no less timely and journalistic than the British balladry which preceded it. If anything, it is more factual, because it has been created not by professional ballad writers who had the constant demands of the press to supply, but by folk composers who depended for their inspiration almost entirely on events of current interest. It is true that some ballads, especially the imitative ones, are so vague and incomplete in their details that there is no good way of connecting them with specific events. Many ballads, however, are rich enough in precise references to enable scholars to authenticate their stories, and in the typical American ballad factual detail takes precedence over both drama and artistry. Belief in the factual basis of both native and imported ballads is, in fact, well established in the minds of American folk singers. This conviction is probably responsible to no small extent for the firm hold which ballads have among the folk. They may look with some suspicion upon fiction, but they take to heart dramatic, and particularly tragic, stories which they believe to be true.

As a rule, it is easier to connect a ballad with a definite event than to discover its author. But tracking down a ballad can become a surprisingly difficult and complex undertaking, as quite a few scholars have discovered. If all ballads were available in their original form, far fewer problems would present themselves. As it is, however, changes are made, by accident or design, so that after a time a ballad may be connected with more than one location or event. The background information provided by singers is frequently unreliable or contradictory. A singer may be firmly convinced that the incident which he has recounted took place within his own region, while another singer hundreds of miles away will make a similar claim. Both will usually offer evidence which the uninitiated might consider reasonable proof of the assertions made. What might be called the alteration of internal evidence is not confined to native ballads; any number of British broadsides and several Child ballads have been similarly treated, thus adding to the confusion. The mere presence of American place names is no clear indication of American origin. The events reported, if they ever actually occurred, may have taken place in England long ago. American ballad enthusiasts are to be congratulated for having overcome many of these obstacles in their successful searches for the facts upon which ballads were built. Obviously, then, when we say that most American ballads are based on fact we do not mean that all statements within a given ballad are to be considered accurate. All available evidence must be analyzed before valid conclusions can be reached.

Belden's footnote to his discussion of "Young Charlotte" offers a good example of the way in which ballad events are localized. Having mentioned Barry's discovery that Seba Smith wrote the ballad, Belden had this to say:

> Doubtless many persons have been frozen to death on a sleigh-ride. . . . Barry's Ohio text in JAFL XXV is said to be derived from a native of Vermont who "knew that the story was as it is related, taking place on New Year's Eve, and . . . either knew the people spoken of, or those who knew them." Fern Bishop, who reports the New York text, had it from her grandmother, who professed to remember the night when the tragedy happened, presumably in Jefferson County, where she lived. And Miss Eddy, Tolman's collaborator, was informed that the song was written about Charlotte Dills, who was frozen to death at Auburn, Indiana, in 1862![4]

It will be observed that each of these statements sounds acceptable when taken alone. Since the ballad mentions no place names, it could easily be claimed for almost any region of snowy winters. Some of the lumberjack ballads offer parallel examples. Singers will positively locate the same ballad event both in Maine and in Michigan.

All the War Ballads can, of course, be connected in a general way with known events, although some of them, like "The Last Fierce Charge" and "The Drummer Boy of Shiloh" might equally well be related to different battles than the ones designated or might even be fictional. In the Ballads of Cowboys and Pioneers the fictional and imitative notes are much stronger, and the settings are only vaguely localized. Only "The Mountain Meadows Massacre" and "The Boys of Sanpete County" have a known factual basis. Again in the Ballads of Lumberjacks we find some fiction and some generalization of incident. At the same time, the factual basis of more than half of them can be demonstrated or reasonably assumed. About seventy-five percent of the Ballads of Sailors and the Sea are based on fact, and the percentage rises even higher among Ballads about Criminals and Outlaws, Murder Ballads, and Ballads of Tragedies and Disasters. In these categories only an occasional piece cannot be related to known persons or events. The fictional note recurs in the Ballads on Various Topics. Only four or five of this group can be definitely tied to specific occurrences. It will be shown in the chapter on Negro ballads that while a factual basis may be suspected for many in that group, it can be demonstrated in only four or five pieces. Approximately two out of every three native ballads, then, can be shown to have a factual basis, while many others probably sprang from actual events. Under these circumstances it is little wonder that singers have great faith in the truth of ballad stories.

---

[4] Belden, *Ballads and Songs*, p. 308.

Since there is nothing to prevent a balladist from using his powers of invention, the investigator who is dealing with a believable story should relate it to some actual occurrence before accepting it as true. The history of the lumberman's ballad "Jack Haggerty" ("The Flat River Girl") is so curious that it may well serve as a warning to those who are inclined to rely heavily on internal evidence. It shows that even ballads which seem to be full of factual details may contain pitfalls for the unwary.

In the ballad, Jack, a raftsman, tells how Anna Tucker, his fiancée, was influenced by her mother to break their engagement and had announced her intention of marrying someone else. Haggerty, who had given the girl expensive gifts and had entrusted his wages to her, expresses his unhappiness and disillusionment, and says that he will leave Flat River and be a wanderer the rest of his life.

Geraldine J. Chickering traced the history of this ballad and uncovered several surprising facts about it.[5] Briefly stated, her findings follow: In 1872 Anna Tucker was the belle of Greenville, Michigan, a town "almost on the banks of the Flat River". Her fiancé, George Mercer, was made foreman of the lumber camp where Jack Haggerty and Dan McGinnis worked. Jealous that such a young man had been placed over him, Dan composed this ballad. He used Jack's name in it, although "Anna had never paid any special attention to Haggerty." Furthermore, "McGinnis did not know Anna Tucker but knew that she was Mercer's fiancée and used this song as a means of hurting him." It should perhaps be added that Mrs. Chickering's principal informant, Anna Tucker's brother-in-law, said that McGinnis and several of the older men in the camp "got their heads together and composed this song." Commenting on his remark, Mrs. Chickering writes: "This hints at a somewhat communal origin of the song. McGinnis, however, seems to have been acknowledged generally as the 'moving spirit' of the group, and is usually accepted as the sole author." We may assume that the author got little more than encouragement from the other members of the group. Mrs. Chickering's conclusion is worth repeating: ". . . It seems most probable that Jack Haggerty did not write nor was he directly responsible for the song which has borne his name throughout the United States and Canada."

Obviously, speculation about the origin of this ballad would have been futile. Written in the first person by a man who conceals his identity, it uses the names of actual places and people to tell a fictional story which could easily be accepted as true. The ballad was generally believed, and Rickaby remarks that "every man who has sung or recited this ballad for me has stoutly averred that he 'knew Jack Haggerty himself' ".[6] Not only that, but Maine lumbermen claimed the unfortunate lover as their own. Mrs. Linscott

[5] "The Origin of a Ballad", MLN 50 (1935), 465-468.
[6] Ballads and Songs of the Shanty-boy, p. 191.

even suggests that the ballad originated in the East and states that "the Flat River is near Greenville, Maine, at the foot of Moosehead Lake."[7] It is indeed fortunate that Mrs. Chickering was able to trace "Jack Haggerty" to its source and thus prevent it from becoming another of the tantalizing mysteries of American balladry.

Among the ballads of doubtful origin, "The Jam on Gerry's Rock" offers a most interesting illustration of the difficulty of tracing a ballad story. It contains the name of the central character, the location of the tragedy, and other specific details which should be of help in establishing its authenticity. Armed with this information, Mrs. Fannie Hardy Eckstorm began in 1904 a search which was to last until 1927 for corroboration of the statements made in the ballad. In a fascinating chapter entitled "The Pursuit of a Ballad Myth" she tells of her quest.[8]

Although some versions of the ballad mention the Saginaw, Mrs. Eckstorm found no evidence that there was ever a Gerry's Rock in Michigan, or that the folksong originated there. Most of her informants believed that the tragedy happened on one of various rivers in Maine or even in Canada. At last she established the fact that there had once been a Gerry's Rock on the East Branch of the Penobscot River. She also found that there was an old and forgotten song about a drowning in the early 1840's which gave the rock its name. This, however, was not the ballad under investigation. She learned also that Canadians located "Gerro's Rocks" on the Seboois River, a tributary of the East Branch, and she found that two men had been drowned at the Grand Falls of the Seboois in the 1860's. Mrs. Eckstorm points out that a Maine man would not use the plural form to indicate the spot where a man had been drowned, or roll his r's to produce a name like Gerro's Rocks, and she concludes that this name is an imaginary one derived by Province men "from the real Gerry's Rock a few miles away."[9] She does not believe that a girl would have been buried beside the body of her fiancé at the scene of his drowning, and she assumes that this romantic ending is fictitious. "An examination of the text," Mrs. Eckstorm writes, "shows that the song must have been composed by a Canadian. The phrasing, the story, and the sentiment are Provincial; so is its ballad form, the prominence given to the generosity of the men, the vocabulary itself."[10] She points out that many Canadians worked in the Maine woods during the Civil War, and she suggests that the ballad was composed by one of these men, when he was working on the Seboois River. He may have derived his tune and later the place name from the old song about Gerry's Rock, and based his story on some local drowning. She summarizes the results of her study as follows:

[7] *Folk-Songs of Old New England*, p. 214.
[8] Eckstorm and Smyth, *Minstrelsy of Maine*, pp. 176-198.
[9] *Ibid.*, p. 191.
[10] *Ibid.*, pp. 193-194.

Nothing about the song of "The Jam on Gerry's Rock" has been settled except that it did not occur at all in the places where it has been located. A part of it surely is fiction, and it may be entirely an invention; yet against this the matter-of-fact account of the breaking of the jam and the evident desire of the river-drivers to show their great respect for Miss Clara and to have the world made aware of their liberality favor its being in the main a true story; and this in spite of the ending being modeled upon some old ballad in which the rose and the brier *motif* unites the lovers in death.[11]

The writer goes on to say later:

If I have lingered long over this song, it is because it is important to know the history of anything which has so profoundly moved the hearts of men. If I have failed, it is because oblivion has already all but closed over the origin of the song and the incident it was based upon, which can hardly lie back of the memory of men now living. So swift is Time the effacer![12]

Mrs. Eckstorm's findings seemed worth outlining here in very brief and incomplete form not only for the reasons she has given but because "The Jam on Gerry's Rock" presents problems not unlike those which, at one time or another, plague all who try to trace popular ballads to their source. Researchers suffer not so much from lack of clues as from lack of facts upon which to base sound theories of origin and development.

The great mass of contradictory evidence which an investigator may gather probably contains many true statements. But one who is acustomed to receiving inaccurate information has no sound method of separating the true from the false. Where folklore is concerned, documentary evidence is usually sketchy or non-existent. Probability must serve in place of fact, and theories built upon probability are never quite satisfactory, particularly if the information available about one ballad produces not one reasonable theory but several.

The task of proving a factual basis for ballads of this kind is not entirely unrewarding, even if the results are sometimes discouraging. A great many ballads, however, contain almost no information which can be used either to date them or to localize them. Unless they can be found in early broadside or manuscript form, they must remain almost as mysterious in origin as some of the older Child pieces. "The Jealous Lover," for example, is one of the most widely sung ballads in America. Its general distribution in the United States and its artistic execution lead one to suspect British origin. Its relation to other British and presumably American murder ballads like "The Wexford Girl," "Poor Omie," and "On the Banks of the Ohio" has more than once been pointed out. Belden lists 21 different names by which the victim is known in various versions of "The Jealous Lover," as well as seven

[11] *Ibid.*, p. 196.
[12] *Ibid.*, p. 198.

names applied to her murderer. Obviously these first names are of no help in tracing the ballad. The central event, murder by stabbing, has long been common in balladry as in life. The ballad offers no additional pertinent information to assist the student in discovering upon what actual murder, if any, it was based. Thirty-five years ago Phillips Barry published an article in which he sought to demonstrate the derivation of "The Jealous Lover" from an early nineteenth century English broadside entitled "Murder of Betsy Smith."[13] Clearly there is a basic similarity between the two stories, as well as some striking parallels in incident. Barry prints six long stanzas from the broadside which he said had 'entered into the composition' of "The Jealous Lover." His third stanza of "Betsy Smith" follows:

> On bended knees she then did fall, in sorrow and despair:
> And loud for mercy she did call; her cries did rend the air;
> With clasped hands and uplift eyes, she cried, "O spare my life,
> And I will never ask of you to make me your wedded wife."

This may be compared with the following stanzas from "The Jealous Lover":

> On bended knees before him
> She pleaded for her life
> Into her snow-white bosom
> He plunged a dragon knife.
>
> "What have I done, dear Edward,
> That you should take my life?
> I always have been faithful,
> And would have been your wife."[14]

The young man proceeds to stab Betsy and is later sent to jail to await execution. In the first of Barry's stanzas, the murderer lures the girl into a 'flowery grove,' intimating that he is about to propose to her. In "The Jealous Lover," Edward invites the girl for a walk, saying that they will discuss their wedding plans. It is easy to understand Barry's reasoning in relating the two ballads. A comparison of the stanzas given, however, can do no more than suggest the most significant difference between them. "The Jealous Lover" is a fine popular ballad, sensitively composed and poetic. The "Murder of Betsy Smith" is a crude and verbose piece of sensationalism written in low broadside style. No demonstrable process of oral transmisssion could within a few decades transform so poor a ballad into one of such relatively high quality. It is remotely possible that some American ballad author wrote "The Jealous Lover" with memory of the other ballad in the back of his mind. But this is mere conjecture. It would be almost as logical to assume that "The Jealous Lover" was known to the English author of "Betsy Smith." In short, since both the American author's identity and the

---

[13] *American Speech* III, no. 6 (Aug., 1928), pp. 441-447.

[14] Hudson, *Folksongs of Mississippi,* p. 186.

event upon which his ballad is based remain a mystery, we have no way of determining whether or not "The Jealous Lover" is based on fact.

At one time it was believed by Cox and others that "The Jealous Lover" was based upon the murder of Pearl Bryan, of Greencastle, Indiana, whose headless body was found near Fort Thomas, Kentucky, in 1896. It has since been pointed out that Pearl Bryan's murder bears no close resemblance to that described in "The Jealous Lover."[15] It is apparent that the folk did little more than insert Pearl's name and that of her lover into the old ballad. We have designated this variant "Pearl Bryan II" to distinguish it from the other two ballads which go into detail about the actual circumstances of the murder.[16] This is another example of localization and the confusion which results from it.[17]

"Pearl Bryan I" is a good example of the type of ballad for which it is relatively easy to establish a factual basis. Brewster's A version, for instance, gives both the location of the crime and the names of the principals, and describes in some detail the events which occurred both before and after the murder. Investigators have had little trouble in finding court records and newspaper accounts to verify the ballad story. Nothing shows more clearly the dependence of the typical ballad author upon facts than the success which students have had in working from the ballads themselves to a knowledge of the events which inspired them.

A case in point is offered by the ballad "Lula Viers," which Jean Thomas heard sung in Kentucky, in the presence of Lula's cousin. Mrs. Thomas's version follows:

> Come all you good people
> From all over the world;
> And listen to a story
> About a poor young girl.
>
> Her name was Lula Vires,
> In Auxier she did dwell;
> A place in old Kentucky,
> A town you all know well.
>
> She loved young John Coyer,
> Was engaged to be his wife;
> He ruined her reputation,
> And later took her life.

---

[15] See "Pearl Bryan" by Ann Scott Wilson in *SFQ* III, no. 1, pp. 15-19.

[16] Some confusion between "Pearl Bryan II" and the next ballad to be discussed, "Pearl Bryan I", will probably exist as long as editors print them together under one title. See for example, Brewster, *Ballads and Songs of Indiana*, pp. 283-289. "Pearl Bryan II" is listed under "The Jealous Lover" in Appendix I.

[17] Chappell, *Folk-Songs of Roanoke and the Albemarle*, pp. 114-116 reports still another variant of "The Jealous Lover" in which the name of Nell Cropsey appears.

They went to Elkhorn City,
Sixty miles away;
And put up at a hotel,
Until the close of day.

And as dark did gather,
They went out for a stroll;
It was in bleak December,
The wind was blowing cold.

They went down to the river,
Cold water was running deep;
John then said to Lula,
"In the bottom you must sleep."

"Do you really mean it, John?
It surely cannot be.
How could you stand to murder
A poor, helpless girl like me?"

She threw her arms around him,
"Oh, John, please spare my life!
I'll go back to my mother,
If I cannot be your wife."

She threw her arms around him,
Before him she did kneel.
Around her waist he tied
A piece of railroad steel.

He threw her in the river,
The bubbles they did rise.
They burst upon the water,
What a sad and mournful sight.

He hastened to the depot,
And boarded a train for home,
Thinking that his cruel crime
Never would be known.

Poor Lula she was missing,
Nowhere could she be found.
They searched the country over,
For many miles around.

John Coyer joined the army,
Four months had come and past.
But in the Ohio River
The body was found at last.

They took her from the River,
And to the near-by town;
The steel that was around her
Weighed over thirty pound.

They held an inquest over her,
The people were in doubt.
They could not recognize her,
They could not find her out.

They sent for a reporter,
His name was Arodent.
He printed it in the paper
And around the world it went.

Her mother was seated in her home
When she read the news.
She quickly left her chair,
To a neighbor told her views.

Saying, "I will send a message,
Or, I will go and see,
If it is my daughter, oh!
It surely cannot be."

She boarded a train for Ironton,
And arrived right at the place.
It was in a morgue there so drear,
She looked on her child's face.

She recognized the clothing,
The poor girl now still wore.
The mother looked upon the corpse,
Fell fainting to the floor.

John Coyer was arrested,
And placed in Floyd County's jail;
But for that awful murder
No one could go his bail.

Soon an army officer came,
And took him off to France.
John Coyer never went to trial,
Nor sought to clear his name![18]

No one hearing or reading this unlyrical and pedestrian chronicle would suppose that the story was fictional. From beginning to end it has every mark of the journalistic report in ballad form. Because its short traditional

---

[18] *Ballad Makin'*, pp. 144-146. Reprinted with the kind permission of Jean Thomas, "The Traipsin' Woman."

life has been confined to the region which produced it, the ballad shows no signs either of corruption or of compression.[19]

In order to verify my belief that the ballad was largely factual, I wrote to the clerk of the Floyd County Court in Prestonburg, Kentucky and asked him for information about the murder. The clerk, Jarvis Allen, replied in part as follows in a letter dated July 26, 1948:

> Lula Viers was killed by John [. . .] at Elkhorn City, Kentucky, approximately October 1917. She was thrown into Big Sandy River, near Elkhorn City, and was not found until from four to six months later at Hanging Rock, Ohio, near Ironton, Ohio.
>
> At the time of her death she was unmarried but had a [child] whose father was supposed to have been John [. . .]. [. . .] left the [child with a relative] at Auxier, Kentucky, and took Lula Viers to get married which was the last trace the family had of her until they found her body in the Ohio River. [. . .] was placed in the Floyd County jail but was later released to join the army.

The almost perfect correlation between Mr. Allen's illuminating statements and those given in the ballad is too obvious to require much comment. The ballad maker's failure to mention Lula's child is in keeping with the conventions discussed early in Chapter III. Whether the accused murderer joined the army before or after he was imprisoned is a minor detail; the statement given in the ballad seems more reasonable. From the foregoing report it can be seen that long after newspapers have yellowed and their contents have been forgotten, a ballad like "Lula Viers" preserves with remarkable accuracy the details of a shocking crime and keeps them fresh in the memory of the folk.

One final example of a ballad grounded in fact may be offered. "The C. and O. Wreck" (1913) has been printed only twice, by Combs, who locates Guyandotte, the scene of the accident, in West Virginia, and by Gardner and Chickering, who include a misleading headnote confusing this disaster with an earlier one.[21] According to the story told in the ballad, Engine 820 crashed through the bridge at Guyandotte about eleven o'clock on the morning of January 1, 1913, killing Ed Webber(s), the engineer, and carrying to their deaths six or seven men who were repairing the bridge at the time. Among the names given in the ballad are those of Lewis Meadows (or Rufe Medders), the bridge foreman, and Fireman Cook. Artistically the ballad has little to recommend it. But despite its crudeness and naïvete and a rather lengthy moralistic ending, it manages to convey a clear picture of the tragedy and to arouse the sympathy of the reader in the fate of the victims.

---

[19] If this ballad survives in tradition, we might expect a gradual wearing away of the latter portion. The piece would then be similar in form to most versions of "The Jealous Lover", which end without reporting the events which follow the murder.

[20] Quoted with the kind permission of Mr. Allen.

[21] See ballads G 3 and G 4 in Appendix I.

No one familiar with the habits of ballad-makers would doubt that "The
C. and O. Wreck" was based upon an actual railroad tragedy. Since it is
always advisable to check the statements made within such a piece, I sent
a letter of inquiry to the Chesapeake and Ohio Railway. Laura E. Armitage,
the company's research analyst, kindly forwarded me information from the
Huntington (W. Va.) *Advertiser* and from the files of the railroad. On
Wednesday evening January 1, 1913, the *Advertiser* carried a detailed account of the accident, which had occurred "shortly before eleven o'clock"
that morning in Huntington.[22] The newspaper report reads in part: "When
the heavy engine reached the center span upon which fifteen bridge workers
were employed, the false work, undermined by the swift current in the river,
began to settle and then before any of the men in danger could get to a point
of safety the whole structure with a tremendous crash plunged into the river,
a twisted mass of iron, wood, and steel." The report states that five bridge
workers were injured and at least five killed, and it mentions the names of
the dead engineer, E. V. Webber, the foreman of the bridge crew, R. H.
Meadows, and the fireman, J. R. Cook. The ill-fated locomotive, Miss Armitage writes, was number 820, as the ballad states; it was later in service
as number 1120.

It is worthy of note that these records not only prove the factual basis
of the ballad but demonstrate the accuracy of some folk composers who felt
obligated to tell his story carefully and truthfully without flights of fancy.
Perhaps the author knew the men involved in the accident and took such
pains partly as a tribute to them.

Ballads of four classes have been discussed: In "Jack Haggerty" we have
fiction masquerading as fact. "The Jam on Gerry's Rock" represents the
apparently factual story which cannot be satisfactorily traced. "The Jealous
Lover" belongs among those timeless and placeless ballads which can almost
never be convincingly connected with actual events. "Pearl Bryan I," "Lula
Viers," and "The C. and O. Wreck" are accurate enough in detail to permit
an investigator to demonstrate positively their factual basis.

Dealing as they do with events of the kind which are frequently used for
full length plays and novels, ballads must of necessity leave much to the
imagination. "Poetry hain't what you'd call truth. There ain't room enough
in the verses."[23] This remark is reported by Charles J. Finger as having
been made by an itinerant ballad singer who felt called upon to elaborate
at great length on each stanza of "Sam Bass." Of course there is always
more to a story than can be told in a few simply worded stanzas. But the
ballad maker is under no obligation to be either subtle or profound. Usually
he is satisfied to report only the obvious actions and reactions which have

---

[22] I understand from Miss Armitage's letter that Guyandotte was a town which became
a part of Huntington.
[23] Finger, *Frontier Ballads*, p. 68.

produced a dramatic event. Sometimes, if he is skilful, he may suggest the complex emotional disturbances of his characters, but as a rule only conventional expressions of emotion are within his power. Dramatic facts, on the other hand, are the raw materials out of which the average folk composer is able to produce a ballad. Without them he would be lost, for he is rarely a creative artist. The ballad which he composes may omit some of the facts, and may leave many questions unanswered, but at least is will be a substantially honest report both in spirit and in substance. No form of literature, oral or written, has a more striking air of reality about it than does the native popular ballad. Invention has been used occasionally in American balladry, but it has never seriously threatened the dominant position of fact.

Chapter VI

American Ballad Forms and Variants

1. BALLAD FORMS

An examination of the Child ballads will show a great many forms in addition to the familiar quatrain of alternating four and three beat lines rhyming abcb. The so-called "ballad stanza" happens to be the vehicle of some of the best known British ballad stories; nevertheless, no ballad scholar will attempt to define balladry in terms of a fixed form. Even if we say that ballad stanzas are short, we are using a relative term that needs qualification and elucidation. Like the British ballads which have influenced them, American ballads exist in a wide variety of stanzaic patterns. The most common forms are the short four-line stanza, and the double-length or "come-all-ye" stanza, also of four lines. Since most ballads have been re-covered from singing, the stanzaic form depends in some cases upon the choice of the editor. Frequently in the "come-all-ye" stanzas the last two lines are no more closely related to the first two than are two consecutive stanzas in the short form. Different versions of the same ballad are not infrequently printed in both forms, even within a single anthology. Thus the sample stanzas given in Appendix I might have been reproduced from other sources in different forms.

As has been said, most American ballad makers seem to have had little knowledge of poetry. We may assume that they have imitated the forms of imported ballads without fully comprehending the material skill which went into the making of many of them. Metrical irregularity is so much the rule in native ballads that one tends to become suspicious of the origin of any piece which is noticeably free from awkwardness.

American authors show a fondness for the three and four-beat lines which have been popular for centuries in English lyric and narrative verse. Great variation will be observed in the number of syllables to a line. Since these ballads are not the work of skilled poets striving for particular effects, nothing would be gained by attempting detailed metrical analyses. It will suffice to discuss form in broad outlines, as the native ballad-makers must have conceived it.

As is usual in English verse, the iambic measure predominates, followed by the anapestic. Fairly regular iambic trimeter may be found in "The Jealous Lover" in which the first and third lines of each quatrain have feminine endings. "Lula Viers" is composed in somewhat irregular iambic quatrains, usually containing three accented syllables to a line. The anapestic measure is frequently used in the three-beat lines of "Grace Brown and Chester Gillette" and may also be found in the much longer lines of "Fuller and Warren". "Poor Omie" is usually printed in six-syllable lines of two stressses each, though it may also appear in tetrameter form.

A "come-all-ye" stanza commonly used in broadsides of the British Isles served as the pattern for many native ballads, particularly those of the shanty-boy. The following first stanza from "Bold McDermott Roe" gives a good example of the form.

> Come all you wild young gentlemen so reckless and so bold
> My hardships and my miseries I'm going to unfold,
> McDermott Roe it is my name, a man of birth well known
> And by my wicked follies to destruction I was prone.[1]

This may be compared with the first stanza of "The Jam on Gerry's Rock":

> Come all ye true born shanty-boys, whoever that ye be,
> I would have you pay attention and listen unto me,
> Concerning a young shanty-boy so tall, genteel, and brave.
> 'Twas on a jam on Gerry's Rocks he met a wat'ry grave.[2]

The following stanza is from "James Whalen":

> Come all ye jolly raftsmen, I pray you lend an ear.
> 'Tis of a mournful accident I soon will let you hear,
> Concerning of a noble youth, Jim Whalen he was call'd,
> Was drowned off Pete McLaren's raft below the upper fall.[3]

The relationship between the American stanzas and the Irish one seems obvious.

It is worth remarking that this come-all-ye line is equivalent to two lines in ballad meter. Thus the first half of one of these stanzas might be written as follows:

> Come all ye true born shanty-boys,
> Whoever that ye be,
> I would have you pay attention
> And listen unto me,

This produces the ballad quatrain of alternating iambic tetrameter and trimeter rhyming abcb. Of course, the content or the music often requires that the stanza be written in the longer form.

A pattern so closely related to that discussed above that it is often indistinguishable from it is the stanza of eight short lines. This might be considered either a come-all-ye stanzas written as an octave or a combination

---

[1] Colm O' Lochlainn, ed., *Irish Street Ballads*, p. 56.
[2] Rickaby, *Ballads and Songs of the Shanty-boy*, pp. 11-12.
[3] *Ibid.*, p. 20.

of two stanzas in ballad meter. Here, too, the tune will sometimes determine the proper printed form. The second stanza from "Kenny Wagner" follows:

> He was captured up in Tennessee
> And put into the jail.
> He had no one to help him out,
> No one to go his bail.
> But Kenny broke the jail one night,
> And he made his getaway.
> He thought that he could go through life
> And never have to pay.[4]

If a stressed syllable is removed from the full-length "come-all-ye" line, a verse of six stresses and thirteen syllables results. The stressed syllable dropped from the middle of the line produces a more marked caesura. The stanzaic patterns based upon this line are familiar both here and abroad. "The Texas Rangers" begins much as do many of the Irish ballads:

> Come all you Texas rangers, wherever you may be,
> I'll tell you of some troubles that happened unto me.
> My name is nothing extra, so it I will not tell—
> And here's to all you rangers, I'm sure I wish you well.[5]

Whether we think of such verses as derived from or responsible for the three-stress line, it is apparent that the two stanzaic patterns are of the same class. The following quatrain from "The Jealous Lover", for instance, could be written as a couplet in the form given above:

> "Come, love, come go, let's wander
> Down by the meadow gay;
> Perhaps this very evening
> We'll plan our wedding day."[6]

A few American broadsides, which were apparently written by professionals, are more skilfully constructed than the average folk ballad. "Brave Wolfe" is cleverly rhymed and uses the caesura effectively. "The *Constitution* and the *Guerrière*" rhymes aabccb, its long "b" lines serving partly as a refrain. The piece seems in strange company here because of its unusual form. One ballad of the Civil War, "The *Cumberland's* Crew", a rollicking piece despite its tragic story, is composed of quatrains in which the lines end alternately in feminine and masculine form and rhyme a b a b. Ballads of this sort, however, are far from typical. Billy Allen's ballad, "The Banks of the Little Eau Pleine" has been shown by Professsor Rickaby to have derived its form and some of its substance from "The Lass of Dunmore", a ballad-like piece of the early nineteenth century, which has some literary

---

[4] Hudson, *Folksongs of Mississippi*, p. 244.
[5] Lomax, *Cowboy Songs*, p. 359.
[6] Hudson, *op. cit.*, p. 186.

merit. Allen's stanzas contain two more syllables to a line than do those in regular ballad meter, and use the anapestic measure freely. Certain other ballads of unusual form may also be based on foreign models.

Other minor stanzaic forms might be mentioned, but enough has been said to show that American ballad composers have used a good many stanzaic patterns. On the other hand, most of these forms are closely enough related to give native balladry as a whole an appearance of consistency. Then, too, those forms which are based upon traditional ballad meter are by far the most popular. Anyone reading through a miscellaneous collection of native ballads or hearing them sung is more apt to be impressed by their sameness of structure than by their variety.

2. BALLAD VARIANTS

The student of balladry comes to expect that any newly recorded version of a native or imported ballad will differ to some extent from all other versions previously reported. The most obvious cause of variation is human forgetfulness. This may result merely in minor substitutions of word and phrase, or it may become progressively serious until it produces corrupt and incoherent texts. The singer's failure to comprehend the meaning of a word or phrase produces similar corruptions. Variation may also be caused by a singer's desire to improve upon the text he has received by substitution, addition, or elimination. The localization of ballad incidents has already been mentioned. It is not uncommon for ballad-singers to censor out certain phrases or stanzas temporarily or permanently. The ballad is then transmitted in its new form to be subjected perhaps to further folk treatment. Then there is the undeniable ability of the folk to create new ballad stanzas which fall neatly into place and become indistinguishable from the old. This process seems always to take place so secretly that it has, so far as I know, never been observed. When or by whom these stanzas are added remains a mystery; some indication of the origin of new forms is given, however, in the unsubstantiated claims of local composition for ballads which are widely distributed.

The substitution of a new phrase for one which has been forgotten does not have the destructive effect in balladry which it would have in great poetry. An approximation of mood and substance will suffice, because one rarely feels that any ballad phrase is too nearly perfect to be tampered with. The priority of one phrase over another is difficult to establish if the original version does not exist; each listener may decide for himself which of several forms he prefers. The following lines from "Henry Green" will illustrate how an equivalent passage varies from version to version. The first passage is from the most complete published text:

> He says, "My dearest Mary,
> If you will be my wife,
> I'll guard you from all peril
> Throughout this gloomy life."[7]

A similar passage was sung in New York State:

> He said, "My dearest Mary, if you will be my wife,
> I'll guard you at my peril throughout this gloomy life.[8]

A Michigan text contains a definite departure from the other forms:

> He said, "My dearest Mary, if you will be my wife,
> I will guard you as the fairest through your remaining life."[9]

The following version comes from Missouri:

> Says he my darling Mary,
> If you will be my wife,
> I'll guard you and protect you
> Throughout this weary life.[10]

Finally we give an Arkansas version:

> Says he Mary, dearest Mary, if you will be my wife
> I'll guard you as a parent all through your gloomy life.[11]

It will be seen that the phrase "if you will be my wife" has remained in all versions, probably because there was no easy way either of forgetting or of altering it. "I'll guard", and in one version the uncontracted form, has also been preserved. The central idea remains the same in all versions, but minor variations occur in the other phrases. The second line of the last version given shows signs of being a corruption from one of the first forms given. When we consider only a pair of lines, the changes seem slight, but carried on throughout a long ballad they result in texts with a large number of minor variations.

We are rarely able to determine the chronology of a series of variant readings except where degeneration is operating. We can assume that certain folk singers have, on occasion, consciously altered the ballads which have come to them. Since many ballads were hastily and awkwardly composed, there is good reason to believe that some of these alterations have strengthened the ballads. It is regrettable that we cannot usually distinguish the revisions from earlier forms. Not only that, but we cannot say with confidence that some of the better substitutions were not themselves the indirect result of forgetfulness. One Ohio version of "McAfee's Confession", for example, sets the murder scene as follows:

---

[7] Flanders & Brown, *Vermont Folk-Songs and Ballads*, p. 66.
[8] Thompson, *Body, Boots and Britches*, p. 442.
[9] Gardner and Chickering, *Ballads and Songs*, p. 346.
[10] Randolph, *Ozark Folksongs*, vol. 2, p. 122.
[11] *Ibid.*, p. 123.

> The act was done one peaceful night
> Quiet reigned, and the stars shone bright:[12]

The more frequently encountered phrase reads:

> 'Twas on a pleasant summer night,
> When all was still, the stars shone bright[13]

It is probable that the rarer form is an innovation, but there is no way of determining whether the alteration was accidental or intentional.

The loss of entire stanzas is the most striking feature of ballad variation. The Flanders and Brown text of "Henry Green" contains twelve double length stanzas, the fairly precise Missouri text contains but six, and another Missouri text printed by Randolph manages to preserve the essentials of the story in only four stanzas.[14] White ballad singers in America are much more likely to drop stanzas than to add them. When this process is carried a little further only a ballad fragment remains. Some of the older and less popular native ballads have suffered especially from this curious sort of erosion. In 1933 Chappell recovered in North Carolina a corrupt fragment of "The Loss of the *Albion*" containing only 16 lines,[15] in contrast to the complete version of 18 stanzas which Harold W. Thompson collected in 1935 from a blind ex-sailor who had learned it in a Scottish port.[16]

Misunderstanding of their phraseology and ignorance of the events which inspired them have resulted in the corruption of various old ballads. In this regard a comparison of the text recovered from singing with an early printed version, when that is available, is highly instructive. Herbert Halpert has printed two versions of "Major André's Capture," the first recovered from singing in 1936, the second reprinted from an 1817 songster. The later version shows that singers will frequently repeat words and phrases which have become meaningless. Two parallel passages will illustrate the degeneration which oral transmission can produce.

> 1817 And begged his assistance, but alas it was too late.
> 1936 He begged on his desistance, till last is was too late.

> 1817 And I trust you can tell me, if the dangers are all o'er.
> 1936 I'll trust to you to tell to me the dangers I a-roar.[17]

Again in Stout's version of "The *Constitution* and the *Guerrière*", a fine old broadside has been reduced to a fragment of twenty lines. In this the line "Commanded by proud Dacres the grandee, oh!"[18] becomes "Com-

---

[12] Eddy, *Ballads and Songs from Ohio*, p. 290.
[13] Cox, *Folk-Songs of the South*, p. 192.
[14] *Op. cit.*, p. 121.
[15] Chappell, *Folk-Songs of Roanoke and the Albemarle*, p. 56.
[16] Thompson, *op. cit.*, pp. 204-206.
[17] *JAF* 52 (1939), 61-63.
[18] Neeser, *American Naval Songs and Ballads*, p. 95.

manded by proud Dekker/Of the Grande O."[19] Despite the requirements of the rhyme scheme, Stout's version of "The Lake of Ponchartrain" becomes simply "Lakes Upon." A typical stanza reads as follows.

> You're welcome, welcome, stranger,
> Although our house is plain;
> We've never turned a stranger out
> Of the Lakes Upon[20]

A Michigan version reads

> We never turn a stranger out from the lake of Pontchartrain.[21]

The French name obviously gave the cowboys trouble, too, for Miss Larkin reports a version entitled "On the Lake of the Poncho Plains."[22] This fails to make sense, but at least it substitutes two familiar words for one strange one.

The addition of entire stanzas is a far rarer phenomenon in white balladry than the loss of stanzas. That it does occur from time to time is well known. The additions of from four to six stanzas to Smith's original text of "Young Charlotte" has been mentioned in Chapter IV. Some of the Western ballads, too, have been recovered in such a variety of variants that composite texts are longer and more redundant than the original versions are likely to have been.[23] Stanza addition seems likely to occur in ballads which are themselves reworkings of older material. Such re-creations tend to give the impression of incompleteness, and consequently would be especially tempting to the improviser. But almost any widely sung ballad may be expected to gain a stanza occasionally. Here again we are faced with the problem of trying to decide which stanzas represent accretions to an author's original. It should be emphasized that the versions of individual singers are almost never of unusual length. But not infrequently we find that one or two new stanzas have appeared while four or five others have dropped out. Almost invariably these rarer stanzas seem completely at home in the ballads. Since many of them contain phrases from other stanzas, perhaps forgetfulness should receive some of the credit for this type of ballad growth.

The importance of native ballad variation should not be overemphasized. By far the largest percentage of variations may be attributed to the imperfect memories of singers. Collectors have pointed out time and again that singers will try to reproduce ballads exactly as they learned them, making no effort

---

[19] Stout, *Folklore from Iowa*, p. 98.

[20] *Ibid.*, p. 91.

[21] Gardner and Chickering, p. 133.

[22] Larkin, *Singing Cowboy*, pp. 31-33.

[23] See for example Lomax's composite text of "The Cowboy's Lament", *Cowboy Songs*, pp. 417-420. His composite version of "The Dying Cowboy", pp. 48-51, may be compared with that printed in this chapter. It contains several stanzas not immediately derived from "The Ocean Burial".

to alter passages which have become corrupt or meaningless. This conviction that ballads should not be tampered with explains why almost identical versions of the more popular ballads are constantly being recovered from widely separated regions. The sharply defined variant types which, over the centuries, have developed, apparently as a slow evolutionary process, in British traditional balladry are rarely to be found in the native balladry of America. Although minor variation is the rule in all oral literature, the native ballads of white singers are relatively fixed both in form and substance. To put the matter simply, good texts of most native ballads do not vary much except in length.

American editors usually include under one number and title all ballads which relate to a particular individual or event. If these versions were simply variants of a single ballad the method would be defensible. As it is, however, we find not variants but separate ballads on the same subject, ballads which could not by any process of simple transmission have developed one from another. To avoid this confusion, I have attached roman numerals to ballads of this kind to distinguish separate texts from variant forms. Thus in Appendix I will be found such titles as "Jesse James I" and "Jesse James II" or following "The Ashland Tragedy" numerals I, II, or III. In ballad making communities it was not at all unusual for several ballads to be written on one dramatic event. Although known to singers under the same title, these ballads have preserved their separate identities. It seems less misleading to keep them separate than to group them.

In cases where one ballad has clearly been derived from another, there is no set rule to determine whether the new form should be considered a variant of the original ballad or a piece with individual identity. Some subjective decisions become necessary. Thus "The Buffalo Skinners" which is modeled on "Canaday-I-O" has been listed as a separate ballad because though its form is unchanged the story it tells is very different. "Michigan-I-O", on the other hand, remains essentially the same as the parent ballad and consequently, is considered merely a variant form of "Canaday-I-O," with which it is listed in the Appendix. Other examples of this kind will be found under "Logan County Jail" and "Charles Guiteau," both of which appear in a variety of localized forms.

Because this is a general study, it has not been thought advisable to include references to all the various titles and proper names which one encounters in different versions of the same ballad. Most of the rarer titles are insignificant as well as unenlightening. No useful purpose would be served by preserving them. On the other hand, I have attempted to include in the index and in the appendices the best known variant titles so that each ballad may easily be located. Like the names of their authors, which are usually lost or changed before ballads have travelled far, most ballad titles seem subject to infinite corruptions and variations. Then, too, a single title may be used for three or four different ballads and songs. I have tried wherever possible to choose primary titles carefully in the hope that some standardization may eventually result; at the same time, I realize the impossibility of finding for every ballad a designation which will be logical, familiar, and distinctive. I have, for example, used the ambiguous title "The Dying Cowboy" in place of the more explicit "Oh, Bury Me Not on the Lone Prairie," partly because the former designation is actually a title and not just a first line, and partly because it seems to be traditionally preferred. In choosing between another pair of titles, I have selected "The Cowboy's Lament" in preference to "The Dying Cowboy" not only to avoid repetition but to preserve the title which western singers say is the correct one.

Much has been said in this chapter about the variations produced by the forgetfulness of singers. Actually the better the ballad the more likely singers are to preserve it nearly intact. If the original author has produced a well-made ballad of universal appeal he may entrust it to the folk without much fear that it will be seriously distorted in transmission. "Young Charlotte," for instance, after nearly a century of folk-handling is still being recovered from all parts of the country in substantially its original form, and many another good native ballad is well preserved in tradition. Loosely constructed and rambling ballads, by contrast, are much more likely to be altered or added to. Some of them even attract stanzas from other ballads; the versions which result present difficult problems of analysis.

An example of this sort of confusion is offered by "Logan County Jail," a rather incoherent piece which some students might wish excluded from the ballad list. It could with some justification be classified simply as a song, but I call it a ballad despite its rambling emotionalism, because it does dramatize a single major event in the life of the narrator. Cox's B version follows:

> When I was a little boy, I worked on Market Square,
> O money I did pocket, but I never did it fair.
> I rode upon the lakes and learned to rob and steal,
> And when I made a great haul, how happy I did feel!
>
> I used to wear the white hat, my horse an' buggy fine;
> I used to court a pretty girl, I always thought was mine,
> I courted her for beauty, her love for me was great,
> And when I'd go to see her, she'd meet me at the gate.
>
> One night as I lay sleeping, I dreamed a mighty dream,
> That I was marching down on the golden stream.
> I awoke all broken-hearted, in Logan County jail,
> And not a friend around me for to go my bail.

Down came the jailer about ten o'clock,
And with the key in his hand he shoved against the lock:
"Cheer up, cheer up, my prisoner!" I thought I heard him say,
"You're going down to Moundsville, seven long years to stay.

Down came my true love, ten dollars in her hand:
"O my dearest darling, I've done all that I can!
And may the Lord be with you, wherever you may go,
And Satan snatch the jury for sending you below!"

Sitting in the railroad, waiting for the train,
I am going away to leave you, to wear the ball and chain.
I'm going away to leave you; darling, don't you cry;
Take a glass of whiskey and let it all pass by.[24]

After the second stanza of his A version, Cox comments that "the part of the song that told about the crime is missing."[25] We do not even know with what crime the prisoner has been charged. This deficiency occurs in every version I have seen; apparently it has not kept the ballad from being popular. Under the title "Dallas County Jail" Randolph prints variants of the ballad in which a cowboy becomes the narrator. The first stanza has been altered in this way:

Well, when I was a cowboy I rode out on the line,
I used to pocket money, an' didn't dress so very fine,
I rode out on the prairie to learn to rob an' steal,
An' when I downed the cowman, How jolly I did feel.[26]

A most interesting variant of the third line occurs in another stanza printed by Randolph. Here misapprehension and forgetfulness have created a proper name:

I rode the Kansas prairies along with Robert Steele[27]

In some Western versions the narrator courts any pretty girl he meets, but in all versions he has one true-love who usually brings him ten dollars and bids him farewell. In place of his sentence of seven years in Moundsville, in other versions the convict is given ten years in Huntsville,[28] twenty-one years in Nashburg,[29] and an unspecified length of time in Hot Springs,[30] the name of the prison depending upon the region in which the ballad is sung. The concluding stanzas differ greatly between versions and establish a variety of moods. In Cox's B version, the prisoner expresses a fatalistic

[24] Cox, op. cit., p. 213. Reprinted by permission of Harvard University Press.
[25] Ibid., p. 212.
[26] Op. cit., vol. 2, p. 33.
[27] Ibid., p. 34.
[28] Ibid., p. 33, p. 35.
[29] Ibid., p. 36.
[30] Ibid., p. 34.

attitude of forced cheerfulness. His C version adds a defiant fifth line:

> Just take a glass of liquor, and let it all pass by;
> For I'll be back next Saturday night, I'm a-comin' back or die.

Randolph's E version begins much like those printed by Cox, and these suddenly dissolve into apparent irrelevancy and incoherence:

> I love my father's children but I love myself the best,
> And them that don't pervide for me will never see no rest,
> A pocket full of money, a pocket full of rye,
> A dram of good old whiskey would pass my troubles by.
>
> My father is a gambler, he learned me how to play,
> He learned me how to stack my cards all on the ace and trey,
> The gambler swore he'd beat me, but likely I did know,
> Ace and deuce all in my hand I'm bound to play high low.[32]

The third stanza of Henry's version also introduces without warning or explanation the subject of gambling:

> When I left on Birmingham, I left her on a bum
> Straightway to Minford and there I just begun;
> Sat down for to gamble; five dollars was the game;
> How I beat that gambler was a scandal and a shame.[33]

The cowboy versions end sentimentally with emphasis on the sadness of the occasion:

> In come my darlin' girl, ten dollars in her hand,
> Sayin' give this to my Willie, it's all that I demand,
> Give this to my young cowboy, to think of olden times,
> An' don't forget the darlin' girl you left so far behind.
>
> While I was in the prison, my father says to me,
> May heaven look down upon you, wherever you may be,
> May heaven look down upon you, wherever you may go,
> An' I could snatch the jury that sent my boy below.[34]

These stanzas are apparently expanded from one like stanza five of Cox's B version. In Randolph's C version the ballad ends with this fifth stanza. Only one last stanza, that which is given below, actually takes the prisoner on his way to the penitentiary.

> As I passed those stations, I heard the people say:
> "Yonder goes that idle bird all bound down in chains,
> All bound down in sorrow, all bound down in shame,
> Carrying him around to Raleigh to wear the ball and chain."[35]

---

[31] Cox, p. 214.
[32] *Op. Cit.*, pp. 36-37.
[33] Henry, *Folk-Songs from the Southern Highlands*, p. 329.
[34] Randolph, *op. cit.*, vol. 2, p. 33.
[35] Henry, *op. cit.*, p. 330.

There is some reason to believe that this ballad has been inspired by or derived from British broadsides. Randolph points out that the stanza which describes the prisoner's dream is paralleled in "Van Dieman's Land" as printed by Mackenzie;[36] the British stanza follows:

O one night as I lay upon my bed I dreamed a pleasant dream;
I dreamed that I was in old Ireland down by a spurling stream,
With a handsome girl upon my side and she at my command,
When I woke quite broken-hearted all in Van Dieman's land.[37]

Under the title "The Bad Boy," Lomax prints a ballad which begins and ends like "Logan County Jail." The first stanza may be compared with that of Cox's B version above:

When I was a young man I lived upon the square,
I never had any pocket change and I hardly thought it fair;
But out upon the highway I went to rob and steal,
And when I met a peddler, oh, how happy I did feel![38]

It would not be surprising to find that "the highway" had once been "the King's highway" in some British ballad.[39] The American ballad's failure to dramatize the crime for which the prisoner has been sentenced also suggests that the piece has been imperfectly reworked in America rather than composed here.

I have discussed the variant versions of "Logan County Jail" at length not because the ballad has any particular merit but because it illustrates what may happen when a loosely organized narrative of wide appeal works its way into tradition. Every stanza undergoes alteration and rearrangement. Some may be dropped completely to make way for new ones. Occasionally one or more of the stanzas may even find their way into entirely different ballads. As long as the ballad is sung, new variants will continue to be collected, because variation always operates strongly in rambling and subjective ballads of this type.

Because I am including in this study a few ballads which are themselves variants of older pieces, I will for purposes of illustration reproduce here both "The Dying Cowboy" and the song from which it was derived. "The Ocean Burial," I feel, should not be called a popular ballad. For one thing its narrative element is extremely weak; for another, its phraseology is certainly not of the folk. The following version was, however, recovered from oral tradition in New England:[40]

---

[36] Randolph, op. cit., vol. 2, p. 32.
[37] Mackenzie, Ballads and Sea Songs from Nova Scotia, p. 305.
[38] Lomax, Cowboy Songs, pp. 161-162.
[39] Willie Brennan (L7 in American Balladry from British Broadsides) "never robbed a poor man/Upon The King's Highway."
[40] From Linscott, Folk-Songs of Old New England, pp. 245-248. This text was contributed to Mrs. Linscott by Phillips Barry and is reprinted here with the kind permission of Mrs. Barry. (See the note on this piece under "The Dying Cowboy" in Appendix I).

"Oh, bury me not in the deep, deep sea!"
These words came low and mournfully
From the pallid lips of a youth who lay
On his cabin couch at the close of day.

He had wasted, and pined till o'er his brow
The death shade had slowly passed and now,
When the land and his fond loved home were nigh,
They had gathered around to see him die.

"Oh bury me not in the deep, deep sea,
Where the billowy shroud will roll o'er me,
Where no light will break through the dark, cold wave,
And no sunbeam rest upon my grave.

"It matters not, I have oft been told,
Where the body may lie, when the heart grows cold;
But grant, oh, grant this boon to me,
Oh, bury me not in the deep, deep sea!

"For in fancy I've listened to the well known words,
The free, wild winds, and the song of the birds;
I have thought of home, of cot and bower,
And of scenes loved in childhood's hour.

"I have always hoped to be laid, when I died,
In the old churchyard, on the green hillside.
By the bones of my father, oh, there let me be!
Oh, bury me not in the deep, deep sea!

"Let my death slumbers be where a mother's prayer
And a sister's tears can be mingled there.
Oh, 'twill be sweet, sweet, ere this heart's throb is o'er,
To know when its fountains shall gush no more,

"That those it so fondly longed for will come
To plant the first wild flowers of spring on my tomb!
Let me lie where those loved ones can weep o'er me.
Oh, bury me not in the deep, deep sea!

"And there is another whose tears will shed
For the one who sleeps far in a cold ocean bed;
In hours that it pains me to think of now,
She has twined these locks and kissed this brow.

"In the hair she has wreathed, shall the sea snake hiss?
This brow she has pressed, shall a cold wave kiss?
For the sake of my loved one that weeps o'er me,
Oh, bury me not in deep, deep sea!

"Oh, bury me not—"And his voice failed there;
But they gave no heed to his dying prayer;
They have lowered him slow o'er the vessel's side,
And above him has closed the dark, cold tide.

Where to dip her light wings, the sea bird rests,
Where the blue waves dance with their foaming crests,
Where the billows bound, and the wind blows free,
They have buried him there in the deep, deep sea!

The Western adaptations show many degrees of variation, from slavish imitation of "The Ocean Burial" to the rather free and original treatment of the version given below. The folk have the good judgment to sing versions of "The Dying Cowboy" which are usually four or five stanzas shorter than the older song. This brings some welcome deletions in the monologue, and increases the reality of the piece. The tendency may be carried too far and result in an unnecessarily abbreviated dying speech, as it does in this otherwise effective version of Belden's:[41]

"Oh bury me not on the lone prairie"—
These words came slow and mournfully
From the pallid lips of a youth who lay
On his cold, damp bed at the close of day.

Chorus:
    O bury me not on the lone prairie,
    Where the wild coyote will howl o'er me,
    Where the wild winds sweep and the grasses wave;
    No sunbeams rest on a prairie grave.

He has wasted and pined till o'er his brow
Death's shades are slowly gathering now.
He thought of his home with his loved ones nigh,
As the cowboys gathered to see him die.

"I've ever wished that when I died
My grave might be on the old hillside.
Let there the place of my last rest be;
O bury me not on the lone prairie!

"In my dreams I saw"—but his breath failed there.
They gave no heed to his dying prayer.
In a narrow grave just six by three
They buried him there on the lone prairie.

May the light-winged butterfly pause to rest
O'er him who sleeps on the prairie's crest;
May the Texas rose in the breezes wave
O'er him who sleeps in a prairie grave.

[41] Belden, *Ballads and Songs* . . . , 390-391. Reprinted with the kind permission of William Peden, Editor, *University of Missouri Studies.*

And the cowboys now as they roam the plain—
For they marked the spot where his bones have lain—
Fling a handful of roses o'er his grave
With a prayer to him who his soul will save.

It will be seen that the chorus, having been derived from stanza 3 of "The Ocean Burial," contains the obviously untrue statement, "No sunbeams rest on a prairie grave." The third stanza of this version is not specific enough, for it fails to explain why the cowboy would prefer "The old hillside" to the lone prairie as a resting place. The "prairie's crest" in the fifth stanza is difficult to visualize, but both this stanza and the one which follows it seem a decided improvement over anything in "The Ocean Burial." In fact, the entire ballad has somehow acquired both the simplicity and the sincerity which are lacking in the song. The sentimentality of "The Dying Cowboy" is less extreme than that of the original, and the latter's morbidity has been noticeably softened.

By way of summarizing our conclusion about native ballad variation we may make the following statements: Because human memory is not infallible, every ballad version recovered will be different in some respect from all others. Although an occasional singer will consciously recompose, localize, improve upon, or add to the ballad which he has received, the typical white singer will try to reproduce the ballad exactly as he learned it. Only a small percentage of ballad variations can be attributed to any other cause than the forgetfulness or misunderstanding of those who sing them.

Chapter VII

The Negro's Contribution to American Balladry

Approximately one-twelfth of the native ballads current in America owe their existence and perpetuation to the Negro. These ballads are sung on occasion by white people, just as the white man's ballads are sung by the Negro. Essentially, however, they belong to the Negro, and they bear many evidences of his proprietorship. Because many of the conclusions about native balladry reached elsewhere in this book do not apply with equal force to Negro balladry, I have decided to treat this phase of the subject separately. At the same time, I will attempt to relate the Negro ballads to those of the rest of the country.

It would be incautious to say that the ballads discussed in this chapter are more than a generous sample of those current among Negroes. Much more collecting must be done before we can make positive statements about the quantity of this material. But we can be certain that some of the most important and widely known Negro ballads are available for study. Furthermore, the ballads which have been printed have so many features in common that we may with some measure of confidence consider them representative.

Since most ballad collecting in America has been regional rather than racial and since nearly all compilers of collections have been white, the partial neglect of Negro material is not surprising. In the North, Negroes live mainly in the large cities, which are usually considered rather barren areas for the collector of folksong. Collectors in the South and Middle West have concentrated largely on the Appalachian and Ozark mountains or on other rural areas of predominantly white population. Most regional collections contain a few Negro folksongs which have found their way into the editor's net. But it has remained for a half-dozen enthusiasts to search out the Negro ballads in colored communities, and to record them directly from singing. Among these was the late Professor Dorothy Scarborough of Columbia, whose delightfully edited collection *On the Trail of Negro Folk-Song* contains many of the ballads discussed here. Two sociologists from the University of North Carolina, Howard W. Odum and Guy B. Johnson, have contributed largely to this field with *The Negro and His Songs* and *Negro Workaday Songs*. In *Steamboatin' Days*, Mary Wheeler has preserved much fine Negro material. The late John A. Lomax and his son Alan, who have done more to preserve and popularize American folksong than any other students, have printed the largest amount of Negro balladry in *American Ballads and Songs, Our Singing Country,* and *Negro Folk-Songs as Sung by Lead Belly.* Finally there is Professor Newman I. White's beautifully and painstakingly edited study *American Negro Folk-Songs.* Though this work presents only a few ballads in fragmentary form, it is invaluable for its documentary and introductory material. This completes the list of collections which pay more than incidental attention to Negro balladry.[1]

The Negro ballads gleaned almost entirely from these anthologies are as moving and dramatic as the best of the white ballads. At once realistic and imaginative, they have a poetic quality which is often sadly lacking in ballads created by white authors, and they suggest almost as much as they express. With few exceptions they deal with crime, usually with murder and its consequences. Because they emphasize character and situation, in contrast to the white ballads, which usually concentrate upon events, the Negro ballads seem to be highly personal expressions of characteristic racial attitudes.

Although the problem of ballad origins is always difficult, and most investigations are unrewarding, not infrequently both the original form of a white ballad and the identity of its author have been discovered. Not so with Negro ballads, for even those of apparently recent origin are already in the strictest sense the possession of the folk. All traditional Negro ballads are anonymous and very few of them can be convincingly connected with actual events. While many white ballads were originally circulated in a relatively fixed broadside form, investigators have apparently not found such early examples of Negro balladry.[2] The white ballad maker frequently wrote a ballad out and had it printed and sold. The Southern Negro composer, who was certainly uneducated and probably illiterate presumably sang his ballad among his people, who were then free to do with it as they would. They could and did add to it, alter it to fit new situations, and pass it along for further folk treatment. As a result, when we speak of a fixed number of Negro ballads, we do so hesitantly, realizing that frequently only a central theme gives one the right to connect one text with another and say that they are variants of the same ballad.

White ballad singers characteristically reproduce ballads as they have learned them, even repeating words and phrases which time or misapprehension have rendered meaningless. Thus most native ballads exist in a fairly definite form and are identifiable even as fragments by certain phrases

---

[1] In addition to the works mentioned, two book-length studies of the Negro ballad hero John Henry have appeared. See the Bibliography under G. B. Johnson and L. W. Chappell.

[2] Professor Johnson discovered a broadside of "John Henry", but he shows that it does not represent the original form of the ballad. See his *John Henry,* pp. 137-140.

or stanzas. The same is not true of Negro balladry. In fact Negro folksongs are full of stanzas or phrases which can be compared to the clichés of English traditional balladry. They pass easily from one folksong to the other, and they are of no help at all in identifying Negro ballads. Most students of the subject have called attention to the Negro's unusual powers of improvisation. He is a far more creative singer than the white man, and he would rather invent a line than repeat one which has no meaning to him. The singing habits of the Negro are admirably summed up in the following passage from Professor White's *American Negro Folk-Songs:*

> Improvisation is not peculiar to Negro folk-song, of course, but it is highly characteristic; it is a racial trait, and it is carried to much greater length than by white people. The next great characteristic is that of variation. . . . In Negro folk-song . . . there is hardly any such thing as a stanza belonging particularly to one song and to that alone. Generally speaking, practically any stanza is at home in practically any song. Since the tune is variable and the stanza is variable, any song is prolonged to almost any length desired, simply by fishing stanzas out of a spacious but none too accurate or discriminating folk memory, augmenting them by improvised lines or stanzas if it seems desirable, and accommodating stanzas and tunes to each other.
>
> Few songs have a fixed beginning and almost none has a definite end.[3]

All these statements about Negro folksong in general can be applied to some extent to Negro ballads. As in all balladry, there is a central event to be recounted. But the Negro is not usually content merely to pass along the ballad as he heard it. In a sense he performs the ballad, sometimes adding comments between stanzas[4] as well as incorporating in it details of interest which could apply to the incident being narrated, and which perhaps make it of more vital concern to the audience of the moment.[5]

It may be said to the credit of the Negro singer that he is not prone to discard established stanzaic patterns; his improvisations will be cast in the mold of the ballad which he is singing. Then the new stanzas may seem completely at home in the old ballad, and the ballad collector is faced with dozens of stanzas to a ballad which needs perhaps fifteen for completeness. To derive a so-called original form from such a mass of material is an obvious impossibility, though some valiant and enlightening efforts in that direction have been made.[6] There is a certain consistency of refrain as well as of stanzaic form in Negro ballads. The familiar "He was her man, but he done her wrong" of "Frankie and Albert"[7] is paralleled in many other

---

[3] P. 26.

[4] See for example, *Negro Folk Songs as Sung by Lead Belly*, pp. 193-201.

[5] Like most general statements about balladry, this has its exceptions. Horace P. Beck gave me a version of the white ballad "Sidney Allen", obtained from the singing of a Negro, which is almost identical with texts printed by other collectors.

[6] See above, footnote 2.

[7] I am assuming that this famous ballad is primarily a Negro product, though the matter may never be definitely settled.

Negro ballads by repeated phrases which are often an integral part of the story being told. These two features of Negro balladry are at times more useful for identification than are minor narrative bits.

In keeping with native balladry as a whole, the Negro ballads make use of a variety of stanzaic forms, but show little concern for the formalities of metrical structure. The quatrain containing four stressed syllables to a line is commonly used. The following stanza from "Bad Lee Brown" is fairly typical:

> Verdic' read murder in de firs' degree.
> I said, "O Lawd, have mercy on me."
> I seed ol' jedge when he picked up his pen,
> Say, "I don't think you'll ever kill a woman ag'in.[8]

Frequently the story is told in couplets expanded to three or four-line stanzas by the use of repeated refrains like "I'm lookin' for that bully of this town,"[9] or "Dese bones gwine to rise again."[10] Another familiar pattern is formed by the repetition of the last line of each stanza, often after a "Lawd, Lawd"[11] or "Po' Boy"[12] to produce a stanza of five lines. The fifth line may be a refrain, sometimes varied, like "Cryin' all I had done gone."[13] Good versions of Negro ballads are usually from 10 to 15 stanzas long, though occasionally one of about 25 stanzas is printed, and the Lomaxes print a version of "Batson", as sung by a Negro nicknamed "Stavin' Chain" which runs to 38 loosely constructed stanzas.[14] Sometimes, however, the singers' habit of improvising and borrowing produces a ballad of more length than coherence.[15]

More than half the Negro ballads are based on murder, a percentage far higher than that of the white ballads. Several possible explanations of this phenomenon spring to mind. For one thing, much native balladry has originated among cowboys, lumbermen, sailors, soldiers and others whose lives were sufficiently dramatic and hazardous to lend themselves to ballad treatment. The Southern Negro's circumscribed life has offered little of comparable excitement to sing about except crime. Then, too, Negro balladry, as the Lomaxes have shown,[16] flourishes in prisons, where songs about crime are presumably of general interest. It may also be suggested that the social distinctions drawn among white men between criminal and non-criminal

---

[8] Lomax, *American Ballads*, p. 90.
[9] "The Bully of the Town".
[10] "Dese Bones Gwine to Rise Again".
[11] "John Henry", Johnson, *John Henry*, p. 92.
[12] "John Hardy".
[13] "Delia".
[14] *Our Singing Country*, pp. 335-341, from L. C. Records 95 A & B.
[15] Thus Lead Belly's long "Ella Speed" contains stanzas that more properly belong to "The Coon-Can Game" and "The Bully of the Town." See Lomax, *Negro Folk Songs* . . . pp 187-192.
[16] Almost all their Negro ballads were collected from prisoners in the South.

have not been equally emphasized among Negroes, who so often have been victims of the white man's laws.

However this may be, Negro and white murder ballads are often quite different in spirit. In contrast to the horror frequently expressed in white ballads at the fact of murder, the Negro ballad usually describes a shooting briefly and rather casually. Trials, hangings, and funerals are then dwelt upon at some length, as are the attitudes of various people concerning the murderer and his victim. Condemnation of the murderer is usually left to the white judge, or perhaps to a relative of the victim. Thus the judge remarks in "Delia":

> ". . . Coonie, if I don't hang you
> I'll give you ninety-nine."

> "Ninety-nine years in prison,
> Workin' 'mong the stone,
> Hope that you'll get sorry
> That you wrecked a home."[17]

Similar attitudes are expressed in "Ella Speed", and "The Coon-Can Game" in both of which the men feel extremely sorry for themselves when they must pay the penalty for having killed unfaithful women.

As a matter of fact, sympathy for the murderer's plight is rather general in the Negro ballads. When Frankie is grieving about her lover's death, her sister says:

> ". . . Why are you weeping so?
> If Albert Gray had been a man of mine,
> I'd killed him long ago" . . . [18]

Again in "Batson", although the prisoner has been accused of murdering his employer's whole family, Lomax says that ". . . the sympathies of the ballad singer rest wholly with the accused, not with his victims."[19] The ballad is primarily an account of Batson's arrest and hanging. Nor do we learn whether Duncan is punished for shooting Brady, whom Lomax describes as a bullying peace officer.[20] Everyone concerned, not excluding Brady's wife, seems pleased at the event. This is not to suggest that Negro singers approve of such murders. But they can understand how, provoked beyond endurance, a man or woman may be driven to kill, and they know, sometimes from personal experience, the devastating effects of long years in prison.

In another class of ballads the victims are shot suddenly, with little or no

---

[17] *SFQ* I, no. 4, p 6.
[18] "Frankie & Albert", Hudson, p. 191, stanza 11. It may be added that in the version quoted Frankie commits suicide. In some versions she is sentenced to death (see Lomax, *American Ballads*, pp. 103-110) ; in others she goes to prison (see Odum and Johnson, *The Negro and His Songs*, pp. 228-230) ; and in still others, she goes free (see Lomax, *Negro Folk Songs*, pp. 192-201).
[19] *Our Singing Country*, p. 335.
[20] *Ibid*, p. 333.

warning and often on what would seem rather slight provocation. Those "bad man ballads" are not always readily distinguishable from the others, but usually one gets the impression from them that the killing is done as an extreme form of meanness or bravado by a bully to whom crime gives a sense of power. Devil Winston was apparently such a man. Having killed Vinie "about a Duke cigarette," he leaves town with a piece of her shoulder in his suitcase. When Mary Wheeler interviewed an old Negress who had known the killer and his victim, she asked if she thought Devil had really taken away part of Vinie's body. Her informant replied, "Yes, Lawd, he sho' did. That nigger wuz jes' onery."[21] Orneriness is apparent, too, in the senseless murder committed by John Hardy. When Hardy's wife pays him a visit just before he is hanged, she says, with a good deal of logic, "Johnny, you were always too mean."[22] And Stackerlee's mother, who might be expected to say a good word for him if anyone would, remarks, "Stacker Lee wuz a bad boy, he wuz a bully from his birth."[23] Bad Lee Brown describes his apparently motiveless murder of Sadie in a few words: "Met my woman an' I blowed her down." The bully then gives a wryly humorous account of his trial:

> 'Bout five minutes befo' Co't begin,
> Jedge charged the jury, twelve honest men.
> 'Bout five minutes aftuh Co't begin,
> Jedge had my verdict in his right han'.[24]

Fate catches up with the bad man, whether he is a murderer or not, as it does with such victims of circumstances as the lovers of Delia and Ella Speed. Dupree, the bandit and killer, is hanged at last. The Bully of the Town is killed by another Negro,[25] and Railroad Bill, as Lomax points out, also falls victim to one of his own race.[26] Lazarus, the thief and bad man, is shot resisting arrest, and Stackerlee is eventually executed for murdering his old friend Billy Lyons.

The attitude of the singers toward these killers seems compounded of fear, admiration, disapproval, and pity. Just as the white outlaw becomes something of a ballad hero, so too does the Negro who flouts the law. Perhaps

[21] *Steamboatin' Days*, p. 108.
[22] Cox, p. 187.
[23] *Steamboatin' Days*, p. 102.
[24] *Ibid.*, p. 111.
[25] "What a picture the song gives of the bully and his pursuer! The boasting braggart sees himself the hero of the whole community, but chiefly among the women. He is better than the police: they will even thank him for his valor. The governor will give him his reward. Everybody he meets he asks about the bully boy, and takes on a new swagger. The scene of the shooting, the reaching for the pistol, and the 'layin'-down' of the bully's body—these offer unalloyed satisfaction to the singer. Altogether it is a great song, and defies a superior picture." Odum & Johnson, *The Negro & His Songs*, p. 205.
[26] *American Ballads*, p. 118.

there is something particularly appealing in breaking the laws imposed by another race. At any rate, collectors have reported that ballad singers take some delight in describing the deeds of these bad men. The terms "bad man" and "bully" certainly do not sound complimentary—and these terms are included in the ballad titles. But they do indicate a certain degree of achievement. Speaking of the "Stacker Lee" songs, Mary Wheeler says ". . . An old Negro named Fred Lee . . . helps us to date the unfortunate story by asserting that he and the rouster Stacker Lee once spent the night in jail together. They were arrested in a saloon fight and put in the same cell. Fred still recalls the incident with apparent satisfaction."[27] Odum and Johnson say: "The Negro loves to boast of being a 'bad man'. 'I bin a bad man in my day,' says the older fellow to the boys about him."[28] There is no more need to assume latent or active criminality in the Negro who sings about murderers and bad men than to suspect the white man who sings of Jesse James or Cole Younger. But we can certainly say that ballads about crime are popular among Negroes.

More should be said about the ballad clichés which were mentioned earlier in this chapter. Pistols are constantly being mentioned, almost always with their calibre reported. Frankie shoots Albert with "a smokeless forty-one";[29] Bill Martin had a "colt 41";[30] Railroad Bill shoots at his pursuer "wid a fo'ty-fo'."[31] Two similar stanzas from different ballads illustrate both the interest in pistols and the borrowing of stanzas:

> Delia, Delia,
> Why didn't you run,
> See dat desperado
> Had a forty fo' smokeless gun . . . [32]

> Brady, Brady, why didn't you run,
> When you saw that Duncan had a forty-four gun? . . . [33]

A note of variety is added in "The Coon-Can Game" when the deserted lover says:

> I pulled out my forty-some odd
> And I shot that dark-skinned child.[34]

Dupree "had a forty-five in his bosom and a Colt kickin' in his hand."[35] Stackerlee has a "smokeless 41" and his victim a "44 special."[36] One more

---

[27] *Steamboatin' Days*, p. 101.
[28] *The Negro and His Songs*, p. 212.
[29] Hudson, *Folksongs of Mississippi*, p. 190.
[30] *American Ballads*, p. 118 ("Ella Speed").
[31] *Ibid*, p. 120.
[32] *SFQ* I, no. 4, p. 4, st. 1.
[33] Lomax, *Our Singing Country*, p. 335, st. 8.
[34] Scarborough, *On the Trail of Negro Folk-Songs*, p. 88.
[35] *Our Singing Country*, p. 329.
[36] *American Ballads*, p .97.

example will suffice: "Dey shot po' Laz'us, shot him wid a great big number, / Number 45, Lawd, Lawd, number 45."[37] This interest in pistols is reminiscent of the days of the old West, when a man's gun was an important part of his equipment. These Negroes' pistols are never merely ornamental; they are used frequently in the ballads and with telling effects.

The death of a well known person calls for another cliché in Negro balladry. The women of the neighborhood dress in red or, more rarely, in black, according to their opinion of the deceased. Thus in "The Bully of the Town" we read:

> Now the wimmins come to town all dressed in red.
> When they heard that bully boy was dead.[38]

The opposite attitude is depicted somewhat differently in "Stagolee":

> All de mans dey shouted, but de womens put on black an' mourned
> Dat de good man Stagolee has laid down, died, an' gone.[39]

The following stanza from a Negro version of "Casey Jones" has, I believe, been incorrectly punctuated. It has more meaning if the internal commas are deleted:

> Womens in Kansas, all dressed in red,
> Got de news dat Casey was dead.
> De womens in Jackson, all dressed in black,
> Said, in fact, he was a cracker-jack[40]

If we assume that their clothing is indicative of their state of mind, we are left without an explanation of the uncharitable reaction of the Kansas women. That a large number of women would celebrate a man's death seems curious until we find an explanation in the killing of Brady, the policeman. The following illuminating stanzas appear in a version of the ballad collected by R. W. Gordon:

> When King Brady was on de beat,
> He 'lowed no ladies to walk de street;
> Now King Brady is daid an' gone,
> An' de ladies walk de street all night long.
>
> When dey heard King Brady was daid,
> Dey all went home an' dressed in red;
> Come back dancin' an' singin' a song—
> King Brady went to hell wid a Stetson on.[41]

It is easy to see how a meaningful and graphic passage in one ballad can become merely a trite and even an illogical phrase in another. A Negro

---

[37] *Ibid.*, p. 92.
[38] *The Negro and His Songs*, p. 204.
[39] *American Ballads*, p. 99.
[40] *The Negro and His Songs*, p. 208.
[41] *Adventure*. July 10, 1923, p. 191. Miss Scarborough prints (p. 86) a stanza similar to the second one given above in which the word "women" appears. Her contributor says, however, " 'Women' is not the word actually used in the song."

ballad can be expanded almost indefinitely by adding such bits. That the additions frequently are inappropriate in their new surroundings is apparently of little concern to the singers.

Another feature of Negro balladry is the statement that the prisoner is held without bail or can find no one to post his bail.[42] Bad Lee Brown says "Had no one to go my bail"[43] and Coonie asks, "Have I now any bond, or can I get one? . . . "[44] Again in John Hardy we read:

> John's father and mother crossed the deep blue sea,
> To get him out on bail;
> Says, "There's no bond for a murdering man."
> So they kept John Hardy in jail.[45]

The custom of contributing toward a funeral is also mentioned occasionally in the ballads. Thus in "Delia", we read:

> "Some give a nickel
> Some give a dime,
> Help to bury,
> This body of mine."[46]

And again in "Stagolee" (or "Stackerlee") :

> "Some give a nickel, some give a dime;
> I didn't give a red copper cent, cause he's no friend of mine."[47]

The finality and sometimes the expense of funerals is frequently spoken of with a succinct vividness characteristic of Negro balladry:

> Fohty dollar coffin, eighty dollar hack,
> Carried po' man to cemetery but failed to bring him back. . . . [48]

The expression is varied slightly in one version of "Frankie and Albert":

> En now it's rubber-tired carriages,
> An' a rubber-tired hack,
> Took old Albert to de graveyard
> An' brought his mother back—[49]

It is also customary in Negro balladry for the victim to beg his assailant not to shoot him any more. Later, at the time of the trial, the prisoner pleads for mercy, but the judge responds with a harsh sentence.

Trains appear frequently in these ballads, as they do in many Negro songs. In "The Coon-Can Game," the murder takes place on a train, and in several ballads, the murderer who has escaped temporarily is captured by the police

---

[42] Such phrases may also be found in white ballads about criminals.
[43] *Steamboatin' Days*, p. 110.
[44] *SFQ* I no. 4, p. 6 ("Delia").
[45] Cox, p. 187.
[46] *SFQ* I no. 4, p. 5.
[47] *The Negro and His Songs*, p. 198.
[48] *Loc. cit.*
[49] *American Ballads*, p. 105.

and returned on a train to stand trial, or is sent to prison on a train. Delia's mother takes a train trip in an effort to forget about her daughter's death:

> Every where the train would stop
> You could hear the people moan
> Singin' dat lonesome song
> "Po' Delia's dead an' gone."[50]

Railroad Bill, as his name would indicate, is a constant rider of trains. John Hardy tries to escape on a train after the murder, and Bad Lee Brown says: "Dey put me on a train, an' dey brought me back."[51]

It will be seen from the foregoing discussion of clichés that anyone wanting to produce a new ballad about a Negro murderer or bad man has a great deal of stock material from which to draw. He has little more to do than fit new names and a new narrative situation into a pattern already established by tradition. Since none of these ballads can be precisely dated, we cannot say definitely that this method has been used, but it is certainly reasonable to assume that it has.

I have found in print only five traditional Negro ballads which do not deal with crime, and four of these I have included with some hesitancy. "Joseph Mica" is so closely tied up with Negro versions of "Casey Jones" that it is difficult to establish its identity as a separate piece. "Dese Bones Gwine to Rise Again" is more unified and polished than most of the ballads under discussion, and may be the work of a white author writing in the idiom of the Negro. The same may be said of "The Blue-Tail Fly", which had its start as a minstrel song. "The Boll Weevil" can be called a ballad only if the definition of the form is stretched somewhat.[52] The central character in this piece is an insect, and the events recounted are fanciful rather than realistic. Furthermore, most versions of the piece do not dramatize and bring to a conclusion a single event. They consist merely of related narrative bits in which time and again the weevil survives the farmer's attempts to destroy him. One feels that the conflict could go on indefinitely. In a few versions, however, the farmer is convincingly defeated. He has lost his entire crop and can get no credit at the store.

Finally there is the great hero-ballad "John Henry", easily the most popular among Negro singers and widely known among whites. The ballad has taken such a strong hold on the folk imagination and exists in so many different forms that two books have been written about it and about the man of whom it tells.[53] John Henry's strength and endurance, his unwillingness to let the steam drill beat his hammer, and his heroic and victorious

---

[50] *SFQ* I no. 4, p. 6.
[51] *American Ballads*, p. 90.
[52] Professor Gerould, however, calls this piece "as good a popular ballad as has sprung up in a great while."
[53] See above, footnote 1.

death make this ballad one of the finest the country has produced. It makes little difference whether John Henry was hammering railroad spikes or mountain stone. Whether he actually lived or not, he is certainly a magnificent figure. The extraordinary variety of incidents recounted in different versions of the ballad show how completely he has endeared himself to his people.

The communal theory of ballad origin, which was rather emphatically dismissed in Chapter IV, recurs again here. In an article on American folk-song, John A. Lomax wrote as follows:

> The "Ballad of the Boll-Weevil" and the "Ballad of the Old Chisholm Trail", and other songs in my collection similar to these, are absolutely known to have been composed by groups of persons whose community life made their thinking similar, and present valuable corroborative evidence of the theory advanced by Professor Gummere and Professor Kittredge concerning the origin of the ballads from which came those now contained in the great Child collection.[54]

I have already excluded "The Old Chisholm Trail" from this study because it lacks the narrative organization of a true ballad, and although I have so designated it, I am not entirely convinced that "The Boll Weevil" deserves to be called a ballad. No one doubts that many people have added stanzas not only to pieces of this kind but to many folksongs which are unmistakably ballads. Unquestionably an occasional added stanza will represent a real contribution to a ballad or song. The fact that a ballad like "Frankie and Albert" has dozens of variants and hundreds of stanzas is no valid argument for the communal theory. Even a large composing group would have to get its story told within the limits of human endurance. Since all the stanzas of such a ballad could not have been composed at once, the inescapable conclusion is that many of them were added to earlier and shorter forms. These earlier forms probably developed from a single version which narrated the central event. There is no reason why ballads of this type could not have originated with individual composers, no matter what alterations have since been made to them.

When Lomax says that "The Boll Weevil" is "known to have been composed by groups of people", he may mean that many people have contributed stanzas to the piece. This much can safely be conceded. But before these stanzas could be added, both the stanzaic form and the fanciful central idea must have been circulated. There is every reason to believe that a single composer was responsible for these. The problem then is to decide how much of the ballad should be attributed to one author. Unfortunately the problem remains unsolved. As has been said, this piece is more loosely constructed

---

[54] "Some Types of American Folk-Song", *JAF* 28 (1915), 16. This passage is quoted by Dorothy Scarborough in her discussion of "The Boll Weevil" (*On the Trail of Negro Folk-Songs*, p. 76) and by Louise Pound, *Poetic Origins and the Ballad*, p. 215.

than most Negro ballads; it can be indefinitely extended because its conflict does not have to be resolved. Recurring incidents in versions from widely separated areas indicate, however, that "The Boll Weevil" was first circulated in a form containing these incidents. I am inclined to believe that there was an original Boll Weevil ballad of individual composition which told as much of a story—which, indeed, is very little—as is found in most versions collected from singing today. Despite his unqualified statement, Mr. Lomax has not offered proof that this piece developed entirely under group influence. Furthermore, as Miss Pound says, pieces of this sort are not to be compared with the well-organized narratives of the Child type, or with the more artistic American ballads.[55] Even if arguments for communal composition based on pieces of this sort were effective, they would have no validity for balladry as a whole.

I have not the slightest doubt that such effectively told Negro ballad stories as "Frankie and Albert", "John Hardy", and "John Henry" are basically individual compositions, no matter to what extent they have been added to and altered over the years.

The Negro singer is dramatist first, moralist second, if at all, in contrast to the white singer, who often lets his moralizing interfere with an otherwise vivid story. The Negro uses words well, if not always in an orthodox manner. And he is so keenly aware of the truth and realism of the story he tells that he holds his hearers by his own sincerity. Limited as they are in range and incident, these narrative folksongs of the Negro are moving and intense, and they have added immeasurably to the richness of American balladry.

---

[55] *Poetic Origins and the Ballad*, pp. 218-220.

Chapter VIII

The British Ballad Tradition in America

For many years the inhabitants of the Southern Appalachians have been spoken of as the Americans of purest Anglo-Saxon stock. It has often been pointed out that their language contains many words and expressions which were current in Elizabethan England. Because these people were for a long time largely illiterate and because their way of life had changed little since their arrival as immigrants, it was thought that they would possess the largest body of English folksong still extant in America. The successful activities of collectors in that part of the country lent support to this theory. Many fine old ballads were recovered from traditional singing, more than Professor Child had ever imagined were sung in the United States. These gold nuggets of folklore inspired further mining, until within a few decades the Southern Mountains had been extensively searched for balladry. As the list of rediscovered Child ballads grew, there developed beside it a longer list of obviously or presumably imported ballads which had not been honored by a place in Child's collection. A third class of ballads also appeared, those which both internal and external evidence showed had had their origin and development in this country. In addition to this constantly growing group of ballads, collectors discovered a large amount of native and imported song, some of which, though partly narrative in form, fell short of fitting the usual concepts of balladry. The conclusion was inescapable that British oral tradition was extremely active among the mountaineers.

Southern ballad collectors have discussed in some detail the ancestry of their informants. Their investigations tend to reinforce the popular concept that the mountaineer is of almost pure British stock. The first scholar to publish an anthology of mountain balladry was Cecil Sharp, who came from England in his quest for survivals of traditional British folksongs. His investigations of the singers and their music led him to believe that they had originally emigrated from England and the lowlands of Scotland.[1] Some years later James Watt Raine wrote as follows of the hill folk:

> The Mountain People are the inhabitants of the region whimsically, but happily, called Appalachia. They are the descendants of the Scotch-Irish, driven from the North of Ireland by the stupidity of the Stuart Kings. . . . They turned southward and swarmed down the inviting Valley of Virginia. . . . In this migration they swept along with them Palatine

---

[1] *English Folksongs from the Southern Appalachians*, Vol. I, pp. xxii and xxxiv.

Germans . . . , Huguenots . . . , Quakers from the Western reaches of Pennsylvania, and a good sprinkling of Virginia English. . . . From these pioneers the Mountain People sprang.[2]

By now the French and German elements seem to have been completely assimilated, and the mountain population has taken on an unusually homogeneous character. The names of the mountaineers are almost invariably English or Scottish. With the Scotch-Irish predominating in the Southern Mountains, it is not surprising to find that the Scottish forms of many ballads have been preserved among them. We should also expect the English immigrants to have contributed their share. This, too, has happened. Since English was the language of the mountains, it was only natural that whatever folksong the German and French pioneers brought with them should have become lost as they were assimilated into the English speaking communities.

Thus English and Scottish folksong came to be cherished without competition among people who were largely unable to read and write, but who loved leisure and song. There is every reason to believe that British balladry arrived in the Southern Mountains with the early settlers and increased in bulk as the immigrant population grew. Today, some two hundred years later, imported balladry, Americanized somewhat but in general largely unchanged, holds sway in the Mountains, as elsewhere in this country. We shall discuss later the dominance of the Child ballads and the British broadsides over the ballads which originated in America. First let us examine briefly the ancestry of Americans in other communities which have been found rich in balladry.

Since both Missouri and Arkansas form the western borders of states within the Appalachian range, it would be natural to assume that western migrations carried British ballads into the Ozark country. That this is true has been more than adequately demonstrated both by Vance Randolph's *Ozark Folksong* and by Professor Belden's *Ballads and Songs.* "Since the Ozark country was settled largely by pioneers from the southern Appalachians," writes Mr. Randolph, "it is not surprising that many of the traditional ballads should be known here." He goes on to say, "Working alone, at odd times, I have recovered 41 Child ballads in this region. . . . I believe that the Ozark hill country affords a richer store of traditional ballads than will be found in any other region of comparable area in the United States."[3]

But the pioneer movement was by no means confined to mountainous areas. It fanned out northward and southward as well as westward. And wherever the early pioneers went, their balladry went with them. Before discussing balladry in the more recently settled parts of the country, we might return for a moment to the Southern Highlanders. These Scotch-Irish and others travelled into the Valley of Virginia mainly from the North, that is, from Pennsylvania, where they had found their freedom threatened

---

[2] *The Land of Saddle-bags,* p. ix.
[3] *Ozark Folksongs,* Vol. 1, p. 37.

by the danger of Indian attack. Many of them moved on to settle in the Southern Mountains. Later their descendants moved on across the country to the Ozarks and elsewhere. But as has often been pointed out, it takes no less hardihood to fight difficulties in one spot than to move on to new territory. In short, the pioneers who remained in Western Pennsylvania were people of the same type as those who went south.[4] Naturally they retained their share of British balladry. When early in the nineteenth century the great western migration began, the Pennsylvania pioneers had an important part in transmitting this balladry to the new settlements beyond the Ohio.

It goes almost without saying that the threads of oral tradition are hopelessly tangled. A few wandering singers could introduce complicated patterns of transmission into any region. If I seem to be unduly simplifying the story of our country's settlement, I may be excused on the ground that I am indicating trends in balladry, not writing history. My purpose is to clarify a complex situation by showing that British balladry was distributed over a large part of this country, relatively early in its history, by a homogeneous group of pioneers whose ancestry was British.

Professor A. P. Hudson has carefully investigated the racial stock of the white people of Mississippi, a state which he has found rich in balladry.[5] He demonstrates the fact that the population emigrated, from 1800-1820, principally from Virginia, North and South Carolina, and Georgia, by way of Kentucky and Tennessee or Alabama. Dr. Hudson quotes a census study which indicates that the population of South Carolina in 1900 had probably retained its proportions of 1790, when 82.4 percent of the people were of English origin, 11.7 percent of Scotch, and 2.6 percent of Irish.[6] Similar proportions are given for North Carolina and Virginia. He believes that an even greater proportion of white Mississippians are of British and Irish origin.[7] He concludes that "the folk-songs of the Mississippi collection are a part of the cultural inheritance of people whose ultimate origin is British and Irish, modified by several generations of life in the South."[8]

It is to be observed that in Mississippi the people are predominantly of English rather than Scotch-Irish stock. Thus the second great strain of Child balladry should be found within the state, and within the other southern states from which these people came. As Professor Hudson points out, we cannot always tell whether some ballads are English or Scottish in origin.[9] Without doubt there was much interchange of balladry even within the British Isles. Then, too, the American versions have naturally lost, in

---

[4] See Shoemaker, *Mountain Minstrelsy of Pennsylvania*, p. 4.
[5] *Folksongs of Mississippi*, pp. 3-13.
[6] *Ibid.*, p. 10.
[7] *Ibid.*, pp. 10-11.
[8] *Ibid.*, p. 13.
[9] *Ibid.*, p .50.

many instances, the place names and the dialectal peculiarities which give evidence of their origin. In the long run it makes little difference which side of the Scottish border produced them. The point is that the South has benefited from the full force of both English and Scottish traditional balladry.[10]

If most of the English population of Mississippi came from Virginia, the Carolinas, and Georgia, it is natural to suppose that the non-mountainous areas of the South Atlantic States must have been the storehouse for a large amount of English balladry. Here again the statement of fact might have preceded the conjecture. Professor A. K. Davis' *Traditional Ballads of Virginia*, which is the largest collection of new versions of Child ballad texts so far published in this country, contains many pieces from east of the mountains as does *The Frank C. Brown Collection of North Carolina Folklore*. Professor Reed Smith's small collection of 14 Child ballads from South Carolina makes no claim to have exhausted the field.[11] Some ballad texts from Georgia have been published, but a collection of imported and native ballads from that state has yet to appear. Undoubtedly such a collection would show that the English tradition is strong there.

Having discussed the Appalachians as far north as Pennsylvania, and the South Atlantic States as two important primary areas in which British tradition is nourished, we should perhaps say something about New England before again moving westward. Here as in the South the original population was almost entirely British, and consequently British tradition early assumed prominence in the region. At this late date there is no accurate way of determining when certain old English, Scottish, or Irish ballads entered the northern states. It is difficult to imagine much ballad singing among the Puritans. But the fact remains that fine early texts of Child ballads have been found in New England. A handful of ballad enthusiasts have discovered more Child ballads in Maine than in any other state; and Vermont has produced as many different ballads as Virginia, though by no means so many ballad texts.[12] Nova Scotia, Newfoundland, and New Brunswick have all been found rich in folksong. These Canadian provinces have contributed a wealth of vital balladry to the living tradition of North America, and here again the transplanted cultures of England, Scotland, and Ireland predominate. These northern regions, then, are responsible for the preservation of a remarkable number of British ballads of all kinds. Some of these are still largely in manuscript form,[13] but several volumes of New England

---

[10] This is a partial explanation of the fact that more Child ballads have been found in recent tradition in the United States than in the whole of England. (See Randolph, *Ozark Folksongs*, Vol. 1, p. 37.)

[11] *South Carolina Ballads.*

[12] See Flanders-Barry, *The New Green Mountain Songster*, p. vii.

[13] For example, in the Flanders collection at Middlebury, Vermont, and in the Barry collection at Harvard.

and Maritime balladry have been published.[14]

Once the movements to the Middle West and Far West had begun in earnest, British balladry from the entire Eastern seaboard was carried to all parts of the country, and thus became even more universally established in American tradition. We may not be able to tell where a particular ballad got its start on this side of the Atlantic before travelling West, but the evidence of ultimate British origin is usually clear. One or two examples will suffice. In the introduction to *Ballads and Songs of Southern Michigan* Miss Gardner writes as follows:

> . . . The present collection contains many comparatively unchanged English, Scotch, and Irish songs, many pronouncedly localized American variants of such songs; and some others of a flavor which shows them to have sprung from American life and conditions.
>
> Through their striking similarity to songs and ballads collected in New England, the Middle Atlantic States, Ohio, Canada, Nova Scotia, and Newfoundland, those of the present collection show scarcely less convincingly then does factual history that the pioneers of Michigan came to the state by way of those regions.[15]

"The population of Southern Indiana", writes Paul Brewster in his introduction to *Ballads and Songs of Indiana*, "is largely of Anglo-Saxon stock, with a considerable number of Germans and a sprinkling of Irish, Scotch, French, and Swiss."[16] So the pattern of Anglo-Saxon dominance in language and tradition continued as new states were settled, and British balladry retained its prominent place as America grew. What little ballad collecting has been done on the West Coast indicates, as we would expect, that the Forty-niners and later pioneers took ballads with them around the Horn or across the Western plains. For a long time, however, life in the Far West was so different from the life which they had left that the pioneers may have substituted new songs and ballads for the old to a larger extent than elsewhere.

The last great area to develop, and consequently the last to be considered here, was the western cattle country, that vast, unpopulated region which produced a unique type of American, the cowboy. Because no one has done more to collect and preserve the cowboy's songs and ballads than John Lomax, we turn to his work to discover who the cowboy was and whence he came. In the "Collector's Note" to the original edition of *Cowboy Songs* Lomax wrote as follows:

> Out in the wild, far-away places of the big and still unpeopled West— in the canons along the Rocky Mountains, among the mining camps of

---

[14] See the Bibliography under Barry, Eckstorm, and Smyth; Barry; Flanders and Brown; Flanders, Ballard, Brown, and Barry; and Linscott for New England; Mackenzie and Creighton for Nova Scotia; and Greenleaf for Newfoundland.

[15] P. 4.

[16] P. 13.

Nevada and Montana, and on the remote cattle ranches of Texas, New Mexico, and Arizona—yet survives the Anglo-Saxon ballad spirit that was active in secluded districts in England and Scotland even after the coming of Tennyson and Browning. This spirit is manifested both in the preservation of the English ballad and in the creation of local songs.[17]

In his note to the revised edition, Mr. Lomax has this to say of the Texas cowboys:

> These boys in their twenties, who could ride and rope and shoot and sing, came mainly from the Southern states. They brought the gallantry, the grace, and the song heritage of their English ancestors. Their own rough songs often took the form and manner of English ballads.[18]

The lumbermen of northern Michigan, Wisconsin, and Minnesota were great singers, too, as Professor Rickaby's collection shows.[19] Here in the second half of the 19th century they sang the Old World ballads and created a considerable body of native ones. This time Ireland gets most of the credit for inspiring balladry. Professor Rickaby has this to say:

> An examination of the names of the heroes in the songs recorded in this collection, and of the names of those from whom the songs were obtained, will support the assertion that in the logging camp the hegemony in song belonged to the Irish. Although the Scotch and French-Canadian occur occasionally, the Irish were dominant, and the Irish street-song was the pattern upon which a liberal portion of the shanty-songs were made.[20]

Since many of the same ballads and other similar ones have been sung in the New England woods, these statements may be applied in some degree to the older lumbering regions.

Thus the influence of British balladry, which had been firmly established along the Eastern seaboard in colonial times, grew and developed with the growth of the country and the increase in population, and spread westward with the pioneers until by late in the 19th century there was no considerable area of the country not dominated by British ballads and songs.

If British balladry had been largely forgotten in this country, it would not have been necessary to devote so much space to the origin of people in ballad singing communities. But British influences are much more than merely incidental to a discussion of native American ballads. The fact is that after two centuries of ballad singing in this country, folksongs which originated in the British Isles still outnumber the American products. Not only are more British ballads known to singers than native ones, but the work of collectors indicates that various British ballads are more popular with singers than are the best known of those which developed in this

---

[17] *Cowboys Songs,* Revised Edition, 1938, p. xxv.
[18] Ibid., p. xvii.
[19] *Ballads and Songs of the Shanty-boy.*
[20] *Ibid.,* p. xxxv.

country. Furthermore, certain ballads treated in this book are reworkings of British ballads, and are considered native only because they have been sufficiently altered to achieve separate identity. Professor Louise Pound's statement of many years ago that "American folk-song as a whole has been imported from the Old World" is echoed from time to time even today.[21] If one could accept this statement without qualification, there would be little occasion for a study under the present title. The past 40 years have plainly demonstrated the need for modification of Miss Pound's contention. At the same time, a great deal of evidence can be brought forward to support the view that native American balladry is still in second place.

It may be of interest to illustrate the prominence of British balladry in current American tradition by referring to some of the folksong collections. The following statements should be taken only as approximations for several reasons. Most editors include a considerable amount of both native and imported material which they received in manuscript form, rather than from singing. Some of these ballads had been salvaged from commonplace books and were not traditional with the contributors. Furthermore, so little collecting has been done in comparison with the probable number of folk-singers that it is too early to come to definite conclusions regarding the incidence of either British or American ballads. The collector's habit of searching for specific pieces should also be mentioned. The Child ballads, for example, have been hunted down relentlessly and held onto firmly for future publication. I am inclined to think that many American ballads and some late British ones have been overlooked while the collector's attention was occupied with the older material. Finally there is the difficulty of determining the origin of many ballads, particularly those which are unspecific as to the date or place of the event involved. Where guesswork is involved, general agreement can hardly be expected. It is thought, however, that the following analyses will at least give a general idea of the dominant position of British folksong.

Professor Belden's Missouri collection of nearly 300 titles, for example, can be divided almost equally between ballads and other songs sung by the folk. Disregarding a dozen or so of indeterminate origin, I find that slightly more than one-third of the ballads are American, the rest British. Linscott's *Folk-Songs of New England* contains only 94 texts, approximately one-third of which are ballads. Of the ballads, less than one-third are American. About 30 of the more than 80 ballads in Hudson's collection I would call native to America. According to my count fewer than one-fourth of the ballads in the Gardner and Chickering collection are native. In Cox's *Folk-Songs of the South* the ratio is one American ballad to two British. In the first two of

---

[21] Pound, *American Ballads and Songs*, p. xxvi. Quoted by Hudson, *Folksongs of Mississippi* p. 182.

the four volumes of *Ozark Folksongs* slightly more than one-third of the ballads are American. Certain specialized collections such as those of cowboy or Negro songs naturally contain a preponderance of native material. As far as the general collections are concerned, however, those mentioned above are not unusual in their proportions of native and imported compositions. It would seem a safe generalization to say that anyone making a comprehensive regional collection can expect to find about twice as many British as native American ballads.

When scholarly ballad collections are published it is customary to include or to mention all the texts of each ballad which have been received by the collector. Thus it is possible to gain some idea of the relative popularity of various English and American ballads. Here again appearances may be misleading for the reasons noted above, but the margin of error is certainly not great enough to render comparisons useless. The tables given below indicate the number of texts or fragments of various well-known native and imported ballads reported by four collectors.[22] Following them is given a like table made up from the Library of Congress *Check-List of Recorded Songs*.

"The Jealous Lover", with fifty-eight appearances in the five collections, "The Butcher's Boy", with fifty, and "The Little Mohea", with thirty-nine were excluded because their origin is still somewhat controversial. No elaborate conclusions should be drawn from these tables. They are not designed to list the ballads according to their popularity throughout the country. It should not be inferred, for example, that "The Demon Lover" is the second most popular English ballad or that "McAfee's Confession" is sixth among American products. Similar lists derived from other collections would not only change the order of listing but would result in the appearance of other ballads in the tables.

	Cox	Hudson	Brewster	Belden	*Library of Congress	Total
Barbara Allen	12	16	14	16	64	122
The Demon Lover	21	2	9	9	43	84
Lord Thomas and Fair Annet	11	5	8	12	39	75
Lady Isabel and the Elf Knight	9	4	3	8	33	57
Lord Randall	12	2	1	5	10?	30
The Maid Freed from the Gallows	7	6	1	1	5	20
Total	72	35	36	51	204	398

* In the Library of Congress *Check-List* folksongs are given under a variety of titles without explanation. Most of these figures are only approximate, and those followed by question marks are particularly doubtful.

---

[22] Most collectors refrain from printing long series of nearly identical texts. The custom is to print all significant variants and follow them by summaries of other texts. The collections referred to are Cox's *Folk-Songs of the South*, Hudson's *Folksongs of Mississippi*, Brewster's *Ballads and Songs of Indiana,* and Belden's *Ballads and Songs.*

Young Charlotte	7	3	5	17	16	48
Jesse James I	1	5?	0	5	9?	20
The Cowboy's Lament	5	0	0	7	7?	19
The Dying Cowboy	2	1	0	5	11?	19
Fuller and Warren	1	1	7	4	5	18
McAfee's Confession	7	0	0	6	2	15
Total	23	10	12	44	50	149

It is significant that only two American ballads, "Young Charlotte" and "Jesse James I" appear twenty times or more in the five collections, while the last ballad on the British list has twenty appearances. Since "The Cowboy's Lament" was derived ultimately from English broadsides and "The Dying Cowboy" is a reworking of a ballad-like piece, for only four of the popular American pieces can we insist strongly on both originality and native origin. The outstanding conclusion to be drawn from the tables is that Americans are far more likely to sing British than native ballads, although, of course, the singers are often unaware that their ballads are of foreign origin. While most native ballads are of such recent origin that they never had a chance to travel widely with the folk in their migrations, the old British ballads were able to diffuse under ideal conditions which can never be duplicated. This fact, coupled with the generally higher quality of the imported pieces, makes their popularity easy to explain. Furthermore, many of the British pieces have universal appeal. They treat of humor and romance, of love and jealousy and death. In short, they portray the human drama as it exists wherever people have banded together.

The average folk composer who was tempted to tell similar stories must have realized that he could not produce ballads so well conceived and executed as those already in tradition. If he wanted his compositions to be successful, his only solution was to find subjects which had not been used in the best British ballads or which he could treat with originality. Local tragedies, crimes, and disasters offered one obvious outlet for his talents. He probably knew many ballads of a lower order, either British or American, which dealt with such topics, and he welcomed the opportunity to present new material in a familiar and not too demanding form. If he was a lumberman, or cowboy, or sailor, or if he was engaged in any other colorful activity, he could write about his occupation. Relatively little skill was required to produce such ballads, yet if they were timely and dramatic, they might become locally popular. Encouraged by his success, the balladist would naturally continue to write in the same vein. But the local and limited appeal of his compositions would keep them from attaining wide diffusion or general popularity.

Thus we may explain the continuing dominance of British balladry and the scarcity of native traditional balladry composed on themes of universal appeal. Many of the new ballads eventually ceased to be timely. They gained little or no headway in tradition, while the British ballads which had forced their composition in the first place were still sung. Had there been just a few British ballads, enough to inspire rather than to dishearten American composers, the story might be different. But the imported balladry was monopolistic; it drove composers to produce ballads which could not compete with it. This is not to suggest that a few generations of folk composers in this country could have produced a body of native balladry to rival that of England, Scotland, and Ireland. The best days of balladry had long since passed when our folk authors came on the scene. But at least they would have had a chance to show what they could do with subject matter of more enduring appeal.

Chapter IX

The Spirit of Native American Balladry

Students of folksong have often commented on the variety, the local color, and the diversity of subject matter to be found in native American balladry. They have generally neglected to point out that our balladry also displays a consistency of tone which overcomes barriers of race, occupation, or place of origin and makes it truly an expression of the spirit of the American people. Using the dramatic and often sensational material which has always been the balladists' stock-in-trade, the American ballad-makers have remolded it to their own tastes to produce a body of folksong with national appeal. Considered technically and artistically, our balladry may seem of rather low quality, but it displays a certain refinement in the tastes of composers and singers. I should like to emphasize here the one feature of native balladry which raises it above mere sensationalism and which helps to explain its continuing vitality. This is the sincere tenderness with which the stories are told. Since approximately three-quarters of our native traditional ballads deal with death, this tenderness is usually manifested in deep sympathy for the victims of tragedy. A sensitive understanding of the plight of others is the quality which at once humanizes native balladry and gives it a distinctively American flavor.

Speaking in general terms of American ballads, Professor Gordon H. Gerould remarks: "They are sentimental instead of being poignant with feeling, as is of course true of balladry wherever it has been affected by the disruptive influences of modern times."[1] Quite properly he compares American ballads not with the Child pieces but with the later street ballads of Britain, and he states that "with some few exceptions, they are no better and not much worse than similar ballads that got into circulation after the chapman had pursued his nefarious activities for a couple of centuries."[2] Without attempting to gloss over the deficiencies of our balladry, I should like to make a clearer distinction between the products of the Old World and the New.

The late British street ballads, including those imported to this country and widely sung here, often bear the mark of the professional composers who catered with some skill to the public taste for humor, romance, and

---

[1] *The Ballad of Tradition*, p. 263.
[2] *Ibid.*, p. 262.

sensationalism. They produced cynical and sometimes ribald ballads which display some of the less noble aspects of human nature.[3] They wrote far-fetched love stories about long separations and eventual reunions.[4] And they dwelt with relish on the shocking details of murders and other crimes.[5] The American balladists, on the other hand, though usually less skillful, largely ignored humor and romance and confined themselves to a considerably softened sensationalism in which the purpose was much less to shock than to excite pity and grief. Composition for them seems to have been a labor of love; their ballads are full of warmth and real emotion. We rarely find in the British pieces the notes of sadness and tragedy which pervade American balladry. Admittedly the British have contributed romance and laughter to modern balladry in English, along with their share of sentimentality, but their tragic pieces lack the feeling and the sense of closeness to the victims of disaster which we find in our native compositions. The British balladist is at times a reporter writing about strangers, at times a fictionalist; the American seems usually to be an amateur composer writing of friends and neighbors whose loss means much to him.

Much American balladry is the product of lumberjacks, cowboys, Southern Negroes, mountain people, and others of little formal education. Many of them lived difficult and dangerous lives away from the refining influences of domesticity. One might expect their balladry to be coarse and crude, but it is surprisingly free from unpleasantness or vulgarity. Although speaking in their own idiom for uncritical audiences, American balladists have demonstrated their innate good taste. Whatever crudeness is present in our balladry springs mainly from the literary inadequacies of the composers and singers; it does not extend to the subject matter or its treatment. In place of vulgarity we find a gentleness which at times spills over into sentimentality. But the sympathy expressed in most ballads has a straightforward artlessness which differentiates them from those distressingly contrived parlor songs and newspaper verses which seem primarily designed to cause the shedding of

[3] See for example the following in Randolph's *Ozark Folksongs:* "Johnny the Sailor", I, 250-253; "The Old Black Booger" ("The Old Man Who Came Over the Moor"), I, 291-294; "Father Grumble", I, 318-323; "There Was an Old Miller" ("The Miller's Will"), I, 359-365; and "Johnny Sands", IV, 246-249. Add "Will the Weaver" in W. Roy Mackenzie's *Ballads and Sea Songs from Nova Scotia*, pp. 328-329.

[4] See the following in Randolph, *op. cit.*, Vol. I: "The Brisk Young Farmer", 231-232; "The Banks of Cloddy", 233-234; "The Maiden in the Garden", 258-261; "John Riley", 262-264; "Mary and Willie", 264-265; and "Willie Taylor", 295-296.

[5] See for example Phillips Barry, "Murder of Betsy Smith", *American Speech* III, no. 6 (Aug., 1928), 441: "Her throat was cut from ear to ear . . ." etc., or the piece in John Ashton's *Modern Street Ballads* (London, 1888), pp. 374-376, about "Mary Arnold, the Female Monster", who blinded her baby by "Binding black beetles round its eyes, Placed in Walnut Shells". A particularly gruesome imported ballad is "Squire Nathaniel and Betsy" ("The Old Oak Tree"), in which a murdered girl's corpse is dug up by hunting dogs. For a traditional text, see Greenleaf and Mansfield, *Ballads and Sea Songs of Newfoundland*, pp. 116-118.

tears and which often strike the modern reader as ludicrous.[6] In the more realistic ballads, particularly those based on fact, the story is the thing, and the sympathy expressed or implied is spontaneously called forth by the sadness of the tale. Playing on the sensibilities is rarely an end in itself.

The balladists' hearts go out unreservedly to the innocent victims of sudden and accidental death, the subject which more than any other has inspired native composers and appealed to native singers. The expressions of sympathy which permeate our balladry occasionally occur in almost poetic lines which show flashes of insight just as the better Child ballads do. In these lines the tragedy may be seen through the eyes of one close to the victim, thus increasing its impact, or the balladist may, in a verse or two of description, etch a vivid picture on his listeners' minds. More often, however, in their obituaries of the obscure, the ballad-makers achieve nothing better than bald statements conventionally phrased.

The following stanza from "Only a Miner" ("The Hard-Working Miner") is a typical blend of triteness, poetic inadequacy, and sincere feeling. The author clearly indicates his own emotional involvement in the action:

> He leaves a dear wife, and little ones, too;
> To earn them a living he was striving to do.
> But while he was working for those that he loved,
> He met his sad fate from a boulder above.[7]

In "Willie Down by the Pond" a youth has drowned himself because his girl has coyly concealed her love for him. Here the balladist displays slightly more skill in weaving his own sadness and affection into the narrative and descriptive details:

> Next morning dear Willie was found
> Down in the pond by the mill,
> His blue eyes forever were closed
> And damp were the locks of his hair.[8]

Among the most moving of native ballad scenes occurs in "Springfield Mountain" when the father finds his son dead from the bite of a poisonous snake. He had misunderstood the boy's shout for help as a call to a workman:

> He took him up and he carried him home
> And on the way did lament and mourn,
> Saying, "I heard but did not come,
> And now I'm left alone to mourn".[9]

By concentrating on the father's grief, the balladist achieves a stanza which,

---

[6] See for example "Put My Little Shoes Away", Randolph, *op. cit.*, vol. IV, pp. 178-180; "The Orphan Child", *ibid.*, pp. 194-196; and "The Little Rosewood Casket", *ibid.*, pp. 269-272.

[7] Wayland D. Hand, Charles Cutts, Robert C. Wylder, and Betty Wylder, "Songs of the Butte Miners", *Western Folklore* IX (1950), 16.

[8] Mellinger E. Henry, *Folk-Songs from the Southern Highlands*, p. 239.

[9] Helen H. Flanders and George Brown, *Vermont Folk-Songs and Ballads*, p. 16.

while it leaves much to be desired poetically, has definite emotional impact. Seba Smith's justly popular "Young Charlotte" advances another step toward the objectivity and restraint of the old British balladry. Her fiancé has just discovered that Charlotte has frozen to death during their sleigh-ride:

> He put his arms around her neck
> And kissed her marble brow,
> And his thoughts went back to when she said,
> "I'm growing warmer now".[10]

To say that such a stanza is melodramatic and that its diction might be improved is not to deny that it is unforgettable. Without a word of personal comment or any account of the young man's grief, the author conveys an impression of keen tragedy.

Great disasters on land or at sea call forth tributes from ballad-makers, who try earnestly to encompass the horrors of a tragedy within a few stanzas. (Multiple deaths in one calamity always seem more terrible than the same number geographically distributed.) In "Cross Mountain Explosion" the narrator grieves for the dozens of miners, among them old men and children, who have been trapped below ground.[11] An even more doleful ballad on a similar occurrence is "The Avondale Disaster", which, after an extended and circumstantial account of the tragedy, ends as follows:

> Now to conclude and make an end,
> Their number I'll pen down—
> A hundred and ten of brave strong men
> Were smothered underground!
> They're in their graves till this last day,
> Their widows may bewail
> And the orphans' cries they rend the skies
> All round through Avondale.[12]

Persons of sophisticated tastes may feel inclined to smile at the phraseology of such a stanza, but the true folk singer would never do that. On the contrary, both the singer and his audience might well be tearful by the end of the song. Then, too, one comes from time to time upon stanzas which seem to strike just the right note. There is some poetry in "The *Persian's* Crew", a lament for the officers and men of a schooner which never returned from a Great Lakes voyage:

> Now around Presque Isle the sea birds scream their mournful notes along.
> In chanting to the sad requiem, the mournful funeral song,
> They skim along the waters blue and then aloft they soar,
> O'er the bodies of the Persian's crew that lie along the shore.[13]

---

[10] Emelyn E. Gardner and Geraldine J. Chickering, *Ballads and Songs of Southern Michigan*, p. 128.

[11] George Korson, *Coal Dust on the Fiddle*, pp. 275-277.

[12] Text from the leaflet by George Korson accompanying recording AAFS 76 B from the Archive of American Folk Song, Library of Congress.

[13] Franz Rickaby, *Ballads and Songs of the Shanty-Boy*, p. 166.

The following lines from "The Loss of the *Albion*", though somewhat redundant, have the poignancy which Professor Gerould says is usually wanting, as well as a measure of dignity:

> Our noble captain he was lost,
> And many a seaman bold,
> And many a gallant life was lost,
> And many a heart made cold.[14]

To understand the spirit of native balladry one must realize that expressions of sympathy and grief are not merely conventions of the ballad composers but accurately mirror the feelings of both singers and listeners. The ballad singer accepts the authority of tradition and serves as the preserver and transmitter of a form of history. To him the ballad consists of a series of factual statements in narrative form. The event recounted may have happened—if it happened at all—long before the singer was born, but to him it is as fresh and worthy of attention as a dramatic news story in the morning paper. Vance Randolph and other collectors report that weeping is common during the singing of sad ballads and that singers sometimes interrupt themselves to comment on the story.[15] Since American ballad authors have relied heavily on fact for their inspiration, the faith of the folk in the truth of the stories is largely justified. Thus the folk believe both in the spirit and in the substance of the ballads they sing, and they share vicariously in the events recounted. So it is that a miner, seventy-five years after the event, will sing "The Avondale Disaster" with tears in his voice,[16] or an old sailor will wipe his eyes after a rendition of "The Loss of the *Albion*",[17] though the ship had gone down a century before. Past and present merge in a ballad singer's mind.

Much of the tenderness of American balladry may be traced to the strong religious feeling of the folk, who seem to have an unshakable faith in the nearness of God. For instance, the shanty-boy who is about to die in "Harry Dunn" thinks not only of himself:

> "Oh, come right now. I'm dying;
> My hour will soon be near.
> May the Lord in his good mercy
> Look upon my parents dear.[18]

And the Negro bad man, John Hardy, shows signs of repentance as he nears the gallows:

---

[14] Harold W. Thompson, *Body, Boots and Britches*, p. 206.

[15] See for example Randolph, I, 34-35; Gardner and Chickering, p. 13; and Charles J. Finger, *Frontier Ballads* (New York, 1927), pp. 65-71.

[16] Recording AAFS 76 B from the Archive of American Folk Song, Library of Congress.

[17] Thompson, *loc. cit.*

[18] Earl C. Beck, *Songs of the Michigan Lumberjacks*, p. 162.

> John Harty was standing in his cell,
> With the tears running down each eye;
> "I've been the death of many a poor man,
> And now I'm ready to die,
> O Lord, I'm ready to die.[19]

For a woman who has been poisoned by her husband, Henry Green's wife sounds painfully sentimental, but at least she is well endowed with Christian charity:

> "Since I am on my bed of death and know that I must die,
> I know I am going to my God, the truth I will not deny;
> I know that Henery poisoned me; dear brother, for him send,
> For I do love him now as well as when he was my friend."[20]

This may be contrasted with "Edward" (Child no. 13) in which the youth offers his mother "the curse of hell" for her bad counsel[21] and with "Lord Randall" (Child no. 12) in which the murderous fiancée is bequeathed "a rope for to hang her on."[22] Henry Green is not at all moved by his wife's display of affection, but the typical ballad murderer who appears on the scene suffers greatly from remorse. In a ballad full of religious allusions, Frankie Silvers, just before her execution, speaks with horror of her husband's murder, for which she expects to dwell forever in hell.[23] In "McAfee's Confession" another homicidal spouse grieves for his innocent victim and expresses the hope that her soul is with God.[24]

As pathetic as any native ballad characters are the young men who die away from home at work on land or water. "The Jam on Gerry's Rock" is but one of several ballads which tell of shanty-boys who are pounded to death in the fury of breaking log jams. When at first only young Monroe's head is found, his fellows do not recoil in horror; instead, they lift it gently from the beach and comb down his raven hair; later they bury him sadly beside the river which caused his death.[25] And when Jimmie Judd's body is recovered, the ungrammatical balladist is obviously sincere in his sorrow:

> 'Twould break your heart with pity
> When they brought him out on shore
> For to see such lovely features
> Which the rocks had cut and tore.[26]

The balladists grieve, too, for the men who die in sawmill accidents: for

---

[19] "John Harty", John A. Lomax and Alan Lomax, *American Ballads and Folk Songs*, p. 125.

[20] "Young Henry Green", Gardner and Chickering, p. 347.

[21] Helen C. Sargent and George L. Kittredge, *English and Scottish Popular Ballads*, p. 26.

[22] Arthur P. Hudson, *Folksongs of Mississippi*, p. 69.

[23] "Frances Silvers", Mellinger E. Henry, *Songs Sung in the Southern Appalachians*, pp. 48-50.

[24] Mary O. Eddy, *Ballads and Songs from Ohio*, p. 291.

[25] Fannie H. Eckstorm and Mary W. Smyth, *Minstrelsy of Maine*, pp. 87-89.

[26] "The Beau Shai River" ("Jimmie Judd"), Beck, p. 145.

Harry Bale, who had no parents to comfort him in his last hours,[27] and for John Singleton, whose body will be covered by the winter snows "With a mantle pure and lovely as the spirit that is gone".[28] They are saddened by the deaths of cowboys like Utah Carroll[29] and Little Joe the Wrangler,[30] who die in stampedes, and they bemoan the fate of young sailors lost in storms at sea.[31] Of course the men who die in battle are honored in the ballads as elsewhere. Unfortunately the war songs too often consist of long-drawn-out and highly sentimental death scenes which suggest a Victorian melodrama rather than a battlefield. But occasionally a piece combines restraint with vigor of phrase:

> It lasted full nine hours before the battle was o'er,
> The like of dead and wounded I never saw before,
> Four of as noble rangers as ever roved the West
> Were buried by their comrades with arrows in their breast.[32]

"The Battle of Shiloh Hill" seems born of first-hand experience. "The horrors of that battle did my soul with anguish fill", says the balladist, who must have been there. His account of the two-day engagement recaptures the agony and confusion of war, and ends, as so many American ballads do, with a prayer for the souls of the dead:

> I'll pray to God my Savior, consistent with his will,
> To save the souls of them brave men who fell on Shiloh's hill.[33]

Many further examples could be added to those given, but enough has been said to show that American balladry is characterized by a tender humanity toward all who are faced with tragedy. It is the natural product of a soft-hearted and charitably-minded people who respond generously with aid and sympathy wherever disaster strikes throughout the nation and throughout the world. In place of the kings and nobles of Child balladry we have victims who are poor and almost unknown, but the democratic folk will grieve and pray for them year after year in song. This is the spirit of almost all our balladry. No matter what region of the country produced them, the ballads will have meaning for all who appreciate the value of human life and know the meaning of human suffering. Native balladry may be rugged and colorful or commonplace and sentimental; much of it may be inept, some even illiterate, but above all it shows compassion, neighborliness, and concern for other men's misfortunes.

---

[27] "Harry Bail" ("Harry Bale"), *ibid.*, p. 174.
[28] "John Singleton", *ibid.*, p. 174.
[29] "Utah Carl" ("Utah Carroll"), Randolph, II, 239-241.
[30] "Little Joe the Wrangler", *ibid.*, pp. 234-236.
[31] Several such ballads are printed in Eckstorm and Smyth, *op. cit.*, pp. 286-300.
[32] "The Texas Rangers", Randolph, II, 173.

Appendix I

Contents

Appendix I

Explanatory Notes

This bibliographical syllabus lists the ballads which have appeared in reputable folksong collections, if those ballads have been sung traditionally within the last forty years. Pieces known to have been composed since 1930 are excluded, as are those for which the evidence of currency in tradition is not conclusive. (For ballads of the latter type, see Appendix II). The ballads are grouped according to type, as explained in Chapter II.

The following items of information are provided, if available, for each ballad:

(a) An identifying letter and number. Thus War Ballads are listed under "A", Ballads of Cowboys and Pioneers under "B", etc.

(b) The title usually printed by collectors, followed by any alternate titles which are commonly used.

(c) A summary of the ballad story.

(d) A sample stanza, usually from a traditional text. The first stanza is given unless otherwise indicated.

(e) A list of printed texts of the ballad. The first reference given is that from which the sample stanza was taken. Folksong collections are usually identified by the name of the editor alone; the titles of these collections will be found in the Bibliography.

A typical entry, from "Mary Phagan," follows: "Brown II, 598, 7d; 5; 9 (N.C.); notes." This indicates that three North Carolina texts of the ballad, of seven double-length or come-all-ye stanzas, of five short stanzas, and of nine short stanzas, are printed, along with notes about the ballad, in Volume II of the *Frank C. Brown Collection of North Carolina Folklore*, beginning on page 598.

The abbreviation "refs." at the end of an entry indicates that the editor provides references to other texts of the ballad outside his collection. No attempt is made to list in this syllabus all the texts available for study, but by checking the additional references one may obtain a fairly complete bibliography for each ballad.

Local titles, if they seem significant, are given after the abbreviation of the state or province in which the text was collected. The symbol "m" after the number of stanzas indicates that a melody is provided with the text. The editors of some popular anthologies frequently fail to say where a text was collected; consequently the state from which the piece came may be omitted.

(f) Under "L. C. Records," a list of the non-commercial recordings of the ballad as given in the *Check-List of Recorded Songs . . . in the Archive of American Folk Song*, published by the Library of Congress, 1942, 2 vols., mimeographed. The number of the record is followed by the state in which the piece was collected, but the name of the singer has usually been omitted. Because of title variation, I have had to use some guesswork in compiling these lists. For example, I have assumed that "George Allen" is a variant of "George Alley," an alternate title for "The Wreck on the C. & O." It is to be hoped that the Library of Congress will soon publish a list which describes its folksong holdings more fully.

The designation AAFS followed by a number indicates that the record has been made available to the public by the Library of Congress separately or as part of an album. Otherwise AAFS refers to the collection of texts and recordings in the Archive of American Folk Song.

(g) A discussion of facts and theories pertaining to the ballad, including statements about origin and authorship. References are given to more extended notes and to detailed studies.

While this appendix does not include references to ballads recently reprinted without annotation in purely commercial anthologies and songbooks, it will be apparent that some of the texts here listed are far more authentic than others. Editors of folksong collections frequently give composite texts, fill out their collectanea from print, emend unusual words and phrases, and otherwise alter what the singers have sung. An explanation of such editorial tampering may or may not appear, but even when it does it is too general to explain what has happened to individual texts. The student who examines all texts carefully and reads the accompanying editorial matter will soon learn which editors are the most reliable.

With the exception of ballads first composed for the phonograph industry, I have usually ignored commercial records of native American ballads. Such recordings have appeared by the hundreds in recent years. While a number of them meet all the tests of authenticity, a far greater number must be regarded as at least partially suspect. The kind of study necessary for the adequate treatment of recordings is beyond the scope of this volume. Until such a study appears, the reader is referred to the record review sections of the scholarly folklore journals, to the catalogues of the record companies, and to Ben Gray Lumpkin's *Folksongs on Records, Issue Three*. Also useful is Alan Lomax's discography, pp. 608-615 in *The Folk Songs of North*

America, which is largely derived from Ray M. Lawless's *Folksingers and Folksongs in America*, pp. 485-630. Lawless lists the contents of about seven hundred long-playing folksong records covering the years 1948-1958.

Note: In the following tables of contents for each ballad type, a double line separates the titles included in the first edition of this work from those added in this edition.

WAR BALLADS

A 1 Brave Wolfe
A 2 Major André's Capture
A 3 Paul Jones, the Privateer
A 4 Paul Jones's Victory
A 5 James Bird
A 6 The *Constitution* and the *Guerrière*
A 7 The Battle of New Orleans
A 8 The Texas Rangers
A 9 The Battle of Bull Run
A 10 The Battle of Shiloh
A 11 The Battle of Shiloh Hill
A 12 The Battle of Elkhorn Tavern
A 13 The Battle of Mill Springs
A 14 The Dying Ranger
A 15 The Drummer Boy of Shiloh
A 16 A Soldier from Missouri
A 17 The Last Fierce Charge
A 18 The *Cumberland's* Crew
A 19 The Rebel's Escape
A 20 Hiram Hubbert

A 21 Bold Dighton
A 22 Brave General Brock
A 23 The Sweet Sunny South
A 24 Revolutionary Tea
A 25 The Hunters of Kentucky
A 26 The *Cumberland*

A 1

BRAVE WOLFE

Disappointed in love, Wolfe gives the young woman a ring as a token of remembrance and leaves her. He lands eventually at Quebec and prepares to meet the French in battle. After a talk with Montcalm, the general retires to his lines. Wolfe is mortally wounded, but when he learns that a British victory is assured, he says, "I die with pleasure".

> Cheer up, ye young men all, let nothing fright you;
> Though at your love's pursuits, let that delight you;
> Don't let your fancy move when come to trial,
> Nor let your courage fail at the first denial.

Thompson, 323, 10d (N.Y.). Carmer, 61, 8d, m. Combs, 176, 19 (W. Va.). Flanders & Brown, 55, 12d couplets (Vt.). *The Forget Me Not Songster*, (Phila., n.d.), 100, 19 sts. Greenleaf, 96, 11d, m. (Nfld.). Leach, 717 (the text quoted above); 9d (Va.). Lomax, *FSNA*, 42, 7d, m. (N.Y. "from singing of Frank Warner and Yankee John Galusha"). Lomax, *Folk Song U.S.A.*, 118, 9d (inc. one st. repeated), m. (N.Y. from Frank Warner). Mackenzie, 198, 8d (N.S.); refs. to many broadside and songster texts. Randolph IV, 101, 9d, m. (Ark.). Shoemaker, 108, 19 (Pa.). Thompson, *A Pioneer Songster*, 99, 19 (N.Y. from ms.).

Major-General James Wolfe (b. 1727) died at Quebec Sept. 13, 1759 (see Thompson, 322-323, for further details).

A 2

MAJOR ANDRÉ'S CAPTURE

The young gentleman, John Paulding, escapes from a British prison and helps capture Major André. General Arnold escapes and leaves the British spy to be executed. The penultimate stanza ends: "And every one wish'd André clear, and Arnold in his stead."

> Come all you gallant heroes, I'd have you lend an ear,
> I'll sing you a small ditty that will your spirits cheer,
> Concerning a young gentlemen whose age was twenty-two,
> He fought for North America, with a heart so just and true.

Halpert, *JAF* 52 (1939), 62, 7d (condensed from *The New American Songster*, Phila., 1817); p. 61, 8d lacking five lines (N.J.). Eddy, 258, 11d (from ms.). *The Forget Me Not Songster* (Phila., n.d.), p. 88, 11d. *NYFQ* 10 (1954), 281, 9d (N.Y. from ms.); refs.

Major John André had been sent by Sir Henry Clinton to negotiate with Benedict Arnold, who had offered to yield West Point to the British. After the interview, André was captured in enemy territory. He was found guilty and was hanged October 2, 1780. (Note condensed from Eddy, 259.)

A 3

PAUL JONES, THE PRIVATEER

The Yankee ship with all sails set outruns the British man-of-war which attempts to intercept her. The ballad is concerned mainly with a technical account of the delights of sailing a fine ship.

'Tis of a gallant Yankee ship that flew the stripes and stars,
And the whistling wind from the west-nor'-west blew through her
    pitch-pine spars,—
With her larboard tacks aboard, my boys, she hung upon the gale,
On an autumn night we raised the light on the old head of Kinsale.

Rickaby, 158, 8d ("The Yankee Man-of-War", from Eggleston's *American War Ballads*); 156, 5d, m. (Minn. Sung by M. C. Dean). Beck, *The Folklore of Maine*, 173, 10d (Me.). Colcord, 126, 8d, m. ("The Stately Southerner"). Creighton and Senior, 267, 9d, m.; 7d, m.; 7d (N.S.). Doerflinger, 131, 9d, m. (from ms.; tune from N.Y.). Neeser, 25, 8d (from Luce's *Naval Songs*). Ranson, 82, 16 sts. and alternate verses, m. (Ireland).

According to Miss Colcord, the ballad "recounts an exploit of John Paul Jones off the Irish coast in his privateer, the *Ranger,* which was fitted out in Portsmouth, N.H., in 1777." The incident occurred in 1778. (See Neeser, 25, for further details).

A 4

PAUL JONES'S VICTORY

This patriotic broadside dramatizes Paul Jones's hard-fought and victorious battle off the British coast with two English warships of forty-four and twenty guns.

An American frigate, a frigate of fame,
With guns mounting forty, the *Richard* by name,
Sail'd to cruise in the channels of old England,
With valiant commander, Paul Jones was the man.
Hurrah! Hurrah! Our country for ever, Hurrah!

Neeser, 26, 14 (from a broadside?); frontispiece, 13 sts. (reproduction of a broadside). Brown II, 523, 7; 8 (N.C.). Cazden, 16, 9d, m. (N.Y.); notes. Chappell, 48, 7 m. (N.C.); reprinted by Leach, 713. Creighton and Senior, 226, 6, m. (N.S.). Mackenzie, 206, 7; 5 (N.S.); See for refs. to many appearances of this ballad in songsters and on Brit. and Amer.

broadsides. Ranson, 51, 5 (Ireland). Thompson, *A Pioneer Songster*, 111, 9 (N.Y. from ms.).

"While cruising around the British Isles with a small squadron, Commodore Jones sighted a fleet of forty sail off Flamborough Head on September 23, 1779. They were merchantmen from the Baltic, under convoy of the 44-gun ship *Serapis*, Captain Richard Pearson, and the *Countess of Scarborough*, 20 guns. . . . *The Bon Homme Richard* attacked the *Serapis* single-handed". (Note from Neeser, 26-27. See for further details).

A 5

JAMES BIRD

Bird bids farewell to his family and sweetheart and goes to Lake Erie, where he fights valiantly with Perry, refusing to go below even when seriously wounded. Later he writes to his parents, saying that he must die for having deserted from the brig *Niagara*. The execution is carried out.

> Sons of freedom, listen to me,
> And ye daughters, too, give ear,
> To a sad and lonesome story
> As ever was told you shall hear.

> Farewell, Bird, farewell forever,
> Home and friends shall see no more,
> But his gallant form lies buried
> On Lake Erie's farthest shore.

Eddy, 265, 14½, m. (O. from ms.); the first and last sts. are given above; refs. Belden, 296, 19 (Mo.); refs. Brown II, 525, 20 (N.C.). Burt, 183, 9, m. (Pa. from ms.). Cox, 261, 7 (W. Va.). Hubbard, 287, 20, m. (Utah). *JAF* 35 (1922), 380, 22 (O. from ms.). Pound, 93, 22 (N.Y. via Neb.). Thompson, 345, 20 (N.Y.); historical notes. Thompson, *A Pioneer Songster*, 125, 22 (N.Y. from ms.). *The Forget Me Not Songster*, Phila., n.d., p. 116, 22 sts. L. C. Records 1003 A (O.); 3373 B2 (Cal.); 2298 A4 & B1 (Mich.); 1845 B (N.J.); and 4202 A1 & A2 (Cal.).

"The ballad gives the facts of Bird's career accurately and with considerable fullness." (Note from Tolman and Eddy, *JAF* 35, 380). Bird was executed in 1814.

"This ballad was written by Charles Miner and printed in his paper. *The Gleaner*, at Wilkes-barre, Pennsylvania, in 1814" (note from Belden, 296). "For a detailed study of this old song, see 'The Battle of Lake Erie in Ballad and History' by Charles B. Galbreath, Ohio Archaeological and Historical Publications, Vol. 20 (1911), pp. 415-456" (note from Eddy, 267). "For the original text and an interesting account of the composition of the ballad . . . see Charles Francis Richardson and Elizabeth Miner (Thomas) Richardson, *Charles Miner, a Pennsylvania Pioneer*, pp. 67-76" (note from Rickaby,

221). See also Mary Elizabeth King, "More Light on the Ballad of 'James Bird'," *NYFQ* 7 (1951), 142-144; Charles A. McCarthy, "James Bird: the Man and the Ballad," *KFQ* 6 (1961), no. 4, pp. 3-13; and George Swetnam, "An Early Notice of the James Bird Ballad," *KFQ* 6 (1961), no. 4, pp. 13-17. The 22 st. text from the Richardson book is reprinted in *KFQ* 6 (1961), no. 4, p. 9.

A 6

THE *CONSTITUTION* AND THE *GUERRIÈRE*

(Hull's Victory)

Dacres, the commander of the British frigate *Guerrière*, is confident that he can easily defeat the Yankee ship. But the accurate and effective fire of the Americans causes him to surrender to Captain Hull.

> It oft times has been told,
> That the British seamen bold
> Could flog the tars of France so neat and handy, oh!
> But they never found their match,
> Till the Yankees did them catch,
> Oh, the Yankee boys for fighting are the dandy, oh!

Neeser, 95, 9d (from print). Colcord, 130, 9d, m. Cox, 257, 9d (from ms.); refs. to broadsides and other early printings. *Grigg's Southern and Western Songster* (Phila., 1847), p. 44, 9d. Lomax, *Amer. Ballads*, 507, 13, m. (tune from Colcord). Lomax, *FSNA*, 49, 7d, m. Stout, 97, 2½d (Ia.). Thompson, *A Pioneer Songster*, 119, 10d (N.Y. from ms.). L. C. Record, 4204 A4 (Cal. "Capt. Hull & Proud Dacus").

"This famous single-ship engagement took place on August 19, 1812, off the coast of Nova Scotia. Captain Isaac Hull, commanding the *Constitution*, 44 guns, had sailed from Boston without orders, in the hope of meeting some of the British frigates reported off the coast. In twenty-five minutes the *Guerrière*, 38 guns, Captain R. Dacres, was reduced to a perfect wreck, 78 of her crew being killed and wounded. The *Constitution* had only 7 killed and 7 wounded". (Note from Neeser, 95).

A 7

THE BATTLE OF NEW ORLEANS

The American forces repulse three British charges, inflicting heavy casualties on the enemy. After three hours of fighting, the few remaining British troops are forced to withdraw.

> 'Twas on the eighth of January, Just at the dawn of day,
> We spied those British officers All dressed in bat'l array;
> Old Jackson then gave orders, "Each man to keep his post,
> And form a line from right to left. And let no time be lost."

Paul G. Brewster, " 'The Battle of New Orleans': (An Example of Communal Composition)", *SFQ* 1 (1937), no. 3, p. 25, 4d, m. (Ind.).

The battle was fought in 1815.

Brewster received this ballad in 1935 from a man who believed that it was "composed and sung by the soldiers who fought the battle". The informant's grandfather, who had taken part in the battle, had sung the piece to his children and grandchildren. To call it "an example of communal composition", however, as Brewster does, is to place too much faith in hearsay evidence 120 years old. Moreover, this ballad shows some knowledge of poetic techniques. Undoubtedly it is the work of a single author, who may well have been *one* of the soldiers at New Orleans.

A 8

THE TEXAS RANGERS

The narrator describes the Indian fight in which many white men are killed, and then speaks wistfully of his mother and of the girl he loved and left.

> 'Twas at the age of sixteen I joined the jolly band;
> We marched from San Antonio on to the Rio Grande.
> Our captain he informed us—of course he thought it right—
> "Before you reach that river, my boys, you will have to fight".

Hudson, 227, 8d (Miss.). Belden, 336, 8; 10; 7 of 14 (Mo.); refs. Brown II, 544, 3 8-line d; 7 (N.C.). Cox, 262, 4½d (W. Va.). Flanders-Barry, 226, 7½d, m. (Vt.); notes. Fuson, 191, 9 (Ky.). Henry, *Folk-Songs*, 350, 13 (Ga.); 6d (N.C.). Hubbard, 291, 7d, m. (Utah). *KFR* 1 (1955), 86, 10 (Ky. from ms.). Lomax, *Cowboy Songs*, 359, 10d, m. Lomax, *FSNA*, 331, 7d, m. Lomax, *Our Singing Country*, 245, 9d, m. Morris, 29, 10, m. ("Longstreet's Rangers"); 5d; 6d (Fla.). Pound, 163, 14 (Mo. via Wash.). Randolph II, 170, 12, m.; 6d, m. (Mo.); refs. Sharp II, 253, 5d, m. (N.C. "Come All Ye Southern Soldiers"). L. C. Record 5266A, 6d (Mo.).

In Civil War versions of this ballad, the enemies are Yankees or Rebels rather than Indians.

A 9

THE BATTLE OF BULL RUN
(Manassa Junction)

This piece speaks derisively of the precipitous retreat of the cowardly Yankees near Bull Run, and pays honor to the brave Southern soldiers. Even the ladies who had come to see a Northern victory were forced to flee with McDowell's men.

> In eighteen hundred an' sixty one,
> Way down in old Virginia,
> MacDowell marched with old and young,
> Horse-thieves an' other villains.

Randolph II, 250, 13, m. (Mo.) ; 9 (Ark.).

"The name 'Manassa Junction' refers to a place near the Bull Run battle-field" (Note from Randolph, 250, who refers to another text printed in *Ozark Life.*) The First Battle of Bull Run was fought in July, 1861.

A 10

THE BATTLE OF SHILOH

A Southern account of the hard battle and subsequent retreat of the Yankees, with a stanza of lament for the girls whose men lie dead at Shiloh.

> All you Southerners now draw near,
> Unto my story approach you here,
> Each loyal Southerner's heart to cheer
> With the victory gained at Shiloh.

Sharp II, 172, 10, m. (Va.).
The battle was fought in April, 1862, in Tennessee.

A 11

THE BATTLE OF SHILOH HILL

A veteran of the battle tells of its horrors in rather general terms, hopes that there will never again be such a slaughter, and adds a prayer for the souls of the dead.

> Come all ye valiant soldiers, a story I will tell,
> About the bloody battle that was fought on Shiloh's hill,
> It was an awful struggle that caused your blood to chill,
> All from the bloody battle that was fought on Shiloh's hill.

Randolph II, 272, 6d, m. (Mo.) ; reprinted by Lomax, *FSNA,* 349. Brown II, 535, 6½ (N. C.) ; the editors refer to a text of this piece in *Allan's Lone Star Ballads* (Galveston, 1874), pp. 44-45. Hudson, 260, 3d (Miss.).

This piece has none of the partisan flavor of the preceding one.

A 12

THE BATTLE OF ELKHORN TAVERN (a)

THE PEA RIDGE BATTLE (b)

This involved and partisan ballad tells of the defeat of the Confederate forces by the Federal troops "at a tavern called Elkhorn". The Southern and Northern versions differ materially, but both speak satirically and insultingly of the enemy.

> My name is Daniel Martin,
> I'se borned in Arkansas;
> I fled from those base rebels
> Who fear not God or law.

Belden, 368, 14 (Ark. "The Battle of Elkhorn Tavern").

My name it is Dan Martin,
I was born in Arkansas,
I fled from them dishonored Feds
Who fear not God nor law.

Randolph II, 247, 21 (Mo. "The Pea Ridge Battle"). High 4, 24 lines
(Ark).

The battle of Elkhorn Tavern was fought March 6-8, 1862. For details
see the headnotes to Belden's and Randolph's versions.

A 13

THE BATTLE OF MILL SPRINGS

(Young Edward)

A wounded soldier, lying on the battlefield at Mill Springs, speaks sentimentally of his parents and sister, and of the girl he will never see again.
He kisses the Stars and Stripes and dies with his comrades around him.

> There was a dying soldier boy
> Lay near the battlefield
> His comrades gathered 'round him
> And by his side did kneel.
> At length he raised his drooping head
> And a murmuring word he said:
> "Oh who will care for mother
> Now her soldier boy is dead?

Henry, *Folk-Songs*, 368, 5d (N.C. "The Dying Soldier"). Cox, 264, 9d
(W. Va.). Perrow, *JAF* 28 (1915), 165, 12d couplets (N. C. "Young
Edwards"). L. C. Records 2892 A2 (Tenn.) and 2811 B (Va. "Young
Edward").

"The battle was fought at Mill Springs, Kentucky, on January 19, 1862".
(Cox).

A 14

THE DYING RANGER

The cowboy (or soldier) speaks at length of his sister at home in Texas
(or New England), who will be left alone. His comrades promise to act as
her brothers "till the strongest one shall fall", and the wounded man dies
happy.

> The sun was settin' in the west, it fell with a ling'rin' ray,
> Beneath the shade of the forest where a dyin' cowboy lay,
> Beneath the tall palmetto, beneath the sultry sky,
> Away from his loved old Texas we laid him down to die.

Randolph II, 196, 9d, m.; 7d, m. ("The Dying Cowboy"); 264, 11d, m.
(Mo. "The Dying Soldier"); refs. Belden, 397, 9d, (Mo.) Cox, 263, 6d (W.
Va.). Doerflinger, 274, 10d, m. (N.B.). Finger, 170, 10d. High, 21, 22d lines

(Ark.). Lomax, *Cowboy Songs*, 366, 10d, m. Morris, 47, 10d (Fla.). L. C. Record 2332 A & Bl (Mich.).

A 15
THE DRUMMER BOY OF SHILOH

The soldiers sorrowfully bury the drummer boy "who prayed before he died," using a flag as his shroud.

> On Shiloh's dark and bloody ground
> The dead and wounded lay around.
> Amid these were a drummer boy
> Who beat the drum that day.

Henry, *Folk-Songs*, 366, 6 (N. C.). Brown II, 536, 7; 4d (N. C.); refs. Hubbard, 282, 4d, m. (Utah). Randolph II, 308, 5d (Mo. from ms.); refs. L. C. Record 2850 A2 (N. C.).

"As a piece of sheet music written and composed by Will S. Hays and published by D. P. Faulds, Louisville, Ky., 1862, this song is listed by Dichter and Shapiro (*Early American Sheet Music*, 1941, p. 115)." (Note from Randolph). "This ballad appears in Frank Lum's *The 'Beauty of Broadway' Songster* (N. Y., 1870), p. 13, and in *Allan's Lone Star Ballads* . . . (Galveston, 1874), p. 145." (Note from Brown).

A 16
A SOLDIER FROM MISSOURI
(The Kansas Line)

The dying soldier sends a sorrowful message to his family "up near the Kansas line". He regrets that he has not followed his mother's advice to stay at home. Both his neighbors and the girl he loved had persuaded him to join the rebels.

> A solider from Missouri,
> In early manhood's prime,
> Lay with the dead an' dyin'
> In Mississippi's clime. . . .

Randolph II, 258, 6½d, m. (Mo.).

"This piece is widely known in the Ozark country. It is sometimes called 'The Kansas Line', and there have been numerous attempts to turn the central figure into a dying and repentant Yankee, instead of a dying and repentant Confederate. Professor Belden writes me (Feb. 9, 1930) that there are several similar texts in his collection at the University of Missouri." (Note from Randolph, 258).

A 17
THE LAST FIERCE CHARGE
(The Battle of Fredericksburg; Custer's Last Charge)

Two Civil War soldiers, a boy and a man, are about to ride into battle.

Each asks the other to write a letter for him if he should die. Both are killed, and thus no letter goes to the man's fiancée or to the boy's mother.

> 'Twas just before the last fierce charge
> Two soldiers drew their rein,
> With parting words and shaking of the hands,
> For they ne'er might meet again.

Eddy, 304, 8 (O.); 301, 10d (O.). Belden, 383, 8d; 20, m. (Mo.); refs. Brown II, 539, 18 (N.C.); refs. Fuson, 94, 15 (Ky.). Henry, *Folk-Songs*, 363, 11½ (Ga.). Hubbard, 277, 10d, m. (Utah). Mackenzie, 298, 10d (N.S.). Owens, 120, 15, m. (Tex. "Custer's Last Charge"). Randolph II, 298, 9 7-line sts., m. (Ark.); roughly 8d (Mo.); refs. *WF* 17 (1958), 237, 1 (Ia.).

L. C. Records 3207 A1 (Mo.); 2288 A3 (Mich.); 4214 A2 & B and 3296 B1 (Wis. and Cal. Same singer); 2417 B (Cal. "The Battle of Fredericksburg").

"Patently 'literary' and widely known as this song is, I have not been able to find its authorship, nor have I seen it in print except as a collector's item". (Note from Belden, 383). For a rather artless text in the idiom of the folk, see the Ohio version quoted above.

A 18

THE *CUMBERLAND'S* CREW
(The Sinking of the *Cumberland*)

Despite heavy casualties and their inability to damage the iron ship of the enemy, the seamen of the *Cumberland* fight on heroically until their ship is rammed and sunk.

> Oh comrades, come listen, and join in my ditty
> Of a terrible battle that happened of late.
> May each Union tar shed a sad tear of pity
> When they think of the once gallant Cumberland's fate.

Gray, 162, 14 sts. printed as 7 (Me.); the first half of st. 1 is given above. Beck, 233, 13 (Mich.); reprinted in Beck, *Bunyan*, 249. Cazden, 20, 14 printed as 7, m. (N.Y.); notes. Doerflinger, 134, 8, m. (N.Y. a composite text); refs. Rickaby, 140, 1 st., m. (Minn. from the singing of M. C. Dean, whose full text is in Dean, p. 36). Shoemaker, 217, 7 (Pa.). Broadside in the Harvard Library: Bell and Co., 639 Kearny St., San Francisco, 14 sts. Wolf, p. 28, lists broadsides by Auner, DeMarsan, Johnson, and Wehman. L. C. Records 2236 A2 (Wis.); 1605 B1 (O.); 3815 A1 (Cal.).

"The United States frigate *Cumberland*, commanded by Lieutenant George Morris, was sunk by the *Merrimac* off Newport News, Virginia, on March 8, 1862." (Note from Gray, 162).

See also "The *Cumberland* (A 26).

A 19

THE REBEL'S ESCAPE

The Rebel prisoner puts the guard to sleep with whiskey, escapes to the Licking River, gets across it on a raft, and then goes upriver to see his family. His wife gives him supper and a blanket and advises him to find his way into Southern territory.

> Come all you jolly soldiers, I will sing to you a song,
> I'll try to be brief, I will not detain you long
> Concerning all my troubles and how they did advance,
> And how I got around them and what a narrow chance.

Thomas, *Devil's Ditties*, 146, 5d, m. (Ky. "War Song"). Carmer, 149, 4d, m. (Tenn.).

Mrs. Thomas reports that she first heard the "War Song" from Rebel Jack Hawkins, "a picturesque old character" from Rowan County, Kentucky. Neither she nor Carl Carmer provides any supplementary information about the ballad.

A 20

HIRAM HUBBERT (HUBBARD)

Hiram is captured by Rebels and is cruelly driven ahead of them to the Cumberland River. There he is tried, and, after his captors have sworn against him, is condemned to death. He writes a will in which he bids farewell to his family and friends and then is tied to a tree and shot dead.

> A sad and mournful story
> 'Tis unto you I now will tell,
> Concerning of Hiram Hubbert,
> And about the way he fell.
>
> Hiram Hubbert was not guilty,
> I've heard great many say;
> He was not in this country,
> He was ninety miles away.

Combs, 199, 9 (Ky.); sts. 1 & 9 are given above. Ritchie, *A Garland*, 57, 9d couplets, m. (Ky.). L. C. Record 1544 Bl (Ky.).

"Cette chanson est un echo de la guerre de guerillas dans les highlands pendant la Guerre Civile". (Combs).

A 21

BOLD DIGHTON

More than three hundred seamen are imprisoned by the French on Guadeloupe. Bold Dighton pays five hundred guineas to relieve their distress and is himself imprisoned. He executes a daring escape for all to the ship *Tiger*. The next day the *Tiger* defeats the *Lion* in a hard-fought battle and sails to Antigua.

> Come all you bold heroes that plough the rough main,
> Give ear to our story, the truth I'll explain.
> It was our misfortune which happened in great war,
> And how we escaped from the French at Bastar.

Mackenzie, 217, 26d; 21d (N.S.); notes and refs. Gardner, 235, 22d, m. (Mich.). Thompson, *A Pioneer Songster*, 108, 26d (N.Y. from ms.). *The Forget Me Not Songster*, Phila., n.d., p. 34, 26d.

"The Harvard College Library has two broadside copies of the early nineteenth century. One is headed: 'The Escape from Bassaterre. Being an account of an action fought off Guadaloupe in 1805, where ninety-five Americans, and near three hundred Britons made their escape at that place.—Composed by P. Russel, while lying in irons in the Moro Castle, who received two wounds in the action." (Note from Mackenzie, p. 216).

A 22

BRAVE GENERAL BROCK

(Come All You Bold Canadians)

General Brock and his men travel all night to meet the Yankees. The United States commander at first refuses to surrender but quickly changes his mind after being fired upon and gives up the town and the garrison.

> There was a bold commander, brave General Brock by name,
> Took shipping at Niagara and down to York he came.
> He says, "My gallant heroes, if you'll come along with me,
> We'll fight those proud Yankees in the west of Canaday!"

Doerflinger, 273, 7d, m. (Ont. via N.Y. "Come All You Bold Canadians"); notes.

". . . General Brock, Governor of Ontario, raised a provincial militia in 1812 and marched against General William Hull, United States commander in the Northwest. . . . Brock bluffed Hull into surrendering Detroit, although reinforcements were on the way." (Note from Doerflinger).

A 23

THE SWEET SUNNY SOUTH

The young Southerner has shouldered his rifle and buckled his sword, has bid farewell to his family and his sweetheart, and hopes to return home "when from Union and Yankee our land shall be free."

When the sweet sunny South was in peace and content,
The days of my boyhood I carelessly spent,
From the broad rolling plains to the pure purling streams,
Ever dear to my mem'ry, ever fresh in my dreams.

Gardner, 242, 6d, m. (Mich.). Cazden, 18, 8d, m. (N.Y. "The Bright Sunny South"); notes. Cox, 280, 7d (Ky.). Creighton and Senior, 272, 5d, m.; 7d (N.S.). Mackenzie, 139, 7d (N.S.); refs.

This piece is well above the usual ballad quality. Pointing out that it has been reported mainly from the North, Cazden suggests that it may be of Irish rather than Confederate origin (p. 110).

A 24

REVOLUTIONARY TEA

Angered at her daughter's refusal to pay a tax on tea, the mother sends her a large amount and threatens to whip her unless the tax is paid. The girl defiantly dumps the tea into the ocean.

There was an old lady lived over the sea
And she was an island queen.
Her daughter lived off in a far country
With an ocean of water between.
The old lady's pockets were full of gold
But never contented was she,
She called on her daughter to pay her a tax
Of threepence a pound on her tea,
Of threepence a pound on her tea.

Fowke and Mills, 54, 4d, m. (Ont.). Morris, 19, 8, m. (Conn. via Fla.); refs.

"Then came the Boston Tea Party. On the night of December 16, 1773, fifty of the rebels disguised themselves as Indians and boarded British ships lying in Boston harbor. They burst open 343 chests of tea and dumped them in the ocean—an act of defiance that sparked the American Revolution." (Note from Fowke and Mills).

A 25

THE HUNTERS OF KENTUCKY

The Kentucky men with their rifles protect the New Orleans ladies by forcing the British invaders to flee.

Ye gentlemen and ladies fair,
Who grace this famous city,
Just listen, if ye've time to spare,
While I rehearse a ditty;
And for the opportunity,
Conceive yourselves quite lucky,

> For 't is not often that you see
> A hunter from Kentucky.
> Oh! Kentucky, the hunters of Kentucky,
> The hunters of Kentucky.

Rickaby, 142, 8 10-line sts. (the original text; see below); 141, 1d and chor., m. (Wis.); notes and refs. Henry, *Songs Sung*, 93, 6d and chor. (Tenn.). Randolph IV, 104, 4, m. (Mo.). Thompson, *A Pioneer Songster*, 131, 8d (N.Y. from ms.). *Grigg's Southern and Western Songster* (Phila., 1847), 81, 8d and chor.

"The Hunters of Kentucky . . . was written in 1822 by Samuel Woodworth, the poet of *The Old Oaken Bucket*. It may be found in his *Melodies, Duets, Trios, Songs, and Ballads* (New York, 1826, pp. 221-223) . . ."

"The hunters of Kentucky were the Kentucky riflemen, about two thousand in number, who figured so dominantly in General Andrew Jackson's repulse of the forces of the British General, Packenham, at New Orleans, January 8, 1815." (Notes from Rickaby, 222-223).

A 26

THE *CUMBERLAND*

(Good Ship *Cumberland*)

Although the Union sailors fight gallantly, their shots cannot hurt the ironclad *Merrimac*. When the *Cumberland* refuses to surrender, she is rammed and sinks with the stars and stripes flying from her masts.

> Was on a Monday morning just at the break of day,
> I espied a lofty steamship to an anchor in the Bay,
> When a man from our masthead, our topmast so high,
> "There's something up to windward like a housetop I espy."

Creighton, 282, 5d and chor., m. (N.S. "Maggie Mac"). Brown II, 532, 5d (N.C. "Cumblom"); detailed notes and 5d sts. from a Johnson (Phila.) broadside. Wolfe, 52, lists seven broadsides of this piece in the Library Company collection. A broadside text of 8d sts. with tune is printed in Silber, p. 256.

See the note to "The *Cumberland's* Crew" (A 18).

BALLADS OF COWBOYS AND PIONEERS

B 1 The Cowboy's Lament
B 2 The Dying Cowboy
B 3 When the Work's All Done This Fall
B 4 Utah Carroll
B 5 Little Joe the Wrangler
B 6 Bill Vanero
B 7 The Wandering Cowboy
B 8 A Fair Lady of the Plains
B 9 Sweet Betsy from Pike
B 10 The Buffalo Skinners
B 11 The Sioux Indians
B 12 Pattonia, the Pride of the Plains
B 13 The Trail to Mexico
B 14 Joe Bowers
B 15 The Bucking Broncho
B 16 Zebra Dun
B 17 Tying a Knot in the Devil's Tail

B 18 Strawberry Roan
B 19 The Mountain Meadows Massacre
B 20 The Wild Boy
B 21 Root Hog or Die
B 22 Sweet Jane
B 23 My Heart's Tonight in Texas
B 24 Cowboy Jack
B 25 The Rolling Stone
B 26 The Boys of Sanpete County
B 27 The Horse Wrangler

B 1
THE COWBOY'S LAMENT
(The Dying Cowboy)

Saying that drink and gambling have ruined him, the wounded cowboy gives detailed instructions for his funeral and dies. His comrades mourn their loss.

> As I rode out in the streets of old Laredo,
> As I rode out in Laredo one day,
> I saw a young cowboy all wrapped in white linen,
> All wrapped in white linen and as cold as the clay.

Belden, 393, 5 and chor. (from ms.); 5 and chor., m.; 9 (Mo.); refs. Brown II, 614, 8; add. sts. (N.C.); refs. *Bulletin* no. 7, p. 16, 6½ and chor., m. (Kan. via Mass.); notes. *CFB* 1 (1962), no. 3, p. 20, 4, m.; 6 (Colo. "The Dying Ranger"). Combs, 209, 3½ and chor. (Ky. "Jack Combs". Jack, who is not a cowboy, has been murdered). Cox, 242, 6 and chor.; 3 and chor.; 5 and chor. (from ms.); 4 and chor.; 4 and chor. (W. Va.); refs. Flanders-Barry, 250, 4 and chor. (Vt.); notes. Hubbard, 310, 3 and chor. (Utah). Larkin, 14, 5 sts. Lomax, *Cowboy Songs*, 417, 11, m. (a composite text). Lomax, *FSNA*, 384, 7, m. Lomax, *Folk Song U.S.A.*, 206, 8, m. Mackenzie, 302, 4 and chor. (N.S.). Morris, 41, 5, m.; 7 (Fla.). Pound, 170, 4 and chor. (Ill. via Wyo.). Randolph II, 179, 6, m.; 4 (Ark.); refs. Sandburg, 263, 7, m. Sharp II, 165, 4, m. (Va.). Williams, 419, 3 and chor. (Ky). *WF* 17 (1958), 7, m. (Ia.). L. C. Records 3806 A2, 3808 A2 (Tex. same singer); 1372 B1 (Va.).

"The Cowboy's Lament" is ultimately derived from the British broadside ballad "The Unfortunate Rake" (or "The Unfortunate Lad"), in which a soldier who is dying of syphillis requests a military funeral, saying:

> Muffle your drums, play your pipes merrily,
> Play the dead march as you go along . . .
> (Belden, 392)

That piece was rewritten as "The Bad Girl's Lament" ("The Young Girl Cut Down in Her Prime" (Q 26 in *American Balladry from British Broadsides*. Alternate titles for this piece are "One Morning in May" and "St. James' Hospital". For texts see Hubbard, 272 and Sharp II, 164). The cowboy version, which makes the plea for the dead march the third time is a reworking of "The Bad Girl's Lament". Barry writes: "There is nothing in the traditional history of the air (the one to which all three pieces are often sung) to invalidate the claim of F. H. Maynard that he recreated "The Bad Girl's Lament" as a cowboy song (Sires, Ina, *Songs of the Open Range*, p. 4)." (Note from *Bulletin* no. 7 (1934), p. 18).

133

B 2

THE DYING COWBOY

(Oh Bury Me Not on the Lone Prairie)

The dying cowboy asks to be taken home and buried beside his father in the churchyard, but his request goes unheeded. He is buried on the prairie, "in a narrow grave just six by three."

> Oh bury me not on the lone prairie,
> These words came low and mournfully
> From the pallid lips of a youth who lay
> On his dyin' bed at the close of day.

Randolph II, 185, 10, m.; 8, m. (Mo.); refs. Belden, 388, 7; 7 (from ms.); 6 and chor. (Mo.); 3 (Tex.); 5 (Mo.); refs. Brown II, 613, 10; 3 (N.C.). *CFB* 1 (1962), no. 1, p. 8, 8; no. 3, p. 19, 7, m.; *CFB* 2 (1963), p. 10, 8 (Colo.). Cox, 247, 8; 10 (W. Va.); refs. Hubbard, 313, 8½, m.; 4 (Utah). Hudson, 222, 8 and chor. (Miss.). Lomax, *Cowboy Songs*, 48, 13 sts and 6 choruses, m. ("Amalgamated from thirty-six separate sources"). Lomax, *Folk Song U.S.A.*, 208, 10, m. Pound, 171, 8 and chor. (Wyo.). Sharp II, 236, 1, m. (Ky.); 1, m.; 1, m. (N.C.). Williams, 421, 9 (Ky.). L. C. Records 58 B2 (Tex.) and 3028 B2 (Miss.).

This piece is an adaptation of "The Ocean Burial," which was "written by the Reverend Edwin H. Chapin (1814-1880), a famous Universalist clergyman, and published in the *Southern Literary Messenger* in 1839. It was set to music by George N. Allen, and sung in public at the concerts of Ossian N. Dodge and in innumerable homes." (Note from Linscott, p. 245).

See Francis C. Lathrop, "Commercial Parlor-Ballad to Folksong," *JAF* 70 (1957), 240-246.

For a comparison of "The Dying Cowboy" and "The Ocean Burial", see Chapter VI.

B 3

WHEN THE WORK'S ALL DONE THIS FALL

The cowboy tells his friends that he is planning to return home after many years to see his lonely mother. That night the cattle stampede and he is fatally injured. Before he dies, he asks that his mother be sent his wages, and he wills his saddle and his pistol to two companions. The board marking his grave says that he won't see his mother "when the work's all done this fall".

> A group of jolly cowboys, discussing plans at ease.
> Says one, "I'll tell you something, boys, if you will listen, please.
> I am an old cow-puncher and here I'm dressed in rags,
> I used to be a tough one and go on great big jags.

Lomax, *Cowboy Songs*, 74, 9d and chor., m. Brown II, 618, 10d (N.C.);
refs. *CFB* 2 (1963), 30, 5 8-line d. sts., m. (Colo.). Henry, *Folk-Songs*, 351,
5 8-line d. sts. (Tenn.?); 8 (N.C.). Sandburg, 260, 5 8-line d. sts. L. C.
Records 1577 A & B (Ky.); 2641 B1 (Tex.).

J. Frank Dobie in *WF* 18 (1959), 323-325, attributes this ballad to Mar-
shall Johnson, McLennan County, Texas.

B 4
UTAH CARROLL

When he is unable to save the boss's daughter from stampeding cattle by
lifting her onto his horse, Utah runs off with the red blanket which has
maddened them, leaving her unharmed. The cattle bear down on him, and
he dies under their hooves.

> You ask, my little friend,
> Why I'm always sad and still,
> And my eyes are always darkened
> Like a cloud upon a hill.
> Rein in your pony closer,
> I'll tell to you a tale
> Of Utah Carl, my partner,
> And his last ride on the trail.

Hudson, 224, 14d (Miss.). Larkin, 115, 12d. Lomax, *Cowboy Songs*, 125,
17d, m. (a composite text, partly from Tex.). *Rocky Mt. Coll.*, 22, 10½d, m.
(Tex.). The AAFS has a text, 16d, Utah, contributed by Austin Fife. L. C.
Record 4107 A (Cal. spoken).

"J. T. Shirley of San Angelo, Texas, says that a cowboy on the Curve T
Ranch in Schleicher County wrote this song." (Lomax). The story told in
this melodramatic ballad is probably fictional.

B 5
LITTLE JOE THE WRANGLER

Taken in by the cowboys and taught how to herd cattle, Little Joe dies
under his horse while trying to halt a stampede.

> Little Joe the wrangler, will never wrangle more;
> His days with the "remuda"—they are done.
> 'Twas a year ago last April he joined the outfit here,
> A little "Texas stray" and all alone.

Thorp, 96, 11d. Reprinted by Larkin, 119. *CFB* 2 (1963), p. 35, 11d, m.
(Colo.). Lomax, *Cowboy Songs*, 91, 11d, m. Randolph II, 234, 10 6-line sts.
(Mo.). L. C. Records 654 A (Tex.) and 4116 B (11d, Cal.).

N. Howard Thorp's note: "Written by me on trail of herd of O Cattle
from Chimney Lake, New Mexico, to Higgins, Texas, 1898 . . . It was
copyrighted and appeared in my first edition of 'Songs of the Cowboys',
published in 1908."

B 6

BILL VANERO (PAUL VENEREZ)

Bill is fatally wounded while riding to warn Bessie Lee and other ranchers of an Indian raid. He writes a warning love-letter to Bessie in his own blood. The horse carries the letter, and the ranch is saved.

> Bill Vanero heard them say
> In Arizona town one day
> There's a band of 'Pache Indians
> They're on the trail this way.

Randolph II, 223, 17, m. (Ark.); 11d (Mo.); add. sts.; notes and refs. Kirkland, "A Check List," *JAF* 59 (1946), 427, lists "Bill Venero." Larkin, 27, 12½d (Col. "Billy Venero"). Lomax, *Cowboy Songs*, 197, 13d, m. The AAFS has texts of 12½d (Utah. coll. by Austin Fife) and 14 sts. (Tex.).

Miss Pound says that "The Ride of Paul Venarez" was composed by Eben E. Rexford and was originally published in the *Youth's Companion*. It "was long a favorite with reciters." (*Poetic Origins and the Ballad*, 227).

B 7

THE WANDERING COWBOY

(Home, Sweet Home)

A melancholy cowboy tells his comrades that he left home because, during a quarrel, he had fatally wounded his boyhood friend, who had been a rival for his girl's affections.

> We was layin' on the prairie at French Ranch one night,
> Our heads was on our saddles an' our fires a-burnin' bright,
> Some was tellin' stories an' some was singin' songs,
> An' some was idly smokin' while the hours rolled along.

Randolph II, 204, 5d and chor., m. (Mo. reprinted by Larkin, 143); 3¼d (Mo.); 13 (Ark.). Brown II, 619, 11 (N.C. "A Jolly Group of Cowboys"). Lomax, *Cowboys Songs*, 124, 6d (Tex. "Home, Sweet Home"; reprinted from *PTFS* 6).

B 8

A FAIR LADY OF THE PLAINS

(Death of a Maiden Fair)

The fair lady, who enjoys "red liquor" and can use a six-shooter, is killled by Indians while camping with her husband near a herd of wild steers. The cowboys ride out to avenge her death.

There was a fair maiden;
She lived on the plains;
She helped me herd cattle
Through the cold rain and snow.

Henry, *Folk-Songs*, 358, 10 (Ga. "Death of a Maiden Fair"). High, 24,
16d lines (Ark.). Larkin, 147, 4d (Mo. from Vance Randolph). Randolph II,
199, 4d 6-line sts., m.; 5d; 5d (Mo.); 6, m.; 2½d. m. (Ark.); refs.

The contributor of Randolph's A text told him that this was "supposedly
an old song in 1893". The history of the piece has not been traced.

B 9

SWEET BETSY FROM PIKE

Betsy and Ike, from Pike County, Missouri, arrive in California after many
hardships and a few gay times.

Did you ever hear tell of sweet Betsy from Pike,
Who crossed the wide prairies with her lover Ike,
With two yoke of cattle and one spotted hog,
A tall shanghai rooster and an old yaller dog?

Lomax, *Amer. Ballads*, 424, 14d, m. Lomax, *Cowboy Songs*, 388, 14d, m.
Lomax, *FSNA*, 335, same text (from *Put's Golden Songster*). Belden, 343,
10d (Cal. via Mo.); refs. Hubbard, 300, 10d, m. (Utah). Leach, 750, Belden's
text. Randolph II, 209, 4d; 2d (Mo.); refs. *KFR* 4 (1958), 117, 4d, m.
(Ky.). L. C. Records 3295 A 1 (Wis.); 1697 Al (Ky.); 4099 A 2 (Cal.).

Black and Robertson, *The Gold Rush Song Book*, p. 10, print a text of
11d sts. from *Put's Golden Songster*, by John A. Stone, San Francisco, 1858.
In the preface to his 1855 songster, Old Put, "the most famous of the folk-
composers and song collectors of the period," speaks of himself as the author
of the pieces in his collection. (Note from Black and Robertson). Louise
Pound in "Yet Another Joe Bowers," *WF* 16 (1957), 117, accepts Stone as
the author.

B 10

THE BUFFALO SKINNERS (a)

BOGGY CREEK or THE HILLS OF MEXICO (b)

After a summer of hardships, the buffalo slaughterers kill Crego, their
employer, when he refuses to pay them, and return home.

Come all you jolly cowboys and listen to my song,
There are not many verses, it will not detain you long;
It's concerning some young fellows who did agree to go
And spend one summer pleasantly on the range of the buffalo.

Lomax, *Amer. Ballads*, 390, 11d, m. Carmer, 172, 4d, m. Lomax, *Cowboy
Songs*, 335, 11d, m. (reprinted by Sandburg, 270, 10d, and by Larkin, 83,

8d). Lomax, *Folk Song U.S.A.*, 174, 7d, m. (reprinted by Leach, 773). L. C. Records 2075 A—10 in. and 2088 B—10 in. (both sung by John A. Lomax); 78 A4 (Tex.).

In *Bulletin* no. 6 (1933), 12-13, Mrs. Eckstorm points out that this ballad is a Western adaptation of "Canaday I-O" (C 17). "The date, 1873, in *The Buffalo Skinners,*, is correct; in that year, professional buffalo-hunters from Dodge City first entered the northern part of the Texas panhandle". (See for references and further details.)

What Lomax calls a cowboy version of "The Buffalo Skinners" appears in *Cowboy Songs*, 41-42,, 8d. sts. (Tex.) under the title "Boggy Creek" and in *FSNA*, 380, 6d. Dobie prints the same piece as "The Hills of Mexico", *PTFS* VI, 201-202, 7d. sts., and refers to a fragment called "Boggus Creek" in *PTFS* II. See Dobie's notes. The piece has not been sufficiently reworked to warrant separate listing. L. C. Record, 57 A1 (Tex. "The Hills of Mexico").

B 11

THE SIOUX INDIANS

The central event in this chronicle of a trip across the Western plains is a fierce battle with a marauding band of Sioux. Although far outnumbered, the white men are victorious. They continue their trip and arrive at last in Oregon.

> I'll sing you a song, though it may be a sad one,
> Of trials and troubles and whence first begun.
> I left my dear kindred, my friends, and my home,
> And we crossed the wide deserts and mountains to roam.

Lomax, *Cowboy Songs*, 344, 12d, m. (Tex.). Burt, 142, 35d lines, m. (Utah). *CFB* 1 (1962), no. 1, p. 4, 32d lines (Colo. "Crossing the Plains"). Gordon, *Adventure*, Dec. 20, 1923, 191, 11d (Utah via Ohio). Hubbard, 293, 8d, m. (Ariz. via Utah). Randolph II, 216, 5½d (Ark.). L. C. Records 56 B1 and 3942 B 1 (Tex. Same singer); 662 A 1 (Tex.).

B 12

PATTONIA, THE PRIDE OF THE PLAINS

Indians on the warpath have killed so many rangers that the force at the post must be augmented. The captain sends the narrator for help "to the border of New Mexico." Although wounded by arrows, his swift horse, Pattonia, outruns the pursuers and carries his rider to his goal. The ranger arrives with an arrow pinning his foot to its stirrup.

> You look at that picture with a wondering eye,
> And then to the arrow that hangs by its side,
> You say tell the story, for I know there is one
> For the name of Pattonia is a story I know.

Randolph II, 242, 14½d (Mo. from ms.). Sackett, *Kansas Folklore*, 155, 9½d, m. (Kan.). Fowke, *WF* 21 (1962), 249, 7d (Ont.). Larkin, 111, 16 (N. Mex. "Plantonio"). Lomax, *Cowboy Songs*, 356, 22 (a composite text from Tex. and La., partly from L. C. Record 68 A2 & A3, (Tex.).

This well-made and melodramatic ballad sounds somewhat professional, but it is traditional among the folk. No account of its origin has been printed.

B 13

THE TRAIL TO MEXICO

In 1883 A. J. Stinson hires the narrator to drive a herd into Mexico. When he returns home at last, he finds that his fiancée has married a richer man. She tries to persuade him to stay home where life is safe, but he curses her gold and says, "I'll stay on the trail till the day I die."

> It was in the merry month of May
> When I started for Texas far away,
> I left my darling girl behind;
> She said her heart was only mine.

Sandburg, 285, 8, m. (Tex.). Larkin, 49, 8, m. Lomax, *Cowboy Songs*, 52, 8d and refrain, m. (a composite text). L. C. Records 3658 A2 & B1 (N.Y.) and 658 B1 (Tex.).

Cox, 358, points out that "The Trail to Mexico" is an adaptation of the British piece "Early in the Spring", four texts of which he prints from American tradition, 358-361. The cowboy ballad, however, shows considerable reworking.

B 14

JOE BOWERS

Having gone to California and worked hard to raise money for his marriage to Sally, Joe is understandably upset when he hears from his brother that the girl has married a red-haired butcher and has a red-haired baby.

> My name is Joe Bowers;
> I've got a brother Ike;
> I came from old Missouri,
> All the way from Pike.

> But whether it was a boy or gal child
> The letter never said
> It only said the baby's hair
> Was inclined to be red.

Belden, 342, 8d (Mo. The first and last half-stanzas are given above); see for refs. to early printings and to texts from W. Va., Miss., Ill., Minn.,

Neb., Ida., and Pa. Beck, *Bunyan,* 212, 12 (Mich. a lumberjack adaptation). Brown II, 607, 8d (N. C.). High, 25, 52 lines (Ark.). Hubbard, 302, 8d, m. (Utah). Leach, 751, Belden's text. Lomax, *Amer. Ballads,* 422, 10d, m. Lomax, *FSNA,* 336, 6d, m. (Tex. text from Owens). Owens, 107, 4½d, m. (Tex.). Randolph II, 192, 5d, m. (Mo.); 8d (Ark.); 7d, m. (Mo.); refs. Ritchie, *A Garland,* 55, 4d, m. (Ky.). Williams, 260, 4½d (Ky.).

For a full discussion of the possible authorship of this ballad, see Louise Pound, "Yet Another Joe Bowers," *WF* 16 (1957), 111-120. Miss Pound believed that the most likely author was John A. Stone, whose tombstone reads, "Early California Song Writer; Author of Put's Golden Songster . . . . Crossed the plains from Pike County, Missouri in 1849. Died January 23, 1864." See also the note to "Sweet Betsy from Pike" (B 9).

B 15

THE BUCKING BRONCHO
(The Broncho Buster)

The girl gives her love to the romantic broncho buster, but she warns others that the cowboy will "leave you and go / In the spring up the trail on his bucking broncho".

> My love is a rider, wild horses he breaks,
> But he promised to quit it all just for my sake,
> He sold off his saddle, his spurs and his rope,
> And there'll be no more riding, and that's what I hope.

Randolph II, 229, 4, m. (Ark); frags. (Mo.); Lomax, *Cowboy Songs,* 267, 7 sts. Lomax, *Amer. Ballads,* 417, 7 sts. Thorp, 14, 5 sts. L. C. Records 3641 A1 & A3 (N.Y. Sung by Herbert Halpert).

"Dobie (*Texas Folk Lore Society Publications* 7, 1928, 170-172) mentions one James Hatch of San Antonio, Texas, as claiming the authorship of this piece. 'While I was at Platte City, Nebraska, in 1882 with a trail herd,' says Mr. Hatch, 'I composed "The Bucking Brancho" . . . Billie Davis, . . . also a wrangler, . . . made up the tune.'" (Note condensed from Randolph).

B 16

ZEBRA DUN

The newcomer seems to the cowboys to be an authority on every subject but range life. Nettled by his erudition, the cowboys are delighted when he asks for a fat saddle horse. They give him the outlaw Zebra Dun, and he rides the bucking horse like the veteran he is. When the boss discovers that he can use a lasso, too, he is glad to give him a job. The narrator has learned "that every educated fellow ain't a plumb greenhorn".

We were camped on the plains at the head of the Cimarron
When along came a stranger and stopped to arger some.
He looked so very foolish that we began to look around,
We thought he was a greenhorn that had just 'scaped from town.

Lomax, *Cowboy Songs*, 78, 12d. Gray, 98, 24 (The "North West" via N.B.). Larkin, 35, 8½d, m. Randolph II, 244, 49 lines (Mo. from ms.).

This piece sounds like the composition of a white cowboy, although Lomax's version has this note: "This song is said to have been composed by Jake, the Negro camp cook for a ranch on the Pecos River belonging to George W. Evans and John Z. Means". Craddock (*PTFS* 26, 131) calls this "The Z Bar Dun", a more meaningful title.

B-17

TYING A KNOT IN THE DEVIL'S TAIL

On their way back to camp after a drunken spree, two cowboys meet the devil, who has come for their souls. After a brief struggle, they leave him roped and tied to a tree with his horns trimmed and his hide branded.

Way high up, in the Syree Peaks
Where the yellow pines grow
Old Sandy Bob and Buster Jiggs
Had a round-up camp last fall.

Lomax, *Amer. Ballads*, 407, 15 (Ariz.); reprinted in Lomax, *FSNA*, 388, with tune. Larkin, 66, 14, m. ("Rusty Jiggs and Sandy Sam"). *Rocky Mt. Coll.*, 25, 15, m. (Utah). L. C. Record 755 A1 (N. Mex.).

I have not discovered any information about the origin of this humorous and obviously fictional ballad.

B 18

STRAWBERRY ROAN

The cowboy agrees to ride the untamed horse for ten dollars and brags about his skill. He has trouble saddling the outlaw, and after a short, wild ride finds himself "settin' on nothin'—up there in the sky."

I was laying around town, just spending my time,
Out of a job and not making a dime,
When a feller steps up and says, "I suppose
That you're a bronc' rider by the looks of your clothes."

Lomax, *Amer. Ballads*, 392, 15½, m. (Ariz. Tune from Owen Wister, Pa.); from *Cowboy Songs*, 1938, p. 99. Hubbard, 311, 13, m. (Utah). Morris, 39, 12 (Fla.); notes. Randolph II, 232, 15½ (Mo. from ms.).

"Curley W. Fletcher informed me . . . that he himself composed the poem. His version is published in his *Songs of the Sage* (Los Angeles: Frontier Publishing Co., 1931)." (Note from Lomax, *Cowboy Songs*).

B 19

THE MOUNTAIN MEADOWS MASSACRE

The western emigrants in thirty wagons are attacked by men "in Indian garb and colors." They surrender their arms when Lee, the Mormon leader of the band, promises them protection. As soon as they are defenseless, the attackers slaughter them and divide their property. In the last stanza, the massacre is blamed on Brigham Young.

Come all you sons of liberty,
Unto my rhyme give ear;
'Tis of a bloody massacre,
You presently shall hear.

On a crisp October morning
At the Mountain Meadows green,
By the light of bright campfires,
Lee's Mormon bullets screamed.

Burt, 118, 13, m. (Utah. A composite text). Hubbard, 445, 4½d, m. (Utah). *WF* 12 (1953), 232, 9 (Hubbard's text); 8, m. (Cal.); 12, m. (Wash.); 7 (Nev. from a newspaper).

"The marker at Mountain Meadows bears a bronze plaque on which is inscribed: . . . "In this vicinity—September 7-11, 1857 . . . a company of about 140 emigrants from Arkansas and Missouri . . . enroute to California, was attacked by white men and Indians. All but 17 small children were killed. John D. Lee, who confessed to participation as leader, was legally executed here March 23rd, 1877. . . ."" (Note from Burt). Both Mrs. Burt and Dr. Hubbard say that the ballad is practically taboo in Utah.

See Austin E. Fife, "A Ballad of the Mountain Meadows Massacre," *WF* 12 (1953), 229-241.

B 20

THE WILD BOY

After committing various crimes, the speaker is arrested and sent to Ute jail. He is deserted by all his family except for a rich uncle from the far West who bails him out and pays his debts. He vows not to be a wild boy anymore.

I started up the cow trail
To see some Western land.
I met up with a wild bunch,
And likewise killed a man.

I stole a many a fat horse,
Stole him from the poor,
And over the Rocky Mountains
I made his iron hoofs roar.

Craddock, *PTFS* 6 (1927), 185, 9 (Tex. a composite text?); stanzas 2 and 3 are given above. The editor says that the ballad is sung in New Mexico and West Texas.

B 21

ROOT HOG OR DIE

The speaker gets a job making hay and then loses his money in a poker game. When he becomes drunk on corn liquor he is thrown into jail. A friend pays his twenty-dollar fine. The ballad ends with a warning against poker playing.

> Oh I went to Californy in the Spring of Fifty-six,
> Oh when I landed there I was in a turrible fix,
> I didn't have no money my vittles for to buy,
> An' the only thing for me was to root hog or die.

Randolph III, 163, 7d, m.; 1d, m .(Mo.); refs to various pieces with the refrain "root hog or die."

B 22

SWEET JANE

After bidding farewell to Jane, Willie sails away, spends three years mining gold, sails home to the South, and marries his faithful sweetheart.

> Farewell, sweet Jane, for I must start
> Across the foaming sea.
> My trunk is now on Johnston's barque
> With all my company.

Brown II, 608, 16 (N.C.); refs. Combs, 206, 12 (Ky.).

B 23

MY HEART'S TONIGHT IN TEXAS
(By the Silvery Rio Grande; Texas Jack)

The rancher sends his daughter to England hoping she will marry a nobleman. When an earl proposes to her, she replies that she will marry no one but Texas Jack.

> In the Lone Star State of Texas, by the silv'ry Rio Grande,
> Strolled a couple one fine evening, two sweethearts hand in hand,
> 'Twas the ranchman's pretty daughter and the lad she loved so dear,
> On the morrow they must part for many a weary year.

Carmer, 183, 6d, m. Craddock, *PFTS* 6 (1927), 187, 8 and 2 sts. chorus (Tex.).

B 24

COWBOY JACK

After a quarrel with his sweetheart, Jack leaves and joins a band of cowboys. One night, having sung about a loyal girl, he decides to return and ask forgiveness. He does so only to find that the girl has died breathing his name and is buried on the prairie.

> He was just a lonely cowboy, with a heart so brave and true;
> And he learned to love a maiden with eyes of heaven's own blue.

Lomax, *Cowboy Songs*, 230, 10d couplets, m. ("from *Cowboy Sings*, ed. Kenneth S. Clark (New York: Paull-Pioneer Music Co."). *CFB* 2 (1963), 27, 10d couplets, m. (Colo.). L. C. Record 899 B1 (Tex.).

This sentimental piece is popular on Western phonograph records.

B 25

THE ROLLING STONE

The wife counters each of her husband's arguments for going west and adds, ". . . . the stone that keeps rolling can gather no moss." When at last she warns him that she and their children might be murdered by Indians, he changes his mind and decides to stay on the farm.

> "Since times are so hard, I'll tell you, my wife,
> I've a mind for to shake off this trouble and strife
> And to California my journey pursue
> To double my fortune as other men do;
> For here we may labor each day in the field
> And the winters consume all that summers do yield."

Belden, 351, 7d and refrains (Mo.); refs. Cazden, 56, 7d and refs., m. (N.Y. partly from print). Flanders-Barry, 106, 7d and refs., m. (Mass. "The Wisconsin Emigrant's Song"; tune from Vt.). Fuson, 100, 5d (Ky.). Randolph II, 213, 7d and refs., m. (Mo.). *JAF* 35, 408, 7d and refs., m. (O. text from ms.). *NYFQ* 7 (1951), 65, 7d and refs. (N.Y.).

Cazden writes (p. 121): "The full text, on which we have drawn for completion, was printed in the songbook *Mock-Bird* in 1805. This text in turn is unmistakably a re-writing of a London music hall duet published in *The Vocal Miscellany* (1734), Vol. 1, #115."

B 26

THE BOYS OF SANPETE COUNTY

After ferrying the wagons over Green River, the boys attempt to drive the cattle across. In their struggles with the cattle, which refuse to swim, six young men are drowned.

> We, the boys of Sanpete County,
> In all obedience to the call,
> Started out with forty wagons
> To bring immigrants in the fall.
> Without fear or thought of danger
> Lightly on our way we sped;
> Every heart with joy abounded—
> Captain Seeley at the head.

Hubbard, 404, 4d (Utah); notes and refs. Austin E. Fife collected and deposited in the AAFS a text of 8d sts. from Utah.

"In 1868 Captain William Stewart Seeley of Mount Pleasant went with a [Mormon] Church train to Laramie, Wyoming, to assist Mormon immigrants coming to Utah. The difficulties of Seeley's men while crossing Green River are narrated in this song." (Note from Hubbard).

B 27

THE HORSE WRANGLER (THE TENDERFOOT)

Despite the foreman's assurance that cow-punching is nothing but play, the novice wears himself out trying to keep the cattle (or horses) under control. After being badly injured in a fall, he decides he has had enough.

> One day I thought I'd have some fun,
> And see how punching cows was done;
> So when the round-up had begun
> I tackled the cattle king . . .

Lomax, *Cowboy Songs*, 119, 7d, m. Fowke and Johnston, 96, 5d, m. (Can. "The Tenderfoot"). Sandburg, 274, 6d, m. (Can. via Ore.).

"The original of this song was published in the Miles City (Montana) *Stock Growers' Journal*, Feb. 3, 1894, under the pseudonym of R. J. Stovall. The author's real name is D. J. O'Malley, and he lives at Eau Claire, Wisconsin." (Note from Lomax).

BALLADS OF LUMBERJACKS

146

C 1

THE JAM ON GERRY'S ROCK

Despite some prejudice against Sunday work, young Monroe and six shanty-boys turn out to break a log jam. Suddenly the jam gives way and all are swept into the river. Monroe's body—in some versions, only his head— is found, and he is buried by the sympathetic woodsmen, who take up a collection for his mother. His sweetheart soon dies of grief and is buried beside him near the river.

> Come all ye loyal shanty boys, wherever you may be,
> I would have you give attention and listen unto me,
> Concerning six brave shanty boys, so loyal, true and brave,
> Who broke the jam on Gerry's Rock and met a watery grave.

Eckstorm, 87, 8d; 10d; 10d; 10d (Me.); notes. Barry, 52, 9d, m. (Me. via N.H.; from *Bulletin* no. 12). Beck, 134, 10d, m. (Mich.); reprinted in Beck, *Bunyan*, 126. Beck, *The Folklore of Maine*, 260, 9d (Me.). Brown II, 501, 9d (Wis. via N.C.); 10d (Me.); 10d (N.C.); refs. Cazden, 6, 11d, m. (N.Y.). Cox, 236, 10d (W. Va.); refs. Creighton and Senior, 267, 10d, m. (N.S.). Doerflinger, 238, 9d, m. (N.Y.); 3d (Ont. via N.Y.). Flanders-Barry, 44, 6d, m. (N.H.); notes. Gardner, 270, 10d, m. (Mich.); refs. Gordon, 58, 10d. Gray, 3, 20; 18 (Me.). *KFR* 9 (1963), 54, 6d, m. (Ky.). Linscott, 218, 8d (Me.). Leach, 771, 10d, from Eckstorm. Lomax, *Folk Song U.S.A.*, 170, 7d, m. Morris, 107, 7d, m. (Fla.). Rickaby, 11, 10d, m. (Minn.); 9d, m. (Wis. Reprinted by Lomax, *Amer. Ballads*, 448); 1d, m. (Wis.); 1d, m. (N.D.). Sandburg, 394, 9d, m. (Ore.). Thompson, 259, 10d (N.Y.). L. C. Records 2323 A & B1 (Mich.); 4171 B2 (Wis.); 3670 B1 & 2 (N.Y.); 3571 A1 (W. Va.); 3749 B (N.H.); and other recordings.

Although much valuable research has been done on this fine old ballad, nothing very specific has been learned about its origin or about the facts upon which it may have been based. For a discussion, see Mrs. Eckstorm's chapter, "The Pursuit of a Ballad Myth" in *Minstrelsy of Maine*, 176-198. (A condensed account of her findings is given in Chapter V of this study). See also Barry, *Bulletin* no. 10, 18-20, with another Maine version.

C 2

THE BANKS OF THE LITTLE EAU PLEINE

After hearing a detailed description of her raftsman, the narrator tells the young school-ma'am that he has been drowned and is buried far from the Little Eau Pleine. She curses Wisconsin and Johnny's boss, and says she will give up school-teaching and go where she can never hear "the squeak of a fifty-foot oar".

> One evening last June as I rambled
> The green woods and valleys among,
> The mosquito's notes were melodious,
> And so was the whip-poor-will's song . . .
>
> I happened to see a young school-ma'am,
> She mourned in a sorrowful strain,
> She mourned for a jolly young raftsman
> On the banks of the Little Eau Pleine.

Rickaby, 25, 13d, m. (Wis. As sung by the author. The first half of st. 1 and the last half of st. 2 are given above); 9d, m. (Minn. As sung by M. C. Dean. Text reprinted from Dean, 11). Beck, 119, 13d, m. (Mich. A composite text); reprinted in Beck, *Bunyan*, 201. Carmer, 192, 5d, m. L. C. Record 2263 B2 (Mich. Sung by Bill McBride).

This piece was written by Mr. W. N. ("Billy") Allen, (Shan. T. Boy). "The song is compounded wholly of imagination except for the character of Ross Gamble, who was a well-known pilot on the Wisconsin River at the time the verses were composed. Mr. Allen placed the time of composition 'somewhere in the 70's' ". (196) "The Little Eau Pleine is a small tributary of the Wisconsin River . . . " (198) Rickaby points out that the author's model was an old-world piece called "The Lass of Dunmore". (For a discussion of Mr. Allen's career as a "singer" and author of ballads, see Rickaby xxix-xxxvii; for further comments on this piece, see 196-198.)

"The Shanty Boy on the Big Eau Claire" (C 11) is another of Mr. Allen's ballads.

C 3

THE DROWNING OF JOHN ROBERTS

Swept into the river while trying to break a jam, John Roberts struggles to save himself but drowns after rising three times. His body is brought to the surface three days later. The ballad ends with an admonition to lead a Christian life.

> Dear fellow men, pray lend an ear,
> A melancholy tale to hear;
> One of our mortals numbered he,
> Has gone to long eternity.
>
> He ventured out to break a jam
> Which had commenced on a roll dam,
> And when he started for the shore,
> He sank his last to rise no more.

Barry, 80, 9, m. (Me.). Stanzas 1 and 4 are given above. Gray, 22, 12 couplets (Me.). Eckstorm, 45, 11 (Me.).

John Roberts was drowned in 1852 on the West Branch of the Union River in Maine. (See Eckstorm, 45-48, for details.)

C 4

JIMMIE JUDD (THE BEAU SHAI RIVER)

Jimmie is drowned while trying to break a jam, and his body, with his face torn and cut by the rocks, is recovered the next day after a fisherman's boy sees it floating in the river. The death of the handsome youth is mourned by the girl who loved him, by his aged parents, and by his fellow woodsmen.

> Come all you gallant young men
> Who run the river deep,
> Look on the fate of that young man
> Who lies here underneath.
>
> Down on the Beau Shai River,
> A little below Runtreau,
> He went forth to break a jam
> And with it he went through.

Beck, 145, A: 10 sts. and B: 6d sts. (Mich.); the first half of st. 1 of B and st. 1 of A are given above. Barry, *Bulletin* no. 10 (1935), 20, 6d (Me. "Jimmie Judges"). Gardner, 277, frag. of 18 lines (Mich.). *NYFQ* 14 (1958), 220, 6d, m. (N.Y.).

Beck suggests that the ballad was taken to Michigan from New Brunswick or Maine. No report on its history has been printed. According to Barry, the Bonshee River, which is named in his version, is the Bonnichere River, Renfrew County, Ontario.

C 5

THE WILD MUSTARD RIVER (JOHNNY STILE)

While working on a jam, Johnny gets his foot caught among the logs; he is swept downstream when the jam gives way. His mangled body is recovered and buried by his comrades.

> Come all you brave boys of the river,
> And listen to me for a while.
> I'll tell you what befell him,
> My friend and my chum Johnny Styles.
>
> We were camped on the Wild Mustard River
> Just below the old Tamarack Dam.
> As we arose from our blankets one morning,
> We saw on the rocks a big jam.

Beck, 149, 8, m.; 9; add. sts. (Mich.). Beck, *Bunyan*, 145, 6, m. (Mich.). Fowke and Mills, 178, 9, m. (Ont. "Johnny Doyle"). Gardner, 276, 8 (Mich.). Lomax, *Our Singing Country*, 228, 7, m. (Mich. from L. C. Record 2353). L. C. Record 2266 A1 (Mich.).

C 6
TEBO (THIBAULT)

After being swept into the water, Tebo tries to swim away from the logs, but the jam overtakes him. The comrade who attempts to save him is forced to let him go, and Tebo is drowned. He leaves a widow and five young children, who receive a subscription from the lumbermen.

> It was on the sixth of May, my boys, as you will understand,
> When Sherman ordered out his men all for to break a jam.
> The logs were piled up mountains high, the water so dreadful strong
> That it washed away poor Tebo and the logs that he was on.

Thompson, 275, 7d (N.Y.).

". . . The song about Tebo (Thibault) is still known to a considerable number of people". Dr. Thompson's informant told him that Tebo was a "Canuck" working on a drive in the Jordan River in New York and that the ballad was composed by a man who made other songs popular in lumber camps. (See Thompson, 275-277).

C 7
JAMES WHALEN

Asked by his foreman to work on a jam in rough water, Whalen bravely starts toward it. The jam suddenly breaks, and the youth is hurled into the raging rapids and drowned.

> Come all ye jolly raftsmen, I pray you lend an ear.
> 'T is of a mournful accident I soon will let you hear,
> Concerning of a noble youth, Jim Whalen he was call'd,
> Was drowned off Pete McLaren's raft below the upper fall.

Rickaby, 20, 6d (Minn.); 6d (Ont.). Beck, 141, 5d (Mich.); reprinted with variations in Beck, *Bunyan*, 138. Doerflinger, 243, 5d, m. (N.B.). Eckstorm, 122, 5d (Me.). Gardner, 274, 11 (Mich.). Sandburg, 389, 6, m. (Minn. via Iowa). Tolman, *JAF* 35 (1922), 383, 12 (Minn. via Iowa).

James Whalen was drowned at King's Chute on the "Mississippi River" in Frontenac County, Ontario, Canada, about 1878. The ballad is said to have been composed by John Smith of Lanark Village, Ontario. (See Rickaby, 194-195, for details).

C 8
LOST JIMMIE WHALEN

The grieving girl calls for her drowned sweetheart to rise from his grave. He comes from the waters "a vision of splendor" to see her once more. When she begs him to stay, he replies that Death keeps them apart, but he will try to guard her from danger. He vanishes and she is left alone.

As lonely I strayed by the banks of the river,
I was watching the sunbeams as evening drew nigh;
As onward I rambled, I spied a fair damsel;
She was weeping and wailing with many a sigh.

As she sank down on the ground she was standing,
With the deepest of sorrow these words she did say,
"My darling," she cried, "O my lost Jimmie Whalen,
I will sigh till I die by the side of your grave!"

Barry, 12, 11d, m. (Me.); stanzas 1 and 11 are given above; reprinted from *Bulletin* no. 11, p. 4; reprinted by Leach, 726. Beck, 117, 6d and chorus. (Mich. "Jimmie Whalen's Girl"); reprinted in Beck, *Bunyan*, 139. *Bulletin* no. 11, p. 5, 13d (Me.). Creighton, *Maritime Folk Songs*, 114, 9d, m. and add. tune (N.S.). Creighton and Senior, 186, 9d, m. (N.S.). Rickaby, 24, frag. of 3d (Mich.). L. C. Records 3287 A1 (Wis.) and 2412 A1 & B2 (Mich.).

It is possible that this beautiful Irish ballad originated in America. Barry reports that it was sung in the Maine woods in 1886 and 1894, and says, "No trace of this ballad exists in old country tradition." He describes its background as "Irish folk-tradition, grounded in that rich bed of *synthetic mythology* which should not longer pass for authentic Celtic." (See *Bulletin*, no. 11 (1936), 4-7). This and the preceding ballad presumably refer to the same tragedy.

C 9

GUY REED

While trying to break a log jam, Guy Reed is swept into the river and drowned. The funeral is described at some length. He is buried "by the Order of K. P." in the family plot.

This young man and his companions where the waters they do roam
Was breaking in the landings on the Androscoggin shore.
They picked the face on one of them from bottom to the top
Fully thirty feet this landing had, a perpendicular drop.

Flanders-Barry, 55, 15d, m. (N.H.); refs. Gray, 24, 32 (Me.).

"Guy Reed, the son of Joseph and Remember Mitchell Reed, met his death on 9 September 1897, and is buried in the little West Byron [Maine] cemetery. . . . [Reed's niece] says that he was killed breaking a landing . . . on the Androscoggin River, and that Joe Scott, a friend of Guy's . . . wrote the song and published it in the Rumford Falls *Times*." (Note from Ives, *JAF* 72 (1959), 61. See also the note to "Benjamin Deane" (F 32).

C 10

SAMUEL ALLEN

The rolling dam which Allen is examining is torn away by the rushing water, and he falls into Rocky Brook and drowns.

Ye tender hearted people, I pray you lend an ear,
And when you have my story heard, you can but drop a tear;
Concerning Samuel Allen, a man both strong and brave,
And on a stream called Rocky Brook, he met with a watery grave.

Barry, *Bulletin* no. 9, 19-21, 10d, m. (Me.). Reprinted in Barry, 70.

This accident occurred on a tributary of the Miramichi River in New Brunswick. "The verses are said to have been written by a twelve-year-old boy." (For details and notes, see Barry, *Bulletin*).

C 11

THE SHANTY BOY ON THE BIG EAU CLAIRE

A milliner disapproves of her daughter's love for a shanty-boy and takes her away. The girl dies of grief and scarlet fever, and the distracted lover plunges to his death "on the falls at Mosinee". The milliner becomes bankrupt, and is haunted by the ghosts of the lovers. The ballad satirically advises fair maidens to stay away from rowdy shanty-boys and try to snare "some one-horse farmer's boy."

Every girl she has her troubles; each man likewise has his.
But few can match the agony of the following story, viz.
It relates about the affection of a damsel young and fair
Who dearly loved a shanty-boy up on the Big Eau Claire.

Rickaby, 54, 14d (Wis. author's text); 13d, m. (Wis.). Beck, *Bunyan*, 207, 12 (Mich.). Shoemaker, 183, 10½d (Wis. via Pa.). *JAF* 22 (1909), 259, 9d (Wis. via N. D.). L. C. Records 4167 A1 and 4187 (Wis.)

This ballad was written in 1875 or 1876 by William N. Allen (Shan T. Boy), who said that it had no foundation in fact. (See Rickaby, xxix-xxxvii for an account of the author and 203-205 for a note on this piece.)

"The Banks of the Little Eau Pleine" (C 2) is another of Mr. Allen's ballads.

C 12

THE DEATH OF HARRY BRADFORD

Young Harry, the foreman's son, is crushed to death on the rollway when he is unable to escape the falling logs. This long and moving ballad describes the accident in detail. The stanazs in which the boy's father learns of the tragedy are exceptionally effective.

Come all ye true-born lumbering boys, both fellows young and old,
A story I will tell you that'll make your blood run cold,
Concerning a poor unfortunate lad who was known both far and near.
He was killed on the deck at Essex Mill, as you will quickly hear.

Beck, 137, 15d (Mich.); reprinted in Beck, *Bunyan*, 130.

"Mrs. Ramsey, of Cadillac, says that W. J. Taylor wrote this song about an accident that occurred at Phelps's camp, north of Torch Lake. . . . The

Bradfords lived at Central Lake." (Beck) The third stanza gives the date of the tragedy as Jan. 29, 1902.

C 13

HARRY BALE (DALE, BAIL, BELL)

Young Harry, an orphan, is fatally hurt when he is drawn against the saw in the mill where he works. He dies a day later and is buried as his brothers and sisters grieve.

> Come kind folks, friends, and parents,
> Come brothers, one and all.
> If you'll listen unto me,
> 'Twill make your blood run cold.
> It's of a young unfortunate boy
> That's known both far and near;
> His parents raised him tenderly,
> Not many miles from here.

Gardner, 278, 8d, m. (Mich.) and variant stanzas. Beck, 169, 8d, m. (Mich.). Beck, *Bunyan*, 141, 7d, m. (Mich.). Belden, 419, 7d (Ark.); refs. *JAF* 35 (1922), 375, 4 (Minn. via Iowa). Finger, 33, 8d. Rickaby, 110, 10d (Mich.). L. C. Record 2288 A2 Mich.).

Harry Bahel, age 19, was fatally injured in April, 1879, at a mill in Arcadia Township, Lapeer County, Michigan. The ballad is said to have been composed by his brother Charles. (For details see Beck, 169, who reproduces the inscription from Harry's tombstone, and Gardner, 278).

C 14

HARRY DUNN (THE HANGING LIMB)

Disregarding his mother's advice to stay at home, Harry goes to work in the woods of Michigan. One morning he tells a friend that he has had "an awful dream" and fears there is trouble at home. The same day he is crushed to death by a falling limb. When his body is sent home, his parents die of shock. The ballad ends with a warning to stay away from the woods.

> But Charlie only laughed at him. That pleased him for a time.
> At length he said to Harry, "It is time to fall the pine."
> They worked along until ten o'clock upon that fatal day
> When a hanging limb came down on him and crushed him to the clay.

Gardner, 282, 10d (Mich.); st. 6 is given above. Beck, 160, 19 (Mich. reprinted in Beck, *Bunyan*, 151); 9d (N.S.). Creighton, 280, 37 lines, m. (N.S.). Doerflinger, 222, 2d, m. (Ont. via N.Y.); 9d (N.S. from ms.). Eckstorm, 120, 8½d (Me.). Greenleaf, 329, 9d (Nfld.). Rickaby, 103, 10d (Ont.); 12d (Mich. from ms.). L. C. Record 2349 B3, 2350 A (Mich. Spoken).

Many versions of this ballad address "Canadian boys" in the early stanzas and imply that Harry came from across the border. The piece seems well known in Canada. According to Eckstorm and Smyth, 122, "The song was introduced into Maine from Nova Scotia about 1910 or 1911."

C 15

JOHN SINGLETON

Singleton, the head sawyer in a lumber mill, is fatally mangled in the machinery after being struck by a slab of wood from a hollow log. His body is sent home to Deckerville to be buried by his grieving family. The last stanzas lament the death of the good man.

> On the border of Lake Huron, where the billows wildly roar,
> A bustling little village stands upon the sandy shore,
> Where the buzzing of the busy mill is heard the whole day through
> It was there that poor John Singleton bade this fair world adieu.

Beck, 173, 9d (Mich.).

David D. Smith, whose version is quoted above, said that "the event recorded happened about 1870, when he was a boy, and that the composition was by a John Morrison, of Sanilac County." (Beck).

C 16

THE LITTLE BROWN BULLS

McCluskey bets twenty-five dollars that his steers can skid more logs than Gordon's little brown bulls. Confident of victory, he makes a belt for the steers only to have the bulls beat them.

> Not a thing on the river McCluskey did fear
> When he threw his stick o'er the big spotted steers.
> They were young, quick, and sound, girting eight foot and three,
> Says McCluskey, the Scotchman, "They're the ladies for me."

Rickaby, 65, 14d, m. (Wis.); 1d, m. (Minn.). Beck, 92, 11½d, m. (Mich.); reprinted in Beck, *Bunyan*, 68. Eckstorm, 56, 14d (Me.); reprinted in Barry, 30, with tune. Gardner, 266, 5½d (Mich.). Gordon, 56, 10d. Leach, 775, 14d (N.S.). Lomax, *FSNA*, 110, 8d, m. (Mich.). Lomax, *Our Singing Country*, 224, 14d, m. (Mich. from L. C. Record 2265). L. C. Records AAFS 5, 12d (Wis.); 4186 A & B (Wis.); and 7 others from Mich., Wis., and Cal.

"According to Mr. Fred Bainter, the singer of Version A, the ballad was composed in Mart Douglas's camp in northwestern Wisconsin in 1872 or 1873. It was in this camp and at this date, he said, that the contrast between the big spotted steers and the little brown bulls was waged." (Note from Rickaby, p. 206).

C 17

CANADAY-I-O (a)

MICHIGAN-I-O (b)

COLLEY'S RUN I-O (c)

After a winter of suffering in the woods of Canada, (or Michigan, or Pennsylvania), the lumbermen are glad to leave poor food and beds in the snow and return home.

> Come all ye jolly lumbermen, and listen to my song,
> But do not get discouraged, the length it is not long,
> Concerning of some lumbermen, who did agree to go
> To spend one pleasant winter up in Canada I O.

CANADAY I-O

Eckstorm, 22, 11d (Me.); reprinted by Leach, 774; 7 (Me.). Barry, 26, 11d (from Eckstorm). Gray, 38, 7 (from Eckstorm). Linscott, 181, 7 (Me.).

MICHIGAN I-O

Beck, 9, 7d; 9d (Mich.); both reprinted in Beck, *Bunyan*, 109. Gardner, 261, 8d (Mich.). Rickaby, 41, 4½d (N. D.).

COLLEY'S RUN I-O (THE JOLLY LUMBERMEN)

Beck, 14, 6d (Mich.). Shoemaker, 88, 15½ (Pa.); reprinted by Gray, 41.

Mrs. Eckstorm reports in *Bulletin* no. 6 (1933), 10-13, that "Canaday I-O" was composed by Ephriam Braley, a lumberman of Hudson, Maine, in the spring of 1854. Mr. Braley and other Maine men had spent the winter working at Three Rivers in the Province of Quebec. She calls this piece a revamping of the older English sea-song, Canada I O. (See for further details). See also "The Buffalo Skinners" (B 10).

C 18

THE THREE McFARLANDS

This chronicle of hard work in the snowy woods contains some kind words for Louie Culberson, the "leadin' teamster" and some harsh comments about the bosses, the three McFarlands, who drove the men unmercifully. As the ballad ends, the lumbermen are looking forward to going home and kissing the girls.

> 'Twas on a stormy winter in eighteen seventy-one,
> When fourteen jolly teamsters did join the jolly gang,
> Some of them from Clarenton, some more of them from Ross,
> And five of them from Rumsey that knew not who was boss.

Rickaby, 77, 7d, m. (N. D.); sung by James Gallagher.

Professor Rickaby says, "Mr. Gallagher insisted on calling this ballad, in a deprecatory way, 'just a homemade song', although he knew nothing of what camp it was made in and knew no such people as the McFarlands, or any of the rest; nor could he locate any of the three towns mentioned in stanza 1." (Rickaby, 208).

C 19

THE BACKWOODSMAN (THE GREEN MOUNTAIN BOYS)

The wood-hauler gets drunk during the day and is persuaded to attend a ball. A long night of dancing and drinking follows. The narrator asks the old gossips not to exaggerate their accounts of the event.

> As I got up one morning in eighteen hundred and five,
> I found myself quite happy to find myself alive.
> I geared up my horses my business to pursue,
> And went to hauling wood as I used for to do.

Rickaby, 132, 8d (N.D.). Cazden, 14, 8d, m. (N.Y. "The Cordwood Cutter"). Flanders & Brown, 43, 8d (Vt.). Gardner, 407, 7d (Mich.). Lomax, *Our Singing Country*, 231, 8d, m. (a composite text, partly from L. C. Record 1548). Shoemaker, 54, 8d (Pa. The contributor said that the piece was sung in Penna. lumber camps in the late 50's and early 60's). L. C. Records 1849 (Ky.) and 1521 B2 (Ky.).

"Mr. Paul Lorette of Manchester Center, Vermont, when questioned as to the authorship of this apparently Vermont production, said that three or four of the men in the camp (Chaffee Lumber Camp, Rutland-Chittenden) got together and made up the story—*what one wouldn't think of, another would fill in*" (Flanders and Brown, 43). Perhaps the men merely remembered an old piece and gave it local application.

C 20

BLUE MOUNTAIN LAKE (THE BELLE OF LONG LAKE)

The ballad recounts a fight in a lumber camp between Jim Lou and lazy Jimmie Mitchell, and ends with a humorous reference to the camp cook, Nellie, "the belle of Long Lake."

> Come all you good fellows, wherever you be,
> Come sit down awhile and listen to me.
> The truth I will tell you without no mistake
> Of the racket we had around Blue Mountain Lake.
> Down, down, down derry down.

Flanders-Barry, 176, 7, m. (N.Y.); p. 175, 5, m. (Vt.); notes. Lomax, *Folk Song U.S.A.*, 168, 7, m. (N.Y. As sung by Frank Warner). *NYFQ* 14 (1958), 222, 7, m. (N.Y.). Thompson, 267, only 1 st. given (N.Y. Note,

p. 517: "*Blue Mt. Lake,* said to have been composed by a lumberjack named Oat Bets.") Lomax, *FSNA*, 115, seems to have added some stanzas from this ballad to a piece called "Moosehead Lake".

"The collector crossed trails with this ballad in the home of Mr. Herbert Haley on Shrewsbury Mountain, when he spoke of 'Dorset's Song'. He recalled that Charlie Dorset used to play a fife. He lumbered over on a job Griffith had on Long Lake. There was a fight there where a man licked a man and Dorset made up this song and taught it by playing it on the fife and then singing it to Mr. Haley. . . ." (Note from Flanders-Barry, 175).

C 21

THE DAM ON BALDWIN CREEK

When Bill Reed's cofferdam fails, Old George Shane saves the shingle mill from a flood by piling sandbags between it and the water. Reed errs again in trying to start the sawmill too soon. To Bill's vast disgust, Old George replaces him as boss.

> The dam went out on Baldwin Creek
> On a Wednesday night;
> Bill Reed came up to fix it
> Before it was daylight.

Beck, 81, 8 (Mich.).

"A bit of obscenity creeps into 'The Dam on Baldwin Creek" once in a while. This version . . . is free from it." (Note from Beck, who says nothing of the history of the ballad).

C 22

DRIVING LOGS ON THE CASS

The narrator complains mainly about the scanty and ill-prepared food provided for the lumbermen by "Old Black Joe." The men are successful in breaking jams, and the drive goes well until a shortage of water over the rapids halts it. The boss, Miller, discharges his crew, and after an evening of sociability, they head homeward, thankful that all are alive.

> Come all you river drivers, wherever you may be
> That's standin' round the fire tonight, come listen unto me,
> While I relate the dangers and the hardships that we pass
> While driving logs for Miller on the winding River Cass.

Beck, 74, 11d (Mich.) ; reprinted in Beck, *Bunyan*, 38.

Nothing has been reported concerning the origin of this presumably factual chronicle. Beck says that his version came from the Saginaw River country and that the piece is also known in the Thumb district of Michigan.

C 23

TURNER'S CAMP ON THE CHIPPEWA

This chronicle depicts graphically the lumbermen's life during a winter in the woods of Michigan.

> Come all you jolly lumbermen
> That do a-lumbering go,
> Come listen to my story,
> Which I relate to you.
>
> Of the hardships and the dangers
> We undergo each day
> While working up in Turner's Camp
> On the banks of the Chippewa.

Beck, 44, 20 (Mich.); reprinted in Beck, *Bunyan*, 42.

"This song was composed on the Chippewa River, which runs through Isabella County and empties into the Tittabawassee River at Midland. It is one of the streams of the once heavily timbered Saginaw country." (Note from Beck, who lists the names of ten people who recalled this piece).

This is a borderline ballad. It might have been placed with the ballad-like pieces because it describes a good many typical rather than specific occurrences. On the other hand, it does recount a single extended experience.

C 24

SILVER JACK

When Robert Waite calls the Bible a fable and the Saviour "just a common man", Silver Jack springs to the defense of his mother's religion and beats ·Waite until the infidel admits that he was in error.

> I was on the drive in 'eighty,
> Working under Silver Jack,
> Which the same is now in Jackson
> And ain't soon expected back.

Beck, 96, 16 (Mich. "Lumberjack's Revival"); reprinted in Beck, *Bunyan*, 88. Hudson, 206, 16 (Miss.). Lomax, *JAF* 28 (1915), 9, 8d printed as 7 (Mich); reprinted in *Cowboy Songs*, 234; by Rickaby, 125; and by Lomax, *FSNA*, 119. L. C. Record 2345 B2 (Mich.).

Lomax says, ". . . This particular ballad has a suspicious resemblance to newspaper verse" (*JAF*, 28, 8), and Hudson calls it ". . . a ballad-like piece, suspiciously slangy and journalistic in its technique" (182). Nevertheless, it has had widespread popularity among the folk. It has been reported also from Tex., Neb., Ida., and Ore. (See Beck, 96).

Beck gives a brief history of John ("Silver Jack") Driscoll, who died at

L'Anse, Michigan, April 1, 1895. See also Pound, *Poetic Origins and the Ballad*, 229.

C 25
JACK HAGGERTY (THE FLAT RIVER GIRL)

Jack expects to marry Anna, a blacksmith's daughter. Without warning, she writes that she will marry another man. Blaming the girl's mother for her interference, Jack loses all faith in women.

> I'm a broken-hearted raftsman, from Greenville I came.
> I courted a lassie, a lass of great fame.
> But cruel-hearted Cupid has caused me much grief;
> My heart it's asunder, I can ne'er find relief.

Beck, 124, 8d, m. and four other good Michigan texts. With a historical account. Beck also prints a cowboy adaptation, 131, 6d (Tex.), in which Jim Oxford is jilted by the Salt Creek girl. Beck, *Bunyan*, 182, reprints his first three texts. Beck, *The Folklore of Maine*, 262, 8d (Me.). Brown II, 610, 8d (Wis. via N.C.); refs. Carmer, 17, 4d, m. Cazden, Part II, p. 100, 11d, m. (N.Y.). Doerflinger, 245, 7d, m. (N.B.). Gardner, 267, 9d (Mich.). Linscott, 214, 7d, m. (Me.). Lomax, *Cowboy Songs*, 268, 6d ("The Lovesick Cowboy," another adaptation, Tex.). Rickaby, 3, 13d; 6d, m. (Mich.). Sandburg, 392, 5d, m. (Wis.). *PTFS* 7, 177, 13 (Tex. The Jim Oxford Variant). L. C. Records 2358 A (Mich.) and 4172 A (Wis.).

The origin of this ballad is discussed in Chapter V.

C 26
THE BANKS OF THE GASPEREAUX

Despite the pessimistic predictions of the natives, the Maine lumbermen are able to drive the Gaspereaux successfully. A native girl whom they nickname "Robin Redbreast" and a Yankee woodsman fall in love. Because neither is willing to live away from home, the lovers part, and the lumbermen return to Maine.

> Come all you jolly lumbermen, I'd have for you to know
> The Yankees they'll return no more to drive the Gaspereaux;
> You told them all the lies you could; you were their bitter foe;
> Bad luck attend those wild galoots who live on Gaspereaux.

Barry, *Bulletin* no. 5 (1933), 13, 11d (Me.); reprinted by Leach, 770. Beck, *The Folklore of Maine*, 257, 11d (Me. All but 3 sts. reprinted from Barry). Doerflinger, 245, 8d (Me. from ms.).

"No version of this pretty ballad has, to our knowledge, yet been printed. It may be one of the oldest woods songs, going back to the square-timber era, [before 1850] when Maine men worked on Canadian drives." (Note from Barry, *loc cit.*, who says that the Gaspereaux "is a feeder to the port of St. John.")

C 27

PETER AMBERLEY

Having been fatally injured in the woods of New Brunswick, Peter sends farewell messages to his unkind father, his mother, his sweetheart, and the island on which he was born.

> My name is Peter Emerly as you may understand;
> I belong upon Prince Edward's Island, near by the ocean strand;
> In eighteen hundred and eighty when the flowers bore a brilliant hue,
> I left my native country, my fortune to pursue.

Barry, 68, 9d (Me.). Beck, 32, 8 (N.S.). Beck, *The Folklore of Maine*, 255, 6d, m. (Me.). Doerflinger, 225, 10d, m.; 5d, m.; 9d (N.B.); detailed notes and refs. Eckstorm, 99, 5d; 9d (front print); 5 (Me.). Flanders-Barry, 115, 4½ d, m. (N.H.); refs. Greenleaf, 334, 8d (Nfld.). Mackenzie, 295, 10½d (N.S.). *Bulletin* no. 2, p. 13, 10d (Mass. from a newspaper); add. tunes. L. C. Record 3749 A (N.H.).

"The cross in the small Catholic cemetery a mile or so east of Boiestown, New Brunswick, reads: 'Peter Amberley. Died 1881.'" (Note from Doerflinger, p. 225). Doerflinger demonstrates that the ballad was composed in 1881, not by Lawrence Gorman, as some have thought, but by John Calhoun (1848-1939), a New Brunswick acquaintance of the victim's.

C 28

THE FOX RIVER LINE (THE ROCK ISLAND LINE)

The narrator, along with men of various nationalities, works in George Allan's camp for six weeks but finds himself in debt. He gets another job. Occasionally the lumberjacks and the local girls have a dance.

> I arrived in Fox River February the tenth.
> 'Twas a week in the city with pleasure I spent.
> While a-looking in the paper the notice to find
> Wanted fifty old bums for the Fox River line.

Creighton, 252, 7d, m. (N.S.); notes. Cazden, 52, 10d, m. (N.Y. "The Rock Island Line"; in this version the narrator is a railroad man.)

"It is sung all over the province where the words are changed to suit the locality." (Note from Creighton).

BALLADS OF SAILORS AND THE SEA

D 1 The Bold Northwestern Man
D 2 The Loss of the *Albion*
D 3 Fifteen Ships on Georges' Bank
D 4 The *Persian's* Crew
D 5 The Death of William Gilley
D 6 The Death of Herbert Rice
D 7 Dixie Brown
D 8 The *Bigler's* Crew
D 9 Red Iron Ore
D 10 The Sealers
D 11 The *Eastern Light*
D 12 The *Dom Pedro*
D 13 The *Dreadnaught*
D 14 The Schooner *Fred Dunbar*
D 15 Bold Manan the Pirate

D 16 The Ghostly Crew
D 17 The Beaver Island Boys
D 18 The *Cedar Grove*
D 19 Charles Augustus Anderson
D 20 George Jones
D 21 The Wreck of the *Huron*
D 22 Bound Down to Newfoundland
D 23 The Flemings of Torbay
D 24 The *Titanic* I
D 25 The Gallant Brigantine
D 26 The Coast of Peru
D 27 The Ship That Never Returned
D 28 The *E. A. Horton*

D 1

THE BOLD NORTHWESTERN MAN

Some Indians who have come aboard to sell furs find the *Lady Washington's* chest of arms unguarded and attempt to capture the ship. When they lose control of the situation, a bitter fight ensues in which seventy or more of the savages are killed. The goods which the others have stolen are recovered in an attack on the Indian village.

> Come all ye bold Northwestmen, who plough the raging main,
> Come listen to this tragedy, while I relate the same;
> 'Twas on the "Lady Washington" at Cowper where she lay
> And by Queen Charlotte's Islands in North America.

Barry, *Bulletin* no. 10 (1935), p. 17, 8d (Me.). Smyth, *Bulletin* no. 4 (1932), p. 13, 12d (N.B.); notes. F. W. Howay, "A Ballad of the Northwestern Fur Trade," *New England Quarterly*, I, 71, reprints the original broadside of 14d sts.

This ballad is based on "an attack in June, 1791, by Indians on the *Lady Washington*, Captain Kendrick commanding, anchored in Koyah's Harbor (now Barrell's Sound), named for the chief who led the raid." (Note from Smyth, *Bulletin* no. 4, 14).

D 2

THE LOSS OF THE *ALBION*

When the *Albion*, from New York, is battered in a storm, the captain and many of his crew are swept overboard. After being refused permission "to take a turn at the pumps," a heroic woman named Miss Powell loses her life. Finally the ship is split on the rocks; only one person escapes drowning.

> Come all you jovial seamen
> And listen unto me,
> Till a dreadful story I relate
> That happened on the sea.
>
> The wreck of the *Albion* ship, my lads,
> Upon the Irish coast,
> And all her passengers and crew
> Were most completely lost.

Thompson, 204, 18 (N.Y. Learned in a Scotch port). Chappell, 56, 16 lines (N.C.). Eckstorm, 271, 9d (Me. from ms.). Ranson, 101, 6d (Ireland). Thompson, *A Pioneer Songster*, 154, 9d (N.Y. from ms.). Early printed texts may be found in John Kenedy's *The American Songster*, Phila., 1836, and in *The Forget Me Not Songster*, Phila., n.d., p. 91, 9d.

"The ship *Albion*, Williams master, from New York to Liverpool, was wrecked on the Irish coast, probably not far from Kinsale, at 4 a.m. of the morning of April 22, 1822." (Note from Eckstorm).

D 3
FIFTEEN SHIPS ON GEORGES' BANKS

Fifteen vessels founder on the Banks in a winter storm, and all hands are lost. The ballad laments the fate of the crews and the loss which the widows and children must bear.

> Come all ye bold undaunted ones
> Who brave the winter's frost,
> And ye who sail on Georges' Banks,
> Where thousands have been lost.
>
> It was in the month of February,
> In eighteen sixty-two,
> The vessels sailed from Gloucester,
> With each a hardy crew.

Eckstorm, 281, 13 sts. (sts. 1 & 3 are given above); reprinted by Leach, 781, and by Beck, *The Folklore of Maine*, p. 210; Eckstorm, 283, 12; 6d (Me.). Greenleaf, 260, 9 (Nfld.).

" 'The Fisherman's Memorial and Record Book' . . . gives an account of this great gale of February 24, 1862, when thirteen vessels with their entire crews were lost and two other vessels were lost after the crews had been taken off." (See Eckstorm, 286, for further details).

D 4
THE *PERSIAN'S* CREW

The first stanza tells as much about the event as the narrator knows: the *Persian* was not heard from again after leaving Chicago. Consequently, the remainder of the ballad can only lament the fate of the men lost.

> Sad and dismal is the story that I will tell to you,
> About the schooner Persian, her officers and crew.
> They sank beneath the waters deep, in life to rise no more,
> Where wind and desolation sweep Lake Huron's rock-bound shore.

Rickaby, 164, 9d, m. (Minn. sung by M. C. Dean); 1 st., m. (N.D.). Beck, 231, 6d (Mich.). Colcord, 203, 8d, m. Dean, 29, the text quoted above. L. C. Record 2279 B (Mich.).

Beck, 231, says of this piece, which Rickaby calls an "elegaic ballad", "George Gotham, once a master of Great Lakes boats, thinks that it was composed by the daughter of Dan Sullivan, first mate on the *Persian*."

D 5

THE DEATH OF WILLIAM GILLEY

After less than two months of marriage, the young widow relates, her husband went to sea in a schooner which was never heard from again. She tries bravely to submit to God's will and find solace in her religion.

> Come all ye young widows around,
> Who are mourning the loss of your mates,
> Attend ye to what I now say:
> My heart it is swelling with grief.

Eckstorm, 291, 16 (Me. original broadside) ; 290, 8 (Me. from recitation) ; the editors report having recorded another version from singing.

The broadside is entitled: "Lines Composed for Clarissa, daughter of Mr. Nathaniel and Elizabeth Gott of Mount Desert and wife of Mr. William Gilley who was married the 14th of January, A. D. 1829, and sailed the first day of March on a sealing voyage to the north with Captain Samuel Hadlock and has not returned." Beneath the title is printed "Written by Mrs. Mary Lurvey Stanley of Cranberry Isles." (Eckstorm, 291). Captain Hadlock's ship was the *Minerva*. (Eckstorm, 289).

D 6

THE DEATH OF HERBERT RICE

This lament for Herbert Rice, who was lost off Block Island during a storm, seeks to reconcile the grief of his family with the will of God.

> Come all kind friends and neighbors, too
> And listen to a tale of woe
> A fine young man is lost at sea
> It was poor Herbert's lot to be.

Eckstorm, 298, 6 (broadside). Beck, *The Folklore of Maine*, 164, 6 (Me.).

The broadside bears the following title: "Lines written On the death of Herbert A. Rice, who was lost at sea Nov. 1868. Aged 18 yrs., 9 months." (Eckstorm, 298). The editors report having taken down two versions of "this simple song" from Maine singers in 1925.

D 7

DIXIE BROWN

Homeless and broke, the sailor has to go to sea again. Shipped on board a whaler, he suffers hardships in the Arctic seas. He warns young sailors to marry and settle down.

> As I went walking down the street I met big Dixie Brown
> He looked me in the face, sure, and he eyed me with a frown,
> Saying, "The last time you were paid off, with me ran up a score.
> Now take my advice, give you a chance, and go to sea once more.

Mackenzie, 255, 4d and refrains (N.S.). Doerflinger, 107, 5d. m. (N.S. "Off to Sea Once More"; this is the text printed by Lomax) ; 108, 5d (N.S.) ; refs. Lomax, *Amer. Ballads*, 494, 5d, m. ("Jack Wrack". In this version the sailor has been robbed of his pay by Angelina in Frisco and hence must go to sea once more). Colcord, 180, prints a song called "The River Lea" which she says is an adaptation of this piece.

The history of this piece has not been traced. William Doerflinger wrote Lomax, "I have heard the song under the title Ben Breezer" (Lomax, 494), and Miss Colcord speaks of the sailor as "poor Ben Brace" (180).

D 8

THE *BIGLER'S* CREW

A humorous and rambling account of the *Bigler's* slow trip from Milwaukee to Buffalo.

> Come all my boys and listen, a song I'll sing to you
> It's all about the Bigler and of her jolly crew.
> In Milwaukee last October I chanced to get a sight
> In the schooner called the Bigler belonging to Detroit.

Rickaby, 168, 11d and chor., m. (Minn. Sung by M. C. Dean. Text from Dean, 19). Colcord, 200, 12d and chor., m. ("The Cruise of the *Bigler*"). Creighton, *Maritime Folk Songs*, 141, 3½d, m. (N.S.). Lomax, *Folk Song U.S.A.*, 148, 8d, m. Lomax, *JAF* 28 (1915), 10, 9d and chor. Lomax, *Our Singing Country*, 220, 8d and chor., m. (A composite text, partly from L. C. Records 2323 B2, 2324 A1). Sandburg, 175, frag. of 11 lines, m. (O.). L. C. Records 3405 A2 (O.) ; 3398 B1 & 3 and 3398 A1, 2, & 4 (Mich. Same singer) ; 3398 A3 (Mich.).

Lomax, (*Our Singing Country*, 220) quotes his singer, Captain Asel Trueblood, as saying: "I learned this song a good fifty years ago . . . I've walked the old Bigler's decks many times, though I never sailed on her. She was supposed to be the slowest vessel in the fleet."

D 9

RED IRON ORE

The log of the *E. C. Roberts'* trip from Chicago to Cleveland with a load of ore picked up at Escanaba. The *Roberts* passes the *Minch*, despite the latter's head start, and arrives in Cleveland ahead of the fleet.

> Come all you bold sailors that follow the lakes
> On an iron ore vessel your living to make.
> I shipped in Chicago, bid adieu to the shore,
> Bound away to Escanaba for red iron ore.

Rickaby, 161, 12d, m. (Minn. sung by M. C. Dean). Dean, p. 12. Lomax, *Amer. Ballads*, 47, and *FSNA*, 128, 7d (reprinted from Rickaby). Sandburg, 176 (reprinted from Rickaby?). L. C. Records 2224 A2, B1, & B2 (Mich.); 3402 A2 & B1 (Mich.); and 3405 A1 (O.).

"A Great Lakes ballad celebrating the earlier traffic in iron ore from Michigan. It follows perfectly its model, the sea ballad of the *Clipper Ship Dreadnaught* type, a sort of log of the trip . . ." (Note from Rickaby, 225).

D 10

THE SEALERS

After three days of sailing, the sealers reach the ice jam which is their goal. The crew spend the day clubbing seals, and by evening they have nine hundred pelts. The ballads end as the ships start homeward.

> Come all ye good people, I pray lend an ear,
> Who wish to go seal fishing in the spring of the year;
> There were two schooners and two sloops in the Pool where we lay,
> Being well-manned and rigged and would soon sail away.
>   To me raddy for the diddle all the day.

Eckstorm, 324, 6½d (Nfld. via Me.).

See Eckstorm, 326, for comments on this Newfoundland piece, which describes, in the singer's words, "a true trip, about sixty years ago," [i.e. about 1865].

D 11

THE *EASTERN LIGHT*

This chronicle gives a graphic account of fishing for halibut and cod on the Grand Banks. Strict Captain McCloud drives his men hard until their provisions run out and they must head back toward Gloucester.

> 'Twas of my sad misfortune in eighteen hundred and seventy-three,
> I shipped on board the fisherman right off a drunken spree.

Eckstorm, 326, 18d couplets (Me.). Beck, *The Folklore of Maine*, 214 (text from Mrs. Eckstorm's singer).

"Taken down in October, 1925, from the singing of Captain Archie S. Spruling, of Islesford, Maine, who learned it many years ago on board a fishing vessel. The *Eastern Light*, 70 tons, was built in 1856 and was owned by Maddocks and Company, of Gloucester." (Note from Eckstorm, 326).

D 12

THE *DOM PEDRO*

The ship sails from Boston harbor, runs along Cape Cod, and goes down to the Line. After filling casks with rain-water, the crew start on their long trip to Shanghai. Having reached their destination and discharged their cargo, the sailors look forward to a jolly time on their return.

> It's of a flash packet, a packet of fame,
> She belongs to New York and *Dom Pedro's* her name,
> She's rammed up and jammed up on deck and below,
> We're bound for Shanghai in the *Dom Pedero,*
> Singing down, down derry down!

Colcord, 179, 7, m. L. C. Record 2530 B & 2531 A (sung by Capt. Richard Maitland in N.Y. in 1939, 6 sts.).

"This New York clipper bark, built for the coffee trade with Brazil, was later put into the China run." (note from Colcord). Compare the similar ballad, "The *Dreadnaught*" (D13).

D 13

THE *DREADNAUGHT*

The chronicle of an uneventful trip from England to New York. Most of the stanzas end "She's the Liverpool packet—O Lord, let her go!", and the concluding line boasts, "The *Dreadnaught's* the flier that outsails them all".

> There is a flash packet, flash packet of fame,
> She hails from New York, and the *Dreadnaught's* her name,
> She is bound to the westward, where the strong winds blow,
> Bound away in the *Dreadnaught* to the westward we'll go.

Colcord, 170, 9d, m. Creighton, *Maritime Folk Songs,* 140, 10d, m. (N.S.). Creighton and Senior, 227, 9d, m. (N.S. "The Banks of Newfoundland"). Doerflinger, 126, 6d, m. (N.Y.); 8d (N.Y. from ms.). Neeser, 330, 9d (a broadside text). Rickaby, 150, 8d, m. (Minn. As sung by M. C. Dean. Text from Dean, 58); refs.

"Although not the fastest of the Western Ocean packets, the *Dreadnaught* was probably the best known of them all. She was built at Newburyport, Mass., in 1853, and was 1,413 tons register; a very large ship for those days. During her first eight trips, her average eastern passage was 21 days, 15 hours, and for the western passage, 24 days, 12 hours". The *Dreadnaught* was wrecked off Cape Horn in 1869. (Notes from Colcord, 169-170).

D 14

THE SCHOONER *FRED DUNBAR*

Partly advice to the girls and partly a "moniker song," this balled is principally a chronicle of a trip along the Northern coast from Bagaduce to the Bay Chaleur.

You darling girls of Bagaduce, who live along the shore,
'Tis little do you think or know what sailors do endure;
Or if you did, you would treat them with more respect than before,—
You never would go with a landloper while sailors are on shore.

Barry, *Bulletin*, no. 5 (1933), 15, 11d, m. (Me.).

This piece was composed by Amos Hanson, Orland, Maine; it "has long been a favorite song about Penobscot Bay." (See Barry, *loc. cit.*, for further details).

D 15

BOLD MANAN THE PIRATE

The pirates capture and ransack the *Fame* from New York and murder her crew. To stop an argument among his men, Manan severs the head of a young lady on board whose fate they had been discussing. A merry celebration of the victory follows. The next day, Manan mistakes a warship under Captain Rodney for an East Indiaman. In the ensuing battle the pirate ship is sunk.

> Bold Manan went to sea one day, a dreary day 'twas, too,
> 'Twas thick as any buttermilk among the fog and dew;
> Bold Manan's ship you all may know, no finer ship e'er swam,
> Five hundred and fifty men on board, her guns were forty-nine.

Eckstorm, 262, 13d (Me.); 259, 14d (Me.). Doerflinger, 139, 11d and chor., m. (N.S. "Bold Manning"); refs. Ranson, 59, 10d (Ireland). The AAFS has a text of 25 sts. called "Bill Shepherd's Pirate Song".

"We have never found this song in print, yet it must have been well known and widely distributed in the Northeast; for in March, 1916, Mr. L. I. Flower, of Central Cambridge, New Brunswick, telling about the old woods and the songs sung there forty years before, wrote: 'And Noah Sears's pirate song—I'll never forget a verse of that:

> And then this cru-el ruff-yan,
> Without fear or dread,
> He rush-ed up to this female,
> And snap-ped off her head!' "

(Note from Eckstorm, 264. See for further details) The hyphenation of this stanza and the tenor of the entire ballad suggest that despite its grim subject matter one was not always expected to take it seriously.

D 16

THE GHOSTLY CREW

After assuring his listeners that he is not easily frightened, the sailor tells of the night at sea when a sudden feeling of dread came over him. At once a dozen ghostly sailors came over the side and took their stations. They vanished when the Tower Light came into view. He identifies them as the drowned crew of a vessel run down by his craft some time before on Georges Shoals.

> Right o'er our rail came climbing, all silent, one by one,
> A dozen hardy sailors. Just wait till I am done.
> Their faces pale and sea-worn, all ghostly through the night,
> Each fellow took his station as if he had a right.

Doerflinger, 181, 7d, m. (N.S.) ; stanza 5 is given above. 182, 8d (N.S.) ; notes. Greenleaf, 227, 8d, m. (Nfld.). Beck, *The Folklore of Maine*, 204, 7d, m. (Nfld.). Creighton, 254, 8d, m. (N.S.).

Mr. Doerflinger says (p. 337), " 'The Ghostly Crew', by Harry L. Marcy, appeared in *Fishermen's Ballads and Songs of The Sea* (Gloucester, Mass., Procter Brothers, 1874), p. 46. The book is 'respectfully dedicated to the hardy fishermen of Cape Ann.' The Preface states that 'very many of the ballads are original, having been written expressly for us by the fishermen.' "

D 17

THE BEAVER ISLAND BOYS

Despite his mother's premonitory dream, Johnny and his companions set out across Lake Michigan. Returning from Traverse City, the small boat has almost reached Beaver Island when it overturns in a squall and all hands are lost.

> Come, all brother sailors, I hope you'll draw nigh
> For to hear of the sad news, it will cause you to cry,
> Of the noble Johnny Gallegher, who sailed to and fro,
> He was lost on Lake Michigan where the stormy winds blow.

Lomax, *Our Singing Country*, 216, 9d, m. (Mich. From L. C. Records 2273 and 2274) ; notes.

"It was in '74 that this song was composed by a man by the name of Daniel Malloy. . . . Three men went out of this harbor in a small boat to go to Traverse City for supplies, and they left here in a gale of wind, and she foundered and they were all lost. . . . That was in '73." (Dominick Gallegher, whose father was successfully dissuaded from making the fatal return trip, as quoted by Lomax, p. 215).

D 18

THE *CEDAR GROVE*

The helmsman knows the ship is too close to shore but dares not say so. The lookout's warning comes too late, and the ship crashes into the rocks. She is backed off but later sinks. Miss Farrell, a passenger, is swept away, and the captain and two engineers are lost. The captain's disfigured body is later recovered by divers.

> It's of a noble steamer, the *Cedar Grove* by name,
> She crossed the briny ocean, from London city came.
> She was strongly built on the banks of Clyde, five hundred tons or more;
> But her strength it proved of no avail on the banks of Casno shore.

Mackenzie, 236, 10d (N.S.); notes. Doerflinger, 186, 11d, m. (N.S.); notes.

"The Steamship *Cedar Grove*, of about 2000 tons' register, was wrecked off Casno, Nova Scotia, on the night of November 30, 1882. She had sailed from London, and was bound for St. John, New Brunswick, with a cargo principally of liquors. The captain and two engineers were lost, also a Mrs. Farrell, the only female passenger on board." (Note from Mackenzie).

D 19

CHARLES AUGUSTUS (or Gustavus) ANDERSON

The speaker, a Swede of good upbringing, wishes he could bid farewell to his family before being hanged for mutiny and murder on the *Saladin*. He fears the Lord's judgment but asks his mercy. The ballad ends with Anderson's execution.

> Come all ye human countrymen, with pity lend an ear,
> And hear my feeling story—you can't but shed a tear.
> I'm held in close confinement—bound down in irons strong,
> Surrounded by stony granite walls and sentenced to be hung.

Mackenzie, 289, 14d (N.S.); notes. Beck, *The Folklore of Maine*, 180, 14d (Me.). Creighton, 235, 15d, m. (N.S.). Creighton, *Maritime Folk Songs*, 196, 15d, m. (N.S. "Saladin Mutiny". Reprinted from Creighton). Doerflinger, 291, 2d, m. (N.B.); 14d (N.S. from a newspaper clipping). Greenleaf, 319, 10½d (Nfld. "Fielding"; "Learned from a newspaper text"). L. C. Record 220 B (N.S.).

In 1843 the English barque *Saladin* returning from Valparaiso was captured by her crew led by a passenger, an ex-pirate named Captain Fielding, who incited the men against their harsh master, Captain Mackenzie. The captain, his officers, and some of the crew were murdered, and the mutineers headed for Newfoundland, but having become suspicious of Fielding, they threw him and his son overboard. The ship was wrecked off Halifax, N.S., on April 28, 1844, with six men aboard. Four of these (Anderson, George Jones, Travascus, and Hazelton) were tried and executed. (Note condensed from Mackenzie, *The Quest of the Ballad*, pp. 213-222).

See also the following piece and "Saladin's Crew" in Appendix II.

D 20

GEORGE JONES

George Jones from County Clare gives a detailed account of the *Saladin*
mutiny and its aftermath. (See the preceding piece).

> Good people all, come listen to my melancholy tale,
> My dying declaration which I have pen'd in jail.
> My present situation may to all a warning be,
> And a caution to all seamen to beware of mutiny.

Creighton, 238, 19d, m. (N.S.); notes. Mackenzie, 286, 23 sts. (N.S.
recited); notes.

D 21

THE WRECK OF THE *HURON*

Despite the best efforts of the officers and crew, the Navy ship breaks up
on the rocky coast of North Carolina and one hundred lives are lost.

> On a dark and stormy night
> When orders came to sail
> Mountain high the billows rolled
> And louder blew the gale.
>
> *Chorus:* Toll, toll the bell
> For the loss of the *Huron* crew;
> We'll mourn and weep the sad, sad fate
> Of the noble boys in blue.

Brown II, 670, 7 and chorus; 669, 2 8-line d. sts. and chorus (N.C.); notes.
The U.S.S. *Huron* was wrecked near Oregon Inlet, N. C., November 24,
1877. (Note from Brown).

D 22

BOUND DOWN TO NEWFOUNDLAND

The young captain becomes ill and cannot appear on deck. Unable to take
the ship into Halifax harbor, the crew sails on to Arishat, where, after eight
days, the captain dies of smallpox.

> Saint Patrick's day in sixty-five,
> From New York we set sail.
> Kind Providence did favor us
> With a sweet and pleasant gale.
> We bore away from America,
> As you will understand;
> With courage brave we rode the waves,
> Bound down to Newfoundland.

Doerflinger, 201, 8d, m. (N.S. Tune from Creighton). Creighton, 223, 8d, m. (N.S.). Creighton, *Maritime Folk Songs*, 195, 8d, m. (N.S.). Greenleaf, 317, 2½, m. (Nfld. "The Schooner *Mary Ann*"). Mackenzie, 228, 6d (N.S.).

"This song is of Nova Scotian composition. The singer who delivered it to me stated that it was made by Captain Cale White of Maitland, Colchester County." (Note from Mackenzie).

D 23

THE FLEMINGS OF TORBAY

Two fisherman adrift in a dory suffer from exposure for six days before being rescued unconscious by a coal ship, the *Jessie Maurice*. The captain nurses them faithfully and takes them to a hospital in Quebec.

> The thrilling tale we heard last week is in our mem'ries yet,
> Two fishermen from Newfoundland snatched from the jaws of death,
> Two fine young men born in Torbay they went adrift at sea
> On the eighteenth day of April from the schooner *Jubilee*.

Creighton, *Maritime Folk Songs*, 202, 12d, m. (N.S.). Creighton, 248, 13d, m. (N.S.). Greenleaf, 285, 16, m. (Nfld.).

L. C. Record 35 A & B (from the Creighton collection).

The event here described occurred in May, 1888. The author of the ballad is given as Johnny Burke of St. John's. (Notes from Creighton, 251).

D 24

THE *TITANIC* I

Although the builders thought the ship would never sink, it is doomed. Because the rich would not ride with the poor, the latter, who are below, are the first to die. The passengers sing "Nearer, my God, to Thee" and sixteen hundred people perish.

> It was on a Monday morning about one o'clock
> When the great Titanic began to reel and rock.
> All the people began to cry saying lord I have to die.
> It was sad when that great ship went down.
>
> *Chorus:* Oh it was sad when that great ship went down.
> There were husbands and their wives,
> Little children lost their lives.
> It was sad when that great ship went down.

Brown II, 666, 6d and chorus (from ms.); add. st.; 7 and a chorus like that of "The *Titantic* II" in Appendix II (N.C.). Henry, *Folk-Songs*, 427, 5d and chorus (Tenn.). Randolph IV, 145, 2d and chorus (Mo.). White, 347, 7d and chor.

"On Sunday night, April 14-15, 1912, and Royal Mail Steamer *Titanic*, making her maiden voyage from Southampton to New York, with 2224 passengers and crew, struck at full speed an iceberg and went to the bottom of the Atlantic, with a loss of 1513 lives." (Note from Brown, p. 662).

Brown II, 663-666, prints copies of early broadsides which have a chorus much like that of the traditional piece, although the ballads are otherwise dissimilar:

> Women and children saved their lives;
> Husbands parted from their wives.
> It was sad about the *Titanic* when it got lost.

Seen Appendix II for four more *Titanic* ballads.

D 25

THE GALLANT BRIGANTINE

The sailor meets a beautiful girl who responds politely to his greeting. They chat awhile and she gives him her address, saying that her husband would be glad to see him. He then tells her he is married and has a newborn son. Hand in hand the two stroll to her farm where he meets her husband, has dinner, and spends a pleasant afternoon.

> As I strayed ashore one evening from my gallant brigantine,
> In the island of Jamaica where I have lately been,
> Being tired of my wandering I sat me down to rest,
> And I sang a song of my native land, the song that I love best

Creighton, *Maritime Folk Songs*, 142, 7d, m.; 3d of 9d (N.S.). Cazden, part 2, p. 46, 9d, m. (N.Y. "The Island of Jamaica"). Creighton, 73, 7d, m. (N.S.). Flanders-Barry, 27, 8d, m. (N.H. "Henry Orrison"); notes. L. C. Record 2284 A (Mich.).

This tongue-in-cheek narrative achieves its effect by repeatedly disappointing the listener's anticipation of the stock situations of broadside balladry.

D 26

THE COAST OF PERU

After the lookout sights a whale, the men lower the boats, harpoon the whale, and bring it back to the ship, where the blubber is cut and tried out and the oil is stowed. When the ship is laden, the whalemen look forward to seeing the girls at home.

> Come all you young sailors who cruise round Cape Horn,
> Come all you young tars who follow the sperm,
> For our captain has told us, we hope it is true,
> There are plenty of whales on the coast of Peru.

Doerflinger, 151, 7d (from ms.); refs. Colcord, 194, 5d, m. Thompson, 194, 5d, (N.Y.).

A. L. Lloyd, who sings this ballad on "Thar She Blows!" (Riverside Record RLP 12-635), writes, *The Coast of Peru* was the most important ballad of the South-Seamen, notably those sailing out of Hull."

D 27

THE SHIP THAT NEVER RETURNED

The ship leaves after loving farewells. Among those aboard are a youngest son going away for his health and the captain, who plans to retire after this final trip. But the ship is never heard from again.

> On a summer's day, when the waves were rippled
> By the softest, gentlest breeze,
> Did a ship set sail with its cargo laden
> For a port beyond the seas.
>
> *Chorus:* Did she ever return?
> No, she never returned,
> And her fate is yet unlearned, . . .

Henry, *Folk-Songs*, 369, 6 and chor. (Tenn.). Brown II, 507, 3d and chor. (N.C.); refs. Randolph IV, 140, 3d and chor.; 4d and chor. (Mo.). Sandburg, 146, 6 and chor., m. (Ky.). *JAF* 28 (1915), 6 and chor. (N.C.).

This ballad was written by Henry C. Work and copyrighted in 1865.

What the editors of the Brown collection call a parody of this piece, "The Train That Never Returned," 3d and chor., appears in Brown II, 510 and in Randolph IV, 146.

D 28

THE *E. A. HORTON*

The American ship *E. A. Horton* has been captured by a Canadian cutter and her men have been imprisoned. The captain and his men recapture their ship at night and triumphantly sail her back to Gloucester.

> Ye sons of Uncle Samuel, come listen for awhile,
> I'll tell you of a captain that was made in Yankee style;
> Of the schooner *E. A. Horton* and the bold undaunted band,
> Commanded by brave Knowlton, a true son of Yankee land.

Eckstorm, 314, 8d (Me.); detailed notes, 303-310. Creighton, 314, 6d, m. (N.S.).

The international incident here recounted took place on Oct. 8, 1871, when Canada seized the *E. A. Horton* in Halifax harbor on a charge of fishing inside Canadian waters. The successful return of the ship caused great excitement in the Northeast. (Note condensed from Eckstorm).

BALLADS ABOUT CRIMINALS AND OUTLAWS

E 1 Jesse James I
E 2 Jesse James II
E 3 Cole Younger
E 4 Sam Bass
E 5 Sidney Allen
E 6 Claude Allen
E 7 Kenny Wagner
E 8 Kenny Wagner's Surrender
E 9 Wilkes Lovell
E 10 Wild Bill Jones
E 11 Charles Guiteau
E 12 Ewing Brooks
E 13 Frankie Silvers
E 14 Gambling on the Sabbath Day
E 15 Young Companions
E 16 Twenty-One Years
E 17 Logan County Jail
E 18 Zeb Tourney's Girl
E 19 J. B. Marcum
E 20 The Rowan County Crew

E 21 Harvey Logan
E 22 Daniel Sullivan
E 23 Howard Carey
E 24 Frank Dupree
E 25 Muff Lawler, the Squealer
E 26 The Murder of F. C. Benwell

E 1

JESSE JAMES I

Typical versions contain short but admiring references to the James brothers' depradations, followed by an account of the treacherous murder of Jesse by a member of his own gang, Robert Ford, "the dirty little coward that shot Mr. Howard."

> Now Jesse was a man, a friend to the poor.
> He would never see a man in pain.
> And with his brother Frank he robbed Chicago Bank
> And stopped the Glendale train.

Hudson, 236, 3 10-line sts. (the first four lines of st. 2 are given above); 237, 3 (Miss.). Belden, 401, 8 and chor. (Mo.); detailed refs. Brown II, 558, 9; 6 and chor. (reprinted from *JAF* 22, 246); 4 and choruses (N.C.); refs. Cambiaire, 17, 8 and chor. (Tenn.). Chappell, 192, 7 lines (N.C.). Cox, 216, 19 lines (W. Va.); refs. Gardner, 339, 3, m. (Mich.). Henry, *Folk-Songs*, 321, Cambiaire's singer. Leach, 753, texts from *JAF* and Belden. Leach and Beck, *JAF* 63 (1950), 278, 3 (Va.). Lomax, *Cowboy Songs*, 152, 11 and chor., m.; 3 and chor.; 4; 5 and chor. Lomax, *FSNA*, 351, 9 and chor., m. ("from singing of B. L. Lunsford, L. C. Record 97 B1"). Lomax, *Folk Song U.S.A.*, 296, 9 and chor., m. Owens, 112, 6 and chor., m. (Tex.). Pound, 145, 4 and chor. (S.C.); 2 and chor. (Ia.). Randolph II, 17, 2, m. (Ark.); 7, m.; 9 (Mo. from ms.); 6, m. (Ark.); 6, m. (Mo.); refs. Sandburg, 334, 3 10-line sts., m. (a Negro version); 420, 7 and chor., m. L. C. Records 73 A3 (Ky. via Conn.); 2917 A2 (Tenn.); 1823 B (N.Y.); and eight others from Tex., Tenn., Va., Miss., Cal., and Wash., D.C. Finger, p. 57, reproduces the Wehman broadside.

"Probably the most famous son of Missouri—after Mark Twain—is the bandit who, starting his career with Quantrill's bushwackers, became in the fifteen years following the Civil War the most notorious train- and bank-robber in the country. His career ended when, in 1882, he was shot treacherously by one of his own gang, Robert Ford, who was tempted by the $10,000 reward offered for the capture of James. The story goes that he was shot while hanging a picture on the wall of the house in St. Joseph in which he was living under the name of Howard." (Note from Belden).

E 2

JESSE JAMES II

The ballad first describes the robbing of the Pittsfield bank; then follows an account of Jesse's murder. Planning a train robbery, Jesse reaches for his rifle and knocks down his wife's picture. Stooping to retrieve it, he is shot in the back of the head by Ford.

> Now people may forget a lot of famous names,
> But every nook and corner knows of Jesse James.
> They used to read about him in their homes at night;
> When the wind blew down the chimney they would shake with fright.

Hudson, 235, 8d (Miss.). Brown II, 561, 7d (N.C.). Burt, 192, 8d. Henry, *Folk-Songs*, 320, 8d (Tenn. a confused text). Lomax, *Amer. Ballads*, 131, 4d & chor. (La. via Mo.). Randolph II, 18, 7d, m. (Mo.). See the notes to the preceding ballad.

E 3

COLE YOUNGER

Cole tells of robbing a miner, and, with his brother Bob, murdering a train crew, meeting the James boys in Texas, and finally being captured during the robbery of the Northfield bank.

> I am a bandit highwayman
> Cole Younger is my name,
> For many a depredation
> I have brought my friends to shame,
> By the robbing of the Northfield Bank,
> For which I can't deny,
> Oh now I am a poor prisoner,
> In the Stillwater jail I lie.

Randolph II, 14, 7d; 13, 7½d, m.; 14, 1, m. (Mo.); 4, m. (Ark); notes. Lomax, *FSNA*, 350, 9d, m. ("As sung by Edward L. Crain, Amer. Folk Music, Folkways Disc, No. 15. Apparently Crain learned song word for word from the original edition of *Cowboy Songs*, p. 106, and set his own tune."). L. C. Records 3213 B1 (Mo.); 911 A1 (Tex.); 2279 A (Mich.); 535 B (Tex.), and 4197 B2 (Cal.).

"Cole Younger was a Missourian who rode with Quantrell's guerrillas, and became a captain in Shelby's Missouri Cavalry toward the end of the Civil War. He and his brothers turned outlaw, and robbed trains and banks with the James boys. Captured while trying to loot a bank at Northfield, Minn., in 1876, Cole was sent to prison for murder. Pardoned in 1901, he joined his old comrade Frank James in a Wild West Show venture." (Part of Randolph's note, 12).

E 4

SAM BASS

Having turned from cow-punching to successful train robbery, Sam is eventually betrayed by a supposed friend named Jim Murphy and is shot down by a Texas Ranger.

> Sam Bass was born in Indiana, it was his native home,
> And at the age of seventeen young Sam began to roam.
> Sam first came out to Texas a cowboy for to be,—
> A kinder-hearted fellow you seldom ever see.

Thorp, 135, 11d. (Thorp writes: "By John Denton, Gainesville, Texas, 1879."). Belden, 399, 12 (Mo.). Burt, 199, 3d, m. (Utah); notes, including the inscription from Sam's tombstone. *CFB* II (1963), 28, 11d, m. (Colo.). High, 17, 24d lines (Ark.). Owens, 122, 10d, m. (Tex.); notes. Owens, *PTFS* 26, 139, 10d (Tex.); notes. Randolph II, 70, 10d, m.; 4 sts. from a longer version (Mo.); the editor refers to several other texts and to various sources of information about Sam Bass. L. C. Records 3806A1 and 3808A1 (Tex. Same singer), 3222B1 (Mo.), 2637A1 (Tex.), and 1462A (Ky.).

"Sam Bass the train-robber was killed at Round Rock, Texas, in 1878" (Note from Randolph, 69). For a text elaborated on by the singer in a highly entertaining manner, see Finger, 65-71.

E 5

SIDNEY ALLEN

Sidney starts a pistol battle in the courtroom by killing the judge. He escapes and rides away with his friends and his nephew, but is later recaptured and returned home. Although his family fears he will be electrocuted, he is sentenced to the penitentiary instead.

> Come all you rounders if you want to hear
> The story about a cruel mountaineer.
> Sidney Allen was the villain's name.
> It was in a courthouse he won his fame.

Hudson, 242, 8d (Ala.). Burt, 254, 8d (Nev.); notes. Campbell, *SFQ* 3, 170, 4 8-line d. sts. (Ky.). Gardner, 341, 8d (Va. via Mich.). Henry, *Folk-Songs*, 319, 8d (Tenn. via Mo.). Leach and Beck, *JAF* 63 (1950), 270, 16, m. (Va.). Thomas, *Ballad Makin'*, 155, 7d (Ky.). L. C. Records 2028B—10 in. (Ky.); 2747 A & B1 (Hillsville, Va., spoken, "The Allen Murder Case").

During their trial the Allen family reacted to a jail sentence by starting a shooting affray in the courthouse at Hillsville, Virginia, in 1912. "In less than a minute 200 shots had been fired, the judge, the sheriff, the prosecuting attorney lay dead . . . , and the murderers had swung onto their horses and headed into the mountains". (Note condensed from Hudson, 242, who quotes from the *Literary Digest* of March 30, 1912, 627-628). Claude and Floyd Allen were later tried and executed; Sidney was given a jail sentence. For further details, some of them conflicting, see Hudson and his references and Richardson, 106-107. Richardson prints a late sequel, "The Pardon of

Sydna Allen", 34. See also Lomax's headnote to the following piece which accompanies L. C. Records AAFS 35.

It will be seen that this ballad owes a heavy debt to "Casey Jones".

E 6

CLAUDE ALLEN

This ballad is a lament for young, handsome Claude Allen, who has been executed as a result of the Governor's indifference, leaving his mother and his sweetheart to grieve for him.

> Claud Allen and his dear old father
> Have met their fatal doom at last.
> Their friends are glad their troubles are over
> And hope their souls are now at rest.

Henry, Folk-Songs, 316, 7 (N.C.); 7; 6 (Ga.). Brown, II, 567, 10; 5 (N.C.); notes and refs. Burt, 253, 7 (Nev.); notes. L. C. Records 2908 A2 (Tenn. "The Doom of Claude Allen"); 1351 A1 (Va.); 854 A2 (N.C.); AAFS #35 (Va.).

Claude Allen was electrocuted for killing the sheriff in a courtroom fracas at Hillsville, Va., in 1912. (For details, see Lomax's note accompanying L. C. Record AAFS #35 and the notes and references to the preceding ballad.)

E 7

KENNY WAGNER

After murdering a sheriff in Mississippi, Kenny flees to Tennessee where he is captured. He breaks jail, but is recaptured later in Texarkana by a woman sheriff. Returned to Mississippi, he is given a life sentence. The ballad ends with a warning against law-breaking.

> It was down in Mississippi
> Not many years ago,
> A young man started out in life,
> A life of sin and woe.
> Now Kenny Wagner was his name,
> A bandit bold and free;
> He shot down Sheriff McIntosh
> And fled to Tennessee.

Hudson, 243, 4d (Miss.). *TFSB* 2 (1936), 12, 8 (N.C.).

"Kenny Wagner is an actual Mississippi 'bad man', now serving a life sentence in the state penitentiary for several murders. Two ballads have been composed about him, both of which were popular in Mississippi, Alabama, and Arkansas as late as 1928. See also the following piece. These ballads in the main tell his story accurately so far as they go." (Note from Hudson, 243, who gives further details about Wagner's career).

Professor D. K. Wilgus writes that this and the following ballad were composed by Andrew Jenkins. See the note to "Floyd Collins."

E 8

KENNY WAGNER'S SURRENDER

Except for the casual mention of two additional murders, this first person ballad tells practically the same story as "Kenny Wagner."

> I am sure you have heard my story
> From "The Kenny Wagner Song":
> How down in Mississippi
> I took the road that's wrong.

Hudson, 245, 10 (Ala.); notes; text reprinted by Burt, 216. Brown II, 566, 10 (N.C.). Morris, 90, 8 (Fla.).

See the notes to the preceding ballad.

E 9

WILKES LOVELL

The sheriff's wife tells him that his two prisoners have escaped. He chases them on his white horse, captures them, and returns them to jail. The narrator, speaking from prison, warns his listeners against doing the deed they have done—but the deed remains unnamed.

> 'Twas on the fourteenth day of March,
>   As you will plainly see,
> We broke the locks of Springfield jail
>   Our liberty to get.
> We broke them, yes, we broke them,
>   Swung open wide the door,
> Resolved to leave old Springfield town
>   And get in jail no more.

Flanders-Barry, 217, 4d, m. (Vt.).

"The Honorable Wilkes S. Lovell was sheriff of Windsor County, Vermont, in the 1890's. The story is that the thieves were gypsy horse traders and the crime for which they served six months in jail was the theft of a harness." (Note from Flanders-Barry).

E 10

WILD BILL JONES

The narrator shoots Wild Bill, who has stolen his girl, and is taken to jail. Lula won't bail him out. The ballad becomes confused at this point. After a dialogue with the girl, borrowed, Hudson remarks, from "The Lass of Roch Royal", the murderer talks of going on a spree with the boys because he is about to die.

> One day when I was rambling around,
> I met up with Wild Bill Jones.
> A-walking and a-talking to my Lula girl.
> I bid him to leave her alone.

Hudson, 239, 10 (Miss.). Cambiaire, 19, 4 sts. Chappell, 193, 4 (N.C.).
Henry, *Folk-Songs*, 323, 6½ (N.C.); 4 (Tenn.). Lomax, *FSNA*, 270, 6, m.
(from Richardson's *Amer. Mt. Songs*, p. 36). Randolph II, 105, 8, m. (Ark.);
refs. Sharp II, 74, 3d, m. (N.C.). Williams, 405, 8, m. (Ky.). L. C. Records
2554B and 828B2 (N.Y. via Ky. Sung by Aunt Molly Jackson), 2896 A2
& B1 (Tenn.), 1822A2 (N.Y. Sung by B. L. Lunsford), 2746B4 (Va.),
4139A1 (Cal.), and four more Ky. versions.

The history of this piece has not been traced.

E 11

CHARLES GUITEAU

Having tried unsuccessfully to escape from the law and to plead insanity,
the youthful murderer grieves for his family as he prepares to die.

> Come all ye gentle Christians
> Wherever you may be,
> And likewise pay attention
> To these few words from me,
> For the murder of James A. Garfield
> I am condemned to die,
> Upon the twentieth day of June
> Upon a scaffold high.

Randolph II, 31, 5d, m. (Ark.); 29, 4d, m. (Okla. via Ark.); refs. to
various Southern and Midwestern texts. Arnold, 113, 7½, m. (Ala.). Belden,
412, 4d and chor. (Mo.); refs. to texts from W. Va., N.C., Miss., Ill., Ia.,
and S.D. Brown II, 572, 4d and chor.; 4d and chor.; 10 (N.C.); notes.
Burt, 226, 4d and chor., m. (Pa.). *CFB* I (1962), no. 3, p. 22, 5½d, m.
(Colo.). Hubbard, 252, 2d and chor., m. (Utah). Hudson, 238, 4½d (Miss.).
Kansas Folklore, 159, 5d, m. (Okla.). Lomax, *FSNA*, 273, 3d and chor., m.
Morris, 72, 5d, m. (Fla.). Owens, 118, 5, m. (Tex.). *SFQ* 24 (1960), 282,
4d; 4d (S.C.). *WF* 17 (1958), 235, 4, m. (Ia.). L. C. Records 1812 A1
(N.Y. Sung by B. L. Lunsford); 1361 A2 (Va.); 2968 A2 (Miss.).

This ballad seems to have been sung in the 1870's under the title "John T.
Williams." (See Pound, 251). Apparently it was altered slightly to fit the
assassination of Garfield in 1881. It will be seen that the President's name
is mentioned casually without reference to the national significance of
the murder.

Other pieces based on this pattern are "The Murder of F. C. Benwell"
(E 26); "Story of Gustave Ohr," Eddy, 274, and "Story of George Mann,"
Eddy, 276 (see Appendix II); "Johnny Runks," Gordon, 41; and "Ewing
Brooks," the following ballad.

E 12

EWING BROOKS (MAXWELL'S DOOM)

The murderer tells of his escape to "Frisco" and then to New Zealand where he was arrested and returned to the United States. The pleas of his family having failed, he will be executed. The ballad ends on a sentimental and religious note.

> I come to old America,
> Old England I forsook,
> I took the name of Maxwell,
> Denied of Ewin' Brooks.
> I bein' a very reckless man
> A spendthrift too was I,
> I murdered Arthur Fralow
> My wants to satisfy.

Randolph II, 119, 6d, m. (Ark.). The editor calls this "one of the numerous adaptations of the 'Charles Guitteau' song . . ." See for further comments and for references to related pieces. Belden, 413, 6d (Mo. from ms.); 5d & chorus (Mo. from ms. "Maxwell's Doom").

"The 'Ewing Brooks' mentioned in the song was really Hugh M. Brooks, an Englishman who assumed the name of Walter Lennox Maxwell, and murdered Charles Arthur Preller at the Southern Hotel, St. Louis, in 1885. Brooks fled to New Zealand, but was brought back to Missouri and hanged Aug. 10, 1888" (Note from Randolph, 118. See Belden's headnote for further details about this crime).

E 13

FRANKIE SILVERS

Having been sentenced to die for the murder of her husband, Mrs. Silvers speaks with horror of the deed she has done and of the fate which awaits her.

> This dreadful, dark and dismal day
> Has swept my glories all away.
> My sun gives down, my days are past
> And I shall leave this world at last.

Henry, *Songs Sung*, 48, 15 (N.C. reprinted from *JAF* 45 (1932), 62, which contains a misleading note about the date of the crime). Randolph II, 125, 4, m. (Mo.); refs.

"Charles Silver was murdered Dec. 22, 1831, at Deyton Bend of Toe River, in the Blue Ridge Mountains of western North Carolina. His wife Frankie was convicted of the crime and hanged at Morgantown, N. C., July 12, 1833." (Note from Randolph, 124, who refers to the detailed account given by Muriel Early Sheppard in *Cabins in the Laurel*, 25-39. She writes, 35, that Frankie, "in the last days of her imprisonment . . . contrived a long, gloomy poem which she recited from the scaffold". Mrs. Sheppard prints a text of 13½ stanzas, part of which is reprinted by Burt, p. 17).

E 14

GAMBLING ON THE SABBATH DAY

Having murdered a comrade, the young man is condemned to hang. His family is unable to save him, and after repentant farewells, he dies on the scaffold.

> A poor unworthy boy who dares
> To disregard a father's cares,
> Who smiles to see a sister's tears
> An' scorns to hear a mother's prayers.
>
> From their advice he turned away,
> At dice an' cards he learnt to play,
> An' then a comrade he did slay
> While gamblin' on the Sabbath day.

Randolph II, 41, 8, m. (Mo.); 10 (Ark.); fragments. Henry, *Songs Sung*, 105, 8 (Tenn.).

For a discussion of this ballad with references to another text and to some fugitive stanzas, see Randolph, 40. The piece is said to have been sung by an outlaw named Bill Walker, who was hanged in Missouri in 1889, but its authorship has not been settled.

E 15

YOUNG COMPANIONS

In this confession ballad a young man tells of leaving his devoted mother and sisters and going to Chicago where he "sinned both night and day." His career ends when he murders a "fair young maiden" and is condemned to hang.

> Come all you young companions
> And listen unto me,
> I'll tell you a sad story
> Of some bad company,
> I was born in Pennsylvania
> Among the beautiful hills,
> And the memory of my childhood
> Is warm within me still.

Lomax, *Cowboy Songs*, 212, 6d, m. Hudson, 248, 9 (Miss.). Larkin, 104, 6d. Morris, 75, 12 (Fla.). *PTFS* 6 (1927), 187, 6d (Tex.). Randolph II, 139, 5, m.; 5d (Mo. "Taney County"). L. C. Records 552 A (Tex.); 3017 A2 & B1, 3024 A1, and 3031 A2 (Miss.); 4047 A2 (Cal. "Bad Companions").

Randolph reports having heard this piece "as long ago as 1918." Its history has not been traced.

E 16

TWENTY-ONE YEARS

The prisoner addresses himself principally to the girl for whose sake he has lain forlornly in a dirty jail for six months. He begs her to go to the Governor for him, and to write to him. The ballad ends with a warning to young men not to trust women.

> The judge says stand up, boy, and dry up your tears,
> You're sentenced to Nashville for twenty-one years,
> So dry up your eyes, babe, and say you'll be mine,
> For twenty-one years, babe, is a mighty long time.

Randolph II, 156, 7d; add. sts. (Mo.). Henry, *Songs Sung*, 69, 11 (Tenn.). Morris, 67, 8d, m. (Fla.).

Randolph prints four related pieces under this title. The second of these, "Answer to Twenty-One Years," (157, 6½d, Mo.) is the girl's letter in reply to the one given above. She has been too ill to write, and her plea to the Governor has been fruitless. She promises to come to him when she recovers, and she says, "I'll wait for you, love, for twenty-one years." (This piece appears also in Morris, 69, 4½d, Fla.). In "Ninety-Nine Years," (158, 6d, Mo.) the prisoner is serving time in Nashville for another man's sake. His hopes of a pardon are dashed when he hears that his sweetheart will marry the judge. Finally in "A Sequel to Nine-Nine Years," (159, 6d, Ark.) the prisoner, having been freed, sets out to find the girl he loves. She has been cast aside by the judge after less than a year of marriage and is going to another town to begin life anew.

E 17

LOGAN COUNTY JAIL (DALLAS COUNTY JAIL)

The narrator's illegal activities land him in jail, and he is sentenced to a long term in the penitentiary.

> O, when I was a little boy, I worked in Market Square;
> I used to pocket money, I did not make it fair.
> I rode upon the lakes, to learn to rob and steal,
> And when I made a big haul, how happy I did feel!

Cox, 212, 5½d; 6d; 6½d (W. Va.). Henry, *Folk-Songs*, 329, 6d and chor. (N.C.). High, 35, 18d lines (Ark.). Randolph II, 33, 6d, m.; 5d; 8, m. (these are cowboy versions from Missouri: "The Dallas County Jail"); 6d (Ark.); refs. L. C. Record 847 A1 (Ark.) "The Dallas County Jail." For a full text and a disccussion of this piece, see Chapter VI.

E 18

ZEB TOURNEY'S GIRL

Keeping a promise made to his dying father, Dan Kelly kills all the Tourney men and brings back Zeb Tourney's daughter, whom he loves.

> It was out in the Tennessee mountains,
> Away from the sins of the world.
> There Dan Kelly's son stood leaning on his gun,
> Thinking of old Zeb Tunney's girl.

Hudson, 247, 8 (Ala.). Burt, 251, 8 (N. Mex.). Campbell, *SFQ* 3 (1939), 171, 4d (Ky.). Lomax, *Amer. Ballads*. 135, 4d, m. ("From the singing of 'Slim' Critchlow, Utah Buckaroos"). Williams, 246, 8 (Ky. "From the memory of the editor who learned it from the singing of Vernon Dalhart about ten years ago"). L. C. Record 1345 B1 (Va.).

This melodramatic and almost satiric ballad sounds suspiciously unlike a mountaineer's conception of a feud. Although it is sung in the mountains, its cleverness of phraseology and its emphasis upon local color in lines like "the moon shining down on the still" suggest that its composer was an outsider. The singer of the *SFQ* variant, however, "said the ballad originated in the mountains and concerned an actual feud, but when or where it was first sung he did not know."

E 19

J. B. MARCUM (A KENTUCKY FEUD SONG)

J. B. Marcum is shot dead in the courthouse by Curt Jett. Judge Jim Hargis's attempt to fix the Breathitt County murder jury misfires when the trial is moved to Harrison County. Jett and his accomplice Thomas White are sent to prison.

> It was on the fourth of May,
> Half past eight o'clock that day;
> J. B. Marcum was standing in the courthouse of his town,
> Where Curt Jett was lurking 'round
> Just to get a chance to lay him on the floor.

Henry, *Folk-Songs*, 333, 9 5-line sts. (Ky. via Tex.). Burt, 249, 8 6-line sts. (Miss. via Utah); notes. Combs, 183, 13 6-line sts and chor. (Ky.). *KFR* 5 (1959), 46, 13 6-line sts. and chor. (Ky.). L. C. Records "The J. B. Marcum Song": 1452 A (Ky.), 1521 A & B1 (Ky.), and 1718 A (O.).

This ballad, which is also called "The Hargis-Marcum Feud" or "The Hargis-Callihan Feud", is based on a killing which took place in Breathitt County, Kentucky, in 1905. (See Henry, 333-335). Combs calls the piece an adaptation of "Jesse James."

E 20

THE ROWAN COUNTY CREW (TROUBLE, OR TRAGEDY)

(A Tolliver-Martin Feud Song)

This ballad gives a long and involved account of the Tolliver-Martin feud. John Martin, Floyd Tolliver, Sol Bradley, and a deputy sheriff named Baumgartner are killed. Still the "war" continues. The ballad ends with a warning against strong drink and pistols.

> Come on all young men and ladies, mothers and fathers, too,
> I'll relate to you the hist'ry of the Rowan County Crew,
> Concerning bloody Rowan and her many heinous deeds,
> Now friends please give attention, remember how it reads.

Thomas, *Devil's Ditties*, 148, 14d, m. (Ky. Author's text). Cox, 203, 8½d (W. Va.); notes. Henry, *Folk-Songs*, 331, 13d (Tenn.). Lomax, *Our Singing Country*, 324, 11d, m. (Tex.). Randolph II, 160, 14d, m. (Ark.). L. C. Records 3293 B1 (Wis.); 2847 B1 (N.C.); 1585 B1 (Ky.); 1691 A1 (O.); 2936 B4 (Tenn.); 1016 A1 (Ky. Sung by "Jilson Setters" or James W. Day, the author).

For a good account of this feud, condensed from Mutzenberg's *Kentucky's Famous Feuds and Tragedies*, see James Watt Raine's *The Land of Saddle Bags*, 150-158. Another account is given in *Ballad Makin'*, 1-5. Miss Thomas says that the author of the ballad, James William Day, "sang his ballad for me in that same courthouse yard in Morehead, in the fall of 1936, standing in the selfsame spot where he had stood as a young man the day the 'troubles' started". (*Ballad Makin'*, 4). The shootings took place in 1884.

Cox's "A West-Virginia Feud Song", 205-206, is "a reworking of this song to fit a similar occurrence." (Cox, 203.)

E 21

HARVEY LOGAN

Harvey attracts the attention of the police when he gets into a fight while gambling. He is arrested after a gun battle but escapes from the Knoxville jail by using the jailer as hostage and riding away on the sheriff's horse.

> On one Saturday evenin',
> Just around the hour of two,
> Harvey Logan and his partner
> Was playin' a game of pool,
> O my babe, my honey babe.

Lomax, *Our Singing Country*, 326, 9, m. (Ky. from L. C. Record 1548 A2). Morris, 91, 13 (Fla.); notes.

Harvey Logan was born in Missouri, became a cowboy and later the leader of a notorious gang of outlaws and bank robbers. The ballad recounts his escape from jail in Knoxville, Tennessee, in 1903. Logan committed suicide in 1904 to avoid recapture after being wounded by the police. For a detailed account, see "The Gunman That Jails Couldn't Hold," by Edward H. Smith, *Coronet*, July, 1951, pp. 85-89.

E 22

DANIEL SULLIVAN

When he was a baby, Daniel's mother dreamed of him hanging on a gallows tree in a foreign country. Now that he has stabbed "a nice young man," to death, he is lonely and penitent. He writes to a brother in Liverpool, thinks of his sister and his sweetheart, and asks to be buried beside young O'Brien. He sends farewell to his family from the gallows.

> My name is Daniel Sullivan, I am a righteous man;
> I write a saucy warning, pray take no knife in hand;
> I write a saucy warning, for all young men to mind;
> When you get into a passion, I pray remember mine.

Barry, *Bulletin*, no. 11 (1936), p. 10, 7d, m. (Me.). Beck, *The Folklore of Maine*, 254, 2d, m. (Me.) plus 4 sts. from Barry.

According to Horace P. Beck's informant, Mark Lodge of Danforth, Maine, Daniel Sullivan, a lumberjack from Liverpool, Nova Scotia, was hanged for murder about 1890. (Note from "Down-East Ballads and Songs", unpub. diss., Phila., 1952, p. 226).

E 23

HOWARD CAREY

Howard leaves his aged parents, and despite his mother's warnings against wickedness falls into a life of sin. Saying that whiskey and bad women have doomed him, he hangs himself in a cell at Rumford Falls.

> My name is Howard Carey, in Grand Falls I was born,
> In a pretty little cottage on the banks of the St. John,
> Where the small birds chant their notes so fine, and
>   the trembling waters roar
> And that ivy vine does thickly twine around our cottage door.

Ives, *JAF* 72 (1959), 62, 17d, m. (Me.). Mr. Ives reports the existence of five other texts from N.H., Me., and N.B.

This is another of the ballads tentatively attributed to Joe Scott, along with "Guy Read," (C 9), "Benjamin Deane," (F 32), and "The Plain Golden Band" (H 17). For a detailed discussion, see Edward D. Ives, " 'Ben Deane' and Joe Scott: a Ballad and its Probable Author," *JAF* 72 (1959), 53-66.

E 24

FRANK DUPREE

Frank goes into an Atlanta jewelry store and steals a diamond. In the street outside he shoots a policeman dead and escapes in a flivver. When he returns to see Betty, his sweetheart, he is arrested and sentenced to death.

> I want my buddies and all my friends
> To take this warning from me;
> Stop your drinking, buddies, and live like men;
> Don't live as Frank Dupree.

Morris, 87, 8 (learned indirectly from a phonograph record); 6 (Fla.); notes. Brown II, 570, 7 (N.C.).

"In substantiating the history of this song, Mr. B. Graham West, comptroller for the city of Atlanta, wrote: 'On December 15, 1921, Dupree entered a jewelry store in Atlanta and snatched a diamond ring and, in his attempt to escape, he killed a policeman. . . . Dupree escaped and, after a chase through several states, was captured in Detroit, Michigan. He was returned to Atlanta, tried, convicted, and sentenced to be hanged. Dupree was the last man in Georgia to be hanged, as all subsequent executions have been by electrocution.'" (For further details, including the shooting of Mr. West, see Morris, p. 89).

Morris observes that his B text displays more folk quality than the A text, which is close to that of the original phonograph recording.

Professor D. K. Wilgus informs me that "Frank Dupree" was composed by Andrew Jenkins and is sung by him on Okeh record #40446B. See the note to "Floyd Collins."

See also the Negro ballad "Dupree" (I 11).

E 25

MUFF LAWLER, THE SQUEALER

Muff Lawler goes to the lawyers' office and says he can tell all about both the dead and the living members of the gang, but he is afraid of being shot when he returns to Shenandoah. The lawyers offer to send him to a country where he is not so well known.

> When Muff Lawler was in jail right bad did he feel,
> He thought divil the rooster would he ever heel,
> "Bejabers," says Lawler, "I think I will squeal."
> "Yes, do," says the judge to Muff Lawler.

Korson, Penna. Songs, 399, 5d, m .(Pa. from a L. C. Record); notes.

Michael Lawler, called "Muff" because he raised "mufflers", or fighting cocks, was the leader of the "Molly Maguires", a band of criminals, in Shenandoah, Penna. In 1876 he was convicted of murder but was saved from death by turning state's evidence. (Note from Korson, *Penna. Songs,* p. 398).

Four more ballads about the Molly Maguires are listed in Appendix II, E.

E 26

THE MURDER OF F. C. BENWELL

Birchell tells of luring Benwell to his death, of pretending innocence during his trial, and of being sentenced to hang. His wife bids him a sad farewell, and he dies on the gallows.

> Come all you tender Christians, wherever you may be,
> And kindly pay attention to these few words from me.
> On the fourteenth of November I am condemned to die,
> For the murder of F. C. Berwill, upon the gallows high.

Burt, 228, 5d and chor. (Utah); notes. Pound, 148, 4d and chor. (Neb.); notes. Spaeth, *Weep Some More,* 135, 5d and chor.

Miss Pound's informant wrote: "A young man by the name of Bendall . . . came to Canada about the year 1890 and settled near St. Thomas, Ontario. He soon made friends with . . . J. J. Birchell. Birchell, knowing that Bendall carried much gold on his person, enticed him out on a hunting expedition and very coolly shot him. The lines of *Young Bendall* were composed and set to music by a young school teacher in the neighborhood where the tragedy took place." Mrs. Burt gives the date as 1861 and the names of the men as J. R. Birchell and F. S. Benwell.

Like "Ewing Brooks" (E 12) this is closely related in phraseology to "Charles Guiteau" (E 11).

MURDER BALLADS

F 1   The Jealous Lover
F 2   Pearl Bryan I
F 3   Pearl Bryan III
F 4   Poor Omie
F 5   On the Banks of the Ohio
F 6   Rose Connoley
F 7   Grace Brown and Chester Gillette
F 8   The Brookfield Murder
F 9   The Murder of Sarah Vail
F 10   Lula Viers
F 11   Ellen Smith
F 12   Murdered by a Brother
F 13   McAfee's Confession
F 14   Henry Green
F 15   Nat Goodwin
F 16   Fuller and Warren
F 17   The Vance Song
F 18   Jim Fisk
F 19   Floyd Frazier
F 20   Mary Phagan
F 21   Suncook Town Tragedy
F 22   Poor Goins
F 23   John Funston
F 24   The Peddler and His Wife
F 25-F 27   The Ashland Tragedy, I, II, and III
F 28-F 30   The Meeks Family Murder, I, II and III

F 31   Naomi Wise
F 32   Benjamin Deane
F 33   Marian Parker
F 34   Emma Hartsell
F 35   The Lawson Murder
F 36   The Murder of Laura Foster
F 37   Stella Kenny

F 1

THE JEALOUS LOVER A (FLORELLA, FLOELLA)

Lured into the woods on the pretext of making wedding plans, innocent Florella is fatally stabbed by her angry and jealous fiancé, Edward, who is later imprisoned for life.

Deep. deep in yonder valley
Where the violets always bloom,
There sleeps my own Florella,
So silent in the tomb.

Down on her knees before him
She pleaded for her life.
Into her snow-white bosom
He plunged the fatal knife.

Hudson, 185, 11 (st. 1 is given above) ; 186, 5 (st. 4 is given above) (Miss.). Belden, 325, 9 (Mo.) ; Belden describes 17 other texts in his collection. See for notes and for refs. to texts from Nfld., N.S., Ont., N.H., Vt., Mass., Pa., W. Va., Ky., Tenn., Miss., Ark., Mo., Ill., Mich., Ia., Neb., and Wyo. Brown II, 578, texts of 10, 9, 12, 13, and 5d stanzas and fragments (N.C.) ; notes and refs. *CFB* I (1962), no. 1, p. 14, 5 sts.; I, no. 2, p. 15, 9, m.; II (1963), p. 11, 10, m. (Colo.). Doerflinger, 287, 4½d, m. (N.B.). Hubbard, 68, 7; 8; 10 (Utah). *Kansas Folklore*, 179, 8 m. (Kan.). Leach, 787, text from *JAF* 22 (1909), 370; 10 (Va.). Lomax, *FSNA*, 93, 7, m. Morris, 76, 10, m.; 9 (Fla.). Owens, 100, 11, m. (Tex.). Randolph II, 45, texts, some with tunes, from Mo. and Ark, of 12, 8, 8, 7, 10, 8, and 10 sts.; refs. Williams, 133, 7 (Ky.). *WF* 17 (1958), 235, 4d, m. (Ia.).

L. C. Records 1748 B (Ky. "Floella") ; 1544 A2 (Ky.) and 1547 B2 (Ky.) ; 3028 A1 (Miss.) ; 3203 A1 (Mo.).

Nothing certain is known about the origin of this piece, which is one of the most popular of all white ballads apparently native to this country. Barry has attempted to show that it is a reworking of the 19th century English broadside "The Murder of Betsy Smith" (*AS*, III, 441-447). For a discussion of Barry's article, see Chapter III.

THE JEALOUS LOVER B (PEARL BRYAN II)

In this variant the names of Pearl Bryan and Scott Jackson appear.

Way down in yonder valley
Where the violets fade and bloom,
Our own Pearl Bryan slumbers
In a cold and silent tomb.

And while the birds were singing
So gaily all around,
A stranger found Pearl Bryan,
Cold, headless, on the ground.

Brewster, 286, 12 (Ind.); the first and last sts. are given above. Brown II, 588, 7 (N.C.); notes. Burt, 31, 1 (Utah). Cox, 200, 4½d; 4½d (W. Va.). Morris, 79, 4d (Fla.). Neely and Spargo, 158, 7d, m. (Ill.).

THE JEALOUS LOVER C (NELL CROPSEY II)

The ballad is altered again to apply to a North Carolina murder.

Look down in the low green valley
Where the violets bloom and fade,
'Tis there my sweet Nellie Cropsey
Lies moldering in the grave.

Chappell, 115, 12; 2½, m.; 2, m. (N.C.); notes.

F 2

PEARL BRYAN I

Pearl Bryan leaves home to meet her lover, who, with an accomplice, drives her to Kentucky, where she is decapitated. Her body is found the next day. Some versions depict the girl's sister asking the murderer for her head and describe the trial and sentencing of the criminals.

Now, ladies, if you'll listen, a story I'll relate
What happened near Fort Thomas in the old Kentucky state.
'Twas late in January this awful deed was done
By Jackson and by Walling; how cold their blood did run!

Brewster, 285, 6d (reprinted by Leach, 789); 13; 1d, m. (Ind.); historical notes. Burt, 31, 4d. Henry, *Folk-Songs*, 209, 16 (Ga.). *SFQ* 3 (1939), 17, 9 (W. Va.). Williams, 130, 6d (Ky.).

Pearl Bryan, of Greencastle, Indiana, was murdered by Scott Jackson, the father of her unborn child, and his accomplice, Alonzo Walling. Pearl's headless body was found near Fort Thomas, Kentucky, February 1, 1896. The murderers were executed March 20, 1897. (Notes from Ann Scott Wilson, "Pearl Bryan", *SFQ* III (1939), 15-16.

Students of the ballad have persistently confused this piece with "The Jealous Lover" (See Cox, 198-202; Brewster, 283-289; Wilson, *Loc. cit.*; Henry, *Folk-Songs*, 209-214). This ballad reports the actual circumstances of the crime. Some variants of the older piece are entitled "Pearl Bryan", but in these the names of the girl and her murderer are late interpolations.

F 3

PEARL BRYAN III

Pearl goes to Jackson for aid, but he and his friend plot to take her life and carry out their design.

> In Greencastle lived a maiden,
> She was known the wide world o'er;
> She was murdered by Scott Jackson
> Whom she fondly did adore.

Eddy, 242, 6 (O. from ms.). Henry, *Folk-Songs*, 212, 4d (Ky.).

F 4

POOR OMIE (JOHN LEWIS)

(Little Omie Wise)

At first John tells Omie he will marry her to avoid disgrace, but later he reveals that he intends to drown her. Despite her pleas and her offer to go begging, he throws her into the river. When her body is discovered, John goes to jail for murder.

> I'll tell you a story of little Oma Wise,
> How she got drowned by John Lewis' lie.
> He told her to meet him at the Adams' Springs,
> Some money he would bring her and other fine things.

Henry, *Folk-Songs*, 227, 4d (Tenn.); 221, 15 (Tenn.); 15 (N.C.); 13 (N.C.); 228, 10 (Va.). Belden, 322, 8d couplets (Mo.); 9d (Kan.); notes and refs. to texts from Ky., Tenn., N.C., and Miss. Brown II, 692-695, 8d; 7d; add. sts. N.C.). Burt, 25, 8, m. (Pa.); 2 (Utah); notes and refs. Carmer, 84, 4d, m. Gordon, 11, 18 (N.C.). High, 37, 18d lines (Ark.). *KFR* I (1955), frag. of 4 sts. (Ky. from ms.). Leach, 797, texts from Belden, and *JAF* 20, 265. Lomax, *FSNA*, 268, 13 ("As sung by G. B. Grayson on Amer. Folk Music Folkways Disc. no. 13"). Morris, 85, 7, m. (Fla.). Randolph II, 86, 16; 13 (Mo.); shorter versions from Ark. and Mo.; notes and refs. to texts from Ohio and the South. Williams, 146, 10 (Ky.). *WVF* 7 (1957), 61, 13d couplets (W. Va.). L. C. Records 2829 A1 (Va.) and 2857 B3 (N.C.) "Little Omie Wise"; 57 B1 (Tex.) "Poor Omie Wise"; and other Southern recordings.

Jonathan Lewis was accused of drowning his former sweetheart, Naomi Wise, in Deep River, Randolph County, North Carolina, in 1808. He escaped from jail and was later recaptured, tried, and acquitted. For detailed notes and refs. see Brown II, 690.

For another ballad on the same murder, see "Naomi Wise" (F 31).

F 5

ON THE BANKS OF THE OHIO

A young man drowns the girl he loves, after threatening her with a knife, apparently because she wishes to abide by her mother's decision that she is too young to marry.

> I asked my love to take a walk
> Just to be alone with me,
> And as we walked we'd have a talk
> About our wedding day to be.
>
> I took her by the pale white hand,
> Led her to the river brink;
> There I threw her in to drown,
> Stood and watched her float on down.

Henry, *Folk-Songs*, 220, 5 and chor. (N.C.); stanzas 1 and 4 are given above; 3 and chor. (N.C.). *CFB* II (1963), p. 7, 6, m. (Colo.); p. 8, 4, m. (Colo. "On the Banks of the Old Bayou"). Eddy, 223, 2d, m .(O. "On the Banks of the Old Pedee"). Gardner, 80, 6 (Mich. "On the Banks of the River Dee"); refs. Henry, *Songs Sung*, 76, 3 and chor. (N.C.). Pound, 108, 5 (from ms. "The Old Shawnee"). Randolph II, 137, 4, m.; 1; 5½, m. (Ark.). *WF* 17 (1958), 235, 4, m. (Ia.).

The history of this piece has not been traced, but its similarity to certain English broadsides has been pointed out.

F 6

ROSE CONNOLEY

The narrator has murdered Rose by poisoning her with wine and then running a "skeever" through her. His father had told him that his money would free his son if he were to kill the girl, but the youth is about to die on the scaffold.

> Rose Connoley loved me as dearly as she loved her life,
> And many's the time I've told her I'd make her my lawful wife.
> But Satan and Satan's temptation have overpowered me,
> And caused me to murder that fair young maid they called
>   Rose Connoley.

Cox, 314, 4½d; 5d couplets (W. Va.). Brown II, 249, 6 (N.C.); add. sts. Davis, *Folk Songs*, lists 2 Va. texts of 8 sts each. Kirkland, "A Check List", *JAF* 59 (1946), 461, lists "Rose Conna Lee." Lomax, *Folk Song U.S.A.*, 302, 3d, m. ("Down in the Willow Garden"); reprinted in Lomax, *FSNA*, 267. Treat, *JAF* 52 (1939), 24, 4, m. (Ky. via Wis.) *WVF* 7 (1957), 64, 8 (W. Va.). L. C. Record 1401A2 (Ky.).

F 7

GRACE BROWN AND CHESTER GILLETTE

Having been found guilty of drowning his former sweetheart, Gillette awaits execution. The narrator reflects on the grief of the two mothers involved, comments on the tragic ending of the love affair, and visualizes the fatal boating excursion.

> The dreams of the happy is finished,
> The scores are brought in at last;
> A jury has brought in its verdict,
> The sentence on Gillette is passed.

Thompson, 444, 10 (N.Y.). Burt, 32, 10, m. (notes).

The girl was killed at Big Moose in the Adirondacks, July 11, 1906. This murder became the basis of Dreiser's *An American Tragedy*. (Notes from Thompson, 443, 523).

F 8

THE BROOKFIELD MURDER

Cook shoots Susan Heston from outside her home. Her mother and brother are shocked by the discovery of her body. The ballad ends with a warning to young ladies to "shun such reptiles" as Buzzell.

> The Brookfield murder has come to light,
> By a young man rather short of sight;
> Joe Buzzell he hired and drove young Cook,
> To shoot the girl, so it seems to look.

Linscott, 175, 7, m. (N.H.). This text is used by Earl Rogers on a phonograph record in Musicraft Album #M68.

Angered by Miss Hanson's suit for breach of promise, Joseph Buzzell hired a half-wit, Charles Cook, to kill her. Later he changed his mind but was too late to prevent the murder. The crime took place in New Hampshire in 1847. Buzzell was hanged and Cook was imprisoned for life. (Note from Linscott).

F 9

THE MURDER OF SARAH VAIL

John Monroe, the married father of two children, makes love to Miss Vail, who at length has a child by him. He takes the girl and her baby on a trip, murders them, and hides their bodies. When the crime is discovered, Monroe is sentenced to hang.

> Come all you people lend an ear,
> A dreadful story you shall hear.
> This murderous deed was done of late
> In eighteen hundred and sixty-eight.

Flanders-Barry, 221, 10, m. (Me. via Vt.).

The murders were committed in St. John, New Brunswick, on October 31, 1868. Monroe was hanged in February, 1870. The ballad has also been reported from Bucksport, Maine. (Notes from Flanders-Barry, 223. See for further details).

See also "John A. Munroe" (Appendix II).

F 10

LULA VIERS

John Coyer throws Lula, his fiancée, into the river with a piece of steel tied around her. Her body is discovered several months later. Coyer is arrested, but is turned over to Army authorities before standing trial.

> Come all you good people
> From all over the world;
> And listen to a story
> About a poor young girl.

Thomas, *Ballad Makin'*, 144, 22 (Ky.). *KFR* 2 (1956), 60, 9d (Ky.). L. C. Records 288A and 1456 A 3 (Ky).

For a full text of this ballad with some discussion, see Chapter V.

F 11

ELLEN SMITH

Peter says that he has been falsely accused of murdering his sweetheart. He tells of being captured and sentenced to hang, and he adds, "My soul will be free when I stand at the bar".

> I choked back my tears for the people all said
> That Peter Degraph had shot Ellen Smith dead!
> My love is in her grave with her hand on her breast
> The bloodhound and sheriff won't give me no rest.

Richardson, 32, 10, m (Stanza 6 is given above). Combs, 219, 18 (Ky.); in this version the accused man marries after the murder. Fuson, 132, a 14-line fragment from Ky. in which the speaker admits his guilt. Henry, *Folk-Songs*, 315, a fragment from N.C. Refs. Hudson, 193, 7 (Miss.). Williams, 139, 5 (Ky.).*WVF* 7 (1957), 65, 4½d (W. Va.). L. C. Records 2891 B3 (Tenn.) and 2745 B1 (Va.) "Poor Ellen Smith"; 822 B2 (Ky.

via N.Y.); 1823 A (N.Y. Sung by B. L. Lunsford); 1707 B (Ohio); and four more Southern recordings.

"Peter Degraph did really shoot and kill Ellen Smith (according to the verdict) near Mount Airy, North Carolina. He was executed for the crime, and while he waited for them to take him to the chair he called for a guitar and this song was composed and sung by him. So great was the feeling, for and against Degraph, that it had to be declared a misdemeanor for the song to be sung in a gathering of any size for the reason that it always fomented a riot." (Note from Richardson, 106). The date of the murder is not given.

F 12

MURDERED BY A BROTHER

The brother takes his sister out in a skiff. He denounces her for having brought dishonor on the family and says that he will be revenged on her. After telling her that he has already drowned her lover, he drowns her and rows back alone.

> "Oh come from out the chamber
> In sadness and its gloom,
> And look abroad on nature
> Its beauty and its gloom,
> The air is clad with verdure,
> Music on ev'ry tree.
> Come forth, my sister Helen,
> Come forth and walk with me."

Flanders-Barry, 92, 9d, m. (Vt. Sung by Josiah S. Kennison). L. C. Record 3748 B (Vt. Sung by Kennison).

For comments on this piece with a discussion of ballads with related themes, see Flanders-Barry, 94. The editors say, "Of its history nothing is known; nor has it to our knowledge been recorded by any previous collector."

F 13

McAFEE'S CONFESSION

Orphaned at an early age, McAfee is reared by a kindly uncle. He is a wayward youth, however, and eventually runs away. Having married a good woman, McAfee falls in love with Hettie Stout and decides to kill his wife. On the pretext of giving her medicine, he poisons her as she lies in bed with their baby. As his time of execution nears, the murderer warns young men to live righteously.

> Come all young men and learn of me,
> My sad and mournful history,
> And may you ne'er forgetful be,
> Of all this day I tell to thee.

Belden, 320, 18, m. (Mo. from print) ; 318, 10d (Ind. from ms.). The editor mentions five other versions in his collection. Burt, 22, 17 (Ore.). Eddy, 289, 18 (Ohio). *Kansas Folklore*, 175, 15, m. (Kan.). Leach and Beck, *JAF* 63 (1950), 266, 8½, m. (Va.). Morris, 73, 14 (Fla.). Randolph, II, 27, 10d (Mo. from ms.) ; and two other texts; refs. L. C. Records 1716 A (Ohio) ; 63 A1 (Tex. "Hattie Stout").

John McAfee was found guilty of the murder of his wife and was hanged near Dayton, Ohio, March 28, 1825. (Note from Belden, who gives further details and a dozen references to other texts from nine Southern and Midwestern states).

F 14

HENRY GREEN (THE MURDERED WIFE)

Rich Henry threatens suicide if Mary, who is poor, will not marry him. After a week's marriage, Henry poisons her. She dies forgiving him. He is found guilty and is sentenced to die late in the fall.

> Come listen to my tragedy,
> Good people, young and old;
> I'll tell you of a story
> 'Twill make your blood run cold,
> Concerning a fair damsel,
> Miss Wyatt was her name,
> She was murdered by her husband
> And he hung for the same.

Flanders and Brown, 65, 12d, m. (Vt.). Belden, 321, 3d (Mo.). *Bulletin* no. 12 (1937), 16, 10d, m. (Vt.) ; reprinted by Leach, p. 792. Carmer, 25, 4d, m. Gardner, 346, 11d, m.; 1 (Mich.). Leach and Beck, *JAF* 63 (1950), 268, 13½, m. (Va.). Morris, 131, 8d, m. (Fla.). Randolph II, 121, 4d, m. (same source as Belden's) ; 6d (Mo.) ; 9½d (Ark.). Thompson, 442, 11½d (N.Y.). L. C. Records 1776 B1 (N.J. "Miss Wyatt, 1848") ; 3702 B (N.H. "Young Henery and Miss Ryatt").

The murder story is also told in a different broadside ballad of 24d sts. See *Bulletin* no. 12, frontispiece. This text is reprinted by Burt, p. 8.

Henry G. Green of Berlin, Rensselaer County, New York, who was infatuated with another woman, poisoned his bride, Mary Ann Wyatt Green, in February, 1845. He was hanged in September .(For a complete account see L. C. Jones, "The Berlin Murder Case in Folklore and Ballad", *New York History* XVII (1936), 192-205. Or see Jones' article in *Bulletin* no. 12, 14-18, to which Barry adds a long note.

F 15
NAT GOODWIN

A young mother, lying ill, is denied one last look at the baby who has died after being taken from her. When she recovers, her husband turns her out of the house. After offering to take her back, he becomes infatuated with another woman. He then kills his wife and is convicted of murder when the second woman testifies against him.

> In the little town of Wellsboro,
> Take heed to what I say,
> Close at death door a fair young wife
> On a bed of sickness lay . . .

Gardner, 349, 7d (Pa. via Mich.).

Walter Goodwin's wife was shot September 3, 1897, at Wellsboro, Pennsylvania, and her husband was hanged the following May. The ballad has been ascribed both to the accused man, who may not have done the shooting, and to a woman in a neighboring community. (See Gardner for further details).

F 16
FULLER AND WARREN

Fuller falls in love with and becomes engaged to a young woman who soon announces her intention of marrying Warren. Accusing Warren of having told the girl that he had deserted a wife, Fuller kills him and is hanged.

> You sons of Columbia, your attention I crave
> While a sorrowful story I will tell
> Which happened of late in Indiana State,
> And a hero not many to excel.

Belden, 303, 11; 16 (Mo.); 307, 7 (Kan.); see for details and for refs. to texts from N. B. via Me., Me., W. Va., Miss., Tex., Ark., Mich., and Neb. Brewster, 363, 12; 8d (Ind.). Burt, 51, 11, m. (Ind.). Hubbard, 72, 12 (Utah). Musick, *JAF* 60 (1947), 222, 12 (Ill. from ms.). Randolph, II, 73, 10, m. (Mo.) and fragments; see 72 for refs. L. C. Records 3813 A2 & 3 (Cal.), 864 B (Ark.), 1736 B (Ind.), 1328 A2 (Tex. "Warren and Fuller").

Enraged because Palmer Warren had gained the affections of his fiancée, Amasa Fuller shot him dead at Lawrenceburg, Indiana, on January 10, 1820. The sensational case was closed when Fuller was hanged the following summer. (For detailed accounts of the crime and a discussion of the ballad, see Barry, *Bulletin* no. 8 (1934), 12-13 and no. 9 (1935), 14-17).

Tradition attributes this ballad, with its many Biblical allusions, to an Indiana artist and versifier named Moses Whitecotton. (See Brewster, 363-364).

F 17

THE VANCE SONG

Condemned to die for murder, Vance lashes out at the men who have caused him to be unjustly sentenced. He regrets that he must leave the countryside he loves, and he bids farewell to his family.

> Green are the woods where Sandy flows,
> And peace it dwelleth there;
> In the valley the bear they lie secure,
> The red buck roves the knobs.

Cox, 208, 12 (from a slip printed about 1897); 13 (W. Va.); 211, frag. of 4 sts. (Ky.). Carmer, 119, 4, m. Finger, 81, 13. Hudson, 246, 4 (Miss.). Lomax, *Our Singing Country*, 322, 7, m. Ky. Text and tune from L. C. Record 1592 B1). E. J. Sutherland, "Vance's Song," *SFQ* 4 (1940), 252, 5½d; 7½d (Va.); notes.

"Some hundred years ago, Abner Vance, a Baptist preacher, was hanged at Abington, Virginia, for the killing of Lewis Horton, who had abused Vance's family in his absence. . . . After conviction Vance lay in prison for some time, during which he made a ballad about himself". (Note from Cox, 207, who obtained these details from Vance's great-grandson and who gives similar material from other sources).

F 18

JIM FISK

After speaking of the advantage which rich defendants have in court, the ballad praises Fisk who "never went back on the poor". It speaks of his generosity in sending food to the fire victims in Chicago, and expresses the fear that his wealthy murderer will go free.

> With his grand six-in-hand on the beach at Long Branch
> He cut a big dash, to be sure;
> But Chicago's great fire showed the world that Jim Fisk
> With his wealth still remembered the poor.

Belden, 415, equiv. of 11 sts. (Kan. from ms. St. 8 is given above); notes and refs. to texts from Vt. and Minn. Flanders-Barry, 213, 5½d (Vt.); notes. Sandburg, 416, 4d and refrains, m. (O.); notes. L. C. Records 3755 B (Vt. the text printed in Flanders-Barry); 2332 B2 (Mich.).

James Fisk was shot by Edward Stokes, "his rival for the affections of the actress Josie Mansfield", in the Grand Central Hotel, New York, January 6, 1872. (Note from Belden, 415). Fisk had dispatched "a trainload of food-stuffs for the relief of the Chicago fire sufferers". Stokes, who "was actually penniless," was "finally convicted of manslaughter, for which he served four

years in the New York State Prison". (Notes from Flanders-Barry, 215).
This ballad "is built upon an older homiletic, 'Remember the Poor', of
which there are several copies in the Harvard Library". (Belden, 415).

"A sheet-music copy, 'Jim Fisk, or He Never Went Back on the Poor',
published by F. W. Helmick (Cincinnati, Ohio, copyright, 1874), is inscribed
'Written and sung by William J. Scanlon'." (Note from Flanders-Barry,
215.)

F 19

FLOYD FRAZIER (ELLEN FLANNERY)

Floyd kills Ellen Flannery and hides her body in the woods. The next day,
when neighbors hear her five hungry children crying, a search is started,
and her body is found under a pile of rocks. Floyd is arrested, admits the
crime, and is pronounced guilty.

> Come you people of every nation,
> And listen to my mournful song;
> I will tell you of a circumstance
> Which happened not very long.
>
> Floyd Frazier is now in prison,
> And ought to hang-ed be,
> For the killing of an innocent woman,
> This world may plainly see.

Combs, 179, 16 (Ky.). L. C. Records 1389 A2 (Ky.) and the following
under the title "Ellen Flannery": 2782 B1, 2781 B1, and 2813 A2 (Va.).
The history of this ballad has not been traced.

F 20

MARY PHAGAN

Mary Phagan is beaten to death in the pencil factory by Leo Frank. An
innocent Negro watchman is at first arrested for the crime. Later Frank
is tried and condemned to death.

> Little Mary Fagen,
> She went to town one day:
> She went to the pencil factory
> To get her weekly pay.

Henry, *Folk-Songs*, 336, 13 (Tenn. "Leo Frank and Mary Phagan");
refs. Arnold, 74, 5d, m. (Ala.). Brown II, 598, 7d; 5; 9 (N.C.); notes.
Burt, 61, 5d, m. (Utah); 6 (Ga.); add. sts.; notes. Cambiaire, 104, 4d.
Eddy, 252, 4 (O.). Gardner, 352, 5 (Va. via Mich.). Morris, 81, 17; 10
(Fla.). *JAF* 31 (1918), 264, 20 (Ala.). Carter, *JAF* 46 (1933), 39, 6 (Tenn.
"Little Mary Phagan"). R. M. Schmitz, "Leo Frank and Mary Phagan,"

JAF 60 (1947), 59, 14 (Ky.); full notes. *SFQ* 24 (1960), 7; 11½ (S.C.).
WVF 7 (1957), 65, 8d (W. Va.). L. C. Records 3415 A2 (Wash., D.C.);
1411 A (Ky.); 1812 B2 (N.Y. Sung by B. L. Lunsford); 2876 A2 (Tenn.).

"Little Mary Phagan is a new ballad based on the murder of Mary Phagan
on Aug. 5, 1913 in The National Pencil Co. factory, Atlanta, Ga. Leo M.
Frank and Jas. Conley were suspected of the murder. On Aug. 26, 1913,
Leo Frank was found guilty of murder and sentenced to death, but many
believed him innocent and there was widespread protest. . . . On June 22,
1915, Gov. Slaton commuted Frank's sentence to a life term. On the 17th of
the following August a mob kidnapped Leo Frank from the Ga. State Prison
Farm and lynched him." (Note from Carter, *JAF* 46 (1933), 39-40).

Kirkland, "A Check List . . . of Tennessee Folksongs" *JAF* 59 (1946),
449, lists a broadside under the title "Little Mary Phagon."

F 21

SUNCOOK TOWN TRAGEDY (JOSIE LANGMAID)

Josie is ambushed and brutally slain by LePage while on her way to
school. Her father and brother search for her and find her mangled body.
The murderer is tried at Concord and is sentenced to hang.

> Come all young people, now draw near;
> Attend awhile and you shall hear,
> How a young person of renown
> Was murdered in fair Suncook town.

Flanders & Brown, 72, 9, m. (Vt.). Burt, 57, 3, m. (Vt.).

Josie Langmaid, a student at Pembroke Academy, was murdered in New
Hampshire on October 4, 1875, by a degenerate named Joseph LePage. A
copy of the original broadside is in Phillips Barry's collection. (Note from
Barry, *Bulletin* no. 4 (1932), 20).

Mrs. Burt reports that the N. H. Historical Society has a book on this
case entitled *The Murdered Maiden Student* (1878), as well as the trial
records and newspaper accounts.

F 22

POOR GOINS

Pretending to help Goins escape from bandits, Boggs leads him into their
hands. One of the robbers clubs Goins to death after a rifle shot has caused
the victim's horse to bolt.

> Come all you good people
> That live far and near;
> And I'll tell you of the murder
> That was done on the nine mile spur.

> They surrounded poor Goins
> But Goins got away,
> He went to Ely Boggs's
> He went there to stay.

Thomas, *Ballad Makin'*, 138, 6d (Ky.). Combs, 195, 3d sts. and 3d couplets (Ky.). Kittredge, *JAF* 30 (1917), 361, 9d couplets, m. (Ky.); reprinted by Pound, 118. L. C. Records 2771 A1 and 1748 A1 (Ky.).

In *Ballad Makin'*, p. 138, Goins is described as a horse trader who "made trips along the Clinch and Powell Rivers in Virginny." He was first trapped "on Calahan Creek near the foot of Black Mountain."

˙ F 23

JOHN FUNSTON

John Funston murders and robs William Cartmell on a country road. At first an innocent passerby is held. Later John spends the stolen money too freely and is arrested, tried, and convicted. The latter stanzas recount the events preceding the hanging. Two doctors want to steal the body, but John's little brothers have come with a carriage to claim it.

> John Funston, a youth about twenty years old,
> His courage undaunted, he stood firm and bold;
> He was tall, fair, and handsome, fair hair and blue eyes;
> He sought his own ruin by seeking a prize.

Eddy, 269, 9, m.; 268, 9 (O.). Burt, 81, 6, m.; notes.

The murder took place in Tuscarawas County, Ohio, on September 9, 1825. (See Eddy, 270-271 for details).

F 24

THE PEDDLER AND HIS WIFE

Ambushed while riding in their wagon, the peddler and his wife are murdered and robbed.

> One day the sun was rising high,
> A day in merry June;
> The birds set singing on a tree,
> All nature seems in tune.
>
> A peddler and his wife were travelling
> Along a lonely way,
> A-sharing each other's toil and care,
> They both were old and grey.

Fuson, 116, 7 (Ky.). Cambiaire, 9, 7 sts. Combs, 193, 7 (Ky. "The Irish Peddler"). Henry, *Folk-Songs*, 330, 7 (Ky.). L. C. Record 1405 A1 (Ky.).

"They were robbed and killed on Martin's Fork, of Cumberland River,

Harlan County, Kentucky, about twenty-five years ago". (Note from Fuson, 116).

F 25

THE ASHLAND TRAGEDY I

For details of this crime, see the following piece.

> Dear father, mother, sister, come listen while I tell
> All about the Ashland tragedy, of which you know full well.
> 'Twas in the town of Ashland, all on that deadly night,
> A horrible crime was committed, but soon was brought to light.

Cox, 189, 14d (W. Va. Learned from a printed copy about 1888). Burt, 58, 13d (Mo. via Utah); notes.

One of Cox's informants, who had witnessed the execution of Craft and Neal, said that Elijah Adams, the author of this piece, had a *stack* of ballads on the day of the hanging . . . and sold them as fast as three men could hand them out. (Cox, 189. But see the following ballad).

F 26

THE ASHLAND TRAGEDY II

Two little girls, Fanny Gibbons and her friend, are attacked and murdered by Ellis Craft, William Neal, and George Ellis, who break into the Gibbons house at night. After murdering Fanny's brother, Bobby, the men attempt to fire the house. Ellis is lynched. The other felons are hanged later, but not before three Ashland men have been shot dead by soldiers guarding the criminals.

> Come people dear from far and wide,
> And lend a willing ear to me.
> While I relate the cruel facts
> Of Ashland's greatest tragedy.

Thomas, *Ballad Makin'*, 156, 13 (Ky.); notes. 13 sts. (Ky.).

The ballad gives an accurate but necessarily condensed account of this crime and its aftermath, which occurred in Kentucky in the early 1880's. Craft and Neal were hanged in Carter County in 1884. (see Thomas and Cox, 189).

The singer credited this piece to Elijah Adam of Carter County, Kentucky. (See also the preceding piece. It is not clear which of these pieces Adams composed. Many of the events which occurred between the crime and the executions are recounted in this ballad; consequently it seems a more logical one to have distributed on the day of the hanging).

F 27

THE ASHLAND TRAGEDY III

A more imaginative and less detailed account of the murder than those given in either of the other ballads.

> Oh have you head the story,
> It happened long ago
> Of the Gibbons' children murder,
> And Emma Carico.

Thomas, *Ballad Makin'*, 160, 13 (Ky.).

Bart Blevins, who sang this and the preceding ballad, said that the piece was composed by Bill Terrell, of Gore Station, Ohio, who had "read a heap about the Ashland Tragedy." (Thomas, 159-160. See also 162).

It is unusual for an American ballad composer to recount an event "which happened long ago," especially if, as is implied here, he had no connection with it. But see "Naomi Wise" (F 31).

F 28

THE MEEKS FAMILY MURDER I

Lured away from home, Meeks, his wife and two of their children are murdered and their bodies placed under a pile of straw. A third child, Nellie, is wounded but escapes to a nearby farm to tell the story of the crime. The murderers are captured and jailed.

> About one mile from Browning town, at the foot of Jenkins' hill,
> Took place this awful murder by the Taylors, George and Bill.
> Gus Meek's wife and children were taken from the home,
> Were taken by those Taylors to meet their fatal doom.

Belden, 406, 7d (from ms.); 405, 9; 407, 6d; 3 sts. (Mo.). Burt, 232, 13, m. (Mo.); notes. Randolph II, 108, 11; 8 (Mo.).

William and George Taylor murdered the Meeks family on May 11, 1894, in order to prevent Gus Meeks from testifying against them in a cattle-stealing case. William was hanged for the murder, but his brother escaped from custody and was never recaptured. (For details and references see Belden, 404-405 and Randolph, 106-107).

This piece is said to have been composed by Arthur Wallace, a blind entertainer. Belden points out that it was made before the Taylors were captured in August, 1894.

Five ballads on this murder have been recovered. There has been some crossing over between Ballads I and IV. Ballad III may be derived from one or both of these. Ballad II is a separate piece. Ballad V is a sentimental piece related to III.

See Appendix II for ballads IV and V.

F 29

THE MEEKS FAMILY MURDER II

This tells much the same story as the preceding ballad but omits Nellie's monologue. It reports that the Taylors were convicted of first-degree murder.

'Twas in the lovely Springtime,
In the lovely month of May,
When Meeks, his wife, and children
Were induced to go away.

They were leaving, little dreaming
When they took their midnight flight,
They'd be murdered ere the morning,
In the darkness of the night.

Randolph II, 110, 10 (Mo.). Burt, 235, 3 (Mo.); 149, 1d (Cal.).
Randolph's informant said that this piece "was written by Marion Anderson, Browning, Mo., in the summer of 1894, a few weeks after the murder. . . . Mr. Anderson had it printed on little slips of paper, which he sold for ten cents, and . . . people sang it in that vicinity for many years afterward."

F 30

THE MEEKS FAMILY MURDER III

A short ballad in the first person in which Nellie tells of the murder and asks for the prayers of her listeners.

I'm one of Mister Meeks' little girls,
An' if you'll lend an ear,
I'll tell you-all the saddest tale
That ever you did hear.

We lived upon the Taylor's farm
Not many miles from town
One night while we was all asleep
The Taylor boys come down.

Randolph II, 107, 7, m. (Okla.). Burt, 235, 9, m. (Mo.). notes.
There is a local tradition that Nellie Meeks sang this piece at carnivals in the 90's. (See Belden, 408 and Randolph, 106-107).

F 31

NAOMI WISE

Young Lewis goes for a ride with Naomi and throws her into the river below the old mill dam. When her body is found, he is arrested but not convicted. He is said to have confessed the murder on his deathbed.

Now come all you young people
And listen while I tell
About a maid they called Naomia Wise.
Her face was fair and beauteous;
She was loved by everyone.
In Randolph county now her body lies.

Brown II, 696, 6 6-line sts.; (N.C.). Morris, 86, 6d (Fla.). *WVF* 7 (1957), 66, 7d (W. Va.).

For factual details and references, see the earlier and better known ballad on this murder, "Poor Omie" (F 4).

Dr. Wilgus informs me that this piece was composed by Carson J. Robison, who is also the author of "The Wreck of Number Nine."

F 32

BENJAMIN DEANE

Benjamin prospers in business at Berlin Falls, but thirst for more gold leads him to selling liquor illegally and committing other crimes. His wife leaves him and seeks the protection of another man. Benjamin follows her and in a jealous rage shoots her dead. From prison he warns others against an evil life.

My name it is Benjamin Deane and my age is forty-one;
I was born in New Brunswick in the city of St. John,
Nearby the Bay of Fundy where the seagulls loudly call
As they rock with pride on the silvery tide as the billows rise and fall.

Ives, *JAF* 72 (1959), 53, 19d, m. (Me.); stanza 2 is given above. Mr. Ives has collected three other texts: 16d, m. (Me.); 14d; and 15d, m. (N.B.). He adds that Miss Creighton has a number of variants from Nova Scotia. Creighton, *Maritime Folk Songs*, 189, 25d, m. (N.S.).

Benjamin F. Deane, who was born in St. John, New Brunswick, in 1854, killed his wife in May, 1898, in Berlin Falls, New Hampshire. He spent less than ten years in prison, remarried, and resettled in Berlin, where he died in 1924. (For the full account, see " 'Ben Deane' and Joe Scott: a Ballad and its Probable Author," *JAF* 72 (1959), 53-66. Edward D. Ives in this article attributes "Ben Deane," "Howard Carey," (E 23), "Guy Read," (C 9), and "The Plain Golden Band," (H 17) to Joseph W. Scott, a New Brunswick woodsman, singer, and composer of songs.

F 33

MARIAN PARKER I

Marian Parker is kidnapped from school by a "murderous villain." After her body is found, Young Hickman is arrested, tried, and convicted and awaits execution in San Quentin.

'Way out in California
A family bright and gay,
Were preparing for their Christmas
Not very far away.
They had a little daughter,
A sweet and pretty child;
And everyone who knew her
Loved Marian Parker's smile.

Burt, 65, 5d (Ia.). Mrs. Burt reports receiving only slightly different texts from Ore. and N.Y. Brown II, 603, 7 (N.C.).

Marian Parker, the twelve year old daughter of a Los Angeles banker was abducted and murdered in December, 1927. Her slayer, William Edward Hickman, was executed at San Quentin the following year. For further details, see Burt, p. 64.

A Perfect phonograph record (no. 12429), "Little Marian Parker," sung by Vernon Dalhart, gives the author as Bill Barrett. Dr. Wilgus says that the ballad was copyrighted in 1928 by Triangle Music. Unlike the Burt text but like the Brown text, this version does not mention the death sentence. It was probably composed before Hickman's trial.

See also "Marian Parker II," "Marian Parker III," and "Edward Hickman" in Appendix II.

F 34

EMMA HARTSELL

Emma has been murdered, her throat cut from ear to ear. Two Negroes, Tom and Joe, are hanged for the crime from a dogwood tree. Joe asks for a drink of water before he dies but is refused. The ballad ends, "And Emma Hartsell was her name."

In eighteen hundred and ninety-eight
Sweet Emma met with an awful fate.
'Twas on the holy Sabbath day
When her sweet life was snatched away.

Brown II, 685, 11 (N.C.); notes and refs. There are four other texts in the Brown collection.

Emma Hartsell of Cabarrus County, North Carolina, was raped and murdered on May 30, 1898. Two young Negroes, Joe Kiser and Tom Johnson, were arrested for the crime and jailed. They were removed from the jail by a mob and lynched, protesting their innocence until the last. (Note condensed from Brown).

F 35

THE LAWSON MURDER (CHARLIE LAWSON)

After Lawson kills his wife, his children ask to be spared, but he shoots

all six of them. He closes their eyes, bids farewell to his friends, and prepares
to shoot himself. All are buried in a crowded grave.

> It was on last Christmas evening;
> A snow was on the ground.
> His home in North Carolina
> Where the murderer was found.
> His name was Charlie Lawson,
> And he had a loving wife.
> But we'll never know what caused him
> To take his family's life.

Brown II, 688, 4d (N.C.); notes and refs. to two other N.C. texts. Davis,
FSV, 278, lists a text from Virginia.

"Walnut Cove, N.C., Dec. 25 (AP)—Becoming suddenly insane, a Stokes
county farmer today slew his wife and six children, and, after having laid
them out for burial, went into a patch of woods near his home and killed
himself. The body of C. D. Lawson, the 43-year-old father and husband,
was found about half a mile from the home . . ." (Quoted in Brown from
the N. Y. *Times*, Dec. 26, 1929).

According to Dr. Wilgus, this piece was copyrighted by Wiley Morris and
appears on a Bluebird record.

F 36

THE MURDER OF LAURA FOSTER

Laura's fiancé and his female accomplice stab the girl to death in the
woods and bury her body in a shallow grave. After a long search, her
parents find her body, and a coroner's jury agrees that she has been
murdered.

> A tragedy I now relate.
> 'Tis of poor Laura Foster's fate—
> How by a fickle lover she
> Was hurried to eternity.

Brown II, 708, 21 (N.C.); notes. The editors refer to three other texts
of the same length in the N. C. collection.

Laura Foster was murdered by Thomas C. Dula in Wilkes County, North
Carolina, in 1866. Dula was hanged on May 1, 1868. See Brown for full
details.

Brown II, 712-714, prints two weakly narrative songs on this murder.
The first is the well-known "Tom Dooley (Dula)":

> Hang down your head, Tom Dula,
> Hang down your head and cry;
> You killed poor Laura Foster
> And now you're bound to die.

The second, "Tom Dula's Lament", begins:

> I pick my banjo now,
> I pick it on my knee.
> This time tomorrow night
> It'll be no more use to me.

F 37

STELLA KENNEY

Seventeen-year-old Stella is found murdered with seven gashes in her head. Her uncle, who is married and has three children, is sentenced to life imprisonment for the murder.

> It was one dark and stormy night,
> On the second day of May;
> Stell Kenny she was murdered,
> For home she was on her way.
>
> With her uncle Rob Frazier,
> Where she had been to stay;
> She'd spent ten long month with him
> Before her fatal day.

Thomas, *Ballad Makin'* 151, 14 (Ky.); notes. Williams, 127, 15 (Ky.); notes. Wilgus, *KFR* 5 (1959), 131, Williams' text and another Ky. text of 7d sts; notes. *KFR* 8 (1962), 113, 18 (Ky.).

"According to Flernoy Boggs, a resident of Cherokee, Lawrence County, Ky., the events told about in this ballad occurred in 1917. . . . The motive for murder, a post-mortem examination revealed, must have been pregnancy by her uncle." (Note from Williams, reprinted by Wilgus).

See "Stella Kenny in Song and Story," by Leonard Roberts, *KFR* 8 (1962), 116-124.

BALLADS OF TRAGEDIES AND DISASTERS

G 1
CASEY JONES

Running fast because he is late with the mail, Casey sees another train
ahead. He orders his fireman to jump clear and then dies in the ensuing crash.

> Come all you fellows, for I want you to hear
> The story told of a brave engineer.
> Casey Jones was the fellow's name,
> A big eight-wheeler of a mighty fame.

Hudson, 214, 7 (Miss.). Botkin, *A Treasury of American Folklore* (N.Y.,
1944), 245, 10 m. Brown II, 510, 10 (N.C.); notes. *CFB* II (1963), 37, 9 sts.
and refrain, m. (Colo.). Hubbard, *Railroad Avenue* (New York, 1945), p.
18, 5d. Lomax, *Amer. Ballads,* 34, 7, m. (a Negro version). Morris, 109,
4½ sts., and chorus (Fla.). Pound, 133, 10. Sandburg, 366, 12, m. (see also
368, 4 sts., "Mama Have You Heard the News?"). Spaeth, *Read 'Em and
Weep,* 119, the copyright version. L. C. Records 1551 B2 (Ky.); 3987 B4
(Tex. Negro); 3823 B1 & 2 (Cal.); 1628 A1 (Wash., D.C.); 1330 B1 (Ala.);
1866-10 in. (Canton, Miss. Sung by a friend of Wash Sanders); 3186 A2
(Ark.); 4136 A2 (Cal.); 3076 B2 (Miss.); 356 A (Fla.); 1461 B1 (Ky.).

John Luther ("Casey") Jones, of Cayce, Kentucky, engineer on the
Illinois Central Railroad, died April 30, 1900, at Vaughan, Mississippi, when
his engine crashed into a freight which extended from its siding onto the
main line. His fireman, Sim Webb, jumped in time to save his life. (Note
condensed from Botkin, 241-245, who quotes from *Erie Railroad Magazine,*
vol. 24 (April, 1928), No. 2, pp. 13, 44; vol. 28 (April, 1932), No. 2, pp.
12, 46. Some details from Hubbard, *Railroad Avenue,* 5-23.)

For discussions of the origin of this ballad, see Botkin, 241-245, and
Hubbard, 5-23. Add Lomax, *American Ballads,* 34-39 and *Folk Song U.S.A.,*
248-250. These investigations have failed to clear up certain obscurities. In
1909 Newton and Siebert copyrighted the vaudeville version of "Casey
Jones", with its familiar refrain, and the libellous last line, " 'Cause you've
got another papa on the Salt Lake Line." In this version, Casey is running
toward Frisco. (See text in Spaeth or Lomax, *Folk Song U.S.A.,* 266-269.)
The similar traditional version, with which the copyright version is sometimes
crossed, mentions Memphis and "the old I. C.", and ends with some reflections
on the noble life of a railroad man. (See text in Hudson, Hubbard, or
Botkin.) Perhaps this should be credited to the vaudeville players Bert and
Frank Leighton, whose brother was an Illinois Central engineer (see Hubbard,
19). The piece contains many clever touches and shows a knowledge of
railroading. Although presumably earlier than the copyright form, this is

not necessarily the original ballad on this subject. Credit for the original version has been given to Casey's Negro engine-wiper, Wallace (Wallis, "Wash") Saunders or Sanders, who worked in the roundhouse at Canton, Mississippi. The Lomaxes have created a composite text which they believe represents something near the original. (See "Casey Jones I", *Folk Song U.S.A.*, 264-265 and comments, 249-250). This piece is based upon still older traditional texts of Negro railroad ballads. A related version is given in Sandburg, 368-369. See especially, Odum and Johnson, *The Negro and His Songs*, 207-208. This version mentions Canton, the city toward which Casey was heading when the accident occurred, and contains the perhaps significant line ,"Casey Jones, I know him well". My belief is that the first three stanzas of this brief and fragmentary text come as close as any to Saunders' original.

See also the Negro ballad "Joseph Mica". (I 16) and "Mack McDonald", Cox 231, 8d sts. (W. Va.).

G 2

THE WRECK OF OLD 97

Trying to make up time, an engineer on the Southern Railroad loses control of his brakes between Lynchburg and Danville, goes downgrade at ninety miles an hour, and dies in the wreck with his hand on the throttle.

> Oh, they handed him his orders at Monroe, Virginia,
> Saying, "Steve, you're away behind time.
> This is not Thirty-eight, but it's old Ninety-seven;
> You must get 'er in Spencer on time!"

Hubbard, *Railroad Avenue*, 257, 6 sts (stanza 2 is given above). Brown II, 512, texts of 5, 5, 4, 8, 7, and 6 sts. (N.C.); detailed notes. Cambiaire, 97, 4 sts. *CFB* II (1963), 41, 5, m. (Colo.). Gordon, *Adventure*, Jan. 30, 1924, 191, 14 sts. (a composite text). Henry, *Songs Sung*, 79, 8 (Tenn.). Randolph IV, 132, 10, m. (Mo.); refs. Williams, 335, 5 (Ky.). L. C. Records 1815 B1 (N.Y. Sung by B. L. Lunsford); 3189 A1 (Ark.); 2747 83 (Va.); 1553 B2 (Ky.).

The Southern Railway's mail train "Old 97" was wrecked September 27, 1903, near Danville, Virginia. The engineer, Joseph A. ("Steve") Broady, was killed as were at least ten members of the train crew.

David Graves George, a Virginia mountaineer, who died Jan. 23, 1948, at the age of 82, claimed the authorship of this ballad. He was long involved in a suit against the Victor Talking Machine Company to recover royalties on the five million phonograph records of this piece which the company had issued.

For a detailed account of the wreck and of the court battles, see Freeman H. Hubbard, "The Wreck of Old 97", *Railroad Avenue* (N.Y., 1945), 251-

261.I am indebted to Hubbard's account for the notes given above and to Mr. B. E. Young, Assistant to the President of the Southern Railway System, for providing me with this reference.

G 3

THE WRECK ON THE C & O

This ballad, the chorus of which contains the line, "Many a man's been murdered by the railroad," tells of the death of engineer George Alley, whose engine is wrecked against a rock on the rails. His mother, who had warned him not to run too fast, is with the young man when he dies.

> Along came the old F.F.V., the fastest on the line,
> Running over the C. & O. Road, twenty minutes behind time;
> Running into Sewell, she was quartered on the line,
> And there received strict orders: Hinton, away behind time.

Cox, 224, 9d and chorus (W. Va.). Cox prints four other texts from W. Va. and refers to five more in his collection. His F version is reprinted by Gerould, p. 279, and his D version, with additions, appears in Lomax, *Amer. Ballads*, p. 31. Carter, *JAF* 46 (1933), 41, 6d (Tenn.). *KFR* III (1957), 98, 17d lines; tune p. 110 (Ky.). Morris, 111, 9d (Fla.); refs. Randolph IV, 129, 8½d, m. (Mo.); 3½d, m. (Ark.). L. C. Records 66 B1 (Tex.) and 2916 A1 (Tenn. "George Allen").

George Alley was killed October 23, 1890, near Hinton, W. Va., when his engine was overturned as the result of a landslide.

The ballad is said to have been composed by a Negro who worked in the roundhouse at Hinton. (Notes from Cox. See 221 for details).

G 4

THE C. & O. WRECK (1913)

Although the bridge is weak and men are working on it, the engineer gets a signal to proceed. The bridge collapses, plunging the engine into the river. Ed Webber(s) dies at the throttle, and seven of the thirteen bridge workers are drowned. The ballad ends with a prayer for Ed's wife and eight children and a warning to be prepared for a Christian death.

> It was on a New Year's morning,
> Nineteen hundred and thirteen,
> Engine Eight Hundred and Twenty
> Went down with fire and steam.
>
> It was on this sad morning
> At about eleven o'clock,
> The C. & O. bridge at Guyandotte
> Began to tremble and rock.

Combs, 200, 18 (Ky.). Gardner, 296, 7½d (Mich. from ms.).

Despite the fact that this and the preceding ballad have similar or identical titles, there is no connection between the two pieces.

"Si toutes les chansons du peuple commencaient de cette façon, leur origine, et certainement leur ancienneté, ne seraient pas entourée de mystère." (Combs).

For a discussion of this ballad, see Chapter V.

G 5

HENRY K. SAWYER

Sawyer is fatally scalded when he is pinned beneath an overturned locomotive after a derailment. His rescuers take him to the depot, where he is able to bid farewell to his wife before he dies.

> It was on last Sunday morning,
> Of June the eighth day,
> When Henry K. Sawyer
> From home went away,
> When Henry K. Sawyer,
> A man of renown,
> Took a seat on the tender,
> To ride to Oldtown.

Flanders-Barry, 58, 9d, m. (Me.); reprinted from *Bulletin* no. 9, 17. Barry, 81, 2d, m. (Me.).

"Mr. Sawyer, superintendent of repairs on the Bangor and Oldtown Railroad, was fatally injured when the engine on which he was riding was derailed two miles west of Stillwater, Maine, June 8, 1848." (Note from Barry, 101. See *Bulletin* no. 9 (1935), 18-19, for further details. A condensed account is given in Flanders-Barry, 60, where the editors say that this ballad is "'now nearly extinct.'"

G 6

THE AVONDALE DISASTER I (THE MINES OF AVONDALE)

The miners' families see the breaker burning and realize that there is a fire in the mine. One of two Welshmen who enter the mine to find the victims is suffocated. His partner announces that all the miners are dead. Other volunteers find the bodies of dozens of men in one heap. More than one hundred have died in the disaster.

> On the sixth day of September,
> Eighteen hundred and sixty-nine,
> Those miners all then got a call
> To go to work in the mine;
> But little did they think that day
> That death would gloom the vale
> Before they would return again from
> The mines of Avondale.

Korson, *Minstrels of the Mine Patch*, 189, 10d, m. (Pa. This text is from an old broadside with a few missing words supplied); 9d reprinted by Lomax, *FSNA*, 130. Greenleaf, 123, 8d (Nfld.). Korson, *Penna. Songs*, 386, 10d, m. (Pa.); reprinted by Leach, 783. Shoemaker, 212, 10d (Pa.). L. C. Record AAFS #76 (Pa.).

For details of this disaster, which brought death to 110 men near Wilkes-Barre, Pa., on September 6, 1869, see Korson, *Songs and Ballads*, 131-136. A similar account is given in *Minstrels of the Mine Patch*, 180-182.

G 7
THE AVONDALE DISASTER II

This ballad tells the same story as the preceding one, but dramatizes the grief of the bereaved families in more detail, and adds that the miners' souls may have gone to God "to plead against the company whose greed has caused their death."

> Come, friends and fellow Christians, and listen to my tale,
> And as I sing, pray drop a tear for the dead of Avondale;
> The sixth day of September, in eighteen sixty-nine
> We never shall forget the day until the end of time.

Korson, *Minstrels of the Mine Patch*, 191, 11d (Pa. from ms.). Gardner, 298, 10½d. m. (Pa. via Mich.).

Despite certain similarities between them, this and the preceding piece are separate compositions.

G 8
CHARLEY HILL'S OLD SLOPE

The chain of a mine car breaks while nine miners are riding to the surface on it. The car falls into the mine, and all are killed. Several stanzas describe the grief of the bereaved families.

> Come all ye true born Irishmen wherever you may be,
> I hope you'll attention pay and listen unto me;
> It's of those true-born Irishmen that left their native clay,
> To seek their destination here in Americ-a.

Korson, *Minstrels of the Mine Patch*, 196, 9d (Pa. via Del.).

This accident, which happened in 1865, is described in Korson, *op. cit.*, 185-6. A fuller account is given in *Songs and Ballads of the Anthracite Miner*, 140-6, along with Korson's first printing of the ballad.

G 9
THE CROSS MOUNTAIN EXPLOSION (COAL CREEK DISASTER)

One hundred fifty miners, men and boys, die when an explosion occurs as they work underground. No rescues are possible. Outside, the miners' families grieve.

The ninth day of December,
Nineteen hundred and eleven,
Many were killed in the Coal Creek mine
And I hope they are in heaven.

Henry, *Songs Sung*, 84, 7 (Ky. A confused Text). *KFR* 3 (1957), 99, 7
(Ky.); tune, p. 110. Korson, *Coal Dust on the Fiddle*, 275, 12 sts. L. C.
Records 2539 A (Ky. via N.Y. "Coal Creek Disaster"); 1432 A2 (Ky.).
Korson's note: "Text contributed by Wm. Turnblazer, pres. Dist. 19, UMW.
According to Turnblazer 'This ballad was composed and sung by Thomas
Evans who died a few years ago at Esserville, Virginia. The explosion was
in the Cross Mountain mine at Coal Creek, Tennessee'."

G 10
THE MINERS' FATE

Trapped in a cave-in, five hundred feet underground, the Pittston miners
cannot be saved, nor can their bodies be recovered. This prayerful lament
speaks feelingly of the grief of the bereaved families.

At just three o'clock in the morning
As the whistles gave the death sound,
One hundred brave men that were mining
Were buried alive in the ground.

Korson, *Minstrels of the Mine Patch*, 198, 5d and chor. (Pa.).
For an account of this disaster, which occurred at Pittstown, Pennsylvania,
June 28, 1896, see Korson, 186.

G 11
THE DYING MINE BRAKEMAN
(The True and Trembling Brakeman)

The motorman of a mine train explains that he could not stop in time
to keep the cars from running over his brakeman. The scene then shifts to
the brakeman, who speaks to his sister and then sends messages to his
parents.

See that brave and trembling motorman,
Said his age was twenty-one.
See him stepping from his motor
Crying, "Lord, what have I done?

Korson, *Coal Dust on the Fiddle*, 246, 7, m. (W. Va. Author's text). The
editor reports having recorded two other variants from W. Va. and one from
Va. in the spring of 1940. Kirkland, "A Check List", *JAF* 59 (1946), 468
lists two texts of "True and Trembling Brakeman." Randolph IV, 146, 8
(Ark. "The True and Trembling Brakeman").

A mine worker named Orville J. Jenks wrote this ballad in 1915, shortly
after witnessing the accident referred to in it. (See Korson, 120-121).

G 12

THE DRIVER BOY

Too weak and ill to drive his mule in the mines, the boy is repeatedly whipped by his drunken father. The death of his son from pneumonia brings the father to his senses too late.

> While passing by a house one night I heard a painful cry,
> And gazing in I saw a sight that soon bedimmed my eye.
> A boy was kneeling on the floor, his age was scarce fourteen,
> Upon his pale but handsome face the mark of death was seen.

Korson, *Minstrels of the Mine Patch*, 124, 3 8-line d. sts and 1d st. refrain. Reprinted from *Songs and Ballads,* 114 (Pa. Author's text); *Songs and Ballads,* 115, 4 lines missing (Pa.); variant sts. (Pa.). L. C. Records 1444 A (Ky.) and 2915 A2 (Tenn.).

This ballad was composed in 1900 by John A. Murphy, a miner of Lackawanna County, Pa., who had come upon a drunken father beating his son and had "stepped in and prevented further abuse." The young mule driver subsequently died of pneumonia. (For details, see Korson, *Songs and Ballads . . . ,* 111-114; a condensed account is given in *Minstrels of the Mine Patch*, 106).

G 13

THE BURNING OF THE GRANITE MILL

The ballad recounts some of the horrors of the disaster, and adds that all the victims might have been saved.

> In this world with care and trouble
> Many accidents occur.
> I am going to sing about one
> The saddest you ever heard.
> 'Twas in Fall River City
> Where the people were burned up and killed,
> Imprisoned in a factory
> Known as the Granite Mills.

Flanders-Barry, 229, 6d, m. (Vt.). Beck, *The Folklore of Maine*, 105, 6d (Me.). Creighton, 257, 5d, m. (N.S.).

"The Granite Mill, in Fall River, Massachusetts . . . was burned on September 19, 1874 . . . The fire alarm was not sounded for twenty minutes and in the meantime over fifty persons were trapped in the attic, of whom the *Boston Traveller* of September 20 reported twenty known dead, three missing, and thirty-six injured." (Note from Flanders-Barry, 230).

G 14

THE JOHNSTOWN FLOOD

A distraught father tells some strangers that he and his family had sought safety in the upper part of their house when the flood descended upon them. His children and his wife were then torn from his grasp and carried away by the rushing water. Some men rescued him, and later the bodies of his family were found.

> Is it news you ask for, strangers, as you stand and gaze around
> At those cold and lifeless bodies lying here upon the ground?
> Do you see that lady yonder, with the little girl and boy?
> That's my wife, my darling Minnie, once my household pride and joy.

Pound, 135, 10d (Neb. "The Jamestown Flood"). L. C. Records 3734 B, 3735 A1, 3736 A (Vt.); 3671 B3 (N.Y.).

The great flood at Johnstown, Pa., in which some 2500 lives were lost, occurred May 31, 1889.

This sentimental piece seems too skillfully constructed to have originated with a folk composer. It may have had its start as newspaper verse.

G 15

THE MILWAUKEE FIRE

The fire rushes unchecked through the "oft condemned hotel." Spectators hear the cries of the victims and watch in horror as they are trapped in the flames. A servant girl leaps to her death from the top story, and a mother sees her son engulfed by fire.

> 'Twas the gray of early morning when the dreadful cry of fire
> Rang out upon the cold and piercing air;
> Just that little word alone is all it would require
> To spread dismay and panic everywhere.
> Milwaukee was excited as it never was before,
> On learning that the fire bells all around
> Were ringing to eternity a hundred souls or more
> And the Newhall house was burning to the ground.

Pound, 138, 4d 8-line sts. and refrain (Ia.). Neely and Spargo, 166, 5d; 1d and chorus (Ill.). Wilgus, *KFR* 3 (1957), 101, 6d (Ky.). L. C. Records 2325 B, 2326 A1 (Mich.); 4198 B1, 4198 B2 (Cal.).

Like the preceding piece this may have originated as a newspaper ballad.

"On a January night in 1883 fire destroyed the Newhall House, a leading hotel. Sixty-four persons are known to have perished, though loss of the hotel register made a correct estimate impossible." (Note from *Wisconsin: A Guide to the Badger State; American Guide Series*, N.Y. 1941).

G 16

SPRINGFIELD MOUNTAIN

While mowing his father's field, a youth is bitten by a poisonous snake.
He calls for help, but no one comes to his aid, and he dies unattended.

> On Springfield Mountain there did dwell
> A handsome youth, was known full well,
> Lieutenant Merrill's only son,
> A likely youth, near twenty-one.

Flanders & Brown, 15, 7 (Vt.); the full text of this variant is given in
Chap. II and on L. C. Record 3755 A; reprinted by Lomax, *FSNA*, 13.
Barry, *Bulletin* no. 7, p. 5, 7 (Mass. from ms.); no. 8, p. 6, 6 (from print).
Brown II, 489, 5; 6; 4; frags. (N.C.). Eddy, 248, 7 (O.). Gordon,
Adventure, July 30, 1923, 191, 8 sts. Leach, 720 (Barry's Myrick and
Curtis types). *KFR* 3 (1957), 102, 6 and refrain; tune, p. 111 (Ky.). *NYFQ*
14 (1958), 218, 5, m. (N.Y.). Owens, 257, 8 (Mass. from ms.). Randolph
III, 168, 5 (Mo.).

("Springfield Mountain" has wide currency in tradition as a comic song.
These versions, which usually contain nonsensical refrains, achieve their
effects by exaggerated mispronounciations and ludicrous dialogue. My references are to the serious ballad).

Phillips Barry has made a thorough study of this ballad. (See *Bulletin* no.
7, 4-5; no. 8, 3-6; no. 9, 8-10; no. 10, 6-8; no. 11, 13-15; no. 12, 6-8). He
recognizes four distrinct types, identifiable partly by the names which appear
in them. Of these the Myrick and Curtis types are serious balladry; the
Sally and Molly types are comic pieces. Barry's summary, from *Bulletin* 12,
7, follows:

"One fact, fully documented, has been established: Timothy Myrick of
Wilbraham, Mass., formerly Springfield Mountain, died of snakebite in
Farmington, Connecticut, August 7, 1761, the date recorded on his grave
monument in Wilbraham. It has also been shown that the presence of families
named Curtis, in Springfield and Weathersfield, Vermont, may account for
the name *Curtis* in ballad tradition, side by side with *Myrick*. Of the four
types, the first two, Myrick and Curtis, belong to domestic tradition not
traceable back of the year 1849 . . . : the last two, *Sally* and *Molly*, are of
professional tradition, caught up by the folk, of which the former has a
copyright record of 1836, the latter of 1840. There is no evidence that the
ballad is of earlier date than the second quarter of the last century."

Mr. Barry's suggestion that the ballad originated more than half a
century after the event it records has not, I feel, been convincingly supported.
Furthermore, the evidence that the youth died at Farmington is not conclusive. My belief is that this ballad, like many others, was locally composed
soon after the tragedy it recounts.

G 17

YOUNG CHARLOTTE (FAIR CHARLOTTE)

Vanity prevents Charlotte from wrapping herself in blankets as she starts for a ball on a cold night. After several miles she complains to her fiancé about the cold, but later says, "I'm growing warmer now." When the sleigh arrives at the inn, Charles finds that she has frozen to death. In most versions, Charles soon dies and is buried beside her.

> Young Charlotte dwelt on the mountain side in a bare and lonely spot;
> No cabin there for miles around but her father's humble cot.
> On many a pleasant winter's eve young swains would gather there
> To laugh and pass the hours away for she was wondrous fair.

Flanders-Barry, 111, 10d (Vt.); notes and refs. Belden, 308, 4 full Mo. texts and several fragments. See for refs. to some two dozen texts from 19 states. Brewster, 181, 2 full texts and m. (Ill. and Ind.). Brown II, 492, 21 (N.C.); refs. *CFB* I, no. 1 (Jan. 1962), p. 7, 15, (Colo.). Gardner, 126, 18, m. (Mich.). High, 32, 30d lines (Ark.). Hubbard, 74, 16, m. (Utah). Leach, 723, 17 (Va.); notes. Lomax, *FSNA*, 94, 15, m. ("words and music arranged by Alan Lomax"). Morris, 114, 21, m. (Fla.); refs. Owens, 98, 17, m. (Tex.). Randolph IV, 105, 21½, m.; 5; add. sts.; 11, m. (Mo.). Thompson, 374 ,12d (N.Y.). *WF* 17 (1958), 233, 15, m. (Ia.). L. C. Records AAFS #68 (N.C.), 3211 B1 (Mo.), 3427 A2 (Va.), and 6 others from Cal., N.J., Ind., N.C., Wis., and Tex. Add six more under the title "Fair Charlotte" from Ky., Mo., Ark., Vt., O., and Cal.

Phillips Barry originally accepted the belief that William Lorenzo Carter, of Benson, Vermont, was the author of this ballad. (See *JAF* 25 (1912), 156-168, and *Bulletin* no. 8 (1934), 17-19). Later he discovered that it "was written by Seba Smith (1792-1868) . . . It was published by him in *The Rover*, vol. II, no. 15, p. 225 (Dec. 28, 1843), under the title *A Corpse Going to a Ball*." Barry goes on to say in part, "The incident on which the ballad is based, was known to the author only from an item in the *New York Observer*, Feb. 8, 1840, entitled *A Corpse Going to a Ball*, concerning a certain Miss _____ who was frozen to death, while riding with 'her partner of the evening' to a ball on the eve of January 1, 1840." (*Bulletin* no. 12 (1937), 27).

G 18

STRATTON MOUNTAIN TRAGEDY

A woman perishes in a blizzard, but her baby is found alive the next morning because she has sacrificed herself to wrap the child in her cloak.

Cold was the mountain's height.
Drear was the pastures wild.
Amid the cheerless hours of night,
A mother wandered with her child.
As through the drifts of snow she pressed,
The babe was sleeping neath her breast.

Flanders and Brown, 27, 4, 6-line sts., m. (Vt.).

"The event here described happened at Kelly Stand near the town of Arlington, Vermont." (See Flanders and Brown, 27, for comments and a reference. They say that this piece was printed, copyright, 1843, by Oliver Ditson Company. "The author was given as Seba Smith").

G 19
WILLIE DOWN BY THE POND (SINFUL TO FLIRT)

Though she loves Willie the girl teasingly says she won't marry him. Heartbroken, he drowns himself in the pond by the mill, where he is found with a rose from her hair pressed to his lips.

They say it is sinful to flirt.
They say I've a heart made of stone.
They tell me to speak to him kindly,
Or else leave the poor boy alone.

Next morning dear Willie was found
Down in the pond by the mill.
His blue eyes forever were closed
And damp were the locks of his hair.

Henry, *Folk-Songs*, 238, 6½, m. (Ala.); sts. 1 and 5 are given above; 5; 8, m. (N.C.); 3 and chor. (Ky.); 8 Va.); refs. Brown II, 638, 8 (N.C.); refs. Cambiaire, 90, 8 sts. Owens, 155, 6, m. (Tex.). L. C. Records 2778 B2 & 2747 B2 (Va.).

This piece is probably a product of the Southern Mountains, but I have not discovered any account of its origin.

G 20
MINNIE QUAY (WINNIE GRAY)

Because a young man has slandered her, and as a result her parents have wished her dead, sixteen year old Minnie drowns herself in Lake Huron.

'Twas in the town of Forester,
Along the sandy shore
The voice of one poor Minnie Quay
We'll never hear no more

Beck, 214, 12 (Mich.).

Professor Beck reports having received three texts of this ballad, which, as far as I know, had not previously been collected. "Minnie Quay's tombstone," he writes, "can be found at the little village of Forester, on the Lake Huron shore."

G 21

THE SILVER DAGGER

The marriage of two young people who are deeply in love is opposed by the man's parents because the girl is poor. Hearing of their objection, the girl stabs herself. She is found dying by her lover, to whom she says, "Prepare to meet me on Mount Zion." The young man then kills himself with the dagger she has used.

> Come, young men, pray lend attention
> To these few lines I'm about to write,
> For it is as true as ever was mentioned
> Concerning a fair one, beauty bright.
>
> He then pulled out the silver dagger,
> Pierced it through his own dear heart,
> Saying, "Let this be an awful warning
> To all that does true lovers part."

Hudson, 188, 9 (Miss.); the first and last sts. are given above. Arnold, 75, 5, m. (Ala. "Katie Dear"). Belden, 124, 11 (Ark.); 125, 4 (Mo.). See for refs. to 13 texts from Va., W. Va., Ky., Tenn., Miss., Ark., O., Ill., Wyo., and Mo. Brewster, 211, 8; 10, m. (Ind.). Gardner, 89, 5d (Mich. from ms.); refs. Hubbard, 67, 9, m. (Utah). Leach, 730, 8 (Va.). Morris, *SFQ* 8 (1944), 185, 7, m .(Fla.). Morris, 80, 8 (Fla.). Musick, *JAF* 60 (1947), 218, 12 (O. from ms.). Williams, 116, 7 (W. Va. via Ky.). *WVF* 7 (1957), 60, 9 (W. Va.). L. C. Records 2540 A & B (Ky. via N. Y.); 1341 B (Va.), 2963 A1 (Miss.), 920 A2)Tex.), 3769 B3 and 3770 A1 (N. C.), and 2008 A3-10 in. (Ky.).

G 22

FLOYD COLLINS

Trapped in the cave, Floyd tells his parents that he has dreamed of dying a prisoner there. After days of work by a rescue party, Floyd dies before he can be freed. The ballad ends with a warning to be prepared for death.

> O come all ye good people, and listen while I tell,
> The fate of Floyd Collins, a lad we all know well.
> His face was fair and handsome, his heart was true and brave;
> His body now lies sleeping in a lonely sandstone cave.

Gardner, 308, 5d; 307, 6 (Va. via Mich.). Brown II, 498, 6d and parts of other texts (N.C.); notes. Henry, *Songs Sung*, 82, 6d (Tenn.). *Rocky Mt. Coll.*, 19, 3d (Utah). *TFSB* 16 (1950), 29, 6d, m. (Tenn.). Thomas, *Ballad Makin'*, 110, 5d (Ky.). L. C. Records 1812 A3 & B1 (N.Y.); 2765 B1 (Va.); 843 A1 (N.C.).

"Floyd Collins descended into a 'sandhole' cave, near Mammoth Cave, Kentucky, on January 30, 1925. Missed next day, he was found by his brother, trapped by a landslide. Attempts to rescue him continuing until February 16, when he was discovered to be dead, excited the whole nation." (Note from Brown).

Professor D. K. Wilgus has sent me convincing evidence that the author of this piece was the Rev. Andrew Jenkins, who also composed "Kenny Wagner," "Kenny Wagner's Surrender," "Frank Dupree," and other ballads. For further details, see Chapter IV.

G 23
THREE GIRLS DROWNED

Returning from church the three girls attempt to ford a stream but are swept into it and drowned. The young man with them eventually saves himself.

> In western Pennsylvania fair,
> At Washington three ladies were,
> All teachers in a Sabbath school
> Where children learn the Golden Rule
> To Gravel Run the three did ride,
> To God's own house they did repair
> With young John Ash to worship there.

Gardner, 301, 4d (Pa. via Mich. Sung by E. W. Harns). Brown II, 495, 9 (N.C.).

"Mr. Harns said that these girls were drowned in Elk Creek, which ran through his parents' farm in Erie County, Pennsylvania. His parents knew the girls, who lived only a few miles from their farm, when this tragedy took place in 1849." (Note from Gardner, 301. See for further details and a reference to a longer ms. text from Pa.).

G 24
THE MIRAMICHI FIRE

A great fire ravages an area forty-two miles by one hundred in eight or ten hours, burning forests, houses, ships, and towns and killing or maiming many people. The survivors tearfully bury the dead.

> On the seventeenth evening of October
> Eighteen hundred and twenty-five,
> Thousands of people fell by fire,
> Scorched were those that did survive.

Creighton, Maritime Folk Songs, 201, 21, m. (N.B. A composite text). Beck, The Folklore of Maine, 251, 20 (Me.). Bulletin no. 11, p. 21, 21 (Me. Reprinted indirectly from an old broadside); p. 22, fragments and tunes (Me.).

"One of the worst natural calamities known to have happened on American soil was the series of forest fires in New Brunswick in October, 1825, popularly believed to have merged into one conflagration." (W. F. Ganong, as quoted by Barry in *Bulletin* no. 10, p. 15). Barry adds a contemporary newspaper account which states, "The fire has run over an extent of 100 miles in length and 40 in breadth." The author of the ballad is said to be Thomas M. Jordan (*Bulletin* no. 11, p. 21).

G 25

MEAGHER'S CHILDREN

The children, four and six years old, lose their way and die in the woods. After a week's search by one hundred men, their bodies are found and returned to their grieving parents.

> Good people read these verses which I have written here,
> And if you can peruse them you can't help but shed a tear,
> 'Twas eighteen hundred and forty-two on April the eleventh day,
> Two little girls from Preston Road into the woods did stray.

Creighton, *Maritime Folk Songs*, 204, 15d, m. (N.S. from National Museum of Canada tape 95A). Refs. to other tape recordings from N.S. and N.B., and to L. C. Records 32B & 33A & B and 70B. Beck, *The Folklore of Maine*, 103, 14d (Me. recited). Creighton, 292, 19d, m. (N.S.).

"When Mr. Samuel Jagoe sang this long song through at the Miramichi Folk Song Festival in 1958 he used no gestures nor device, yet his art of story telling in song was so superb that he kept his audience spellbound throughout. Some were even seen with tears streaming down their faces. The incident happened a few miles from my home." (Note from Creighton, p. 205).

G 26

THE WRECK OF NUMBER NINE

The engineer bids farewell to his fiancée and looks forward to his wedding the next day. Rounding a curve, he sees a headlight coming at him, and he is fatally injured in the ensuing collision. He leaves the girl the cottage they were to have shared.

> On a cold stormy night, not a star was in sight,
> And the north wind was howling down the line,
> With his sweetheart so dear stood a brave engineer
> With his orders to pull old Number Nine.

Randolph IV, 134, 3d, m. (Mo.). *Rocky Mountain Collection*, 27, 6, m. (Cal.).

This melodramatic and sentimental piece was composed by Carson J. Robison, the author of "Naomi Wise," and appears on many phonograph records. (Note from D. K. Wilgus).

G 27

THE BROOKLYN THEATRE FIRE

A large audience watches a performance of *The Two Orphans*. Suddenly sparks fly from the scenery and the crowd panics. Next morning the theatre is a black ruin filled with bodies. A mass funeral is to take place at Greenwood cemetery.

> The evening bright stars they were shining,
> The moonbeams shone clear o'er the land,
> The city was quiet and peaceful,
> The hour of midnight close at hand.
> Then hark, hear the loud cry of Fire,
> How dismal the fire bells sound,
> The Brooklyn Theater is burning,
> Alas, burning fast to the ground.

Randolph IV, 137, 4½d (Mo.); refs. Owens, 287, 6, m. (Tex.); notes. *WF* 17 (1958), 240, 1 (Ia.).

Some 300 people died in a fire at a Brooklyn theatre on Dec. 5, 1876, during a performance of *The Two Orphans*. Owens, p. 285, says that his text is a variant of the broadside written by P. J. Downey and published by A. W. Auner of Philadelphia.

G 28

THE HALIFAX EXPLOSION

A ship loaded with explosives is rammed in Halifax harbor by a relief ship. In the ensuing fire and explosion the city is devastated. Twelve hundred people are killed and two thousand injured.

> It was on the sixth of December, nineteen hundred and seventeen,
> That Halifax suffered disaster, the worst she'd even seen,
> It was five minutes after nine, those still alive can tell
> That the beautiful city of Halifax was just given a taste of hell.

Creighton, *Maritime Folk Songs*, 208, 11d, m. (N.S. a composite text). "This graphic description is all too true as those of us who survived remember. I also recall a ballad sheet sold on the streets at this time and regret that I did not have the foresight to buy one." (Note from Creighton).

G 29

JOHN J. CURTIS

While using dynamite, Curtis is buried under an avalanche of coal after an explosion. When he is able to strike a match, he discovers that he is blind. He asks his listeners to be kind to him.

> My name is John J. Curtis,
> My age is twenty-eight;
> I was born in Schuylkill County
> And there I met my fate.

So now with your attention
If you'll be so kind,
I will tell you of that fatal day
That I was stricken blind.

Korson, *Penna. Songs,* 392, 5d, m. (Pa. from a L. C. Record); notes. Korson, *Minstrels,* 201, 4d, m. (Pa.); notes.

"John J. Curtis was blinded while at work in the Morea colliery, Schuylkill County, Pa., in 1888. Led by a boy, he roamed the anthracite region singing this ballad, and selling broadsides on which it was printed. The text was made for him by the Lansford bard, Joseph Gallagher, from whom I obtained it in 1925." (Note from Korson, *Penna. Songs,* pp. 391-392).

G 30
THE CHATSWORTH WRECK

A happy excursion to Niagara Falls ends when the train crashes through a burned bridge and is wrecked with the loss of one hundred lives.

From city, town, and hamlet
There came a happy throng
To view the great Niagara.
With joy they sped along,
The maiden and her lover,
The husband and the wife,
The merry pattering children
So full of joy and life.

Chorus: But oh, how much of sorrow
And oh, how much of pain
Awaited those who journeyed
On that ill-fated train!

Belden, 422, 5d and chorus (Mo.); notes. Randolph IV, 128, 3½d, m. (Mo.); refs.

"The accident described in this song occurred in August, 1887, on the Toledo, Peoria and Western Railroad. A sixteen-coach excursion train from Peoria to Niagara Falls went through a bridge near Chatsworth, Ill., killing 81 persons and injuring 372—the worst railroad disaster in the history of Illinois." (Note from Randolph). According to Belden, the Chatsworth *Plaindealer* on August 12, 1937, reprinted this ballad under the title " 'The Bridge Was Burned at Chatsworth' (Words and Music by T. P. Westendorf)."

G 31
THE SHERMAN CYCLONE

The storm comes quickly, accompanied by lightning and thunder, destroys buildings, kills and injures many people, and departs.

Kind friends, if you will listen,
A story I will tell;
'Tis of a great tornado
You all remember well;

It reached the town of Sherman
The fifteenth day of May,
And a portion of our city
Was completely swept away.

Owens, 129, 8d, m. (Tex.); notes. L. C. Records 4135 B2 (Cal.) and
926 A2 (Tex.).

The Sherman tornado occurred on May 15, 1896.

The author of the ballad was a blind entertainer, Mrs. Mattie Carter East,
who sang at picnics and religious meetings and sold broadsides of her songs
at ten cents each. (Note from Owens).

G 32

THREE PERISHED IN THE SNOW

As they all struggle through the snow, the children ask their mother to
make them warm, but the next morning the three are found dead, clasped
in each other's arms.

'Twas on a dreadful stormy night,
The snow was falling fast,
A woman and three little babes,
Were traveling through the blast.

Arnold, 98, 5, m. (Ala. Learned in 1885). Cazden, 50, 3d and refrain, m.
(N.Y.); notes. L. C. Record 1353 A 2 (Va.).

According to Norman Cazden, "the words and music by one Eddie Fox,
as sung by Fred Waltz of Sweatnam's Minstrels" appeared in 1878. "A
full text appears in *Wehman's Song Book No. 2*, 1890." (p. 122).

G 33

ONLY A MINER (THE HARD-WORKING MINER)

No one is able to help the miner when a boulder suddenly falls upon him.
He has left a wife and little ones and is now "at rest in his grave."

Only a miner, killed in the ground;
Only a miner, and one more is gone.
With our hearts full of sadness, we'll bid him farewell;
His mining is over, poor miner, farewell.

Wayland D. Hand, Charles Cutts, Robert C. Wylder, and Betty Wylder,
"Songs of the Butte Miners," *WF* 9 (1950), 15, 2d and chor., m. (Mont.
the chorus is given above); refs. Emrich, *CFQ* 1 (1942), 222, 3 and
chor., m. (Colo.). Lomax, *Amer. Ballads*, 437, 3d and chor., m. (Ky.).
Randolph IV, 127, 3d, m. (Ark.).

"Only a Miner" is as much a lament as a ballad, but the essential facts
of the tragedy are recorded.

See also "Only a Brakeman" and "Only a Cowboy" in Appendix II.

BALLADS ON VARIOUS TOPICS

H 1   An Arkansas Traveller
H 2   Ten Thousand Miles from Home
H 3   The Dying Hobo
H 4   The Roving Gambler
H 5   Death Is a Melancholy Call
H 6   Wicked Polly
H 7   The Little Family
H 8   The Little Mohea
H 9   The Lake of Ponchartrain
H 10   The Chippewa Girl
H 11   On the Banks of the Pamanaw
H 12   The Lonesome Scenes of Winter
H 13   The Young Man Who Wouldn't Hoe Corn
H 14   The Queenstown Mourner
H 15   Olban, or The White Captive
H 16   Tittery Nan

H 17   The Plain Golden Band
H 18   Morrissey and the Russian Sailor
H 19   Morrissey and the Black
H 20   Heenan and Sayers
H 21   The Fellow That Looks Like Me
H 22   I Wonder Where's the Gambler
H 23   The Old Maid and the Burglar
H 24   The Warranty Deed
H 25   Courting the Widow's Daughter
H 26   The Girl That Wore a Waterfall
H 27   Ten Broeck and Mollie
H 28   The Banks of Brandywine
H 29   The Blooming Bright Star of Belle Isle
H 30   Jerry, Go and Ile That Car
H 31   Christine Leroy

H 1

AN ARKANSAS TRAVELLER

The traveller's unfavorable first impression of poverty-stricken Arkansas is fully confirmed. He is "a different man," as his employer said he would be, when he leaves, but the change has been brought about mainly by malnutrition.

My name is Bill Stafford, I came from Buffalo Town;
I've travelled this wide world over, I've travelled this wide world round;
I've had my ups and downs in life, but better days I've saw;
I never knew what misery was till I came to Arkansas.

Cox, 239, 6d; 7d; 5d (W. Va.). Brewster, 265, 9d; 4d (Ind.). Belden, 424, 7d (Mo.); roughly 7d (Mo. from ms.); see for comments and refs. to 8 more texts from the South and Midwest. Brown II, 382, 9d; 6d (N.C.). Lomax, *FSNA*, 322, 7d, m. Lomax, *Folk Song U.S.A.*, 240, 10d, m. Owens, 226, 5d, m. (Tex.). Randolph III, 9d, m.; 9d; 1½d (Ark.); 7d (Mo.); 1d (Ark.). 5½d, m. (Mo.); refs. *Rocky Mt. Coll.*, 21, 7d, m. (Utah). *TFSB* 16 (1950), 52, 8d, m. (Tenn.). L. C. Records 3346 B1 (Cal. "Bill Stafford"), 1731 A (Ind.), 15 9A (Ky.), and 6 under the title "The State of Arkansas" from N. Y. via Ky., (827 A1), Ky., Tex., Ark., (865 B2), and Miss.

This piece is not the same as the humorous sung and spoken dialogue "The Arkansas Traveler," for a version of which see Henry, *Folk-Songs*, 361-362.

H 2

TEN THOUSAND MILES FROM HOME

(A Wild and Reckless Hobo; The Railroad Bum)

Neither a kind-hearted girl nor one he becomes "struck on" can hold the railroad bum when he hears the call of a train. Despite his loneliness, he keeps wandering from town to town.

My pocket-book is empty,
My heart is full of pain
Ten thousand miles away from home,
A-beating a railroad train.

Hudson, 250, 8 (Miss. "The Railroad Bum"). Brown III, 426, 3d and chorus (N.C.). Cambiaire, 3, 7d (same source as Henry's); 6 sts. without the love motif. Fuson, 128, 13 (Ky.); reprinted by Lomax, *Amer. Ballads*, 29. Henry, *Songs Sung*, 107, 6d (Va. "A Wild and Reckless Hobo"). Lomax, *FSNA*, 419, 5½d, m. Randolph IV, 360, 2d, m. (Mo.). Stout, 113, 5d (Iowa).

L. C. Records "A Wild and Reckless Hobo": 1988 A & B1-10 in. (Ky.);
1461 A1 (Ky.); 2027 A2-10 in. (Ky.).

John Greenway in *JAF* 70 (1957), 231-234, says that this piece was composed by Jimmie Rodgers, a popular singer from 1927-1933, whose phonograph records sold in the millions. "There is scarcely a word [of his various
compositions] that cannot be traced to song and sung phrases of hoboes and
Negro railroad workers."

H 3

THE DYING HOBO

After speaking to his partner about the hoboes' paradise he will find after
death, the hobo dies. His partner steals his hat and shoes and catches the
eastbound train.

> The train pulled in on a siding
> On a cold November day;
> Beside a western water tank
> A dying hobo lay.

Hudson, 252, 5; 7 (Miss.). Brown III, 427, 5; 2d sts. of longer text (N.C.).
Cox, 252, 4d (W. Va.). Finger, 105, 4d, m. (N. Mex.). Gray, 102, 8 (Me.).
Hubbard, 309, 3d (N. Mex. via Utah). Randolph IV, 360, 4d (Mo.). Spaeth,
Weep Some More, My Lady, 131, 4d.

See William Wallrich, "U. S. Air Force Parodies Based upon 'The Dying
Hobo'," *WF* 14 (1955), 236-244.

H 4

THE ROVING GAMBLER
(The Gambling Man)

The gambling man falls in love "with a pretty little girl". Captivated by
him, she takes him to the parlor and cools him with her fan. Almost immediately, she decides to leave home and mother and travel with him wherever
he goes.

> I am a roving gambler;
> I've gambled all around;
> Whenever I meet with a deck of cards,
> I lay my money down.

Henry, *Songs Sung*, 98, 7 (Tenn.). Belden, 375, 10 (Mo. from ms. "The
Guerrilla Boy"); 6, m. (Mo. "A Roving Soldier"); notes and refs. *CFB* I
(1962), no. 3, p. 7, 8, m. (Okla. via Colo.); III (1963), p. 23, 4d, m. (Colo).
Gardner, 200, 7 (Mich. "The Roaming Gambler"). Lomax, *Amer. Ballads*,
150, 5½d, m. (Utah). Owens, 183, 7, m. (Tex.). Randolph IV, 357, 6, m.;
6½; 8 (Ark.); refs. Sandburg, 312, 11d couplets, m.; 6d couplets ("The
Gamboling Man," from *Delaney's Songbook No. 23*. The traveller falls in
love with a London girl). Williams, 417, 8, m. (Ky.). L. C. Records 60 B1

(Tex.); 827 B2 (Ky. via N.Y.); 1594 A1 (Ky.); 859 B2 (Ark.); and 2638
A1 (Tex.).

The variant forms of this piece are legion, and it has become almost
inextricably entangled with other folksongs. For references to a great many
songs containing similar stanzas, see Belden's headnote. In most of these
the narrative element is slight. Lomax, *American Ballads*, 170-173, prints a
generous sample of those stanzas which are often sung with parts of "The
Roving Gambler". See also *Cowboy Songs*, 163-167; Randolph II, 317-318,
with references. As Belden says, it is undoubtedly a derivative of "The Roving
Journeyman", a British ballad which appears on broadsides by Catnach, Such,
and others and in Baring-Gould's *Songs of the West* (London, 1895, Part I,
5d, m.). Cazden's "The Roving Pedlar," Part II, p. 98, seems to be a variant
of the British ballad.

H 5

DEATH IS A MELANCHOLY CALL

The narrator watches the funeral of a youth who has trifled away his days,
and observes that his relatives and friends are troubled by the thought that
his soul is in hell.

> Death! What a solemn call to all,
> A sudden judgement to use all.
> Death takes the young as well as the old,
> And in the winding sheet doth fold.

SFQ 3 (1939), 111, 5 (Ky. "A Solemn Call to All"). Belden, 464, 7 (Mo.
from ms.); 6 (Mo.); 8 (Mo. from ms.); refs to 5 texts from Tenn., Ind.,
and the Southern Highlands. Musick, *JAF* 70 (1957), 349, 2 (W. Va.).
Randolph IV, 15, 7, m. (Mo.); refs. Scarborough, 95, 5 (N.C. "The Lost
Youth"). *WVF* 5 (1955), 32, 3, m. (W. Va.).

Pieces of this type are frequently sung at mountain funerals. See Marie
Campbell's "Funeral Ballads of the Kentucky Mountains", *SFQ* 3 (1939),
107-115. See also Barry article referred to under "Wicked Polly" (H 6).

H 6

WICKED POLLY

Sinful Polly, who would "go to frolics, to dance and play," plans to turn
to God when she gets old. She becomes sick, however, and dies in agony,
realizing that her soul is going to hell.

> Young people who delight in sin,
> I'll tell you what has lately been,
> A woman who was young and fair
> She died in sin and sad despair.

Brewster, 303, 6 (Ind.). Belden, 460, 9 (Ark.); 13 and chor. (Mo. "a single-sheet ballad"); 24 (Kan. from a ms. written "'more than eighty years ago'"); see for refs. to 10 other texts from Jamaica, R. I., W. Va., Ark., Ind., Ia., and Va. Brown III, 92, 8 (from ms.); 7; 4 and chor. (N.C.). Eddy, 305, 12 (O.). Lomax, *FSNA*, 71, 7, m. Morris, 171, 5, m. (Fla.); refs. Owens, 110, 7, m. (Tex.). Randolph IV, 16, 6, m. (Ark. via Okla.); 7; 5, m.; 2 (Ark.); 6 (Mo.); refs. L. C. Records 852 A2 (Ky.) and 983 A2 (Fla.).

Belden refers to Barry's article "An American Homiletic Ballad," *MLN* 28 (1913), 1-5, in which this and the preceding piece are considered as variants of one ballad.

H 7
THE LITTLE FAMILY

Mary and Martha are happy until their brother Lazarus becomes ill and dies. Hearing of his death, their friend Jesus comes to them and prays for Lazarus, who then rises from the grave. The ballad ends with advice to love Jesus and do His will.

> There was a little family that lived in Bethany;
> Two sisters and a brother composed this family;
> With singing and with praying, like angels in the sky,
> Both morning and at ev'ning they raised their voices high.

Gardner, 366, 6d, m. (Mich.). Belden, 447, 7d (from a ms. of 1865); 11 (Mo.); refs. Brown III, 651, 7d; add. sts. (N.C.). Cox, 407, 6½d; 5½d (W. Va.). Eddy, 295, 7½d, m. (O.). Henry, *Folk-Songs*, 417, 12 (Tenn.); refs. High, 31, 20d lines (Ark.). Hudson, 212, 16 (Miss.). Leach, 735, 16 (Va.). Randolph IV, 48, 12, m. (Ark.); 5d (Mo.); refs. L. C. Records 2913 A2 (Tenn. "Family Lived in Bethany"), 2956 B (Miss.), 3264 B1 (Ill. Sung at Nat. Folk Festival), 1475 A2 & B (Ky.), 1492 A & B1 (Ky. "There Was a Little Family in Bethany"), 2866 A1 (N.C. "Mary, Martha & Lazarus), 3233 A1 (Ark. "Martha and Mary"), 1013 B (Ky, "Mary and Martha.").

H 8
THE LITTLE MOHEA

The Indian girl invites the stranger to live in her cottage in the coconut grove. He replies that he must return to his true love in his own country. They part, and he last sees her waving to him from the shore as his ship sails. The girl at home proves untrue, and the sailor longs to return to the lass of Mohea.

> As I went out walking for pleasure one day,
> In sweet recreation to wear time away—
> As I sat amusing myself on the grass,
> Oh, who could I spy but a fair Indian lass!

Hudson, 162, 9; 7 (Miss.). Barry, 86, 9, m. (Me. from Eckstorm). Belden, 144, 9 (Mo.); detailed refs. Brown II, 340, 8½ (N.C.); refs. *Bulletin* no. 6 (1933), p. 15, 7, m. (Me. via Vt.); 3½, m. (Me.); detailed notes. Cambiaire, 62, 9 sts. *CFB* I (1962), no. 2, p. 16, 7, m.; 16 couplets; 6, m. (Colo.). Cox, 372, 7; 6; 3½ (W. Va.). Henry, *Folk-Songs*, 284, 9, m. (Ala.); 9 (Tenn.); 8; 7 (N. C.); 6 (Tenn.); 4 (Ky.). Hubbard, 96, 9, m. (Utah). Leach, 725, 8 (Va.). Lomax, *Amer. Ballads*, 163, 18 couplets, m. (Ky. from Wyman). Morris, 356, 7, m. (Fla.). Owens, 102, 8, m. (Tex.). Randolph I, 280, 9, m. (Mo.); 6 (Ark.); refs. Williams, 218, 6 (Ky.). L. C. Records 2877 B1 (Tenn.); 2856 B1 (N.C.); 1488 A2 (Ky.); and 16 other recordings.

According to Kittredge, " 'The Little Mohea' appears to be a chastened American remaking of the favorite English broadside song of 'The Indian Lass' " (*JAF* 35 (1922), 408. For variants in North American tradition, see Mackenzie, 154, and Halpert, *JAF* 52 (1939), 65). Barry points out, however, that the British broadsides mention New Orleans. The girl in "The Indian Lass" is presumably an American Indian. Barry concludes that "The Little Mohea" was originally the story of a romance between a pioneer and an Indian, and that it became the well known sea song current in American tradition, with its scene changed to Maui, one of the Hawaiian islands. The English broadside, he believes, developed from the American sea ballad. (See *Bulletin* no. 6, 15-18, and Barry's conclusion condensed in Flanders-Barry, 146).

One of the most poetic and romantic of American ballads, "The Little Mohea" in theme and phraseology is a decided improvement over "The Indian Lass". Still it seems more logical to believe that the American piece developed from the British one and that the widely distributed "sea song" with its island setting, rather than the unknown "pioneer ballad" was the original American version.

H 9

THE LAKE OF PONCHARTRAIN

After a wearisome trek, the traveler meets a Creole girl, who conducts him to her father's house and treats him kindly. She refuses his proposal of marriage, saying that she has a lover at sea for whom she is waiting. He promises to drink to her health in "each social circle."

> 'Twas on a bright May morning I bid Orleans adieu
> And steered my course for Jackson, where I was forced to go.
> Of course it was for money, and of no credit gained;
> But it's left me here to wander on the lake of Ponchartrain.

Gardner, 133, 6d (Mich.); refs. Flanders-Barry, 147, 5d, m. (Vt.). Larkin, 31, 5d (A cowboy variant, "On the Lake of the Poncho Plains"). Randolph IV, 413, 3, m. (Mo.). Stout, 90, 4d (Ia.). Tolman, *JAF* 35 (1922), 387, 5d

(Ia.). L. C. Records 2264 B3 (Mich.), 1562 A2 (Ky.), and 3224 B1 (Mo.).

"It is very probable that the author knew and imitated 'The Little Mohea'." (Flanders-Barry).

H 10

THE CHIPPEWA GIRL

Having met an Indian girl, the rover immediately proposes marriage. She refuses him, saying both that she is too young and that her parents would disapprove of such a match. The two part, apparently without regrets. The brief ballad ends with some unrelated comments on marriage.

> As I was roving one morning in June
> Among the pretty roses as they were in bloom,
> I spied a fair damsel all out in the rain;
> She was washing her linen in the Chippewa stream.

Beck, 111, 5d (Mich.). Mackenzie, 150, 6d, m. (N.S.).

"Several lumberjacks from the Saginaw valley know this song. It is not a true shanty-boy ballad, but it grew up where the Chippewa Indians dwelt and was sung in the shanties of the upper part of the Lower Peninsula of Michigan. I expected to find it in Wisconsin, but did not, though it may be there." (Note from Beck, 111).

H 11

ON THE BANKS OF THE PAMANAW

The Indian girl is alone because all the members of her family have died and her lover has deserted her. She refuses the white man's offer to take her "to a paleface counteree" because she has made a vow to spend her life "on the banks of the Pamanaw."

> While strolling out one evening,
> In the latter part of June,
> The sun had sunk far in the west,
> And brightly shone the moon.
>
> I strolled away from camp, my boys,
> To view the scenery round;
> 'Twas there I spied this Indian maid
> A-sitting on the ground.

Beck, 112, 12, m. (Mich.); reprinted by Lomax, *Amer. Ballads*, 451 and in Beck, *Bunyan*, 197.

Nothing definite is known about the history of this appealing old ballad, although Beck suggests that it originated "on the Red River of the North, south of Winnepeg . . . in . . . North Dakota", or perhaps in Wisconsin.

H 12

THE LONESOME (STORMY) SCENES OF WINTER

When the narrator insists on an answer to his proposal of marriage, the girl scornfully refuses him, saying she has another suitor. He reprimands her for her snobbery and love of wealth and plans to go far away as a soldier or sailor. In some texts the girl changes her mind only to have the man say he has found another sweetheart and she may do the same.

> Lonesome seems the winter,
> The chilling frost and snow;
> Dark clouds around me hover;
> The wind has ceased to blow.
>
> I went the other evening
> My true love for to see.
> I asked her if she'd marry me;
> She would not answer me.

Belden, 195, 10 (Mo.); refs. Creighton and Senior, 209, 6d, m.; 6d; 5d; 5½d (N.S.). Henry, *Folk-Songs*, 298, 9 (Tenn.); 11 (Ga. "Pretty Polly"). *JAF* 29 (1916), 200, 3 (Ga.). Kittredge, *JAF* 20 (1907), 273, 5d (Ky.).

This piece is similar in subject matter to ballads P 10-P 12 in *Amer. Balladry from Brit. Broadsides*.

H 13

THE YOUNG MAN WHO WOULDN'T HOE CORN

The young man allows the weeds to choke his corn and then loses his entire crop in a September frost. When he goes courting, the girl learns that he has not hoed his corn and refuses to marry him.

> Now I am going to sing you a song,
> Concerning a young man who couldn't hoe corn.
> The reason why I cannot tell,
> For this young man was always well.
>
> Then why do you ask of me for to wed
> As long as you cannot raise your bread?
> Single I am and single I'll remain;
> For a lazy man I won't maintain.

Flanders and Brown, 74, 6 (Vt.). Belden, 440, 7 (Mo.); see for refs to texts from W. Va., Tenn.—"Harm Link," Miss., Ind., Iowa, and Neb. Brewster, 307, 4 (Ind.). Brown II, 247, 5 (N.C.). Eddy, 243, 7 (O. "The Lazy Man"). Lomax, *Folk Song U.S.A.*, 230, 7. Owens, 219, 7, m. (Tex.). Randolph II, 196, 7, m. (Ark.); refs. L. C. Records 55 A3 (Tex.); 1744 B (Ind.); 870 A1 (Ark. "The Lazy Young Man").

The history of this ballad has not been traced, but Lomax, (*Folk Song U.S.A.*, 223) suggests that "Frontier Americans . . . carried it westward with them from New England and the Southeastern states into the corn belt of the Middle West."

H 14

THE QUEENSTOWN MOURNER

(In the Township of Danville)

The mourner tells of his courtship and marriage and of the sudden death of his beloved young wife. The ballad, which emphasizes the transiency of human life, is strongly moralistic and religious in tone.

> In the township of Danville I courted my love,
> And the truth that I told her, not worthy I was,
> And if she looked for riches to turn me away,
> And not to encourage my suit for one day.

Flanders & Brown, 29, 7d, m. (Vt.) "In the Township of Danville"); 20d (from an old broadside). L. C. Record 3715 A & B, 3716 (Vt.).

H 15

OLBAN (ALBAN) or THE WHITE CAPTIVE

Alban, the Indian chieftan, rescues the captive, Amanda, from torture by his tribe and escorts her to safety in his canoe.

> The moon had gone down o'er the hills of the West;
> Its last beam had faded on Moosilauk crest.
> 'Twas a midnight of horror! the red meteor flashed,
> And hoarse down the mountain the cataract dashed!

Flanders-Barry, 256, 14, m. (Vt. text from ms.). Barry, 36, 13, m. (Me. The original text). Hubbard, 98, 14, m. (Utah). Morris, 128, 10 (O. via Fla.). Peabody, *JAF* 25 (1912), 169, 10½, m. (Tex.). *KFQ* 5 (1960), no. 4, p. 16, 7d (Pa.). Randolph IV, 118, 3½d (Mo.); 11d (Ark.); notes and refs. Will, *JAF* 22 (1909), 256, a frag. of 27 lines (N.D. "Amanda, the Captive"). The AAFS has a 13 st. text of this piece, collected by Austin Fife in Utah, entitled "The Chief of the Utes."

" 'The White Captive' was written in his youth by the Reverend Thomas C. Upham, afterwards . . . Professor of Moral Philosophy at Bowdoin College . . . It was first printed for the author in the *Columbian Sentinel* [Boston], September 19, 1818." (Note from Flanders-Barry, 258. See for further details. For a longer account with the original text and two traditional melodies, see Barry, *Bulletin* no. 8 (1934), 19-24.) "The only authentic detail of the story is the *red meteor....*" (Note from Barry, *Maine Woods Songster*, 98).

H 16

TITTERY NAN

Joe Dimsey steals Josiah's mare, but the old man recovers his horse and pummels the thief.

> On Saturday night the wind blew west,
> Tittery Nan tum ta-ri-o,
> There was a husking in the east,
> Fairy-nay, Tory-no,
> Tittery Nan tum ta-ri-o.

Linscott, 292, 6, m. (Me.). Barry, *Bulletin* no. 6, 13, 5, m. (Me.). (Barry refers also to four variants printed in the Boston *Evening Transcript*. At least two of these are from Maine.)

This little piece with its gay refrain is hardly more than a nonsense song, but, as Mrs. Linscott says, "It is probably founded on fact." Brevity alone should not exclude it from the ranks of balladry.

H 17

THE PLAIN GOLDEN BAND

The girl asks her fiancé to take back his engagement ring because she has momentarily believed false stories about his devotion and has stained the band by being unfaithful.

> Saying, "Take back this ring that I fain would retain,
> For wearing it only causes me pain.
> I have broken the vows that I made on the strand.
> Now take back, I pray you, that plain golden band."

Doerflinger, 248, 9d and chor. (N.S.); stanza 3 is given above; 247, tune from N.B. Ives, *JAF* 72 (1959), 59, 11d, m. (Me.).

Though somewhat sentimental and "literary," this piece has been credited to the New Brunswick logger Joe Scott, who may also have composed "Guy Read," (C 9), "Benjamin Deane," (F 32), and "Howard Carey," (E 23). See Edward D. Ives, " 'Ben Deane' and Joe Scott: a Ballad and its Probable Author," *JAF* 72 (1959), 53-66. In a letter to Mr. Ives, Peter Jamieson, who worked with Scott in New Hampshire, wrote: "After knowing him about a month, one night as him and I were talking, one of our crew started to sing The Plain Golden Band. He stopped talking to me, and as I turned to him he was sobbing and tears running down his cheeks. After a while he turned to me and said, 'I am the author of that song and you have found me right where the song said you would. Still true to the vows I made....' "

H 18

MORRISSEY AND THE RUSSIAN SAILOR

A Russian challenges the boxing champion, Morrissey, in Tierra del Fuego. The hero says he can lick Yankees or Russians and adds, "To the honor of old Paddy's land, these laurels I still will wear." Although he is knocked down twice, he finally gives the Russian his finishing blow in the twenty-eighth round.

> Come all ye brave sons of old Ireland, attention I do pray,
> While I relate the praises of an Irish hero brave,
> Concerning of a dreadful fight took place the other day,
> Between a Russian sailor boy and gallant Morrissey.

Barry, 32, 8d, m. (Me.). Dean, 4, 11d, (Minn.). Finger, 44, 14d, m. Mackenzie, 332, 7d (N.S.) ; refs. Rickaby, 173, text from Dean. Sandburg, 398, 12d, m. (text from Dean).

John Morrissey was born in Ireland in 1831 but moved to Troy, N. Y., as a young boy. He advanced from brawling to professional pugilism in 1852 and in 1860 defeated John C. Heenan for the championship. He then retired from the ring, made Saratoga Springs a famous gambling resort, and later was twice elected to Congress. He died in 1878. (Note from Russell Crouse, *Mr. Currier and Mr. Ives*, (N.Y., 1930), pp. 85-88).

I was uncertain whether to include this and the following two pieces in *Native American Balladry* or in *American Balladry from British Broadsides*. The first two certainly sound Irish, but since the heroes were Americans and since the ballads have been reported from tradition only in America, I have decided to give them here.

H 19

MORRISSEY AND THE BLACK

The fight begins at six in the morning. Up to the fourteenth round, Morrissey is taking hard blows, but he is revived by his second and knocks out his opponent in the twenty-fifth round.

> Come all you true Irish boys, please listen to me.
> I will sing you the praises of John Morrissey,
> Who has lately been challenged for ten thousand pounds
> For to fight Ned the black of Mulberry town.

Mackenzie, 334, 9d (N.S.). Greenleaf, 355, 8d (Nfld.). Horace P. Beck has collected a fragment of this ballad from Maine.

See the notes to the preceding piece.

H 20

HEENAN AND SAYERS

Heenan goes from America to England to fight the British hero. His opponent draws first blood, but by round thirty-seven, when Heenan is winning, the Britons stop the fight and call it a draw.

> I tell of merry England and plucky old John Bull,
> Where Britons fill their glasses and fill them brimming full,
> To drink a toast and sing the praise of Britain's fighter brave,
> Tom Sayers who the honour of his nation sought to save.

Finger, 48, 8d. Beck, *The Folklore of Maine*, 267, 8d, m. (Me.). Dean, 24, 9d (Minn.). Hubbard, 362, 8d, m.; 6d and chor. from ms. (Utah. "Johnny Bull"). Rickaby, 177, 9d (Minn. from Dean); notes.

The match between John C. Heenan (The Benicia Boy) and Tom Sayers took place April 17, 1860. It was stopped in the forty-second round. *The Encyclopedia Brittanica*, Eleventh Ed., says that it was the last of the bare-knuckle fights and the most famous boxing match of modern times.

See the notes to "Morrissey and the Russian Sailor" (H 18).

H 21

THE FELLOW THAT LOOKS LIKE ME

The speaker is first taken for his double in Central Park and made to pay a bill he does not owe. He is then beaten for wronging a man's daughter and later arrested as an escaped criminal. Tried and convicted, he is set free only when the police find the right man, "the ugliest wretch that ever was on earth."

> In sad despair I wandered, my heart was filled with woe,
> While on my grief I pondered; what to do I did not know,
> Since cruel fate has on me frowned, and trouble seems to be
> That there is a fellow in this here town the very image of me.

Mackenzie, 351, 5d and two choruses (N.S.); refs. Randolph III, 219, 8 (Mo.); refs. Hubbard, 329, 6d and two choruses, m. (Utah).

"This song is in the sheet music collection in the Harvard College Library, 'By J. F. Poole. Copyright by Frederick Blume. District Court, Southern District, New York, 1867.' It was much esteemed in the late sixties as a popular song and as a choice bit of music-hall entertainment, and it was included in several of the songsters of the period. See for instance: *'The Fellow That Looks Like Me' Songster* (New York, Robert M. DeWitt, 1867) . . . " (Note from Mackenzie).

H 22

I WONDER WHERE'S THE GAMBLER

Assisted by his friends, the gambling man staggers home in pain. He is put to bed, and his mother asks the Lord to forgive him. Conscious of his sins, the gambler says it is too late to pray.

> The poor man he gambled,
> He gambled all night long.
> He gambled till the broke of day,
> And he rose from the table,
> And he throwed his cards away.
>
> *Chorus:* I wonder where's the gamblin' man,
> I wonder where he's gone.

Wilgus, *KFR* 3, 106, 6 sts. and chorus, tune p. 111 (Ky.). Henry, *Songs Sung*, 96, 4 6-line sts. and chor. (Ky. In this version, the gambling man has been shot). Sharp II, 204, 1, m. (Ky.).

H 23

THE OLD MAID AND THE BURGLAR

(The Burglar Man)

While the burglar is hiding under her bed, the old maid removes her teeth, her glass eye, and her wig. She discovers him and threatens to blow off the top of his head unless he marries her. He replies, "Woman, for the Lord's sake, shoot!"

> One night last week a burglar bold
> Tried to rob a house.
> He crept up to the window
> As quietly as a mouse.

Hudson, 249, 6 (Miss.). Brown II, 465, 7 (N.C.). L. C. Records 1388 B2 (Ky.) and 844 A1 (N.C. 7 sts. "The Burglar Man"). Davis, *Folk-Songs*, 178, lists three Virginia texts.

H 24

THE WARRANTY DEED

(The Wealthy Old Maid)

When the bride prepares to retire for the night, she first washes away the roses from her cheeks, then removes her wig and her false teeth, and finally casts aside her cotton padding. The bridegroom flees. His mistake was in not insisting on a warranty deed.

> There once was a lawyer whom I call Mister Clay,
> He had but few clients and those did not pay,
> At length of starvation he grew so afraid,
> That he courted and married a wealthy old maid.

Randolph III, 221, 9d, m. (Mo.); refs. Sturgis, 26, 6d, m. (Vt.).

H 25

COURTING THE WIDOW'S DAUGHTER

(Hard Times)

The young man goes secretly to call on his sweetheart. Their laughter awakens the widow, who wants a husband herself. When the caller insults her, she beats him with a broomstick and he flees on his horse.

> One Saturday night I went to a house,
> And through a dark entry I crept like a mouse;
> I went for the purpose my true love to see.
> She opened the door; I entered straightway,
> And it's hard times.

Belden, 248, 7 (Mo. fro ms. of ca. 1870) Cox, 511, 6 sts. of this piece with 7 of another (W.Va.). Lomax, *Our Singing Country*, 124, 6, m. (a composite text; "Johnny McCardner"). Randolph III, 107, 7½, m.; 6 (Mo. "The Widow's Old Broom"). Treat, *JAF* 52 (1939), 23, 7, m. (Ky. via Wis.).

H 26

THE GIRL THAT WORE A WATERFALL

The speaker sees the girl first in a drygoods store and later at a picnic. He walks her home and is surprised by the girl's husband. The visitor is beaten black and blue and robbed of his watch, chain, and money.

> Come all of you that's been in love,
> Come sympathize with me,
> For I have loved the fairest girl
> That ever you did see,
> Her age it was but sweet sixteen,
> She was a figger fair an' tall,
> She was a handsome critter
> But she wore a waterfall.

Randolph III, 111, 5d, m. (Mo.); refs. Davis, *Folk-Songs*, 144, 12, m. (Va. ref. only). Henry, *Folk-Songs*, 307, 12 (Ky.). The last line of a lumberjacks' song collected in Quebec in 1957 reads, "Fitzsimmons sang about the girl that wore the waterfall." (Fowke and Mills, p. 174).

"A 'waterfall' is a mass of artificially curled hair, worn at the back of the head . . . " (note from Randolph).

H 27

TEN BROECK AND MOLLIE

After staying behind for a while, the bay horse Ten Broeck tells his rider to let him run, and he then beats Mollie with ease.

Run, old Molly run, run old Molly run;
Ten Brook's gonna beat you to the bright shinin' sun.

Ten-Brooks was a big bay horse, he rode that shaggy mane,
He run all 'round Memphis, he beat the Memphis train.

Wilgus, *KFR* 2 (1956), 80, 9 sts. as sung by Bill Monroe, formerly of
Kentucky; 79, fragments of 5 and 3 sts. (Ky.); add. sts.; 9 sts. (Ky. via
Ill.); notes and refs. *KFR* 2 (1956), 141, fragments of 3 and 2 sts. (Ky.).
Jansen, *KFR* 4 (1958), 149, 2½d (Ky.). All texts display extreme verbal
variation.

"The July 4, 1878, match race in which the Kentucky thoroughbred Ten
Broeck defeated the mare Miss Mollie McCarthy went into the record books
as the last four-mile heat race in American turf history." (Note from Wilgus,
"Ten Broeck and Mollie: a Race and a Ballad," *KFR* 2 (1956), 77).

H 28

THE BANKS OF BRANDYWINE

The sailor asks the lovely maid to forget Henry, her fiancé, saying first
that he is probably unfaithful and then that he is already married. When
she swoons he reveals that he is Henry.

One morning very early, in the pleasant month of May,
As I walked out to take the air, all nature being gay,
The moon had not yet veiled her face, but through the trees did shine,
As I wandered forth to take the air on the banks of Brandywine.

Mackenzie, 186, 8d (N.S.); refs. to texts in many American songsters.
Carmer, 5, 4d, m. Gardner, 193, 9d (Mich. from ms.). *The Forget Me Not
Songster* (Phila., n.d.), 16, 9d. *WVF* 5 (1955), 33, 13d lines, m. (W.Va.).

The Brandywine is the creek near Philadelphia where Washington's forces
were defeated by the British in 1777. See the note to the following piece.

H 29

THE BLOOMING BRIGHT STAR OF BELLE ISLE

The girl tells the stranger that she is poor and works hard but will remain
faithful to her vows and wait for the lad who has left her. The disguised
speaker then reveals that he is her lover and the two are married.

One evening for pleasure I rambled
To view the fair fields all alone,
Down by the banks of Loch Erin,
Where beauty and pleasure was known.
I spied a fair maid at her labor,
Which caused me to stay for awhile;
I thought her the goddess of beauty,
The blooming bright star of Belle Isle.

Greenleaf, 268, 4½d, m. (Nfld. text from a printed folksong collection).
Fowke and Johnston, 144, 7, m. (Nfld.).

This is a Newfoundland product in the English or Anglo-Irish broadside
tradition. For similar stories, see ballads N 28-N 43 in *American Balladry
from British Broadsides.*

H 30

JERRY, GO AND ILE THAT CAR

Larry Sullivan rides a handcar for forty years as a foreman of section
gangs. He takes pride in keeping the tracks in good shape and in never
having had a wreck. As he lies dying he asks to be buried beside the tracks,
and his last words are, "Jerry, go and ile that car."

> Come all ye railroad section men, I hope you will draw near
> And listen to the story that I will tell you here
> Concerning Larry Sullivan, alas he is no more,
> 'Twas over forty years ago he sailed from Erin's shore.

Fowke, *WF* 21 (1962), 254, 9d (B.C.). Sandburg, 360, 6d, m. (N.M.).
WF 11 (1952), 183, an Oregon text referred to.

"Captain Cates' [the singer's] father . . . crossed the plains in the 1880's
when the railroad was being built across western Canada. There he learned
'Jerry, Go and Ile That Car' which was originally sung along the Santa Fe
and probably brought to Canada by migrant railroad workers." (Note from
Fowke).

H 31

CHRISTINE LEROY

The speaker tells her brother how the beautiful seductress gained her husband's affection and blames them both for her impending death.

> No, brother, I'll never grow better,
> It is useless to tell me so now,
> For my broken heart only is waiting
> For its resting place under the sod.
>
> I was only dreaming, dear brother,
> How happy our home was with joy,
> Till a serpent crept into our Eden
> In the fair form of Christine Leroy.

Randolph IV, 314, 10, m. (Ark.); add. lines (Mo.). *JAF* 52 (1939), 28,
4d, m. (Ky. via Wis.). *WF* 17 (1958), 242, 9, m. (Ia.).

BALLADS OF THE NEGRO

I 1

JOHN HENRY

In a contest with a steam-drill, John Henry and his hammer are victorious, but the effort costs the Negro steel-driver his life.

> John Henry was a poor little boy
> Sitting on his father's knee.
> He said, "The Big Ben Tunnel on the C and O
> Going to be the death of me".

Johnson (see below), 127, 7 (W. Va. via Va.); 89, 12 (broadside); the author prints 28 other texts, many with tunes, 90-136. Chappell (see below), prints 30 texts. Brown II, 623, 8 (N.C.); notes. Henry, *Folk-Songs*, 446, 9 and 2 fragments; notes and refs. Leach, 756, texts from Johnson. Leach and Beck, *JAF* 63 (1950), 273, 3, m. (Va. a cante-fable variant). Lomax, *Amer. Ballads*, 5, 22, m. (a composite text); 5. Lomax, *Folk Song U.S.A.*, 258, 17, m.; 8, m. (from L. C. Record AAFS no. 15). Lomax, *JAF* 28 (1915), 14, 11. Lomax, *Our Singing Country*, 259, 9, m. (Ark. from L. C. Record 2668 or AAFS no. 15). Morris, 182, 8, m. (Fla.). Sandburg, 24, 12, m. White, 189, notes and fragments. Williams, 327, 9 (Ky.). L. C. Records AAFS no. 15 (Ark.); 2943 A2 & B1 (Ala.); 2551 A1 (Ky. via N.Y.); 2916 B2, 2917 A1 (Tenn.); 3167 B1 (N.C. Sung by B. L. Lunsford); and recordings from 32 other singers from Fla., Ky., S.C., Va., Miss., Ga., Mich., and Wash., D.C.

Professor Johnson writes: "I prefer to believe that (1) there was a Negro steel driver named John Henry at Big Bend Tunnel, that (2) he competed with a steam drill in a test of the practicability of the device, and that (3) he probably died soon after the contest, perhaps from fever." The Big Bend Tunnel on the Chesapeake and Ohio Railroad, nine miles east of Hinton, W. Va., was under construction from 1870-1872. (Notes from Johnson, 54, 27.)

The following exhaustive studies of the John Henry tradition have been published:

Louis W. Chappell, *John Henry: A Folk-Lore Study*, Walter Biedermann, Jena, Germany, 1933. Reviewed by Barry, *Bulletin* no. 8, 24-26.

Guy B. Johnson, *John Henry: Tracking Down a Negro Legend*, Chapel Hill, 1929.

I 2

JOHN HARDY

The Negro bad man John Hardy threatens to kill the first man who wins his money in a gambling game. Another Negro (in some versions, a Chinaman) is the victim. Hardy is arrested and sentenced, and dies on the gallows.

> John Hardy was a desp'rate little man,
> He carried two guns ev'ry day,
> He shot down a man on the West Virginia line,
> You oughta seen John Hardy gettin' away, poor boy,
> You oughta seen John Hardy gettin' away.

Lomax, *Folk Song U.S.A.*, 306, 9, m. Brown II, 563, 8; 9; 4 (N.C.). Cox, 178, nine W. Va. texts of 7, 9, 6, 7, 10, 8, 5, 12, and 13 sts. Gordon, *Adventure*, July 10, 1923, 192, 3 sts. Johnson, *John Henry*, 135, 9 (from Columbia record no. 167 D). Leach, 759, texts from Cox and from *JAF* 22 (1909), 247. Leach and Beck, *JAF* 63 (1950), 275, 2, m. (Va.). Lomax, *Amer. Ballads*, 124, 6, m. (Va. via Ida.). Lomax, *FSNA*, 271, 10, m. (adapted and arranged by Alan Lomax). Morris, 93, 7, m. (Fla. Text from L. C. Record 957 A1. It was learned from a phonograph record). Randolph II, 144, 4, m.; 5½ m. (Ark.); 6½ (Mo.). Sharp II, 35, 9, m. (N.C.). N. J. H. Smith, *PTFLS* VII, 115, 6, m. (N.C.). Williams, 407, 7 (Ky.). *WVF* 5 (1955), 36, 2 (W.Va.). L. C. Records 2896 B2, 2897 A1 (Tenn.); 1814 B2, 1814 B4, 1815 A2 (N.Y. Sung by B. L. Lunsford.); 4085 B1 (Va.); 4148 B3 (Cal.); 2994 B2, 2995 A1 (Miss.); and seven other Southern recordings.

Professor Cox located John Hardy's execution order in the court house at Welch, McDowell County, West Virginia. Hardy had been convicted of murder and was sentenced to be hanged January 19, 1894. He is said to have wantonly killed another Negro, whom he had accused of stealing twenty-five cents. Having "got religion" in prison, he died in a penitent mood. (For a detailed account, see Cox, 175-177, where, however, John Hardy and John Henry are sometimes confused.)

I 3

FRANKIE AND ALBERT

Frankie shoots Albert when she finds him with another woman. Albert dies forgiving Frankie and she grieves. In some versions she is arrested and sentenced; in others she goes free.

> Frankie was a good girl.
> And everybody knows
> She paid one hundred dollars
> For Albert a suit of clothes.
> He's her man, but he's done her wrong.

Hudson, 189, 15 (Miss.). Belden, 331, 29 (a composite text); see 330 for notes and refs. to texts from W. Va., Ky., Tenn., N.C., Ga., Ala., La., Tex., and Ark. Brown II, 589, 18; 9; 4; parts of other texts (N.C.); notes and refs. Leach, 761, texts from *JAF* 45 (1932), 142. Leach and Beck, *JAF* 63 (1950), 271, 8, m. (Va.). Lomax, *Folk Song U.S.A.*, 312, 17, m. Morris, 126,

14, m. (Fla.). Randolph II, 127, six texts from Ark. and Mo. of 13, 8, 10, 13, 13, and 7 sts. with two tunes; notes and refs. Williams, 136, 11 (Ky. "Albert and Maggie"). L. C. Records 2803 A2 & B1 (Tenn.); 1817 B3, 1818 A (N.Y. Sung by B. L. Lunsford); 2835 A3 (Va.); and other recordings.

"John Huston, author of the play *Frankie and Johnny* (New York, 1930) thinks that the song refers to the killing of Allen Britt by Frankie Baker, which occurred in St. Louis in 1899. Al Britt was an 18-year old black boy who lived with mulatto Frankie. . . ." George Milburn said in a letter to Vance Randolph," . . . The Frankie song may have been applied to Frankie Baker's case, but there is ample evidence that the ballad was being sung in widely separated sections of the country long before 1899. . . ." (Notes from Randolph II, 126). The ballad is sometimes known to folk singers as "Frankie Baker." Many conflicting reports concerning the age and factual basis of this piece have been circulated, but so far research has failed to settle its origin.

I 4

THE COON-CAN GAME

The narrator goes to the depot, sees his woman on a train, boards it and shoots her. Arrested, tried, and sentenced he forlornly laments his fate in prison.

> I sat down to a coon-can game,
> I couldn't play my hand.
> I was thinkin' about the woman I love
> Run away with another man, (Poor boy!)
> Run away with another man.

Scarborough, 87, 7, m. (Tex. With the last line of each stanza repeated as a refrain). Finger, 74, almost identical with Scarborough's. Lomax, *Our Singing Country*, 309, 7, m. (Ky. from L. C. Record 1542, "As I Set Down to Play Tin-Can"). Owens, 179, 4d. m. (Tex. "Po' Boy"). Sandburg, 310, 6d, m. (Ark. and Cal. A composite text); 3d and chor., m. ("Po' Boy"; in this the narrator is jailed for robbing a railroad mail car); p. 456, 3, m. ("Ten Thousand Miles Away from home"). Smith, *South Carolina Ballads*, 48, 11 (Mont. "The Game of Coon-Can"; reprinted from *Adventure*, Dec. 20, 1925, with Gordon's comments; in this text, which borrows liberally from other ballads, the narrator shoots the man who stole his girl).

I 5

DELIA (HOLMES)

Coonie kills his sweetheart when she breaks her promise to marry him. Her mother grieves at Delia's death. Coonie writes a letter from jail, where he has been sent for 99 years, asking the governor to pardon him.

Delia, Delia,
Why didn't you run,
See dat desperado
Had a forty fo' smokeless gun,
Cryin' all I had done gone.

Chapman J. Milling, *"Delia Holmes—A Neglected Negro Ballad," SFQ* 1
(1937), no. 4, p. 4, 23 sts. and chor., m.; frag. of 6 sts.; frag. of 2 sts.
(S.C.); see for notes and refs. to three printed fragments. L. C. Records
4070 A2 (Ga.); 3789 A1, 2 & 3 (S.C. Sung by Dr. Milling).

Will Winn, the Negro singer of Milling's first variant "states that 'Delia'
originated following a murder in Georgia, having been composed about 1900
by a white minstrel of Dallas, Texas, known as "Whistlin' Bill Ruff. The
song, however, seems too typically Negroid to admit of this explanation."
(Note from Milling, 3).

I 6

ELLA SPEED

(Bill Martin and Ella Speed)

Bill Martin shoots his woman because she is unfaithful to him. He is
sentenced to be hanged (or is given life imprisonment).

All you young girls better take heed,
Don' you do like po' Ella Speed;
Some day you will go for to have a lil fun
An' a man will do you like Bill Martin done.

Lomax, *Amer. Ballads*, 117, 8, m. (a composite text; the last stanza is given
above). Lomax, *Negro Folk Songs*, 187, 17, m, (with every line repeated).
Sandburg, 28, 8, m. (Tex. via N.Y. "Alice B."). L. C. Records 3990 A1
(Tex.): 120 B2, 125 B, and 54 A & B (La. Sung by Lead Belly); 215 B2;
2606 A2 (Tex.). These recordings were made from the singing of Negro
prisoners.

"Lead Belly says that not long before he moved to Dallas, Bill Martin
shot down Ella Speed in the street and that along with the other musicians
of that area he composed this ballad." (Lomax, *Negro Folk Songs*, 187).

I 7

DEVIL WINSTON

Devil, a Negro bad man, kills his woman after an argument with her,
and is hanged.

Devil lef' Nine Hundred wringin' wet with sweat,
"Goin' to hunt fo' Vinie, ef I don't I'm goin' to fall dead."
Devil, oh Devil, what's that in yo' grip?
"Piece uv Vinie's shoulder, an' I'm goin' to take a trip."

Wheeler, 109, 6d couplets, m. (Ky.). *KFR* 3 (1957), 103, 2½ (Ky.). Phonograph Record "The Hanging of Devil Winston" sung by Conrad Thibault, Decca Album no. 451.

George Winston (Devil) was executed for the murder of Vinie Stubblefield at Paducah, Kentucky. (See Wheeler, 105-108 for details.)

I 8

BAD LEE BROWN

(Little Sadie)

After killing his woman, the bully tries to run away, but he is arrested, tried, and sentenced to ninety-nine years.

> Late las' night I was a-makin' my rounds,
> Met my woman an' I blowed her down,
> Went on home an' I went to bed,
> Put my hand cannon right under my head,
>
> Here for de res' of my nachul life,
> An' all I ever done is kill my wife.

Lomax, *Amer. Ballads*, 89, 12, m. (Miss. "Bad Man Ballad," partly from L. C. Record 1859, 8 sts.). St. 1 and the last half of st. 10 are given above. Brown II, 597, 8 (N.C. "Sadie"). Cambiaire, 22 (same source as Henry's). Henry, *Songs Sung*, 39, 6 (Tenn. "Little Sadie"). Randolph II, 117, 2, m.; 1½ (Mo.). Wheeler, 110, 10, m. ("Late One Night"). Williams, 410, 9 (Ky.). L. C. Records 2851 B1 (N.C. "Little Sadie"); 384 B (Fla.); and the following under the title "Bad Man Ballad"; 706 A1 (S.C.) and 2591 B2 (Ark.).

I 9

BRADY

(Duncan and Brady)

Duncan kills Brady the policeman because he has wrecked Duncan's combination grocery and barroom. Mrs. Brady takes the news calmly and remarks to the children, "Well' all draw a pension when your daddy die".

> Duncan, Duncan was a-tendin' bar
> When in walked Brady with a shinin' star;
> Cried, "Duncan, Duncan, you are under arrest!"
> And Duncan shot a hole in Brady's breast.

Lomax, *Our Singing Country*, 333, 10, m. (a composite text, with tune from L. C. Record 1865. "Duncan and Brady"). Brown II, 571, 2 and chor. (N. C.); notes and refs. Gordon, 45, 2 sts. Gordon, *Adventure*, July 10, 1923, frag. of 5 sts. Odum and Johnson, *The Negro and His Songs*, 208, frag. of 4 sts. Sandburg, 198, frag. of 1d, m. (Neb. via Mo.); 4 sts. and 2 refrains, from R. W. Gordon's collection. Scarborough, 85, fragments and 7 sts. (Tex.). L. C. Records 1787 A2 (N.Y. Sung by B. L. Lunsford); 3978 B3 (Tex.); 1329 A2 & B2 (Ala.)

I 10

BATSON

Batson is arrested for murder and is sentenced to die. The ballad describes in detail the prisoner's conversations with the sheriff and with members of his own family, and gives a graphic account of the hanging.

> Batson been working for Mr. Earle
> Six long years today,
> And ever since he been working for Mr. Earle,
> He never got a pay.
>   Cryin', "Oh, Mamma,
>   I didn't done the crime".

Lomax, *Our Singing Country*, 335, 38, m. (La. Sung by "Stavin' Chain"; From L. C. Record 95 A & B). Gordon, 45, parts of two fragments. The editor describes Batson as "a Louisiana murderer of about 1901".

"Stavin' Chain said that this long, shuffling, and bloody story. . . . concerns a Lake Charles, Louisiana, murder. Batson, he told us, was a white day laborer, accused of murdering his employer, along with his whole family. They were found in an open field with only a little red soil thrown over their bodies. Inquiry fails to confirm Stavin' Chain's story. . . ." (Note from Lomax, 335).

I 11

DUPREE

Determined to get a diamond ring for Betty, Dupree the bandit kills a jeweler during a holdup, later shoots several policemen, and is finally arrested, tried and hanged.

> Betty tol' Dupree,
> "I want a diamond ring."
> Dupree tol' Betty,
> "I'll give you anything."

Odum and Johnson, *Negro Workaday Songs*, 55, 9; roughly 8d sts. (Ga. "Dupree Tol' Betty") See comments. Lomax, *Our Singing Country*, 328, 23 couplets, m. (Ohio). Tune from L. C. Record 713 B1 (Fla.).

"One of the most interesting aspects of this Dupree song is that it may be compared with the Atlanta ballad of the white *Frank Dupree* as popularly sung on the phonograph records. . . . There is little similarity of expression between the white version and the Negro one." (Note from Odum and John-

son, 55.). For the white ballad and for further details see "Frank Dupree"
(E 24).

I 12

POOR LAZARUS
(Bad Man Lazarus)

Lazarus becomes a fugitive after breaking into the commissary. He is
pursued into the mountains and shot by the sheriff's men. Returned to the
work camp, he asks for a drink of cool water and dies. Hearing of his death,
his mother remembers all the trouble he has caused her.

> So dey shot po' Laz'us, shot him wid a great big number,
> Dey shot po' Laz'us, shot him wid a great big number,
> Number 45, Lawd, Lawd, number 45.

Lomax, *Amer. Ballads*, 91, 11d couplets with 1st line repeated, m. (a composite text). Lomax, *Folk Song U.S.A.*, 308, 13d couplets with 1st line
repeated, m. Lomax, *Our Singing Country*, 342, 28 sts., m. (a composite
text). Odum and Johnson, *Negro Workaday Songs*, 50, 25 sts. with much
repetition (Ga.); 9 (N.C. "Billy Bob Russell"); notes. L. C. Records 3089
A1 (Miss.), 355 B (Fla.), 2709 A1 (Fla.), and 1305 B1 (Ala.), under the
titles "Old Bad Lazarus", "Old Bad Laz'us", "Bad Laz'us", and "Bad Man
Laz'us". In addition there are 17 recordings of "Po' Lazarus", mainly from
Southern Negro prisons.

I 13

RAILROAD BILL

Railroad Bill's depredations are finally ended when he is shot by his
pursuer.

> Some one went home an' tole my wife
> All about—well, my pas' life.
> It was that bad Railroad Bill.
>
> I went down on Number One,
> Railroad Bill had jus' begun,
> It's lookin' fer Railroad Bill.
>
> Railroad Bill mighty bad man,
> Shoot dem lights out o' de brakeman's han'.
> It's lookin' fer Railroad Bill.

Odum and Johnson, *The Negro and His Songs*, 198, 5, 10, 9, 5, and 9 sts.
The first stanzas given above are from the first three versions. Burt, 201, 7 sts.
Leach and Beck, *JAF* 63 (1950), 279, 8, m. (Va.). Lomax, *Amer. Ballads*,

118, 16, m. (a composite text, from Odum and Johnson). Scarborough, 251, 10 (Odum and Johnson's second version); 4 sts. and 2 sts. (from Perrow, *JAF* 25); see for comments. L. C. Records 1801 B1 (N.Y. Sung by B. L. Lunsford); 1327 B2 (Ala.); 3039 B2 (Miss.); 1315 B2 and 1323 A3 (Ala. same singer).

Mrs. Burt (*Amer. Murder Ballads*, pp. 200-202) refers to an article by J. B. Harlan in the Louisville and Nashville employees' magazine for May, 1927. Harlan directed the hunt which led to the death of Morris Slater ("Railroad Bill"), who terrorized Florida and Alabama from 1894 to 1897.

I 14

THE BULLY OF THE TOWN

The pursuer finally finds and kills the bully who has terrorized even the police. Apparently relieved, "All the wimmins come to town all dressed in red."

> The bully, the bully, the bully can't be found;
> If I fin' that bully, goin' to lay his body down.
> I'm lookin' for that bully of this town.

Odum and Johnson, 204, 9 sts. Stanza 2 is given above. Reprinted by Leach, 767. Leach and Beck, *JAF* 63 (1950), 279, 2, m. (Va.). Wheeler, 100, 1d, m. ("Stacker Lee No. 1"). L. C. Records 3391 A3 (La.), 2595 A1 (Tex.), and 180 A2 (Tenn.).

Spaeth, *Read 'Em and Weep*, 212-214, prints "The New Bully", 7 6-line d. sts. m. copyright 1896 by Charles E. Trevathan, as sung by May Irwin in "The Widow Jones." "A Negro melody which he [Trevathan] had picked up in the South made such a hit that Miss Irwin insisted on his making a complete song out of it." (See Spaeth, 212, for details.) Thus the "coon song" seems to have grown out of the traditional ballad.

I 15

STAGOLEE (STACKERLEE)

Irked that his old friend Billy Lyons has beaten him in a gambling game, Stagolee shoots him dead. The bad man is arrested, tried, and hanged. Each incident is dramatized in some detail, largely by means of colorful dialogue.

> 'Twas a Christmas morning,
> The hour was about ten,
> When Stagalee shot Billy Lyons
> And landed in the Jefferson pen.

Lomax, *Amer. Ballads*, 94, 10 (Tex.); 40d couplets (a composite text). Gordon, 44, 8 (a composite text).

> I got up one mornin' jes' about four o'clock;
> Stagolee an' big bully done have one finish fight.
> What 'bout? All 'bout dat Stetson rawhide hat.

Odum and Johnson, *The Negro and His Songs*, 198, 5 sts.; 196, 11 sts., the latter reprinted by Gerould, 288, and by Scarborough, 92; both reprinted by Leach, 765. Scarborough, 93, 6 sts. Spaeth, *Weep Some More*, 132, 24 sts. (first printed by R. W. Gordon in *Adventure*). Wheeler, 101, 6, m. L. C. Records 61 A2 (Tex.); 231 A (Ala.); 1479 B1 (Ky.); 239 A2 (Ark.); 700 A2 (Fla.); 1835 A2—10 in. (La.); 733 A (Miss.); 180 A1 (Tenn.); and 8 others from the South.

I 16

JOSEPH MICA (MIKEL)

(The Wreck of the Six-Wheel Driver)
(Been on the Choly So Long)

Determined to maintain his schedule, the engineer runs too fast to avert a collision with another train. Many are injured in the ensuing crash.

> Joseph Mikel was a good engineer,
> Told his fireman, well, oh, not to fear.
> All he wanted was to keep her good and hot.
> Says, "We'll make Paris 'bout four o'clock."

Lomax, *American Ballads*, 39, 4d ("The Wreck of the Six-Wheel Driver"). Sandburg, 364, Lomax's text. Odum and Johnson, *The Negro and His Songs*, 208, 3sts. Reprinted by Scarborough, 250.

The Lomaxes, *American Ballads*, 36-42, print what seem to be fragmentary texts of several Negro railroad ballads related to "Casey Jones". Among these is "Jimmie Jones", which is said to have inspired the more famous piece, and which ends, "Kase he's been on de cholly so long", a phrase equivalent, according to Lomax to "out on the hog" or "on the bum". "The Wreck of the Six-Wheel Driver" is very similar to Negro versions of "Casey Jones". Its stanzas end, "For I've been on the Charley so long". (Cf. Lomax's L. C. Record 604 A1, Tex., "Been on the Cholly So Long") Odum and Johnson's fragment mentions both Joseph Mica and Jim Jones. In *Folk Song U.S.A.*, 264-265, the Lomaxes have constructed a hypothetical "Casey Jones I" based on the related pieces printed in *American Ballads*. See their notes, 248-250.

I have included "Joseph Mica" not so much to establish its identity as a distinct ballad as to emphasize the extreme instability and confusion which are characteristic of Negro balladry.

See also "Casey Jones".

I 17

THE BOLL WEEVIL

In various fancifully described encounters between the boll weevil and the farmer, the almost indestructible insect usually triumphs.

> First time ah saw de Boll Weevil
> He was settin' on de squah.
> Next time ah saw dat Weevil
> He was settin' everywhah,
> Jes' a-lookin' foh a home,—lookin' foh a home!

Scarborough, 78, 6 (Tex.); stanza 2 is given above; notes and add. sts. Brown III, 245, 10; 4 (N.C.). Hudson, 199, 11 (Ala.). Lomax, *Amer. Ballads*, 112, 21, m. (a composite text from Tex. and Miss.). Lomax, *FSNA*, 535, 6, m. (Ala.). Lomax, *Folk Song, U.S.A.*, 236, 11 and chor., m. (a composite text). Morris, 188, 8, m. (Fla.). *PTFS* 26 (1954), 165, 16 (Tex.). Richardson, 90, 10, m. (Boll Weevil Blues"). Sandburg, 8, 12, m. (from John Lomax); 252, 12, m. L. C. Records AAFS no. 16 (Ala.); 4070 A1 (Ga.); 3988 A2 (Tex.); 3187 A1 (Ark.); 273 A1 (La.); 727 B1 (Va. "Boll Weevil Been Here"); 3989 A1 (La. "Boll Weevil Blues"); and other Southern recordings.

Sandburg writes, 252, "Gates Thomas recorded three boll weevil verses in 1897, many more in 1906. . . ." John Lomax first heard this piece sung in Texas in 1907 (see *Folk Song U.S.A.*, 225). The insect is said to have crossed the Rio Grande shortly before 1900.

For some comments on this piece see Chapter VII.

I 18

DESE BONES GWINE TO RISE AGAIN

A seriocomic account of the creation of Adam and Eve, the temptation, the fall, and the expulsion from Eden.

> De Lord he thought he'd make a man—
> Dese bones gwine to rise again;
> Made him out-a dirt an' a little bit o' sand—
> Dese bones gwine to rise again.

Lomax, *Amer. Ballads*, 597, 18 (mainly from S.C.; reprinted in Lomax, *FSNA*, 476, 13 sts.). Arnold, 148, 11, m. (Ala.). Brown III, 580, 8 (N.C.). Sandburg, 470, 16 sts. White, 83, 12 (Ala. "Creation").

Professor White says that this piece "is found in several printed collections of Negro songs, and is often sung by white people as a picnic song." (p. 83).

I 19

THE BLUE-TAIL FLY

When his horse is bitten by a blue-tail fly, the Negro's master is thrown into a ditch and killed.

> When I was young I used to wait
> On Massa an' hand him de plate,
> An' pass de bottle when he get dry
> An' bresh away de blue-tail fly.

Scarborough, 201, 7 and chor., m. (Va.). Brown III, 496, 7 and chor. (N.C.). Finger, 166, 6 sts. Lomax, *FSNA*, 505, 7 and chor., m.

"The first known copy of this song appeared in the *Ethiopian Glee Book* in 1844 as *Jimmie crack corn*. It was one of Abraham Lincoln's favorites". (Note from *The People's Song Book*, N.Y. 1948, p. 26, with a text of 5 sts. and m.).

I 20

WILLIE WARFIELD

The speaker kills Willie Warfield in a poker game and is jailed. His father cannot or will not help him, but his girl pawns her jewels and has him released on bail.

> Willie Warfield was a gambler,
> A gambler he remained.
> Started out last Sunday morning
> To have one more poker game.
> Every man ought to know when he loses.

Wilgus, *KFR* 3 (1957), 104, 11, with same last line throughout.

Wilgus (*KFR* 3, 171) reports that a version of this piece under the title "Spotty and Dudie," from Letcher Co., Ky., is sung by Paul Clayton in "Cumberland Mountain Folksongs" (Folkways FP-2007).

Appendix II

Most of the following pieces have appeared only once in folksong collections. If content and structure alone are considered, they clearly deserve to be called ballads. Furthermore, some of them are known to have been sung traditionally, while others seem to have enjoyed brief local popularity in song. But traditional balladry, which is always in a state of flux, loses pieces as well as gains them, and it is possible that many of the narratives listed here are no longer sung. I have also included certain pieces which may never have attained the status of folksong. For example, verse narratives may occasionally be learned from their authors or from manuscript or print and passed along to collectors without tunes and without the necessary intermediate steps of folk transmission. Until good texts of these relatively obscure pieces are collected from traditional singing, it has seemed wiser not to include them among the ballads which are known to be current as folksong.

(No attempt has been made to list ballads which are almost certainly extinct or which give no evidence of having passed into the memories of the folk.)

A key to the letters following the ballad titles is given below:

A Ballads printed only once, with little indication of where, when, or from whom the singer learned them.
B Ballad texts printed with insufficient annotation.
C Ballads contributed to collectors without evidence that they were still being sung.
D Ballads recovered from manuscript or from print.
E Ballad texts obtained directly or indirectly from their authors.
F Traditional ballads sung only by people who have since died.
G Ballads not reported from traditional singing since 1920.
H Ballads recovered only in garbled or fragmentary form from singing.

Note: These ballads are classified according to type, as in Appendix I, and are numbered with a prefixed "d" for "doubtful."

A WAR BALLADS

dA 27: LOVEWELL'S FIGHT   D

The British defeat the Indians at Pigwacket in 1725.
Barry, *Bulletin* no. 4, 3-5.

This old ballad has been sung in N. H. and Mass. within recent years, according to information available in Barry's ballad collection in the Houghton Library at Harvard, but no recent traditional texts have been printed.

dA 28: BRADDOCK'S DEFEAT   B
A relic of the French and Indian War.
Lomax, *American Ballads*, 526, 8½ sts.

dA 29: THE DYING SERGEANT   D
A British soldier is fatally wounded in the American Revolution.
Flanders-Barry, 118, 14 sts. References.

dA 30: ON THE EIGHTH DAY OF NOVEMBER   H
Indians defeat American soldiers in Ohio in 1791.
Eddy, 262, 3d, m. (Ohio).

dA 31: THE BATTLE OF POINT PLEASANT   D
American soldiers defeat the Indians on the banks of the Ohio.
Pound, 93, 4 sts.

dA 32: THE BATTLE OF BRIDGEWATER   C, G
A vivid account of the battle with the British in 1814.
Cox, 259, 8d (W.Va.).

dA 33: THE *SIR ROBERT PEEL*   A
Canadian rebels burn a British ship, 1838.
Fowke and Mills, 76, 6d, m. (N.Y.).

dA 34: SAMUEL YOUNG   G
A Kentucky boy dies in Mexico, 1848.
Sharp II, 271, 6, m. (N.C.).

dA 35: VIRGINIA'S BLOODY SOIL   F
The narrator's captain is killed in the battle of the Wilderness.
Warner, *NYFQ* 17 (1961), 95, 9d (N.Y.). Lomax, *FSNA*, 99, 7d, m. (N.Y. "from singing of Yankee John Galusha, as recorded by Frank Warner").

dA 36: THE RED, WHITE, AND RED   F
The Confederate soldiers defeat the Yankees at Big Bethel.
Warner, *NYFQ* 17 (1961), 91, 4d and chor., m. (N.Y.). Brown II, 529, 4d couplets and chor. (N.C. "On the Plains of Manassas"); notes. (The fragmentary Brown text seems to be a recomposition of the Warner ballad to apply to the later battle. Both contain a couplet like the following:

> We had a nice little fight on the fourth of last June,
> When MacGruder of Bethel wiped out Picayune.

dA 37: THE VICTORY WON AT RICHMOND   C, G

An account of a Southern victory in the Civil War.

Cox 266, 9 (Va.). 9 sts. (Va.).

See also the following fragment of Civil War Ballads printed in Cox's collection:

The Yankee Retreat	268	H
Bull Run	269	H
War Song	270	H

dA 38: PRAIRIE GROVE   H

A Civil War battle in Arkansas in 1862.

Randolph II, 275, 3 d. sts. m. (Mo.) Notes.

dA 39: ANDERSONVILLE PRISON   D

A Northern soldier is shot to death in the Southern prison and dies in a comrade's arms.

Randolph II, 306, 13 (Mo.). 13 sts. (Mo.).

dA 40: OLD EARLY CAMPED AT FISHER'S HILL   A

Gen. Sheridan repulses Gen. Early's attempt to drive him from the valley.

Thomas, *Ballad Makin'*, 58, 5 6-line sts. (Ky.).

B BALLADS OF COWBOYS AND PIONEERS

dB 28: MUSTANG GRAY   B

A lament on the death of a hard-fighting Ranger.

Lomax, *Cowboy Songs*, 363, 11, m.

dB 29: JOHN GARNER'S TRAIL HERD   B

The cowboys drive a beef herd north from Texas.

Lomax, *Cowboy Songs*, 25, 10d.

dB 30: THE CROOKED TRAIL TO HOLBROOK   B

The hardships of life on the trail are remembered.

Lomax, *Cowboy Songs*, 27, 8d (Ariz.).

dB 31: GEORGE BRITTON   A, B

George is injured in a stampede on the Lone Star Trail.

Lomax, *Cowboy Songs*, 18, 8, m. (Tex.).

dB 32: ON THE TRAIL TO IDAHO   B

Another account of the hardships of trail-riding.

Lomax, *Cowboy Songs*, 24, 7 (Tex.).

dB 33: WHEN I WAS A BRAVE COWBOY   A, B, H

Beset by cold and danger, the cowboy wishes he were safe at home.
Lomax, *Cowboy Songs*, 228, 6, m. (Tex.), from L. C. Record 650 A1.

dB 34: THE LLANO ESTACADO   B

A cowboy dies of thirst and heat while trying to satisfy a heartless woman's whim.
Lomax, *Cowboy Songs*, 313, 9 sts.

dB 35: BROWN-EYED LEE   C

The complaint of a cowboy unlucky in love. (1889).
Dobie, *PTFS* VI, 216, 32, m. (Tex.); Lomax, *Cowboy Songs*, 214; Larkin, 62.

dB 36: LITTLE JOE THE WRANGLER'S SISTER NELL   B

The cowgirl learns about her brother's death. (A sequel to "Little Joe the Wrangler").
Randolph II, 236, 12d (Mo.).

dB 37: TO THE WEST AWHILE TO STAY   A, B, H

A lonely cowboy hears of his mother's death.
Randolph II, 208, 6, m. (Ark.).

dB 38: THE GOL-DARNED WHEEL   A, B, G

A cowboy takes a wild ride on a high-wheeled bicycle.
Lomax, *Cowboy Songs*, 269, 26d couplets, m. (Tex.).

dB 39: THE BROKEN RING   B

A cowboy prevents his girl from marrying another man by returning with his half of a broken ring.
Fowke, *WF* 21 (1962), 250, 4½d (Ont.).

dB 40: THE INVASION SONG   A

Canton's crew kills Nate and Nick in a cattle war, Wyoming, 1892.
Burt, 173, 7d (Wyo.).

dB 41: WINDY BILL   C

Bill loses his bet that he can rope Blackie, an outlaw steer.
Lomax, *Cowboy Songs*, 113, 6d, m.

dB 42: ANNIE BREEN   A

Texas Joe dies after shooting the villain who brought death and dishonor to the girl Joe loved.
Finger, 77, 8d, m. (Tex.). Reprinted by Lomax, *Cowboy Songs*, 225.

dB 43: THE KILLER   D

A cowboy shoots "Two-Gun Blake" and avenges Nell.
Lomax, *Cowboy Songs*, 172, 12d.

dB 44: THE BUFFALO BULL FIGHT   H

A man shoots a bull and a battle with the herd ensues.
Davidson, *JAF* 58 (1945), 284, 8 sts. from a historical source. Hubbard, 447, 13 sts. and chorus (Utah. Only 4 sts. and chorus from tradition). "On the Road to California or The Buffalo Bull Fight", a fragment of this ballad was contributed to the Library of Congress collection from Utah by Austin E. Fife.

dB 45: ONLY A COWBOY   A

The cowboy has died and is sleeping "on the old staked plains."
Lomax, *Cowboy Songs*, 116, 4d and chor. (Tex.).
See also "Only a Brakeman (II, G) and "Only a Miner" (G 33).

C BALLADS OF LUMBERJACKS

dC 29: DRIVING SAW-LOGS ON THE PLOVER   E

A youth belatedly takes his mother's advice and returns from the woods to the farm.
Rickaby, 89, 7d, m. (Wis.) ; Carmer, 173.

dC 30: A HORSE TEAMSTER   C

Paddy's little bay horses help Brady get his logs up a hill.
Beck, 84, 7 (Mich.).

dC 31: SHANTY TEAMSTER'S MARSEILLAISE C (recited)

The teamsters leave a job, complaining about their slave-driving boss.
Rickaby, 113, 12 (N. Dak.).

dC 32: CHANCE McGEAR   B, C

Chance is killed while loading logs in Michigan, 1892.
Beck, 166, 17 (Mich.). Reprinted in Beck, *Bunyan*, 164.

dC 33: THE RIVER IN THE PINES   C

Charlie Williams' bride waits all her life for him, but he has drowned in Wisconsin.
Rickaby, 119, 8d, m. (Wis.).

dC 34: LES REEDER   A

A youth dies when he is struck by a rolling log.
Beck, 175, 9 (Mich.). Reprinted in Beck, *Bunyan*, 149.

dC 35: THREE MEN DROWNED   A, H

The men drown when their boat is dashed against a rock.
Rickaby, 129, 3d (N. Dak.).

dC 36: 'TWAS ON THE NAPENE   C
A youth drowns while rafting logs.
Beck, 143, 8 (Mich.).

dC 37: THE KID   A (recited)
A youth dies when he is thrown from atop a load of logs.
Beck, 157, 11d (Mich.).

dC 38: FRANK FARROW   E
Frank is crushed to death by a falling tree.
Thompson, 275, 5d (N.Y.).

dC 39: THE FATAL OAK   E
Three youths drown when a tree capsizes their raft.
Rickaby, 116, 18 (Wis.). Notes.

dC 40: JOHN LADNER   D
John is killed by falling logs. (Maine, Nov., 1900).
Barry, *Bulletin* no. 11, 19 (broadside); reprinted in Barry, 72.

dC 41: JOHN ROBERTSON   A
John dies saving young Joe McCarthy's life when a tree falls toward them.
Beck, 154, 18, m. (Mich.). Reprinted in Beck, *Bunyan,* 168.

dC 42: THE MAN FROM CONNER'S CREW   A (recited)
A tenderfoot is saved from drowning by a man from Conner's crew.
Beck, 77, 25 (Mich.).

dC 43: COME ALL YOU JACK PINE SAVAGES   C, E
A lumberjack recommends Dr. Jones, who cured his toothache.
Beck, 61, 6d (Mich.).

dC 44: WHEN O'CONNER DREW HIS PAY   A
O'Conner lands in jail after a spree.
Beck, 89, 8 (Mich.). Reprinted in Beck, *Bunyan,* 52.

dC 45: THE COOK AND THE TEAMSTER   C, G
After losing a fight with a teamster, the cook leaves camp.
Eckstorm, 108, 12 (Me.).

dC 46: THE BURNING OF HENRY K. ROBINSON'S CAMP   E
The lumber camp burns, without casualties, in Maine in 1873.
Eckstorm, 48; *Bulletin* no. 12, 20, 15d, m. Notes.

dC 47: SANDY STREAM SONG   D
The lumbermen's trip to Sandy Stream is interrupted by a fire. (1874)
Eckstorm, 51, 21 (Me.) Notes; Gray 31.

dC 48: PAUL BUNYAN'S BIG OX   A (recited)
A typical sketch of Paul and the blue ox.
Beck, 259, 10 (Mich.).

dC 49: JOE THOMAS   A, B
Joe's canoe is swamped when he attempts to break a log jam.
Carmer, 31, 4d, m. (N.Y.).

dC 50: SHANTY BOY'S ILL FATE   A
A young lumberjack is killed by a falling branch or "widow-maker."
Beck, *Bunyan*, 136, 8 (Mich.).

dC 51: THE DYING HOOPMAKER   A
The hoopmaker has been crushed by a falling tree.
Beck, *Bunyan*, 176, 10d (Mich.).

dC 52: YOUNG FORBEST   A
A boy is crushed to death by logs.
Doerflinger, 224, 6, m. (N.B.).

dC 53: TOMAH STREAM   A
The hardships of life at a miserly contractor's lumber camp.
Doerflinger, 216, 9d, m. (Me.).
The author of this piece was Larry Gorman.

dC 54: SHANNEL'S MILL   A
A man flees the police after a fight and finds work in a sawmill.
Kaiser, *NYFQ* 11 (1955), 134, 10d and chorus (N.Y.).

D BALLADS OF SAILORS AND THE SEA

dD 29: DIXEY BULL   C, D
Dan Curtis kills Dixey Bull, the pirate, in a fierce duel.
Eckstorm, 249, 29 (Me.). Notes.

dD 30: THE DEATH OF CAPTAIN FRIEND   C (recited)
The captain dies not long after his wife is drowned.
Eckstorm, 293, 13 (Me.).

dD 31: THE LOSS OF THE *SARAH*   A (recited)
Sixteen lives are lost when the *Sarah* goes down. (1835).
Eckstorm, 280, 12 (Me.).

dD 32: THE *UNION* OF SAINT JOHN   C (recited)
All hands are lost when the brig capsizes off the Maine coast.
Eckstorm, 273, 18 (Me.) ; 276, the original broadside, 15d sts.

dD 33: THE SPANISH CAPTAIN   A
The Spanish captain and his wife and daughter die when the *Margarita*
is wrecked.
Greenleaf, 275, 11d, m. (Nfld.).

dD 34: THE *GREENLAND* DISASTER   A
Forty-eight men from the sealer *Greenland* die in a storm on the ice.
Greenleaf, 299, 13d, m. (Nfld.).

dD 35: THE WRECK OF THE *FLORIZEL*   A
The steamer is wrecked off Newfoundland during World War I.
Greenleaf, 283, 7d, m. (Nfld.).

dD 36: THE *SOUTHERN CROSS*   A
A sealing vessel with 170 men disappears, 1914.
Greenleaf, 281, 8d, m. (Nfld.).

dD 37: THE LOSS OF THE *DRUID*   H
The unseaworthy *Druid*, from Lunenburg, is battered by a storm off
Bermuda.
Doerflinger, 195, 4 sts. and chorus, m. (Ont.).

dD 38: THE LOST BOYS OF EAST BAY   E?, H
Sixteen young fishermen die in a Florida hurricane, 1894.
Morris, 104, 4d and chorus, m. (Fla.).

dD 39: SALLY GREER   A
An Irish immigrant ship is wrecked off Canada (1833?).
Fowke and Mills, 92, 6d, m. (Ont.).

dD 40: THE *TITANIC* IV   H
Sixteen hundred die in the *Titanic* sinking.
Randolph IV, 144, 5 (Mo.).

dD 41: THE *TITANIC* V   H
Another ballad on the same subject.
Gardner, 295, 5 sts. and chorus (Mich.).

dD 42: THE SCHOONER *KANDAHAR*   H
The narrative of a trip from Lunenburg to the West Indies.
Doerflinger, 196, 8d, m. (N.S. Text and tune from different sources).

dD 43: CORBITT'S BARKENTINE   H

The *George E. Corbitt* sails from Annapolis, N.S., to British Guiana, 1883.
Doerflinger, 189, 15d, m. (N.S. Partly from ms.).

dD 44: THE *DONZELLA* AND THE *CEYLON*   H

The *Ceylon* beats the *Donzella* in a race from Lunenburg to Puerto Rico.
Doerflinger, 192, 14d, m. (N.S. via Ont. Partly from ms.).

dD 45: *SALADIN'S* CREW   H

About to be hanged, Hazleton laments his fate.
Creighton, 241, 7d, m. (N.S.).
See D 19 and 20 in Appendix I.

dD 46: THE *UNICORN*   A

A sailor's account of the hardships of a trip to Liverpool.
Creighton, 326, 7d, m. (N.S.).

dD 47: JOLLY FISHERMEN   A

Three fishermen in a dory are almost drowned in a storm.
Creighton, 269, 6d, m. (N.S.); notes.

dD 48: GUYSBORO SONG   A

Among the narrator's many misfortunes ashore and at sea are two broken
knees.
Creighton, 259, 11d, m. (N.S.).

dD 49: LOSS OF THE *PHILOSOPHY*   A

Only three crewmen survive when the *Philosophy* is lost returning to St.
John from Havana.
Creighton, 275, 8d, m. (N.S.).

dD 50: THE *MARY L. MACKAY*   A

A drunken crew makes record time from Portland to Yarmouth in a gale.
Creighton, 284, 13d, m. (N.S.); notes.

dD 51: CAPTAIN CONROD   A

When his money is gone, the drunken sailor ships on board the brig
Mary and suffers under stingy Captain Conrod.
Creighton, 232, 13d, m. (N.S.); notes.

dD 52: CASNO STRAIT   A

The sailors save their ship in a gale when the drunken captain refuses to
shorten sail.
Creighton, 230, 8½ sts., m. (N.S.).

E BALLADS ABOUT CRIMINALS AND OUTLAWS

dE 27: FEUDING SONG   H

An account of a long and bloody mountain feud.
Campbell, *SFQ* 3 (1939), 166, 12 (Ky.).

dE 28: THE STARTING OF A FEUD   A

Ike routs a gun-toting braggart.
Campbell, *SFQ* 3 (1939), 168 7 (Ky.).

dE 29: THE DOOM OF CAMPBELL, KELLY, AND DOYLE   C

Three of the Molly Maguires are condemned to death.
Korson, 263, 8d (Pa.). See note below.

dE 30: HUGH McGEEHAN   C

One of the Molly Maguires protests his innocence.
Korson, 264, 12d (Pa.). See note below.

dE 31: MICHAEL J. DOYLE   C

Another of the imprisoned men denies his guilt.
Korson, 261, 9d (Pa.). See note below.

dE 32: THOMAS DUFFY   D

Duffy dies bravely on the gallows.
Korson, 265, 10d (Pa.). See note below.
NOTE: The last four ballads listed above deal with members of a gang
called the "Molly Maguires", who terrorized the Pennsylvania coal regions
in the 1860's and 1870's. The pieces are printed in *Minstrels of the Mine
Patch. See Korson's* notes, 240-255.

dE 33: QUANTRELL   H

Quantrell and his raiders come "to burn Lawrence."
Finger, 64; Lomax, *American Ballads*, 132, 4d and chorus, m. (Utah).

dE 34: HARRISON TOWN   Text 1: A
                                Text 2: C

The captured Arkansas outlaw hopes his horse will be well cared for.
Randolph II, 142, 3d, m.; 143, 8 (Ark.).

dE 35: SAINT LOUIS, BRIGHT CITY   B, H

A young robber finds himself in jail.
Randolph II, 151, 3½ m. (Ark.).

dE 36: MOONLIGHT AND SKIES   B
The young prisoner is lonely for moonlight and skies.
Randolph II, 162, 12d couplets, m. (Mo.).

dE 37: COTTON THE KID   D
A young outlaw escapes from prison.
Randolph II, 173, 7d, (Mo.).

dE 38: THE STORY OF GEORGE MANN   D
Mann tells his story of the murder for which he and Ohr must die. (This
and the following are pieces of the "Charles Guiteau" type).
Eddy, 276, 6d (O.); notes.

dE 39: THE STORY OF GUSTAVE OHR   D
Ohr's story of the murder. (See the preceding piece).
Eddy, 274, 6d, m. (O.). The murder took place in 1879 in Ohio.

dE 40: JAMES MUNKS'S CONFESSION   C
James must die for murdering a man with a tomahawk.
Eddy, 256, 10 (Ohio).

dE 41: THE TENNESSEE KILLER   C
The killer is about to be hanged in Arkansas.
Randolph II, 166, 8 (Ark.).

dE 42: TALT HALL   C, D
Talt, a murderer, is about to be hanged in Richmond.
Combs, 181, 9 (Ky.). Notes.

dE 43: THE GAMBLER   H
Members of the gambler's family see him hanged.
Belden, 472, 4 and refrain (Mo.); Randolph II, 81, 5 and refrain, m.
(Mo.); 82, 3 and refrain, m. (Ark.). Notes.

dE 44: JESSE JAMES III   A, C, G
Jesse and Frank escape some enraged Mexicans by swimming the Rio
Grande.
Belden, 403, 11 (Mo.).

dE 45: THE WILD MONTANA BOY   B
The outlaw youth is eventually shot down. (An adaptation of the
Australian ballad, "Jack Donahoe").
Lomax, *Cowboy Songs*, 167, 7d (Mo.).

dE 46: THE DYING DESPERADO   B
The outlaw reminisces about his killings and about his girl.
Lomax, *Cowboy Songs*, 223, 11d (Tex.).

dE 47: BURY ME OUT ON THE PRAIRIE   B

A cowboy turns criminal because of a woman and meets death.
Lomax, *Cowboy Songs*, 300, 6d, m. L. C. Record, 3030 A1 (Miss.).

dE 48: HARRY ORCHARD   A

Orchard has killed ex-Governor Steunenberg with a bomb, 1905.
Burt, 94, 7 (Ida.).

dE 49: EDWARD HICKMAN   C

Hickman kidnaps and murders Marian Parker and is sentenced to die.
Brown II, 606, 12 (N.C.).
This is one of Andrew Jenkins' ballads. (See Chapter IV). He sings it
on Okeh record 45197.

dE 50: THE OLD ROCK JAIL   D

The prisoner's parents die of grief when he is jailed.
Williams, 415, 10 (Ky.).

dE 51: THE ALBANY JAIL   E

The narrator is jailed for drunkenness and fighting.
Cazden, *NYFQ* 16 (1960), 100, 5d, m. (N.Y.).

dE 52: SING-SING   E

An attempted jailbreak fails.
Cazden, *NYFQ* 16 (1960), 95,, 4d, m. (N.Y.).

dE 53: THE NEWBURGH JAIL   A

The speaker escapes from Governor's Isle and later from Newburgh jail
in a boat.
Cazden, 64, 13 sts. and refrain, m. (N.Y.); reprinted in *NYFQ* 16 (1960),
101.

F   MURDER BALLADS

dF 38: COLONEL SHARP   D

Sharp is murdered at the request of the girl he has seduced.
Perrow, *JAF* 28 (1915), 199, 15d (N.C.); notes. Reprinted by Leach,
p. 790.

dF 39: POLLY WILLIAMS   C

The man who has seduced her murders Polly (Penna., 1810).
Lomax, *Amer. Ballads*, 159, 10d, m. (Pa.); notes. Burt, 35, 9d (of 12d)
(Pa.); notes.

dF 40: THE MURDER OF MRS. BROUGHTON   D

Mrs. Broughton is murdered by two Negroes.
JAF 22 (1909), 68, 7d (Ky.).

dF 41: GLADYS KINCAID I   A

Brodus Miller, a Negro, kills Gladys.
Henry, *Songs Sung*, 57, 4d (N.C.).

dF 42: GLADYS KINCAID II   A

Miller is shot dead by his pursuers.
Brown II, 687, 7 (N.C.).

dF 43: THE JANIE SHARP BALLET   C, D

A lament for Janie, who has been raped and murdered.
Hudson, 194, 12 (Miss.); notes.

dF 44: MARIA BEWELL   D

A man murders his adopted daughter when he is unable to seduce her
(Ohio, 1832).
Eddy, 271, 22 (O.).

dF 45: NELL CROPSEY I   G

Jim is suspected of murdering Nell, whose body cannot be found.
Chappell, 108, 6 (N.C.); notes.

dF 46: JOHN A. MUNROE   H

Munroe is hanged for murdering Sarah Vail. (See also "The Murder of
Sarah Vail" (F 9).
Barry, *Bulletin* no. 5, p. 17, 3¼d, m. (Me.).

dF 47: THE MURDER OF CHARLES STACEY   D

Charles is murdered by three men, one of them his rival in love.
Randolph II, 165, 6 (Mo.); notes.

dF 48: WILLIAM BAKER   C

Baker is to be hanged for murdering Prewitt.
Combs, 197, 13 (Ky.).

dF 49: THE MEEKS FAMILY MURDER IV   G

A lament for Nellie follows an account of the murder.
Belden, 408, 8, 5½d, and 3 sts. (Mo.). See also F 28-F 30.

dF 50: THE MEEKS FAMILY MURDER V   C

Nellie offers some comments on the tragedy.
Belden, 411, 4½d and chorus (Mo.).

dF 51: PEARL BRYAN IV   D
Another ballad on the Pearl Bryan murder. See F 2 and F 3.
Eddy, 241, 6d (O.).

dF 52: JOHN FERGUSON   D
John is stabbed to death near a "grocery" (liquor) store.
Williams, 242, 20 (Ky.).

dF 53: LOTTIE YATES   A
Yates murders his wife and is lynched.
Williams, 173, 30d (Ky.).

dF 54: JESSE ADAMS   C
Jesse murders his unfaithful wife.
Williams, 170, 13 (Ky.); reprinted in *KFR* 8 (1962), 19.
Note: The Shearin and Combs "Syllabus," p. 18, lists two texts of "The Cause and Killing of Jesse Adams," 25 sts. (Ky.).

dF 55: ELK RIVER BOYS   A
"Poor Jay" of Elk River is murdered by his wife's lover.
Musick, *JAF* 70 (1957), 350, 10, m. (W. Va.).

dF 56: MARIAN PARKER II   A or C
A lament for the girl who has been killed and dismembered.
Brown II, 604, 5d (N.C.).
Dr. Wilgus has several records of this piece, including Gennett #6362, sung by and credited to John McGhee.

dF 57: MARIAN PARKER III   A or C
A more detailed account of the kidnapping of Marian.
Brown II, 604, 10 (N.C.). See also "Marian Parker I" (F 33) and "Edward Hickman" (II, E).
This is one of Andrew Jenkins' ballads (see Chapter IV); he sings it on Okeh record 45197.

dF 58: THE HENNESSY MURDER   H
The Chief of Police of New Orleans is killed, 1890.
Burt, 165, 2d and chorus, m. (Utah).

dF 59: PRINCE EDWARD ISLAND MURDER   A
William Millman shoots Mary Tuplin and throws her body into the river.
Creighton, 306, 13½d, m. (N.S.); notes.

dF 60: THE MILLMAN SONG   A
A different ballad on the crime mentioned above.
Doerflinger, 285, 10½d, m. (N.B.).

dF 61: ARCH AND GORDON   H

Archibald Brown, son of the Governor of Kentucky, and his paramour, Mrs. Gordon, are shot by Gordon, 1895.
KFR 6 (1960), 53, 5, m.; 4 (Ky.) ; notes.

dF 62: THE DEATH OF SAMUEL ADAMS   C

Schuster's gang murders Adams at Auxier, Ky., 1930.
Thomas, *Ballad Makin'*, 242, 12 (Ky.) ; notes. *KFR* 6 (1960), 123, 12 (Ky.).

dF 63: GRUVER MEADOWS   A

Gruver kills his wife on their Blue Ridge mountain farm.
WVF 9 (1959), 48, 5d (W. Va.).

dF 64: MURDER OF QUIET DELL   A, H

Powers courts a widow, imprisons her and her son, and murders them.
WVF 7 (1957), 67, 7½ (W.Va.).

G BALLADS OF TRAGEDIES AND DISASTERS

dG 34: MARTHA DEXTER   B, G

Martha is thrown from her horse and drowned in the river.
Belden, 417, 14½ (Mo.).

dG 35: LORA WILLIAMS   A

A girl drowns herself rather than swear out a warrant against her lover.
Thomas, *Ballad Makin'*, 140, 10 (Ky).

dG 36: THE HARTFORD WRECK   C

Many are killed in a train wreck. (Vt., 1887).
Flanders-Barry, 156, 6 6-line sts., m. (Vt.). Notes.

dG 37: THE BRUSH CREEK WRECK   C

Several are killed in a train wreck. (Mo., 1881).
Belden, 421, 5½d (Mo.). Notes.

dG 38: THE WRECK AT LATONA   D

The engineer and fireman die when the brakes fail.
Cambiaire, 107, 7 (Tenn.).

dG 39: THE BURNING OF THE BAYOU SARA   G, H

A river vessel is destroyed by fire. (Mo., 1885).
Belden, 423, 6 and chorus (Mo.). Notes.

dG 40: THE MINES OF LOCUST DALE   C

Four miners die in an explosion. (Nov. 18, 1875, Pa.).
Korson, *Minstrels*, 193, 9d (Pa.).

dG 41: THE WRECK ON THE SOMERSET ROAD   A, H

The crew is killed when robbers derail a train.
Lomax, *Our Singing Country*, 254, 5 sts. and chorus, m. (Ky. from L. C.
Record 1532 A2 & B2).

dG 42: THE GIRL WHO WAS DROWNED AT ONSLOW   A

A girl drowns in a sleighing accident.
Mackenzie, 371, 7 (N.S.).

dG 43: McLELLAN'S SON   A

A boy is accidentally shot dead.
Mackenzie, 363, 8 (N.S.).

dG 44: THE McDONALD FAMILY   B

The family dies in a forest fire, Michigan, 1871.
Beck, *Bunyan*, 172, 16 (Mich.).

dG 45: SANTA BARBARA EARTHQUAKE   A

Many are killed in the earthquake.
Henry, *Songs Sung*, 86, 8 (Tenn.).

dG 46: LEE BIBLE   H

The auto racer dies in an accident, Daytona Beach, 1929.
Morris, 106, 6½ m. (Fla.).
This is one of Andrew Jenkins' ballads. (See chapter IV). He sings it on
Okeh record 45343.

dG 47: WEST PALM BEACH STORM   B

The 1928 Florida hurricane is regarded as God's punishment of the wicked.
Morris, 101, 9 sts. and chorus, m. (Fla. from L. C. Record 977 A1).

dG 48: AARON HART   E (indirectly)

Aaron, age 3½, is lost in the woods for three days.   and C
Morris, 121, 10d (Fla.); another text referred to.

dG 49: ONLY A BRAKEMAN   A

A Texas-Pacific brakeman is killed by a train.
Randolph IV, 125, 5d and chor., m. (Mo.).

dG 50: ONLY A MINER KILLED IN THE BREAST   B

When a rock strikes a miner's head, he falls dead at his partner's feet.
Emrich, *CFQ* 1 (1942), 220, 4d and chor., m. (Colo.).
See also "Only a Miner" (G 33) and "Only a Cowboy" (II, B).

dG 51: THE WRECK OF THE ROYAL PALM   A

Many are killed in a head-on collision on the Southern Railway, 1926.
Brown II, 521, 6d (N.C.).
Prof. Wilgus identifies this as another of Andrew Jenkins' ballads. See the notes to "Floyd Collins."

dG 52: THE WRECK OF THE *SHENANDOAH*   A

The Navy dirigible is wrecked in Ohio, 1925.
Brown II, 522, 7 (N.C.).

dG 53: FIRE TRAGEDY   A

Two babies die in a fire.
KFR 9 (1963), 55, 7, m. (Ky.).

H BALLADS ON VARIOUS TOPICS

dH 32: BIG BILL SNYDER   F, G

Snyder is killed by a man in Indian disguise during an anti-rent war in New York State (ca. 1840).
Gardner, E. E., *Folklore from the Schoharie Hills*, 32, 4 and chorus. Notes.

dH 33: CHINKAPIN   C and ultimately D

Pioneer boys trade buffalo hides for hunters' dress and tame wild horses. (This may never have been sung.)
Eckstorm, 373, 31 (Me.).

dH 34: THE BEAR HUNTERS OF 1836   D

A hunter kills three bears in a cave.
Eckstorm, 367, 18 (Me.). Notes, 366-370.

dH 35: THE HOG-THORNY BEAR   C

The bear hunters mistakenly tree a porcupine.
Flanders-Barry, 219, 10 (Vt.).

dH 36: BILL HOPKINS' COLT   A

Bill's unpromising colt proves to be a winning trotter.
Flanders & Brown, 39, 23, m. (N.H.).

dH 37: THE CHAMPION OF MOOSE HILL   C

Muck Mace, the champion boxer, is downed when Mrs. Giles strikes him with a club.
Eckstorm, 126, 8 (Me.).

dH 38: JIM CLANCY   F?
A Bangor water works employee goes on a spree.
Eckstorm, 131, 10 (Me.).

dH 39: STEAM BOAT BILL   B
This humorous piece tells of Bill's death in a steamboat explosion.
Henry, *Songs Sung*, 100, 3d, 8-line sts. and choruses (Tenn.) L. C. Record 3186 Bl (Ark.).

dH 40: JACKSON   B
The returned soldier scornfully rejects a gold-digger whom he once loved.
Sandburg, 430, 8d, m.

dH 41: OLD JOE   H?
An old Cranberry Islander marries a young girl, (1853).
Eckstorm, 334, 15 (Me.) A composite text. Notes.

dH 42: I WAS SIXTEEN YEARS OF AGE   B, C
A woman gives her flirtatious husband a beating.
Henry, *Folk-Songs*, 314, 10 (Ga.).

dH 43: THE IRON MOUNTAIN BABY   G
A baby who was thrown from a train is adopted and raised by a farmer. (Mo. 1902).
Belden, 419, 14 (Mo.). Notes.

dH 44: 'TWAS IN THE TOWN OF PARSBORO   A
Dunkerson challenges McLellan to a fight and is badly beaten.
Creighton, 324, 8d, m. (N.S.).

dH 45: AS I WENT OUT FOR A RAMBLE   A
The hobo leaves town when he cannot overcome the disapproval of his girl's parents.
Lomax, *Our Singing Country*, 267, 10, m. (Ky. from L. C. Record 1542).

dH 46: YOUNG BILLY CRANE   A
A girl wants to follow her unfaithful lover to sea.
Doerflinger, 259, 8d, m. (N.B.).
This ballad is attributed to Larry Gorman. Since the editor has changed the names of the principals, the present title will be useless in identifying the ballad.

dH 47: PRETTY POLLY OF TOPSHAM   F
Polly renounces her sea-captain lover in favor of a minister named Ellis.
Barry, *Bulletin* no. 2, p. 16, 10d, m. (Me.).

dH 48: PERIGOO'S HORSE A

Pranksters shave and paint a stranger's horse in Boiestown.
Doerflinger, 266, 11 sts. and chorus. (N.B.).

dH 49: THE MESSENGER SONG C (recited)

A Miramichi horse tells of escaping from his cruel owner.
Doerflinger, 266, 4½d (N.B.).

dH 50: RUFUS'S MARE A

Tozer takes back his mare from Rufus after the latter has healed her.
Doerflinger, 264, 13, m. (N.B.).

dH 51: CASEY'S WHISKEY A

Two Irishmen on a drinking spree get in trouble with an Irish policeman.
Creighton, 150, 5d and chor., m. (N.S.).

dH 52: McCARTHY'S SONG A

On a spree in Halifax, the narrator is beaten and otherwise mistreated.
Creighton, 288, 14d, m. (N.S.) ; notes.

dH 53: LAURA BELLE A

Laura is chased from Charlie's house by his irate wife.
KFR 8 (1962), 53, 8 (Ky. Reprinted from Williams).

I BALLADS OF THE NEGRO

dI 21: BUGGER BURNS C

No one grieves when the bad man is shot dead.
Lomax, Our Singing Country, 331, 11, m. (Ky.). A composite text. Notes.

dI 22: EDDY JONES B, H

A lament for Eddy, who died "with a special in his hand."
Odum and Johnson, The Negro and His Songs, 205, 7 couplets.

dI 23: IDA RED B

The Negro thief regrets that a jail term will keep him away from Ida.
Lomax, American Ballads, 110, 6 6-line sts. (Tex.).

dI 24: ENGINEER RIGG C (fragmentary)

Many Negroes die in a train wreck.
White, 220, 4 (N.C.). Notes.

dI 25: JAY GOULD'S DAUGHTER   B
(Charley Snyder)

A confused railroad narrative related to the Negro versions of "Casey Jones".

Sandburg, 364, 4, m. (from Lomax); Lomax, *American Ballads*, 41, 5 ("Charley Snyder").

dI 26: THE *TITANIC* II   B

The captain's confidence in the doomed ship is finally shaken, and the women and children are saved.

Sandburg, 254, 7 and chorus, m. (Ga.).

dI 27: THE *TITANIC* III   H
(God Moves on the Water)

Not even their wealth can save the men on the *Titanic*.

Lomax, *Our Singing Country*, 26, 5 sts. and chorus, m. (Tex.).

dI 28: MIAMI HURRICANE (HAIRIKIN)   B

God's hurricane punishes the wicked in Miami, 1928.

Morris, 103, 5 6-line sts (Ga. via Fla.).

This is related to the preceding piece.

Appendix III

BALLAD-LIKE PIECES

American folksong collections contain a great many pieces which have some of the characteristics of popular balladry. They are sung traditionally, with variations, and frequently they have a marked narrative element. Admittedly, it is difficult to draw the line between ballad and non-ballad, but having tested hundreds of folksongs in terms of the definition given in Chapter I, I have decided to exclude from consideration pieces of the following types:

1. Songs weak or disunified in narrative action.
2. Folksongs and chanteys in which the lyric element is dominant.
3. Satirical and fanciful pieces having little basis is reality.
4. Melodramatic and sentimental pieces, usually of professional origin.

The alphabetical list which follows is far from exhaustive; it is offered merely by way of illustration. For purposes of identification, single textual references are provided. The arabic numeral in parentheses relates each title to one of the categories given above.

The Baggage Coach Ahead, Pound, 131 (4)
Billy the Kid, Lomax, *American Ballads*, 136 (1)
The (Little) Black Mustache, Henry, *Folk-Songs*, 295 (1)
The Blind Child, Belden, 275, (4)
The Blue Juniata, Hudson, 210 (2)
Brother Green, Belden, 377 (1)
Calomel, Brewster, 308 (3)
Careless Love, Lomax, *Folk Song U.S.A.*, 64 (2)
Cocaine Lil, Sandburg, 206 (3)
Davy Crockett, Lomax, *American Ballads* (3)
The Days of Forty-Nine, Lomax, *Cowboy Songs*, 378 (1)
Down in the Valley (Birmingham Jail), Lomax, *Folk Song U.S.A.*, 62 (2)
The Dreary Black Hills, Belden, 349 (1)
The Drunkard's Doom, Randolph II, 392 (4)
The Drunkard's Lone Child, Henry, *Folk-Songs*, 382 (4)
The Dying Californian, Belden, 350 (4)
The Dying Nun, Belden, 218 (4)
The Erie Canal Ballad, Lomax, *American Ballads*, 455 (1)
The Farmer's Son and the Shanty-Boy, Rickaby, 48 (1)
The Fatal Wedding, Belden, 141 (4)
The Gypsy Warning, Cox, 439 (4)

Hell and Texas, Randolph II, 217 (3)

The Hell-Bound Train, Beck, 246 (3)

I Wish I Was Single Again, Belden, 437 (1)

Joe Turner, Sandburg, 241 (2)

Just Before the Battle, Mother, Cox, 277 (4)

Kitty Wells, Cox, 395 (4)

Little Nell of Naragansett Bay, Brewster, 345 (4)

The Little Rosewood Casket, Belden, 220 (4)

Lula Wall, Henry, *Songs Sung*, 37 (1)

The Midnight Special, Lomax, *American Ballads*, 71 (2)

Mother and Daughter, Belden, 266 (1)

The Ocean Burial, Linscott, 245 (4). For the complete text see also
Chapter VI.

Old Blue, Hudson, 201 (1)

The Old Chisholm Trail, Lomax, *Cowboy Songs*, 58 (1)

Old Dan Tucker, Lomax, *Folk Songs U.S.A.*, 92 (1)

Old Smokey, Lomax, *Folk Songs U.S.A.*, 60 (2)

Pretty Sairey, Brewster, 362 (2)

Reuben Ranzo, Colcord, 70 (2)

Rio Grande, Colcord, 86 (2)

Sally Brown, Colcord, 82 (2)

Santa Anna, Colcord, 84 (2)

Shenandoah, Lomax, *Folk Song U.S.A.*, 138 (2)

Tom Dooley, Lomax, *Folk Song U.S.A.*, 300 (2)

The Travelling Coon, White, 349 (3)

Whoopee Ti Yi Yo, Git Along Little Dogies, Lomax, *Cowboy Songs*, 4 (1)

Willy the Weeper, Sandburg, 204 (3)

Appendix IV

Although they are not readily distinguishable from native products, many of the following folksongs have been traced to British broadsides. The others, which are marked with asterisks, I assume to be British on the basis of internal evidence. This list is in no sense exhaustive; it is designed merely to differentiate some of the less obviously imported pieces from those of native origin. A single textual reference is given with each title.

*The Banks of Newfoundland, Eckstorm, 219
Billy Boy, Belden, 449
*Blow the Man Down, Colcord, 54
*Bold Daniels, Rickaby, 153
*The Bold Pirate, Eckstorm, 254
The Boston Burglar, Cox, 296
The Bramble Briar, Cox, 305
The Butcher's Boy, Randolph I, 226
Captain Kidd, Mackenize, 278
The Drunkard's Dream, Cox, 398
*Fair Fanny Moore, Flanders-Barry, 233
The Fair *Princess Royal*, Greenleaf, 78
Father Grumble, Randolph I, 318
*The *Flying Cloud*, Belden, 128
The Frog's Courtship, Randolph I, 402
*A Gay Spanish Maid, Randolph I, 434
George Reilly, Cox, 323
The Girl I Left Behind Me, Belden, 198
The Greenland Whale Fishery, Eckstorm, 226
Jack Donahoe, Lomax, *Cowboy Songs*, 209 (from Australia)
Jack, the Sailor Boy, Gardner, 403
Jack Williams, Mackenzie, 291
*James Ervin, Gardner, 233
Johnny Germany, Belden, 155
Johnny Sands, Belden, 237
The Lily of the West, Belden, 132
*The Major and the Weaver, Henry, *Folk-Songs*, 306
One Morning in May (The Nightingale), Randolph I, 266
Pretty Polly, Randolph I, 112

Bibliography

(Editors' names are used in the appendices to designate collections here marked with the asterisk).

AAFS refers to the Archive of American Folk Song in the Library of Congress.

*Arnold, Byron. *Folksongs of Alabama.* University, Alabama: The University of Alabama Press, 1950.

Ashton, John. *Modern Street Ballads.* London: Chatto and Windus, 1888.

*Barry, Phillips. *The Maine Woods Songster.* Cambridge: Harvard University Press, 1939.

Barry, Phillips. "Native Balladry in America," *JAF* 22 (1909), 365-373.

Barry, Phillips, Fannie Hardy Eckstorm, and Mary Winslow Smyth. *British Ballads from Maine.* New Haven: Yale University Press, 1929.

Bascom, Louise Rand. "Ballads and Songs of Western North Carolina," *JAF* 22 (1909), 238-250.

*Beck, Earl Clifton. *Songs of the Michigan Lumberjacks.* Ann Arbor: University of Michigan Press, 1941.

Beck, Earl Clifton. *They Knew Paul Bunyan.* Ann Arbor: University of Michigan Press 1956.

Beck, Horace P. *The Folklore of Maine.* Phila. and N.Y.: J. B. Lippincott Co., 1957.

*Belden, Henry Marvin. *Ballads and Songs Collected by the Missouri Folk-Lore Society.* (*The University of Missouri Studies*, Vol. 15, No. 1). Columbia, 1940; 2nd ed., 1955.

Boatright, Mody C., Wilson M. Hudson, and Allen Maxwell. *Folk Travelers: Ballads, Tales, and Talk.* (*Publications of the Texas Folklore Society*, No. 25). Dallas: Southern Methodist University Press, 1953. (Cited as *PTFS* 25).

*Brewster, Paul G. *Ballads and Songs of Indiana.* (*Indiana University Publications*, Folklore Series No. 1). Bloomington, 1940.

*Brown. *The Frank C. Brown Collection of North Carolina Folklore.* 7 vols., Durham: Duke University Press, 1952-1961. (Vol. II: *Folk Ballads from North Carolina*, ed. Henry M. Belden and Arthur Palmer Hudson, 1952; Vol. III: *Folk Songs from North Carolina*, ed. Henry M. Belden and Arthur Palmer Hudson, 1952; Vol. IV: *The Music of the Ballads*, ed. Jan Philip Schinhan, 1957; Vol. V: *The Music of the Folk Songs*, ed. Jan Philip Schinhan, 1961).

Bulletin of the Folk-Song Society of the Northeast. Nos. 1-12. Cambridge, Mass., 1930-1937. (Cited as *Bulletin*).

BTFS. Bulletin of the Tennessee Folklore Society. Marysville, Tenn., 1935—.

*Burt, Olive Wooley. *American Murder Ballads and Their Stories.* New York: Oxford University Press, 1958.

*Cambiaire, Celestin Pierre. *East Tennessee and Western Virginia Mountain Ballads*. London: The Mitre Press, 1934.

*Carmer, Carl. *Songs of the Rivers of America*. New York: Farrar and Rinehart, 1942.

Carter, Isabel Gordon. "Songs and Ballads from Tennessee and North Carolina," *JAF* 46 (1933), 22-50.

*Cazden, Norman. *The Abelard Folk Song Book*. New York: Abelard-Schuman, 1958.

Cazden, Norman. "Regional and Occupational Orientation of American Traditional Song." *JAF* 72 (1959), 310-344.

*Chappell, Louis W. *Folk-Songs of Roanoke and the Albemarle*. Morgantown, W. Va.: The Ballad Press, 1939.

Chappell, Louis W. *John Henry: A Folk-Lore Study*. Jena, Germany: Walter Biedermann, 1933.

CFQ. California Folklore Quarterly. (See under *Western Folklore*).

Child, Francis James. *The English and Scottish Popular Ballads*. 5 vols. Boston and New York: Houghton, Mifflin and Co., 1882-1898.

Clark, Andrew. *The Shirburn Ballads: 1585-1616*. Oxford: The Clarenden Press, 1907.

*Colcord, Joanna C. *Songs of American Sailormen*. New York: W. W. Norton, 1938.

CFB. Colorado Folksong Bulletin. Boulder: University of Colorado, 1962—.

*Combs, Josiah H. *Folk-Songs du Midi des États-Unis*. Paris: Les Presses Universitaires de France, 1925.

*Cox, John Harrington. *Folk-Songs of the South*. Cambridge: Harvard University Press, 1925.

Creighton, Helen. *Maritime Folk Songs*. East Lansing: Michigan State University Press, 1962.

*Creighton, Helen. *Songs and Ballads from Nova Scotia*. Toronto and Vancouver: J. M. Dent, 1933.

*Creighton, Helen and Doreen H. Senior. *Traditional Songs from Nova Scotia*. Toronto: The Ryerson Press, 1950.

Davis, Arthur Kyle, Jr. *Folk-Songs of Virginia: A Descriptive Index and Classification*. Durham: Duke University Press, 1949.

Davis, Arthur Kyle, Jr. *Traditional Ballads of Virginia*. Cambridge: Harvard University Press, 1929.

*Dean, Michael C. *The Flying Cloud and One Hundred and Fifty Other Old Time Songs and Ballads*. Virginia, Minnesota: The Quickprint, 1922.

Dobie, J. Frank. *Follow de Drinkin' Gou'd*. (*Publications of the Texas Folk-Lore Society*, No. VII). Austin, 1928. (Cited as *PTFS* VII).

Dobie, J. Frank. *Texas and Southwestern Lore*. (*Publications of the Texas Folk-Lore Society*, No. VI). Austin, 1927. (Cited as *PTFS* VI).

*Doerflinger, William Main. *Shantymen and Shantyboys: Songs of the Sailor and Lumberman*. New York: The Macmillan Co., 1951.

*Eckstorm, Fannie Hardy and Mary Winslow Smyth. *Minstrelsy of Maine.* Boston and New York: Houghton, Mifflin Co., 1927.

*Eddy, Mary O. *Ballads and Songs from Ohio.* New York: J. J. Augustin, 1939.

Entwistle, William J. *European Balladry.* Oxford: The Clarendon Press, 1939.

*Finger, Charles J. *Frontier Ballads.* New York: Doubleday Page and Co., 1927.

Firth, C. H. *An American Garland: Being a Collection of Ballads Relating to America, 1563-1759.* Oxford: B. H. Blackwell, 1915.

Flanders, Helen Hartness. *A Garland of Green Mountain Song.* (*Green Mountain Pamphlets,* No. 1) Northfield, Vt., 1934.

*Flanders, Helen Hartness, Elizabeth Flanders Ballard, George Brown, and Phillips Barry. *The New Green Mountain Songster: Traditional Folksongs of Vermont.* New Haven: Yale Univ. Press, 1939. (Cited as *Flanders-Barry*).

*Flanders, Helen Hartness and George Brown. *Vermont Folk-Songs and Ballads.* Brattleboro: Stephen Daye Press, 1931.

*Flanders, Helen Hartness and Marguerite Olney. *Ballads Migrant in New England.* New York: Farrar, Strauss, and Young, 1953.

The Forget Me Not Songster, Phila. and Baltimore: Fisher and Bros., n. d.

*Fowke, Edith and Richard Johnston. *Folksongs of Canada.* Waterloo, 1954.

Fowke, Edith and Richard Johnston. *Folksongs of Quebec.* Waterloo, 1957.

*Fowke, Edith and Alan Mills. *Canada's Story in Song.* Toronto: J. H. Gage Co., 1960.

Friedman, Albert B. *The Viking Book of Folk Ballads of the English-Speaking World.* New York: The Viking Press, 1956.

*Fuson, Harvey H. *Ballads of the Kentucky Highlands.* London: The Mitre Press, 1931.

Gardner, Emelyn Elizabeth. *Folklore from the Schoharie Hills, New York.* Ann Arbor: Univ. of Michigan Press, 1937.

*Gardner, Emelyn Elizabeth and Geraldine J. Chickering. *Ballads and Songs of Southern Michigan.* Ann Arbor: Univ. of Michigan Press, 1939.

*Gerould, Gordon Hall. *The Ballad of Tradition.* Oxford: The Clarendon Press, 1932.

*Gordon, Robert Winslow. *Folk-Songs of America.* New York: National Service Bureau, 1938 (mimeographed).

Gordon, Robert Winslow. "Old Songs That Men Have Sung." A department in *Adventure,* July 10, 1923-Nov. 10, 1927.

*Gray, Roland Palmer. *Songs and Ballads of the Maine Lumberjacks.* Cambridge: Harvard Univ. Press, 1924.

*Greenleaf, Elizabeth B. and Grace Mansfield. *Ballads and Sea Songs from Newfoundland.* Cambridge: Harvard Univ. Press, 1933.

Greenway, John. *American Folksongs of Social Protest.* Phila.: Univ. of Penna. Press, 1953.

Greenway, John "Jimmie Rodgers—a Folksong Catalyst." *JAF* 70 (1957), 231-234.

Henderson, W. *Victorian Street Ballads*. London and New York: Charles Scribner's Sons, 1938.

*Henry, Mellinger Edward. *Folk-Songs from the Southern Highlands*. New York: J. J. Augustin, 1938.

*Henry, Mellinger Edward. *Songs Sung in the Southern Appalachians*. London: The Mitre Press, 1934.

*High, Fred. *Old, Old Folk Songs*. Berryville, Ark., n. d .

*Hubbard, Lester A. *Ballads and Songs from Utah*. Salt Lake City: The Univ. of Utah Press, 1961.

*Hudson, Arthur Palmer. *Folksongs of Mississippi*. Chapel Hill: The Univ. of North Carolina Press, 1936.

Ives, Edward D. " 'Ben Deane' and Joe Scott: a Ballad and Its Probable Author." *JAF* 72 (1959), 53-66.

Ives, Edward D. "The Life and Work of Larry Gorman: a Preliminary Report." *WF* 19 (1960), 17-23.

Jackson, George Pullen. *Down-East Spirituals and Others*. New York: J. J. Augustin, 1943.

Jackson, George Pullen. *Spiritual Folk-Songs of Early America*. New York: J. J. Augustin, 1937.

Jackson, George Pullen. *White and Negro Spirituals*. New York: J. J. Augustin, 1943.

Jackson, George Pullen. *White Spirituals in the Southern Uplands*. Chapel Hill: The Univ. of North Carolina Press, 1933.

Johnson, Guy B. *John Henry: Tracking Down a Negro Legend*. Chapel Hill: The Univ. of North Carolina Press, 1929.

JAF. Journal of American Folklore. Published by The American Folklore Society, 1888—.

KFR. Kentucky Folklore Record. Bowling Green: The Kentucky Folklore Society, 1955—.

KFQ. Keystone Folklore Quarterly. Williamsport, Pa.: Lycoming College, 1956—.

Kirkland, Edwin C. "A Check List of the Titles of Tennessee Folksongs." *JAF* 59 (1946), 423-476.

Kittredge, George Lyman. "Ballads and Rhymes from Kentucky." *JAF* 20 (1907), 251-277.

Kittredge, George Lyman. "Ballads and Songs." *JAF* 30 (1917), 283-369.

Korson, George. *Coal Dust on the Fiddle: Songs and Stories of the Bituminous Industry*. Phila.: Univ. of Penna. Press, 1943.

Korson, George. *Minstrels of the Mine Patch: Songs and Stories of the Anthracite Industry*. Phila.: Univ. of Penna. Press, 1938.

Korson, George. *Pennsylvania Songs and Legends*. Phila.: Univ. of Penna. Press, 1949.

*Larkin, Margaret. *Singing Cowboy: A Book of Western Songs*. New York: Knopf, 1931.

Lawless, Ray M. *Folksingers and Folksongs in America: A Handbook of Biography, Bibliography, and Discography.* New York: Duell, Sloan and Pearce, 1960.

Laws, G. Malcolm, Jr. *American Balladry from British Broadsides: A Guide for Students and Collectors of Traditional Song.* (*Publications of the American Folklore Society, Bibliographical and Special Series,* Vol. VIII). Phila., 1957.

Laws, G. Malcolm, Jr. "Anglo-Irish Balladry in North America." *Folklore in Action: Essays for Discussion in Honor of MacEdward Leach.* (*Publications of the American Folklore Society, Bibliographical and Special Series,* Vol. XIV). Phila., 1962, pp. 172-183.

Laws, G. Malcolm, Jr. *Native American Balladry: A Descriptive Study and a Bibliographical Syllabus.* (*Publications of the American Folklore Society, Bibliographical Series,* Vol. I). Phila., 1950.

Laws, G. Malcolm, Jr. "The Spirit of Native American Balladry," *JAF* 64 (1951), 163-169.

Laws, G. Malcolm, Jr. "W. Roy Mackenzie, 1883-1957," *Ballads and Sea Songs from Nova Scotia by W. Roy MacKenzie.* Reprint edition. Phila.: Folklore Associates, 1963, pp. i-ix.

*Leach, MacEdward. *The Ballad Book.* New York: Harper and Bros., 1955.

*Leach, MacEdward and Horace P. Beck. "Songs from Rappahannock County, Virginia," *JAF* 63 (1950), 257-284.

Leach, MacEdward and Tristram P. Coffin. *The Critics and the Ballad.* Cardondale: The Univ. of Southern Illinois Press, 1961.

*Linscott, Eloise Hubbard. *Folk Songs of Old New England.* New York: Macmillan, 1939; London: Archon Books, 1962.

Lomax, Alan. *The Folk Songs of North America.* New York: Doubleday, 1960.

Lomax, Alan and Sidney Robertson Cowell. *American Folk Song and Folk Lore: A Regional Bibliography.* New York: Progressive Education Assoc., 1942.

Lomax, John A. "Some Types of American Folk-Song," *JAF* 28 (1915), 1-17.

Lomax, John A. and Alan Lomax. *American Ballads and Folk Songs.* New York: Macmillan, 1934.

Lomax, John A. and Alan Lomax. *Cowboy Songs and Other Frontier Ballads.* (Revised and enlarged). New York: Macmillan, 1938.

Lomax, John A. and Alan Lomax. *Folk Song U.S.A.* New York: Duell, Sloan & Pearce, 1947.

Lomax, John A. and Alan Lomax. *Negro Folk Songs as Sung by Lead Belly.* New York: Macmillan, 1936.

Lomax, John A. and Alan Lomax. *Our Singing Country.* New York: Macmillan, 1941.

Lumpkin, Ben Gray. *Folksongs on Records, Issue 3.* Denver: Alan Swallow, 1950.

*Mackenzie, W. Roy. *Ballads and Sea Songs from Nova Scotia.* Cambridge: Harvard Univ. Press, 1928.

Mackenzie, W. Roy. *The Quest of the Ballad.* Princeton: Princeton Univ. Press, 1919.

Mills, Alan. *Favorite Songs of Newfoundland.* Toronto, 1958.

*Morris, Alton C. *Folksongs of Florida*. Gainesville: Univ. of Florida Press, 1950.

Musick, Ruth Ann. "Ballads and Folksongs from West Virginia," *JAF* 70 (1957), 336-357.

*Neely, Charles and John W. Spargo. *Tales and Songs of Southern Illinois*. Menasha, Wisconsin: George Banta Pub. Co., 1938.

Neeser, Robert W. *American Naval Songs and Ballads*. New Haven: Yale Univ. Press, 1938.

NYFQ. New York Folklore Quarterly. Ithaca: Cornell Univ. Press for the New York Folklore Society, 1945—.

Odum, Howard W. and Guy B. Johnson. *The Negro and His Songs*. Chapel Hill: The Univ. of North Carolina Press, 1925.

Odum, Howard W. and Guy B. Johnson. *Negro Workaday Songs*. Chapel Hill: The Univ. of North Carolina Press, 1926.

O'Lochlainn, Colm. *Irish Street Ballads*. (Revised ed.). Dublin: The Sign of the Three Candles, 1946.

*Owens, William A. *Texas Folk Songs*. (*Publications of the Texas Folk-Lore Society*, no. 23). Dallas, 1950.

Perrow, E. C. "Songs and Rhymes from the South," *JAF* 25 (1912), 137-155; 26 (1913), 123-173; 28 (1915), 129-190.

*Pound, Louise. *American Ballads and Songs*. New York: Charles Scribner's Sons, 1922.

Pound, Louise. *Folk-Song of Nebraska and the Central West, A Syllabus*. (*Nebraska Academy of Sciences Publications*, Vol. IX, No. 3). Lincoln, 1914.

Pound, Louise. *Nebraska Folklore*. Lincoln: Univ. of Nebraska Press, 1959.

Pound, Louise. *Poetic Origins and the Ballad*. New York: Macmillan, 1921.

PFTS. Publications of the Texas Folk-Lore Society. See under Boatright, Dobie, and Owens.

Raine, James Watt. *The Land of Saddle Bags: A Study of the Mountain People of Appalachia*. New York: Council of Women for Home Missions and Missionary Education Movement of the United States and Canada, 1924.

*Randolph, Vance and Floyd C. Shoemaker. *Ozark Folksongs*. 4 vols. Columbia: The State Historical Society of Missouri, 1946-1950.

*Ranson, Joseph. *Songs . . . of the Wexford Coast*. Enniscorthy, Ireland: Redmond Bros., 1948.

*Richardson, Ethel Park. *American Mountain Songs*. New York: Greenberg, 1927.

*Rickaby, Franz. *Ballads and Songs of the Shanty-boy*. Cambridge: Harvard Univ. Press, 1926.

Ritchie, Jean. *A Garland of Mountain Song from the Ritchie Family of Viper, Kentucky*. New York: Broadcast Music, Inc., 1953.

Ritchie, Jean. *Singing Family of the Cumberlands*. New York: Oxford Univ. Press, 1955.

Rocky Mountain Collection. Salt Lake City: Intermountain Folkmusic Council, 1962.

Sackett, S. J. and William E. Koch. *Kansas Folklore.* Lincoln: Univ. of Nebraska Press, 1961.

*Sandburg, Carl. *The American Songbag.* New York: Harcourt, Brace & Co., 1927.

Sargent, Helen Child and George Lyman Kittredge. *English and Scottish Popular Ballads.* Cambridge: Houghton, Mifflin Co., 1904.

*Scarborough, Dorothy. *On the Trail of Negro Folk-Songs.* Cambridge: Harvard Univ. Press, 1925.

*Sharp, Cecil J. *English Folk Songs from the Southern Appalachians.* Edited by Maud Karpeles. 2 vols. London: Oxford Univ. Press, 1932.

Shearin, Hubert G. and Josiah H. Combs. *A Syllabus of Kentucky Folk-Songs.* (*Transylvania Studies in English*, II). Lexington, Kentucky, 1911.

Sheppard, Muriel Early. *Cabins in the Laurel.* Chapel Hill: The Univ. of North Carolina Press, 1935.

*Shoemaker, Henry W. *Mountain Minstrelsy of Pennsylvania.* Phila.: Newman F. McGirr, 1931.

*Silber, Irwin. *Songs of the Civil War.* New York: Columbia University Press, 1960.

Sires, Ina. *Songs of the Open Range.* Boston and New York: C. C. Birchard and Co., 1928.

Smith, Reed. *South Carolina Ballads.* Cambridge: Harvard University Press, 1928.

SFQ. Southern Folklore Quarterly. Gainesville: The University of Florida in Cooperation with the Southeastern Folklore Society, 1937—.

Spaeth, Sigmund. *Read 'Em and Weep: the Songs You Forgot to Remember.* New York: Doubleday, Page & Co., 1927.

Spaeth, Sigmund. *Weep Some More, My Lady.* New York: Doubleday, Page & Co., 1927.

*Stout, Earl J. *Folklore from Iowa.* (*Memoirs of the American Folklore Society*, Vol. XXIX). New York, 1936.

*Sturgis, Edith B. and Robert Hughes. *Songs from the Hills of Vermont.* New York: G. Schirmer, Inc., 1919.

TFSB. Tennessee Folklore Society Bulletin, Nashville, 1935—.

Thomas, Jean. *Ballad Makin' in the Mountains of Kentucky.* New York: Henry Holt and Co., 1939.

*Thomas, Jean. *Devil's Ditties: Being Stories of the Kentucky Mountain People and the Songs They Sing.* Chicago: W. W. Hatfield Co., 1931.

*Thompson, Harold W. *Body, Boots, and Britches.* Phila.: J. B. Lippincott Co., 1939.

Thompson, Harold W. and Edith E. Cutting. *A Pioneer Songster: Texts from the Stevens-Douglass Manuscript of Western New York, 1841-1856.* Ithaca: Cornell Univ. Press, 1958.

*Thorpe, N. Howard. *Songs of the Cowboys.* Cambridge: Houghton Mifflin Co., 1921.

Tolman, Albert H. "Some Songs Traditional in the United States," *JAF* 29 (1916), 155-197.

Tolman, Albert H. and Mary O. Eddy. "Traditional Texts and Tunes," *JAF* 35 (1922), 335-432.

Warner, Frank M. "A Salute and a Sampling of Songs," *NYFQ* 14 (1958), 202-223.

Wells, Evelyn K. *The Ballad Tree: A Study of British and American Ballads, Their Folklore, Verse, and Music.* New York: The Ronald Press, 1950.

WVF. West Virginia Folklore. Fairmont: W. Va. Folklore Soc., 1951—.

WF. Western Folklore. (formerly *California Folklore Quarterly*), Berkeley and Los Angeles: Univ. of California Press for the California Folklore Society, 1942—.

*Wheeler, Mary. *Steamboatin' Days: Folk Songs of the River Packet Era.* Baton Rouge: Louisiana State Univ. Press, 1944.

*White, Newman I. *American Negro Folk-Songs.* Cambridge: Harvard Univ. Press, 1928.

Wilgus, D. K. *Anglo-American Folksong Scholarship Since 1898.* New Brunswick: Rutgers Univ. Press, 1959.

Will, G. F. "Songs of Western Cowboys," *JAF* 22 (1909), 256-261.

*Williams, Cratis Dearl. *Ballads and Songs.* (Kentucky Microcards. Series A. Modern Language Series. Sponsored by the South Atlantic Modern Language Assoc. No. 15). Lexington, 1937.

*Wolf, Edwin, 2nd. *American Song Sheets, Slip Ballads, and Poetical Broadsides, 1850-1870: A Catalogue of The Collection of The Library Company of Philadelphia.* Phila.: The Library Company of Philadelphia, 1963.

*Wyman, Loraine and Howard Brockway. *Lonesome Tunes: Folk Songs from the Kentucky Mountains.* New York: H. W. Gray Co., 1916.

Index of Ballads and Songs

References to Appendix I are Printed in Italics